EGYPT LAND

New Americanists

A SERIES EDITED BY DONALD E. PEASE

SCOTT TRAFTON

# Egypt Land

RACE AND NINETEENTH-CENTURY

AMERICAN EGYPTOMANIA

Duke University Press   Durham and London

2004

© Duke University Press

All rights reserved

Printed in the United States of America on acid-free paper ∞

Designed by CH Westmoreland

Typeset in Quadraat by Tseng Information Systems, Inc.

Library of Congress Cataloging-in-Publication Data appear

on the last printed page of this book.

FOR MICHELLE

# Contents

# Illustrations

# Acknowledgments

"To write rapidly about Egypt is impossible," apologized explorer, feminist, and agent of British empire Amelia Edwards in 1877. "The subject grows with the book, and with the knowledge one acquires by the way. It is, moreover, a subject beset with such obstacles as must impede even the swiftest pen; and to that swiftest pen I lay no claim."[1] As ambivalent as I might be concerning the source of this quotation, I find myself hard pressed to disagree with its significance: for those who have known me while I have lived and labored in Egypt Land, it goes without saying that this process has taken far too long and I have incurred far too many debts along the way for me to do any kind of justice to those I owe here. Yet of course I must make a way out of no way, and so first things first: this project was originally drafted as my dissertation for the Department of English at Duke University in 1998, and the people who oversaw it in that stage were generous in their contributions and extraordinary in their support and have remained my models for intellectual and political engagement ever since—Cathy Davidson, Barbara Herrnstein Smith, Nahum Dimitri Chandler, and Wahneema Lubiano. In the years that have followed, Nahum and Wahneema especially have been my constant friends, linked most importantly by our loves of jazz and trashy Hollywood movies, respectively, and to them I cannot express the depth of my thanks.

This project was also fortunate enough to have been funded by two separate fellowships at the Smithsonian Institution, one in 1997 at the Archive Center of the National Museum of American History, under the director-ship of Fath Davis Ruffins, the other in 2001 at the Smithsonian Ameri-can Art Museum (until recently the National Museum of American Art), under the directorship of William Truettner. My fellow fellows and the staffs at both of these institutions were critical in helping me to maintain my sanity as well as my sense of direction. Additional support was also provided by the College of Arts and Sciences of George Mason University; a Mathy Junior Faculty Research Grant in the spring of 1999 and a dean's research leave in the spring of 2002 provided me with that most indispens-able of academic commodities, time. Research support was provided over the years by Paula Redes-Sidore, Adrianna Pavlides, and especially Nadine Meyer. Without all of this assistance for this book, no doubt I would still be trying to finish it.

Since arriving at George Mason, I have been surrounded by friends and colleagues with an outrageous array of skills and talents, all of which are matched only by their kindness and camaraderie: special thanks are due to Denise Albanese, Zofia Burr, Peter Brunette, John Burt Foster, Deborah Kaplan, David Kaufmann, Rosemary Jann, Barbara Melosh, Paul Smith, Chris Thaiss, Steven Weinberger, Alok Yadov, Peggy Yocom, and especially, Cindy Fuchs and Jeanette Roan. Particular thanks are especially due, how-ever, to my colleagues in the Program for African American Studies, who have been there for me from can't see to can't see: Rose Cherubin, Yevette Richards Jordan, Phillis Slade-Martin, Jeffrey Stewart, and especially Keith Clark, Marilyn Mobley McKenzie, and Michelle Smith-Bermiss. I could not imagine a more welcoming and supportive location.

Outside Mason but still conspicuously close to this project, several people have been critical in their insights and support: Dwight McBride, Malini Johar Schueller, Natalie Houston, and especially Dana Nelson and Gayle Wald. I hope they know how treasured their encouragement has been. At Duke University Press, the comments of Robert Levine and an-other reader showed the kind of attention and enthusiasm for this project throughout the long revision process that most writers can only dream of. The legendary patience and understanding of Ken Wissoker and Christine Dahlin were needed at every stage as well, and their benefits are evidenced by whatever success I have managed to achieve.

And then there are the people who have known me for an embarrass-ingly long time yet who still have for whatever reason decided to remain my friends and have even offered their support of this book along the way. James Wolf, twice a roommate of mine and now a staff member of the Library of Congress, contributed crucially timed and thankfully obsessive research skills which helped bring this project to a close—not to mention a spare bed to sleep on at his and his wife Anna's house during one summer in 1997. Robert Reid-Pharr, who needs to give me a call sometime, could be included in this list for a multitude of reasons but is officially acknowledged here because he hates acknowledgments pages just like this one. And Greta Ai-Yu Niu, who like James and Robert has known me through some truly bad hairstyles, has been the sort of friend who comes along once in a lifetime.

I must also thank the members of my family from whom I would never hear the end of it if I did not, and who I would then have to face every Juneteenth: my brothers Greg and Michael Trafton (who published his book before me), my sisters Wendy and Anne Rosamond, my stepbrothers Jonathan Silberberg and Adam Kass, and my once and future stepmothers Lynn Townsend and Miriam Kass. A family as big as Texas, and as essential as a junk drawer. Likewise, properly acknowledging one's parents at a moment like this is a ritual as necessary as it is impossible: Dorothy Louise Rosamond Trafton Dockal Remington Rosamond—Dot—has been a source of more humor and recipes than I could ever hope to remember, and with my father, John Gregory Trafton III, to whom an earlier version of this manuscript was dedicated, I have shared so much that I can only begin to frame it all.

But then, of course, there's the one last and most important name. One night long ago in the middle of an empty street in Durham, I promised that this version of this manuscript would bear a single name, and now, finally, I am able to honor that promise. Moving from place to place with me like a refugee from someone else's war, tolerating my moods and indulging my habits, making me travel and letting me sleep, always there when the hurricanes blow and the dogwoods bloom: an indescribable togetherness has attended every word written here. It is of course too much to try and express how I feel, and certainly a book is hardly adequate evidence, but this book is dedicated, as it has in many ways always been, to Michelle.

# "An Inspired Frenzy

# or Madness"

"If we observe the patient for a time," wrote Emil Kraepelin, nineteenth-century German psychologist and coiner of the term *manic depression*, "[we] see that, in spite of his good education, he lies in bed for weeks and months, or sits about without feeling the slightest need of occupation. He occasionally composes a letter to the doctor, expressing all kinds of distorted, half-formed ideas, with a peculiar and silly play on words, in very fair style, but with little connection. . . . As the illness developed quite gradually, it is hardly possible to fix on any particular point of time as the beginning."[1] This book could have been used as evidence in one of Kraepelin's case studies: it had its beginnings in a series of questions, which led to the repeated recognition of a series of lacks, which I then slowly began to trace. Initially, I was interested in exploring the relationships between the rise of nineteenth-century racialized science and the rise of American Egyptology; the final results of those explorations are seen here, but as I continued to conduct research I became aware of some significant gaps in the scholarship of the period. The foremost study of these initial connections was—and still is, I would argue—William Stanton's 1960 *The Leopard's Spots*, and, well researched as it is, it is, to put it mildly, something of an apology for one of the major collective characters in this study, the proslavery American School of Ethnology. The availability of sources on the American School has improved significantly since this project was begun—and as such this book is one of several now available that reassess the role Egyptology played in discourses of race and the biology of racialization—but it is still the case, I think, that this study addresses several other absences in American and African American cultural scholarship.

The best known and most comprehensive study of the imagery of ancient Egypt in nineteenth-century American culture prior to this one is an instructive case in point: John Irwin's 1980 *American Hieroglyphics* was and still is a landmark analysis of many of the same problematics under investigation here, but, brilliant as Irwin's text is, it stands at something of a conspicuous distance from issues of race and American racialization. Owing, no doubt, to the theoretical preoccupations of his brand of 1970s deconstruction, Irwin manages to produce, for example, a reading of the concluding section of Edgar Allan Poe's racially overwrought *Narrative of Arthur Gordon Pym*, which, even in the context of nineteenth-century American fascinations with ancient Egypt, provides an analysis of a set of black/white and master/slave oppositions that does not specifically thematize race.[2] Indeed, as this project progressed it became clear that Irwin's text was more the rule than the exception: while there were numerous treatments of the separate concerns that eventually contributed to its major arguments, there was no comprehensive study of the relationship race had to what I here term American Egyptomania.[3]

To be sure, there are studies of many of the subfields that inform *Egypt Land*, and over the years during which this project took shape they have only increased in number and quality: Dana D. Nelson's *National Manhood*, Malini Johar Schueller's *U.S. Orientalisms*, Theophus H. Smith's *Conjuring Culture*, Teresa Goddu's *Gothic America*, Wilson Jeremiah Moses's *Afrotopia*, Shawn Michelle Smith's *American Archives*, Eddie S. Glaude Jr.'s *Exodus!*, Hilton Obenzinger's *American Palestine*, Maurice O. Wallace's *Constructing the Black Masculine*, Reina Lewis's *Gendering Orientalism*, John Davis's *The Landscape of Belief*, Inderpal Grewal's *Home and Harem*, Bruce A. Harvey's *American Geographics*, and a number of essays and collections of essays on Cleopatra, Orientalism, and Egyptomania in general.[4] But what this study attempts to do is bridge many different fields and present a new synthesis of the contributions of several divergent areas of research: literary history, cultural history, art history, scientific history, Orientalism, Afrocentricity, white historiography, black historiography, queer historiography, and more.

During the realization of this attempt, however, it became clear to me that there were several additional deficiencies in the existing scholarship available to a project such as this: most of the studies of the history of American interest in ancient Egypt conspicuously avoided the issue of race, and those that did attempt to breach the questions of racialization and Egyptian historiography—however scandalously their appearance was received—were almost exclusively European in interest and focus or treated a time period other than the nineteenth century.[5] This European bias, in fact, characterizes much of the scholarship to which I refer: of the existing studies of Orientalism, for example, nearly all are either British or European in terms of their primary source materials, twentieth century in their time frame, or oriented toward an "Orient" that is not primarily North African. Not until Schueller's 1998 U.S. Orientalisms did a comprehensive study exist that treated nineteenth-century American Orientalism at length, much less with an eye toward contemporary race theory, and what works like Schueller's represent is a body of long overdue cultural reevaluations to which I hope this study contributes in some small way.

The texts that treat Egyptian imagery in a context of the nineteenth-century American politics of race are, moreover, characteristically divided in ways that made one of the main motions of this project that of negotiation—between fields that are concerned with the signs of the sacred and those that are more focused on signs of the secular. Certainly the tradition of scholarship treating African American religious inscriptions of the signs of ancient Egypt is especially rich, and without it this work would not have been possible; yet in writing this book it seemed to me that too few previous studies recognized the extent to which black Americans in the nineteenth century were also engaged in a more secular politics of Egyptomanic signifying—or, if they did, they did so to the exclusion of a systematic reevaluation of the sacred discourses with which the signs of a proto-Afrocentric Egypt must then engage.[6] This is not exclusively the case, of course—Smith's 1994 Conjuring Culture is an excellent example of recent attempts to provide an account of African American Egyptian imagery that does not rely on undertheorized distinctions between "sacred" and "secular"—but there is no question that Egypt Land developed in large part out of an urge to do justice to what I saw as a heterogeneity and complexity of African American representations of ancient Egypt that had previously been undersold.

I was thus also concerned to provide an account of American interests in ancient Egypt that highlighted what I saw as the radical interactions between various factions of nineteenth-century American culture: sacred and secular, professional and popular, classicist and Orientalist, Aryanist and Afrocentrist, black and white. Indeed, if there is any one single contribution I hope to make with this study, it is along these lines; I do not so much ignore boundaries between such various groups as I recognize their extreme permeabilities. What Egypt Land attempts to describe is a radical dialogicism at work in the racially fraught historiographic idioms of nineteenth-century American culture; in doing so, I hope to suggest that this wildly contingent structure can provide some insights about the larger workings of nineteenth-century American racial and national identity.

These realizations led me to make two commitments to the concerns of this project: one, that it would be irreducibly interdisciplinary; and, two, that it would base its arguments as much as possible on relatively lesser known source materials. Of course, the latter commitment proved the most difficult, but what I believe Egypt Land does is present a range of relatively canonical source materials next to potentially less common ones, and I do hope that readers will find the materials that emerge from these interactions both familiar and fresh. In doing so, I have relied on the resources of a wide variety of libraries, rare book rooms, archives, and special collections across the United States — especially those of Duke University, the University of North Carolina at Chapel Hill, the University of Texas at Austin, the Library of Congress, and various branches of the Smithsonian Institution — and it goes without saying that the fruits of Egypt Land presented here would have been patently impossible without them. That it is possible that the study of race and American Egyptomania lends itself in particularly effective ways to such a dialogic project has been suggested to me many times, yet I also continue to carry with me a sneaking suspicion that the influence has in fact been the other way around.

Egypt Land is thus a manifestly intercultural text. It partakes of a polysemity that is characteristic of its subject matter, no doubt, but even though it did not begin as a study of interracial dialogicism it has certainly ended up that way. And while I have throughout this study wrestled with the impulses toward an encyclopedism clearly diagnosable as manic, I nevertheless ultimately hope that what I present here engages in dialogue with the many areas in which I have resided, if even for a brief time, and does not seem to dismiss them. An "inspired frenzy or madness" is one of the definitions other than that of Kraepelin's provided for the suffix -mania by the Oxford English Dictionary, and, as I hope will be clear, I have made every effort to respect the breadth of scholarship that attends every field I have relied on for aid and comfort during my days as an Egyptomaniac. And, although the frenzy has now passed, if nothing else has come of those days, the pages that follow are evidence that the madness has left its mark.

# "This Egypt of the West"

## MAKING RACE AND NATION ALONG

## THE AMERICAN NILE

"For America, read Africa; for the United States, Egypt," wrote African American race theorist, spiritualist, and amateur Egyptologist Paschal Beverly Randolph in 1863: "change a few phrases into their required equivalents, and in this account of a modern colony, you have the story of the old Nilotic civilizations."[1] In this, his signature treatise on history, chronology, and the origins of races, Randolph saw a relationship between two countries of both metaphor and literal link: between Egypt and America there existed a set of connections, which, when properly interpreted, could reveal signs and wonders of revolutionary importance. "We know that these palmy days stretch away vastly beyond the horizon of Time," he wrote. "Little by little we are unravelling the tangled skein of Time and human history."[2] In its combination of racialized theorizing, biblical controversy, historiographic melodrama, political urgency, speculative intellectualism, and popular Egyptology, Randolph's text represents a cluster of consanguinated issues that this book will be concerned to trace. "Reader, let us imagine ourselves to be on the banks of the Nile," Randolph wrote. "We are there. Tread lightly, my fellow-traveler; we are on holy ground, here in Egypt, holy by reason of the awful shadows that enshroud its past."[3]

Randolph was one of many in nineteenth-century American culture who understood the relationship between modern America and ancient Egypt to be one based on close family ties: mirror images, twinned and inseparable. Witness some scenes from Washington, D.C.: the Washington Monument stands forever taller than any other structure in the nation's capital; Egypt and America sit side by side in the main reading room mural of the Library of Congress; and, in the last hours before the signing of the Emancipation Proclamation of 1863, an assembled force of African Americans gathered together in the shadow of the White House and sang an adaptation of the spiritual from which this study takes both its impetus and its title:

> Go down Moses,
> Way down in Egypt Land;
> Tell old Pharaoh,
> Let my people go.

> Go down Abraham,
> Away down in Dixie's Land;
> Tell Jeff Davis
> To let my people go.[4]

Throughout American history the iconography of empire—that of its wielders as well as its resisters—was lavishly drawn from that of ancient Egypt.

That this equation was no simple matter was an open secret; all of the multiple meanings and ambiguous connotations of what was both one of history's most famous empires and its most infamous slave society would be transferred in radically transformative ways to the United States. "A view of the national sin of America," wrote abolitionist E. S. Addy in 1838, "is like discovering the object of worship in the old temples of Egypt, where, after the stranger had walked bewildered through the vistas of superb architecture, he came at last to the filthy idol—a mouthing and obscene ape, playing its pranks on a throne of gold!"[5] Even in antislavery circles the sign of Egypt was constantly shifting, however, and was structured by a kind of

Edwin Blashfield, *The Evolution of Civilization*, 1895. (Rotunda Dome Collar
Mural, Main Reading Room, Jefferson Building, Library of Congress,
Washington, D.C. Prints and Photographs Division, Library of Congress.)

radical split. "The phoenix fire of Egypt revives again," wrote a contributor enigmatically to *The Colored American* in 1840: "[I]n America the face of
things appertaining to the rights of man are fast changing."[6] Yet, speaking
of the moment when she first escaped from slavery, the famously metaphorical Sojourner Truth reported: "I left everything behind. I wa'n't goin'
to keep nothin' of Egypt on me."[7] This is the kind of structure this project
will be concerned to describe: a sort of doubled doubleness in American
national and racial identity in which a doubled relationship is evident between nineteenth-century America and ancient Egypt and brought into
view by the doubled relationship African Americans had with America.

This doubled structure of the American Egypt attends its appearances
throughout the nineteenth century. "The oldest people of the world sends
its morning greeting to the youngest nation," read the inscription on the
two identical pylons that served as the entrance to the Egyptian Court of
the Centennial International Exhibition held in Philadelphia in 1876, and
this dual configuration would be reiterated at the end of the century, at
the World's Columbian Exposition in Chicago in 1893, when the two rep-

lica obelisks fronting either side of the Chicago re-creation of the Temple of Luxor would bear matching inscriptions in hieroglyphics: one a dedication to Rameses II, pharaoh during the days of the temple, the other a dedication to Grover Cleveland, president during the days of the World's Fair.[8] Yet an inescapable feature of this relationship was its recursivity: for every moment of the conscription of Egyptian imagery into the services of empire or authority, there was a corresponding moment of opposition and confrontation. "We have for years been fraternally outraged, and the present calls upon us for action," wrote black nationalist and black Freemason Martin Robison Delany in 1853. "From whence sprung Masonry, but from Ethiopia, Egypt, and Assyria—all settled and peopled by the children of Ham?"[9]

Thus, one of the primary arguments of this book is that much of nineteenth-century American racial and national identity can be said to partake of a schematic split structured by the conflictual visions of ancient Egypt. More than this, however, I am arguing that this split in itself—that is, this split *as* a split, as necessarily doubled—is indicative not exactly of a doubled identity per se, but rather of an overall and widespread instability in American racial and national identity that, through American visions of ancient Egypt, was often stylized as a split. In fact, when African Americans in particular insist on a stylized duality in American racial and national identity—efforts realized most famously, of course, at the turn of the twentieth century in the early work of W. E. B. Du Bois but which this study will insist existed in a variety of ways all across the century that preceded his famous formulation—they do so in large part as a way to gain a stylized purchase on the multilayered operations of American racialization and they also do so principally through the figure of ancient Egypt. There is perhaps no better analytic frame for the violent crucible of race and nation that was the nineteenth-century United States than the figure of ancient Egypt: a land that represented the origins of races and nations, the power of empires and their inevitable falls, and the stories of despots holding people in bondage and of the exodus of the saved from the land of slavery.

This coupled correlation took many different forms at many different times and for many different people; the studies that make up this book have in large part emerged from the interactions between the two constantly shifting sides of what might be thought of as Egypt's split personality. That Africa, for African Americans, is a figure that is itself structured by a kind of doubled doubleness—as we will see in a series of what are themselves split figurations of the sign of ancient Egypt—is evidence of the sort of shape I wish to describe. And in point of fact what this study argues is that what American Egyptomania reveals about American racial and national identity is not just a structurally stylized schematic split but also the mechanics of the *instability* of that split: throughout this book emphasis is placed on the mechanics, the erotics, and the aesthetics of a series of related disruptive figures—the breach, the rupture, undressing, panic. Time and again what American Egyptomania provides is both the means for representing violently opposed and mutually exclusive identities, spaces, or states of being and the means for representing just how irreducibly impossible such separations ultimately are. What these oddly but conspicuously familiar shapes reveal is evidence not just of attempts to structure racial instability—into sets of binary systems in particular—but evidence of the very instability of such attempts as well. That ancient Egypt as a figure carried so many sets of these conflicting operations of stabilization and destabilization is, I believe, evidence of the indispensability to nineteenth-century American identities of the signs of Egypt.

At times Egypt was a symbol split by the politics of power and oppression: half secular greatness, pure and progenitive, half religious oppression, despotic and destructive. At times it was divided along the lines of liberation: operating at once as a sign of righteous insurrection, yet also as a sign of freedoms freely squandered. At times it was a figure of strict and serious rationalism, early parent to mathematics and the sciences, yet also one of the antirational, a signifier of magic, mystery, and the unknown, a figure of esoteric secrets encouraging unrestrained speculation. At times it was half classical patriarch, part of the grand triumvirate of grand ancient civilizations, a third of the holy trinity of Greece, Rome, and Egypt, and yet also half Orientalist fantastic, an interracialized hallucination of sex, decadence, and degeneration, home to the most extreme projections of overwrought Otherness nineteenth-century American culture could imagine. The power and privilege claimed by Egypt as a multivaried sign in nineteenth-century American culture derived in large part from the heterogeneous and often unpredictable uses resulting from the exhanges between the sides of such a split sign—a sign of ancient and modern, religious and secular, proper and shocking, oppression and resistance, civilized and savage, black and white. It is these complex and contradictory cultural interoperations, and the products that emerge from them, that this study places under the heading of American Egyptomania and situates in a space radically racialized and radically fraught, referred to throughout as Egypt Land.

## "Come Forth with the Signs and Wonders"

This study is concerned with the complex interrelations between two main cultural formations in nineteenth-century American culture: those of representations of ancient Egypt, and those of what are variously referred to as race. Densely interwoven and often lengthily stretched, the connections between the cluster of discourses that informed, produced, and resulted from nineteenth-century American interests in ancient Egypt and those that were involved in the construction of race and racialization were thoroughly indebted to one another. As Du Bois wrote in 1946: "[I]t is especially significant that the science of Egyptology arose and flourished at the very time that the cotton kingdom reached its greatest power on the foundation of American Negro slavery." [10] Significant, indeed: as a land of scandals, contradictions, and directly opposed interests, in nineteenth-century America the problems of writing the history of Egypt were of a piece with the problems of the politics of race. Ancient Egypt and its representations were crucibles for conflicting and often contradictory assumptions about some of the most critical and foundational social and political issues in operation throughout America in the nineteenth century, and throughout the century the signs of Egypt were associated with a disruptive power reserved for few others. Indeed, to this day, to bring attention to the relationship here under investigation—even to raise the question of the issue of race in the context of the study or teaching of the history of the Nile Valley—is to create an almost immediate scandal.[11] Yet my concern here, among other things, is to show how routine scandals like this have been. With varying degrees of specificity and varying degrees of success, debates over issues understood to be crucial to concepts of "America" would return again and again to ancient Egypt. From visions of Cleopatra to the tales of Edgar Allan Poe, from the works of Pauline Hopkins to the construction of the Washington Monument, from the measurement of slave skulls to the singing of slave spirituals: in all of these diverse social arenas, claims about and representations of ancient Egypt served as linchpins for discussions about nineteenth-century American racial and national identity.

FIG. 44.

AMUNOPH I.
(A *Grecian* countenance.)

FIG. 45.

His wife.

AAHMES-NOFRE-ARI.
(Strong *Semitic* features.)

FIG. 46.

Son of the above.

His wife.

THOTMES I.
(Strikingly *Hellenic*.)

19

FIG. 47.

AAHMES.
(Absolutely *Jewish*.)

"The Caucasian Types Carried through Egyptian Monuments." (From Josiah Clark Nott and George Robins Gliddon, *Types of Mankind*. Philadelphia: Lippincott, Grambo, 1854, figs. 44–47, p. 145. Library of Congress.)

In a sense, then, the basic argument of this book is quite straightforward: a wide range of Americans throughout the nineteenth century used images and discourses of ancient Egypt as ways of managing contemporary domestic conflicts arising from the politics of race and race-based slavery, and the terms of this management were both literal and metaphorical. They were literal in that, for example, "actual" Egyptians—especially those who were long dead—were used as critical features in the emergent biological taxonomies of the period to justify the enslavement and oppression of "actual" Americans—especially those who were black. "[F]or the sake of illustrating that, even in Ancient Egypt, *African slavery* was not altogether unmitigated by moments of congenial enjoyment, not always inseparable from the lash and the hand-cuff," wrote Josiah Nott and George Gliddon in 1854, "we submit a copy of some Negroes 'dancing in the streets of Thebes,' by way of archaeological evidence that, 3400 years ago, 'de same ole Nigger' of our Southern plantations could spend his Nilotic sabbaths in saltatory recreations, and 'Turn about, and wheel about, and *jump Jim Crow!*'"[12] They were metaphorical in that, for example, biblical traditions of representing ancient Egypt were seized on and mobilized as weapons in the more discursive struggles over abolition and its aftermaths. "Hear, O Israel! and plead my cause against the ungodly nation!" wrote African American Jewish poet Adah Isaacs Menken in 1868. "Come forth with the signs and wonders, and thy strong hands, and stretched-out arms, even as thou didst from Egypt!"[13]

Thus, if one were given to schematization, American Egyptomania can be said to have operated schematically in at the very least a triangulated way: white Americans, black Americans, and ancient Egyptians existed in a radically counterpositioned but radically relational fashion, each admitting the significance of a mutually recognized territorial dispute. "A superficial criticism, guided by local and temporary prejudices," wrote black nationalist Edward Wilmot Blyden in 1882, "has attempted to deny the intimate relations of the Negro with the great historic races of Egypt and Ethiopia."[14] But a better schematization would be quadrilateral: white America, black America, white Egypt, and black Egypt. "The question, in regard to the priority of erection between the pyramids of Meroe, and those of Memphis," wrote Gliddon, one of the century's most famous white Egyptologists, forty years before Blyden, "merges into the still more interesting fact of their having been built by the same race of men, who were not Africans, but Caucasians."[15] American representations of ancient Egypt were as radically split as America itself.

Or not; what something like a quadrilateral scheme would indicate would be, at the very least, an attempt to represent the enormous fluidity with which "black" and "white" and "Egypt" and "America" slid into each other and then out again. Black Americans paid strict attention to developments in white Egyptology—though until after Reconstruction American Egyptology could hardly be said to have existed as such—and yet this attention was not always suspicious; excerpts from the writings of white Egyptologists and white travelers to the valley of the Nile were routinely published in black newspapers, periodicals, and other writings, sometimes framed with sarcastic comments undermining the authoritativeness of the source, sometimes not. "The black man was the first skillful animal on the earth," wrote the self-emancipated David Dorr after traveling to Egypt in the early 1850s, "because Homer describes the Egyptians as men with wooly hair, thick lips, flat feet, and black, and we have no better authority than Homer."[16]

And the reverse was true as well; as is not recognized nearly often enough, white Americans were regularly rapt when confronted by the voices of black Egypt. Indeed, the blackening of Egypt was as much a factor in the formation of white Egyptology as the whitening of Egypt was for black folks, both up close and at a distance, at least in terms of dynamic if not in documented quantity. A basic dynamic of suspicion, panic, opportunism, and signifying characterized all sides of American Egyptomania, from black Egyptologists' seizure of the claims of the blackness of ancient Egypt understood to have been made by Herodotus to the defensive distance adopted by white Egyptologists from what was, even—or especially—to the most racist of them, an unavoidable association between Egypt and the blackness of Africa which was seen to surround it. "Another popular fallacy, and one which, being very prevalent, produces many erroneous deductions," wrote Gliddon, "is the supposition that . . . Ham who, as the father of the Egyptians, has been therefore made the parent of other so-called African nations."17 Indeed, even the most racist constructions of Egypt as white carry within them a recognition of the instability of their structures: Egypt was white but blasphemously pagan, Egypt was white but decadent and doomed to destruction, Egypt was white but held the Hebrews in bondage, Egypt was white but succumbed to amalgamation. Even at its whitest, Egypt cast a dark shadow.

So in another sense, the basic argument of this book is not that straightforward. Instead, this book argues that American Egyptomania consisted of radically intersected and overlapping webs of discourses and practices that were spread widely across different racial or social groups, were utilized by these groups in some wildly inventive and often contradictory ways, and were not merely products of preexisting or racially configured social divisions but were in fact constitutive of them. Such distinctions, then—between "literal" and "metaphorical" or "white" and "black"—are sloppy and unsatisfying, relying as they do on a legacy of other such binary distinctions which work to oversimplify a profoundly complicated situation; moreover, as we will see, such epistemological divides based on either "race" or competing "truths" emerged in what for this study are their most relevant forms only through the very crucible of American Egyptomania, and thus were not so much the terms of the conflict as its spoils.

Thus it is a categorical mistake to understand Egypt as either representationally monolithic or racially stable on either side of the black/white divide, for both black and white Americans were aware of the radical contradictions contained—or not—by their own visions of ancient Egypt, and even given a relatively clear politics of racialized self-definition the meanings of ancient Egypt were still fragmented, juggled, opposed, and explosive. Nineteenth-century racial and national identities were constructed by and through such contingent and conditional claims to ancient truth. Egypt was a land of mystery, magic, and paganism, but it was also a land of lasting monuments, ancient wisdom, and powerful rulers and their slaves. Egypt was potentially a great civilization or a land built on the backs of the oppressed, or both. Either way, it was a land shaped by racialized, historicized, Americanized conflict.

What follows this introduction, then, is an argument structured as a series of overlapping concerns spread over five chapters, each organized around relatively distinct divisions of subject matter. These chapters break down roughly along disciplinary lines; although an ongoing question for the overall argument of this book has been how to extend a set of theoretical discussions past a disciplinary boundary, I have tried my best to respect both the professional idioms of each chapter and the initial impulses behind the total project. Put more plainly, each of the five chapters of this book bases its discussions on a more or less different manifestation of nineteenth-century American Egyptomania: the development of American Egyptology and the rise of racialized science; the narrative and literary tradition of the imperialist adventure tale, and specifically how it relates to the trope of the hollow earth; the cultural politics of the architectural movement known as the Egyptian Revival; the nineteenth-century fascination with the figure of Cleopatra; and the complex interactions between ostensibly competing visions of ancient Egypt in nineteenth-century African America. The boundaries between these manifestations are, however, often hard to draw, and so a series of theoretical shapes emerge from these discussions that also map onto each chapter, if less neatly: the figure of radical interplay between white and black Egyptomanias, read as a reciprocal relationship between intimate enemies; the figure of the terrestrial rupture, read as a punctiform sign of colonial instability; the figure of the breach, read as a form of racialized anxiety; the figure of layered interiority, read alternately as a concern with raciological, sexological, and gynecological secrets; and the figure of radical improvisation, read as a strategy of antiracist resistance. That the individual arguments of each chapter are as convoluted as this brief summary suggests will not, I hope, be as maddening as a mania.

Often, as we will see, what happens in American Egyptomania is that various forms of racial, social, or otherwise cultural anxiety are repeatedly yoked together and frequently form a kind of characteristic dyad: burial and excavation, puncture and containment, secrecy and revelation, rationalism and irrationalism, discipline and resistance, black and white. Yet what makes the study of nineteenth-century American Egyptomania so crucial to an understanding of the very dyadic formations it would seem to have had a stake in constructing is this: as often as a dualistic shape arises in the spaces of American Egyptomania, it appears with a corresponding sign of its own dissolution. Egypt brings wisdom to the dumb only with a curse, treasures are revealed to the hunter only to be lost, ancient mummies disrupt the modern age only to crumble to dust, fantastic races are revealed to the mundane only to disappear, pharaohs keep slaves only to have them escape; slaves pass from Egypt only to return.

This makes the history of American Egyptomania an acutely anxious one, as well as acutely racialized: what it represents are impossible dreams of eternal separation; unmanageable partitions between epistemologically distinct states; fantasies of social, cultural, or chronological segregation in a land that resists it at every turn. This is not to say, of course, that the racialized history of American Egyptomania does not return again and again to the imagery of ostensible containment and its uncontainable corollaries; thus the recursive patterns of discovery and loss, translation and confusion, excavation and destruction, confinement and escape, bondage and freedom, surface and depth, black and white. So what seems to be clearest of all in these doubled formations of American identity are the insistence of the shapes themselves, as well as regular returns to their motivating iconography; these intertwined patterns of disruption and reestablished composure, like all opponents in dramas of mutual exclusion, rely on each other for constant companionship.

Thus, what emerges from this book as a whole is an argument that can be more or less succinctly presented: the cultural politics of nineteenth-century American Egyptomania describe *a carceral aesthetics of racialized anxiety*. Put less succinctly: images and representations of ancient Egypt operated as fiercely contested sites for the expression of widespread anxieties relating to issues of social control, the principal features of these expressions are dialectics of containment and escape, and the resulting effects of these dialectics are a racialized metaphysics of national interiority in nineteenth-century American culture. Sometimes this interiority is associated with the racialized body—in the layers of skin containing expressive essences thought so determinative for cultivation and civilization; sometimes it is associated outright with concepts of criminality—in the iconography of Egyptian prisons; sometimes it is associated with less prosecutable but no less pathological threats to American identity—in the construction of the gynecological, ethnological, or sexualized interiors represented by the disruptive figure of the transgressive Cleopatra; sometimes it is explicitly eruptive—in geological visions of the hollow earth holding evolutionary explosions; sometimes it is more metaphorically irruptive—in political incursions by African Americans into the historiographic structures of white identity. But usually it is associated with the fears and fascinations of interior space, and always it is driven by the anxieties of race.

American Egyptomania places the relationships among these widespread logics of interiority, transgressivity, criminality, and control in sharp relief. In other words, in this book most of the various and varied cultural forms associated with American Egyptomania are understood to derive from most of the most commonly recognized crises in nineteenth-century American cultural life—urbanization, imperialism, chronology, historiography, shifts in gender roles, racialization, emancipation, and the long shadow of race-based slavery—and most of the impacts made by the products of American Egyptomania recursed back to further complicate the politics that first gave them shape. Prisons, cemeteries, re-creations of tombs; mummies, harems, and images of bondage and exodus; gender, geology, and Freudian psychoanalysis; Aryanism, Ethiopianism, and the early formulas for Hollywood monster movies: in nineteenth-century American culture, all of these national formations are continually linked to issues of race, chronology, and notions of civilization, and thus all of them both produced and were in part produced by American Egyptomania.

## "This Egypt of the West"

The history of American interest in ancient Egypt is a long one, dating to the early days of the colonies, and thus writing a history of American interest in ancient Egypt approaches the condition of attempting to write a history of America itself. But familiar as we might be with the importance of the uses by the early colonists of a specifically biblical Egypt—traditions theorized most famously by Perry Miller, Sacvan Bercovitch, and Werner

Sollors—ancient Egypt has, in American life and letters, also always played a relatively more secular role.[18] However, for the earliest American settlers, Egypt's secular presence was one of relative *absence*; it was something of a neglected stepchild for colonial and Federalist American identity, especially when placed in such sharp contradistinction to its importance as a religious figure.

So, speaking for the moment strictly about Egypt as a term of the secular, while a famously historiographic self-fashioning structured much political philosophy during the colonial period, it was, of course, Greece and Rome that formed the most common references to the ancient world in America prior to the nineteenth century. Really only in the history of the Masons does one find sustained attention to Egyptian history and imagery placed in service of the construction of a secular American national identity before the nineteenth century, and even then Masonic secularism was an odd kind of secularism: partially historicized, partially sacralized, and altogether based on composite fragments of materialism, mysticism, historicism, and spiritualism, which, in their *assemblage*, would make Freemasonry a kind of example of the impossibilities of the blurred boundaries between sacred and secular that are so characteristic of nineteenth-century American Egyptomania.[19]

Like most other studies, then, this book finds its history of American Egyptomania beginning in 1798, with the invasion of Egypt by Napoleon Bonaparte. In fact, most of the few American travelers to the Nile Valley before 1800, such as John Ledyard, friend and correspondent of Thomas Jefferson, were relatively unimpressed with Egypt and its legacy. "Cairo is a wretched hole," Ledyard wrote Jefferson in 1788. "Sweet are the songs of Egypt on paper."[20] Even the Nile itself was a severe disappointment and an occasion for a lesson on not believing everything you read: "You have heard and read much of this River, and so had I: but when I saw it I could not conceive it to be the same—it is a mere mud puddle compared with the accounts we have of it. What eyes do travellers see with—are they fools or rogues. This is the mighty sovereign of rivers—the vast nile, that has been metaphored into one of the wonders of the world—let me be carefull how I read—and above all how I read Antient history!"[21] The wonders of Egypt, it seemed, were not worth the trouble it took to see them. "I saw three of the pyramids as I passed up the River," Ledyard mentioned to Jefferson, "but they were 4 or 5 leagues off. If I see them nearer before I close my letter and observe any thing about them that I think will be new to you, will insert it."²² Evidently, Ledyard did not find the pyramids worth any extra effort; he mentions nothing else.

By 1837, however, the famous American travel writer John Lloyd Stephens was rhapsodizing ecstatically over "the great and interesting objects which are the traveler's principal inducements and rewards, the ruined cities on its banks, the mighty temples and tombs, and all the wonderful monuments of Egypt's departed greatness. . . . Of them I will barely say, that their great antiquity, the mystery that overhangs them, and their extraordinary preservation amid the surrounding desolation, make Egypt perhaps the most interesting country in the world."²³ And twenty years after Stephens, Herman Melville would have an altogether different reaction: "I shudder at the idea of ancient Egyptians," he wrote. "It was in these pyramids that was conceived the idea of Jehovah. Terrible mixture of the cunning and awful. . . . It is all or nothing. It is not the sense of height but the sense of immensity, that is stirred. After seeing the pyramid, all other architecture seems but pastry. . . . Its simplicity confounds you. Finding it vain to take in its vastness man . . . measures the base, & computes the size of individual stones. It refuses to be studied or adequately comprehended. It still looms in my imagination, dim & indefinite."²⁴ Certainly, Melville's almost tortured theo-philosophical vacillations mark a moment in the development of his thinking—and, indeed, in American transcendental thought in general—when a violent opposition between equally positioned philosophical concepts no longer produces an adequately formed sublime.²⁵ It must at least be recognized, however, that, in addition to marking a clear distinction between eighteenth- and nineteenth-century receptions of ancient Egypt, the vehicle for this transition is placed in an epistemologically unstable symbolic geography concerned with the boundaries of the origins of history that was being mapped onto a metaphor of America.

That representations of the ancient world played an overdetermined part in the formation of variously configured American identities was especially the case in the nineteenth century, when the definitions of "America" were being so visibly manufactured. The materials of this manufacture were often pointedly historiographic and even more often anciently so: as has frequently been noted, America during the nineteenth century was a land called "republic"; it had a national architecture based on superannuated forms; and it had cities named Athens, Sparta, Columbia, and Rome. But the national architecture for this ostensibly Christian nation was taken from non-Christian cultures, and it also had cities named Memphis, Cairo, Alexandria, and Thebes. It had the same Grecian forms for state capitols as for plantation big houses, it was excavating in its own earth the ruins and evidences of its own history of ancient civilizations, and it had as its central suture throughout almost all of its first full century a 2,300 mile seam referred to over and over again as "the Nile of America."

"It is the great body of the republic," Abraham Lincoln would say, precisely one month before signing the final Emancipation Proclamation, of the Mississippi River valley. "The other parts are but marginal borders to it."[26] Lincoln was making his comments in the context of a secessionist debate over the proposed separation of the United States into two or more autonomous regions as a solution to the Civil War; the issue at this moment in both his speech and his presidency was one of both geographical and metaphorical national identity. "Physically speaking, we cannot separate," Lincoln wrote. "There is no line, straight or crooked, suitable for a national boundary, upon which to divide."[27] But separation, of course, certainly had its advocates: "one section of our country believes slavery is *right*, and ought to be extended," he summarized, "while the other believes it is *wrong*, and ought not to be extended. This is the only substantial dispute."[28]

Speaking in the critical days after Antietam, less than three months after the issuance of the preliminary proclamation, Lincoln was only too aware that for a number of reasons a multitude of issues were converging on the problem of control of the Mississippi. "In the production of provisions, grains, grasses, and all which proceed from them, this great interior region is naturally one of the most important in the world," he wrote. "But separate our common country into two nations, as designed by the present rebellion, and every man of this great interior region is thereby cut off."[29] In addressing Congress, Lincoln was attempting to draw a picture of the United States as a country not divided by a boundary but joined by a seam. "True to themselves," he wrote of the inhabitants of the valley, "they will not ask where a line of separation shall be, but will vow, rather, that there shall be no such line," and four short paragraphs after this passage he proposes the adoption of a constitutional amendment abolishing slavery. Should, however, the crux of the war continue to involve the Mississippi Valley, "we shall be overwhelmed by the magnitude of the prospect presented . . . [by] this Egypt of the West."[30]

Lincoln was relying on one of the great metaphors of American national identity: the Mississippi River as the Nile River, and by extension America as Egypt itself, that is, as a great and powerful empire marked by the sign of a mighty river and its delta. This project will have more to say about these twinned and yet oppositional metaphors, but for now it is important to mark the overlapping significations they had in 1862. At a moment of national crisis based on the politics of race and race-based slavery, Lincoln invoked the land which was not only famous for its role as the earliest and ostensibly greatest of all civilizations, and not only infamous for its role as a biblical slaveholder, but as a metaphor was also particularly well suited as a vehicle for the incompatibilities, contradictions, and violent oppositions operating across the United States. The significational slippages and uncontainable messages delivered by Lincoln's invocation of the Nile and its country spilled out across his land like the racialized and sectionalized strife that was the occasion of his address in the first place. The Mississippi River valley thus took on a sharply specific, doubled, meaning: not only a geographic metonym of the Nile but the very sign of the politics of slavery. "Egypt of the West," indeed.

## "We Americans Are the Israel of Our Time"

The reasons for these intimacies of contact between ancient Egypt, nineteenth-century America, and the signs of race were primarily threefold. First, there was a simultaneity in timing: with the Louisiana Purchase concluded only five years after 1798, Napoleon's invasion of Egypt coincided almost exactly with the earliest explorations of the American West. And for the geographically overwhelmed surveyors and explorers this synchronous timing was further cemented by the immediately exported analogy between the Nile and the Mississippi. "This noble river," asserted the first promoter of the city of Memphis, Tennessee, "may, with propriety, be denominated the American Nile. . . . The general advantages of Memphis, are owing to its being founded on the Mississippi, one of the largest and most important rivers on the globe." [31] As Lincoln's comments over forty years later would make continuingly clear, the semiotic and ideological links between the Nile and the Mississippi were formative links for the iconography of western expansion.

Second, there was a twinned development in American ethnology. Or, more specifically, there was a development in ethnology of two twinned sites of interest: Egypt and America. "Veritable specimens of black, wooly-headed negroes," wrote Virginia-born Mississippi ethnologist Edward Fontaine in 1877, "are represented by the old Egyptian artists in chains, as slaves, and even singing and dancing, as we have seen them on Southern plantations in the present century."[32] Samuel George Morton, for example, craniometrist father figure of American ethnology, wrote two major works: the *Crania Americana* of 1839, and the *Crania Aegyptiaca* of 1844, and, as we will see in chapter one, American ethnology was founded on this relationship between *Aegyptiaca* and *Americana*, between Egypt as a site of racialized theorization and America as its investigational counterpart. The racialized, chronologically disruptive figures of Egypt and America were radically dialogic, producing fields of study that at times had no boundaries at all.

The relationship Egypt had with America was not, however, only one of western expansion or ethnological data and racial theorization. America was seen to have its *own* antiquity, with its own accompanying chronological scandals, rivaling those of Egypt itself. This bipartite division, moreover, was not confined to scientists such as Morton. Stephens, the most significant and popular American travel writer of the nineteenth century, friend and theoretical ally of Morton, also made a career out of exploring the same two general regions of such importance to American ethnologists, Egypt and Central America. "The magnificent tombs of the kings at Thebes rose up before me," he wrote of excavating skeletons near Ticul and exploring the labyrinth at La Cueva de Maxcanú: "Every step was exciting, and called up recollections of the Pyramids and tombs of Egypt."[33] The pyramids of the Yucatán and the pyramids of Egypt have an iconographic relationship that remains lucid and robust to this day, but it began in the early days of the nineteenth century with the coeval rise of American ethnology, American archaeology, and American Egyptomania.

Both ancient and newly discovered, both racially charged, the relationship between Egypt and America was altogether intimate. Antiquity became a primary sign of this relationship in the complicated days of the all too self-consciously young American republic, in the days of the Greek Revival and the words *American republic*. Antiquity became a central feature of the *new*, and its operations were conducted in large part through the sign of ancient Egypt. "America will become another Egypt to Antiquarians," wrote a contributor to *The Colored American* in 1839, "and her ruins will go back to the oldest periods of the world, showing doubtless that the ancestors of the Montezumas lived on the Nile."[34] The sign of antiquity and yet something always already new: this is another mark of American Egypto-mania.

Third among the reasons for this relationship is the complex inter-actions between the two most famous roles ancient Egypt had in nine-teenth-century American culture: Egypt as a land of secular empire, uti-lized as a sign of America's imperial power; and Egypt as a land of religious despotism, utilized as a sign of America's sacred covenant with the Judeo-Christian God. "We Americans are the peculiar, chosen people," wrote Mel-ville in 1850, "the Israel of our time; we bear the ark of the liberties of the world."[35] The most recognizable modes of biblical identification in nineteenth-century nation making by far, the covenental, exegetical, and jeremiadical invocations by white Christians of America not as the land of Egypt but of its opposite—and thus of themselves not as Egyptians but as those once held captive by Pharaoh—were forced to undergo radical change in the face of the efforts of *actual* slaves to free themselves from the Egypt that was America. "African American dramatic reenactments of the deliverance of the nation of Israel were inversions of America's national community," writes Eddie Glaude. "The New Israel was Egypt, and blacks were demanding that Pharaoh (white Americans) let God's people go."[36] In the racially overwrought nineteenth century, the uneasy and often ex-plosive interactions between the competing, conflictual, and often concil-iatory identities of these two Egypts—one scriptural, oppressive and evil, one profane, worldly and redeemable—took on especially sharp meanings: Egypt the wicked enemy of an angry Jehovah, and Egypt the imperial home of God's chosen people.

"Typology helps to create ethnicity," writes Werner Sollors, "and eth-nicity feeds on typology," and indeed, virtually every scholar writing on what Sollors famously codified in 1986 as typological ethnogenesis has had to either address or avoid the contradictions resulting from the inter-actions between the figurative white slaves of exegetical typology and the literal black slaves bound in the white promised land.[37] These contradic-tions were, of course, foundational for the typological imagery of African American Christianity, but what makes them especially important here are not only their manifold variations on the themes of antiquity, empire, op-pression, and deliverance which were crucial in the rise of racialization, be it biological or typological, identity or anatomy, black or white—but also the ways in which the secular positioning of Egypt as a figure of imperial parentage interacted with the well-known figure of Egypt as a land of religious domination. Alongside the famously biblical and terrible Egypt of nineteenth-century America moves Egypt as a land of the secular and the splendid, as a contrapuntal sign in relation to the well-worn shapes of religious figuralism, and, particularly in the context of the politics of race and race-based slavery, American Egyptomania both describes and is described by the relationship between the two.

This relationship was made all the more complicated due to the Bible's ongoing status as a source of historiographic authority during the century that saw the rise of positivist science and its contributions to systems of hierarchical racialization. Indeed, for this as well as many other reasons this rise was in large part located in the Nile Valley: as the source of the most direct challenges to the integrity of biblical chronology, the monuments of ancient Egypt were placed in open conflict with the Bible in its role as secular record and made to function as a wedge between Egypt as a land of scriptural metaphor and Egypt as a land of scientific truth, yet both were concerned to either attack or defend the justifications for American race-based slavery. "Persistent preoccupations with the Bible and biblical geography stood at the ideological core of American colonial expansion," writes Hilton Obenzinger; "representations, controversies, and anxieties involving the certainties of religious and national identities contend upon a heightened field of mythic meanings."[38] Moreover, as both Obenzinger and John Davis remind us, black and white directions noticeably diverged upon arriving in the Holy Land and mapped differential identities on typological terrain. "Egypt, rather than Israel, was the locus of black interest in Bible lands," writes Davis, and Obenzinger elaborates: "unlike its African American intertexts," he writes, "Anglo-Christian typological imagery tends to be concerned not with Egypt as its most important site, but with the desert, the wilderness, or other figures of exodus' aftermath, and with Zion, Canaan, or other figures of the Promised Land."[39]

Indeed, it is important to realize that both black and white Americans were confronted with the dueling politics of the sacred and the secular Egypt: both groups were invested in identifying with the Hebrew slaves held in Egyptian bondage, and both groups were invested in identifying with the pharaohs who built the monuments. Even as black Americans could represent themselves as both the victims and the descendants of pharaonic Egyptians, white Puritan deliverance from the Egypt of England eventually led them to a nation's capital marked with an obelisk of the Egyptian Revival. Even as Harriet Tubman was known as "the Moses of her people," Martin Delany could write that "the literature of the Israelites . . . was derived from the Africans, as they must have carried with them the civilization of those peoples and that country, in their memorable exodus, as the highest enconium upon Moses in the Scripture is that he 'was learned in all the wisdom of the Egyptians,' "[40] and Benjamin Franklin's early proposal for the Great Seal of the United States featuring Moses leading the chosen people out of Egypt would eventually be replaced on its reverse by the iconography of Egypt, crowned by an all-seeing eye. Whether written as divinely emancipated refugees or as divinely sanctioned empire, the conflicting identities of providential chosenness were best scripted by American Egyptomania in their divine contradictions.

"The pyramid signifies Strength and Duration," explained Charles Thomson, final designer of the Great Seal, in 1782, interpreting the image that now most recognizably appears on the back of the one-dollar bill: "The Eye over it & Motto allude to the many signal interpositions of providence in favour of the American cause."[41] The Egyptomanic iconicity of the seal was flexible enough to indicate both a secular primogeniture and a sacred mandate, both an unchanging antiquity and a *novus ordo seclorum*, "a new order of the ages," and the presence of a pyramid on the currency of a nation supposedly founded on an exodus from the land of the pyramids plainly illustrates the manifest anxieties constantly moving through the land of the American Jeremiad. Indeed, this manic logic was such an image's most effective reflection: that its cathected discrepancies spin so wildly apposite along the lines of race, nation, empire, and deliverance seems an apt metaphor for America itself. Thus, nineteenth-century American Egyptomania can be said to have arisen, perhaps most clearly, from the explosive interactions and irregular overlaps between these readily raced, multifold signs of the sacred and secular Egypt: as the land of both covenental typology and historical authority, both imperial identification and retributional redemption, of slaves holding slaves while both, at times, wishing to be pharaohs.

## Black Orientalism

"It was more to see Frederick Douglass than to see the Great Pyramid," wrote Douglass himself of an encounter he had with an American family on the Giza Plateau in 1887. "It was a day to be remembered. When we were going, there came into our compartment of the car, an American family party, discussing their plans. The gentleman took Mr. Douglass for an Arab, and thought he did not understand a word he said. When the recognition was made there was great handshaking." [42] In this scene, we can once again see the irregular revolutions of self and other, African and American, and America and Egypt that are characteristic of American Egyptomania. In this exchange, Douglass himself is rendered an exotic artifact: first mistaken for "an Arab" because of his color, then recognized for who he is for the very same reason, marveled over both because of his celebrity in America and because of the novelty of meeting him in Egypt.

It was, no doubt, admittedly striking, Douglass's presence at the Great Pyramid; African American travelers to Egypt were understandably rare, even as late as 1887. But what this anecdote presents is equally a sign of a greatly underrecognized feature of nineteenth-century black cultural life: black Orientalism. Occupying the spaces between European American imperialism and African American oppression, between white ambivalence and black identification, between interrconnecting images of pharaohs, slaves, homeland, and exodus, black Orientalism was structured by as many contradictions and overlapping valences as other branches of a more general Orientalism. This scene, however, should indicate some of its complexities: a black American being mistaken for an Arab by a white American, during simultaneous moments of imperial privilege, under the shadow of the Great Pyramid, and then being happily recognized as someone who used to be a slave.

Partaking in Douglass's case of a rewriting of the largely white Grand Tour, in which a relatively wealthy African American introduces himself into a history that had been at once ignorant of him and yet entirely concerned with him, this moment of black Orientalism is configured on all sides by unpredictable recognitions and odd absences. No mention is made at all, for example, of the racialized controversies surrounding the signs of Egypt, yet Douglass blinks in and out of Egypt like a raced apparition, in a celebration of post-Emancipational mobility. "How delightful for me," Douglass writes, "visiting the valley of the Nile . . . standing on the pyramids of Egypt, and looking into the stony eyes of the Sphinx, I—who in my boyhood felt myself doomed to drag out a miserable existence as a slave, chained to one hated spot on the earth, now roaming in freedom over many of the most interesting spots on the earth's surface." [43] One of the most iconographic African American antislavery activists in history was visiting one of the most iconographic African locations in the world, which itself had been—and still was—a symbolic battlefield for issues of race and race-based slavery: "Our tour has been all that we could ask," Douglass admits, "and much more than we expected." [44]

Douglass was, however, neither the first black American nor the first former American slave to visit the monuments of ancient Egypt. Perhaps the most important has now become David Dorr, author of the 1858 *A Colored Man Round the World*, which opens with an explicit invocation of the Orientalized imagery of an empire of the East, though strikingly reversed. "The author of this book," writes Dorr, "though a colored man, believes that he has the right to say that, in his opinion, *the American people are to be the Medes and Persians of the 19th century.*" [45] Dorr clearly identifies with the ancient Egyptian victims of the invading Persians, yet this victim status is only provisional: "The remains of Thebes stand like Catskill mountains, unshocked," he writes, in metonyms both of America and of African identity. "Two great streams rises [sic] in the Mountain of the Moon, in Abyssinia, and unites in Nubia, and flows through Egypt, and makes what we call 'The Nile.' " [46] And in Dorr's account we can see a black Orientalism that is every bit as configured by presence and absence, by the twinned operations of identification and misidentification, as Douglass's. "In going to these Pyramids, one walks over a pavement of dead bodies," Dorr writes. "I sunk in the sand, one hundred yards from the pyramid of Cheops, and my foot caught in the ribs of a buried man, which I afterwards learned to be a mummy. Oh, mummy!" [47]

Dorr intrudes violently into a history from which he was being just as violently excluded, and yet he presents his understanding of the racialized issues crunching under his feet as surprisingly complex and curiously bittersweet. "No king, perhaps, of the earth is so absolute in will over his people as the present Pacha of the Turkish empire," he writes, suggesting that as a fugitive slave he knows something about power and the dream of absolute will. "The kings of old times, no doubt, were powerful in their absolute sway. . . . Such were Egyptian kings of olden time, though black." [48] Dorr admits a colored kinship with the figures of power so famously associated with the history of Egypt, one that invokes both the ancient classical empire and the modern Orientalized one, yet even in doing so he articulates a distance from them. A striking example of the complexity and heterogeneity of representations of ancient Egypt in circulation for African Americans during the nineteenth century, and a rare instance of international mobility for a fugitive slave in the 1850s but also one enabled by the same structures of colonialism and imperialism that produced more well-known appearances by its white relatives, Dorr's incursion into the pyramid is a signature moment in black Orientalism.

The same is true of the long effort of black nationalist Edward Wilmot Blyden. "The Oriental world," he wrote in 1875, "is daily getting to be 'nearer seen and better known,' not only in its outward life, but in those special aspects which . . . differentiate Eastern from Western races."[49] Blyden's extended analysis marks one of the better-known engagements of a nineteenth-century black intellectual with questions usually understood to have then been the province of white scholars and travelers—that of the influences of Islam in Africa—but in addition to the many other issues in play in his text his interest serves as a central moment in black Orientalism. Made available through many of the same mechanisms that served European American communities, information and opinions regarding "the Orient" were presented to and re-presented by African Americans with much the same energy. "To students of general literature in Europe and the United States," Blyden wrote, "until the last few years, the Orientals most celebrated in religion or politics, in literature or learning, were known only by name." But now, he asserted, "drawn away from the beaten track of Roman and Greek antiquity . . . the Western student finds rewards far rarer and richer than he had anticipated."[50]

Representing a long legacy of combined affects—sympathy and fantasy, identification and disidentification—Blyden's black Orientalism is a Reconstruction example of the kind of Afrocentric attitudes toward the complex cultural and religious histories of North Africa that would earn him a place in black history as one of the founders of pan-Africanism. Indeed, Blyden's status as an early exemplar of the imbrications of black Orientalism and Afrocentrism is confirmed through his own travel writings; his 1873 *From West Africa to Palestine* stands as one of the clearest expressions of nineteenth-century vindicationist Afrocentrism ever written, made all the more so due to Blyden's physical visit to the Great Pyramid. "Feelings came over me far different from those which I have felt when looking at the mighty works of European genius," Blyden rhapsodized from the Giza Plateau. "I felt that I had a peculiar 'heritage in the Great Pyramid.' . . . The blood seemed to flow faster through my veins. I seemed to hear the echo of those illustrious Africans. I seemed to feel the impulse from those stirring characters who sent civilization into Greece—the teachers of the father of poetry, history, and mathematics—Homer, Herodotus, and Euclid. . . . I felt lifted out of the commonplace grandeur of modern times."[51] Blyden, a Christian missionary based in Liberia, found an important ally in Afrocentric constructions of the black Orient: by identifying with ancient Egyptians, he was able to claim kinship with the modern inhabitants of the Arab world while asserting his moral, cultural, historical, religious, and racial superiority over them. This would be nothing new in the history of black missionaries, nor in that of black Orientalism. His Afrocentric project used the cultures of Africa the ancient as leverage against the cultures of Africa the modern.[52]

The situation in which Blyden—whose eugenicist beliefs about lighter-skinned members of the African diaspora would come to mark his attitudes more and more over the years—was placed was of course unusual, and he did in fact find himself in a difficult position: being driven by evangelical Christian zeal but unable to restrain his appreciation for the benefits enjoyed by Africans under Islam. "When the religion was first introduced," he wrote of Islam, "it strengthened and hastened certain tendencies to independence and self-reliance which were already at work. . . . Christianity, on the other hand, came to the Negro as a slave. . . . The Oriental aspect of Islam has become largely modified in Negroland, not, as is too generally supposed, by a degrading compromise with Pagan superstitions, but by shaping many of its traditional customs to suit the milder and more conciliatory disposition of the Negro."[53] As most scholars have noted, Blyden proved extremely sympathetic toward the traditions of Islam in Africa, finding in them what Richard Brent Turner calls "a monotheistic alternative to the racism of Christianity."[54] "To those acquainted with the interior of Africa—to the Mohammedan world of North Africa and Arabia," wrote Blyden, "it is well known that numerous characters have arisen in Africa— Negro Muslims—who have exerted no little influence in the military, political, and ecclesiastical affairs of Islam, not only in Africa, but in the lands of their teachers."[55] Thus, while it was in many ways beholden to the machineries of whiteness which produced more mainstream Orientalist fantasies, black Orientalism nevertheless operated with some important differences.

"While European Orientalists were busy creating negative and exotic representations of Islam," Turner argues, "Blyden was doing something quite different with the religion: he began with his positive impressions of the black Islamic experience."[56] Certainly the history of the interactions between African Americans and Islam during the nineteenth century is one in which Blyden features prominently and one that has recently received some much overdue attention; accordingly, a full exploration of the multilayered relationships between African American Muslim communities and what I am here calling black Orientalism is one that extends past the boundaries of this study.[57] But surely Turner is downplaying the issue somewhat when he writes that "much of Blyden's work was tinged with a subtle Christian missionary agenda" and that he, perhaps unwillingly, operated as an ambivalent apologist for nineteenth-century colonialism.

Gayraud Wilmore presents the matter less equivocally: "Like many others of the time, Blyden seems to have had no special problem with what today would be regarded as black American cultural and political imperialism in Africa."[58] And even though Turner goes on to provide a more carefully nuanced account of Blyden's relationship with black civilizationism, he nevertheless exhibits some of the same curious blind spots as other scholars of nineteenth-century American Islam: colonialism is often understood to have brought Christian Americans to Islamic Africa, not to mention Islamic Africans to Christian America, but less is it understood to have also brought Islamic Africa to Christian Americans. And, while I do not wish by any means to infer that the belief systems of black American Muslims can be reduced to the history of either Orientalism or Egyptomania, I am interested in highlighting in this context the interactions between nineteenth-century African American constructions of "the Orient"—of which Blyden and his eventual all but official conversion to Islam formed an important part—and the racialized operations of American Egyptomania and American Afrocentrism.

To be sure, what I am here calling black Orientalism overlaps in significant ways with the history of African American international travel. This is especially obvious given the examples I have chosen; Douglass, Dorr, Blyden, and the man whose quotations opened this introduction, Paschal Beverly Randolph, all traveled to Africa as a symbolic sign of their membership in the diasporic removal from it, were all part of the vanguard of nineteenth-century black travelers, particularly in terms of travel to Egypt, and their writings reflect a particularly important stage in the development of the early black tourist industry in Africa. Yet what is also evident in the texts of black Orientalists is what Malini Johar Schueller calls "the patriarchal imperatives of Orientalist discourse." Writing of Dorr, Schueller argues that he needed the epistemic possibilities of Near Eastern Orientalist discourse, a discourse he could enter into not as a novelist, as could white USAmericans, but through the only form permitted an African American—the nonfictional and testimonial. . . . Dorr retained within his travel narrative many of the tropes of popular Near Eastern Orientalism; in particular, the narrator is especially attracted to the role of knowing, empowered hermeneute elsewhere accorded the USAmerican embodying the nation. . . . Exploiting the patriarchal imperatives of Orientalist discourse answered the needs of Dorr as an African American to affirm his selfhood in a culture that denied him legitimacy both as a subject of a nation and as a male subject.[59]

The recursive designs of the black diaspora returned princes to Egypt, crowned as African American men.

Masculinity, then, is one of the enabling structures of black Orientalism in this formation; the embodiment permitted black men abroad, while acting as a corrective to the infantilizations and symbolic castrations of slavery, was nevertheless enabled by the patriarchal imperialism authorized by Orientalism. "I would have given five pds to lift her veil," Dorr writes of a Turkish woman he sees while abroad. "I know she was pretty, her voice was so fluty, and her hands so delicate, and her feet so small, and her dress so gauzy."[60] This imbrication of black masculine embodiment and patriarchal Orientalism is borne out even by Douglass, whose observations of Egypt were not complete without a final note marking him with an embodied imperialist patriarchal masculinity. "And women in Egypt!" he concludes. "A plaything and a beast of burden and that is all! Beaten and divorced by the husband at his merest whim, she never knows when she is to be driven from her house and children. It is all dreadful!"[61]

Equally related to the traditions of African American travel writing as to those of white Orientalism, I am not proposing that black Orientalism is a distinct and separable discourse. Rather, like all Orientalisms, black Orientalism—derived from African journeys like those of Douglass, spiritualist theories like those of Randolph, painterly historicism like that of Henry Ossawa Tanner, biblical figuralism like that of countless black Christians, and speculative Egyptology like that of Martin Delany (who, with his Niger expedition, his history of Prince Hall freemasonry, and his Afrocentric *Principia of Ethnology*, claims a role in the history of black Orientalism that can hardly be overestimated)—is a radically heterogeneous discourse, made up of what Lisa Lowe calls "the nonequivalence of various orientalisms." "I argue for the conception of orientalism as heterogeneous and contradictory," Lowe writes. "To this end I observe, on the one hand, that orientalism consist[s] of an uneven matrix of orientalist situations across different cultural and historical sites, and on the other, that each of these orientalisms is internally complex and unstable." [62] In these four examples of black Orientalism—a fugitive slave before the Civil War, an ex-slave after the Civil War, an egocentric missionary colonialist with a pointedly political grasp of the contemporary issues of Islamic Africa, and a suicidal spiritualist who created a sacralized, depoliticized, universalized Africa— we can see the structures of white Orientalism referenced and even relied on yet transformed at every turn.

And, to be sure, the contingent structures of and extremely flexible boundaries between "sacred" and "secular" constructions of the land of Pharaoh in African American discursive traditions highlight the extent to which black Orientalism depended on black Christianity—and thus domestic black resistance—as well as the extent to which "ancient" and "modern" Egypt shimmered regularly into one another. But all partook of a high degree of self-referentiality, and all took place in the context of transnational American imperialism, which allowed, however ambivalently, for the presence of Frederick Douglass on the top of the Great Pyramid. In ways not possible within the structures of whiteness, in ways only possible within the context of a domestic American imperialism—an imperialism of the interior experienced by Africans in America every single day—to construct the black Orient was to construct the black self. "Come all the way from Cairo town," went one verse of a black folk song from the region of southern Illinois known as Little Egypt, "And I never had but one dime to spend." Yet even in Little Egypt the black Orient bespoke of the ambivalences of masculinity:

> There was an old girl who lived in Cairo town,
> And I wish to the Lord that she was dead.[63]

## "Isis Unveiled"

One of the most instructive examples of nineteenth-century black Orientalism available can be seen in the career of Paschal Randolph—especially insofar as it represents the acute mixture of racialist fantasies and white

Orientalism so characteristic of nineteenth-century spiritualism, a combination of what Schueller has analyzed as "the sacralization of the Orient" and a particularly interesting instance of what Russ Castronovo calls the "Africanist sources of white parapsychology." [64] "In popular discourses of the white unconscious," writes Castronovo, "elements of African mysticism retained by diasporic black populations surfaced in antipolitical forms. . . . Abolitionism . . . staged a deeply conflicted circum-Atlantic performance that triangulated a newly discovered white unconscious amid enslaved black bodies. . . . The persistence of racial oppositions within spiritualism . . . betrays how the postpolitical world of the afterlife does not simply reflect but actively constructs hierarchies." [65] To be sure, the figure of Randolph presents something of an unusual case study in nineteenth-century African American cultural life, but it also speaks to the heterogeneity and complexity of black intellectualism of which it is sometimes easy to lose sight.

One of the only publicly visible black spiritualists remembered today, Randolph confined his most explicit antislavery opinions to only a few of his numerous works, and when he felt fully accepted by neither black activists nor white spiritualists he eventually chose to identify himself with the spiritualists. He did so despite his conflicts with the famous theosophist Madame Helena Petrovna Blavatsky; "Now the nigger is shooting at me!" Blavatsky was reported to have said once while witnessing Randolph attempting to murder her through astral projection from thousands of miles away.[66] Indeed, Randolph's relationship with the mostly white spiritualists, theosophists, Rosicrucians, and other unorthodox thinkers who formed the admittedly infighting nineteenth-century international occultist community was one marked by an ambivalence structured by a racism that Randolph repeatedly encountered yet constantly attempted to overcome — even though he was, however, ultimately unsuccessful. His life was brought to an end in July 1875 when, plagued by years of alternating embattled notoriety, intellectual misunderstanding, professional neglect, and alcoholism, he finally committed suicide. The only major scholarly work on Randolph places him almost exclusively in the context of white colleagues, peers, and enemies, in fact, but it makes equal sense to place him in a context of mostly black intellectuals working from within the spaces of Egyptology, ethnology, and abolitionist activism.[67]

As Randolph's career shows, however, one of the principle offshoots of the dramatic conceptual debates between science and religion that helped produce American Egyptomania during this time was spiritualism. And spiritualism—as well as the closely related idioms variously defined as occultism, mysticism, and popular metaphysics—not at all coincidentally would continue an extremely intimate idiographic relationship with the imagery and iconography of ancient Egypt, even to the late twentieth-century movement known loosely as New Age. The first comprehensive history of American spiritualism, for example, Emma Hardinge's *Modern American Spiritualism* of 1870, features as its frontispiece the literally radiant disembodied head of a long-haired, bearded, even Christ-like white man gazing down from the sky on an ancient Egyptian pyramid.[68] Spiritualism at the very least must be considered one of the central players in the tumultuous drama of epistemological absolutism that unfolded during the nineteenth century—featuring science and religion on center stage in a battle over transcendent truth—speaking many of the same lines even while having, to continue the metaphor, much less influential agents, and its claims to importance were marked not only by its rhetoric but by its uses of the iconography of ancient Egypt.

The importance of the iconography of ancient Egypt to discourses of the metaphysical, paranormal, and supernatural can hardly be overestimated. Seen most clearly in Blavatsky's 1877 *Isis Unveiled*, spiritualism, theosophy, and other occultist discourses seized on both the iconography of ancient Egypt and the possibilities offered by its manias to attempt to self-fashion a discourse with as much claim to transcendental truth and antiquarian validity as what would later be known as professional Egyptology. "Who will dare to lift the Veil of Isis?" Blavatsky asked, already knowing the answer. "The cold, stony lips of these hardy sphinxes keep their secrets well. Who will unseal them? . . . How came Egypt by her knowledge? When broke the dawn of that civilization whose wondrous perfection is suggested by the bits and fragments supplied to us by the archaeologists? . . . The key is in the esoteric doctrine."[69] Nor were such intertwined traditions ever separate from the discourses of human origin, speculative chronology, and race theory that first gave them rise. "It has been lately found that the ancient Egyptians were of the Caucasian type of mankind," wrote Blavatsky, providing epigrams by none other than George Robins Gliddon and citing Samuel George Morton and his *Crania Aegyptiaca*. "If they were less copper-colored than the Æthiopians of our modern day, the Æthiopians them-

Emma Hardinge, *Modern American Spiritualism: A Twenty Years'
Record of the Communion between Earth and the World of Spirits,*
frontispiece. New York, 1870. (Rare Book and Special
Collections Division, Library of Congress.)

selves might have had a lighter complexion in days of old."[70] In esoteric mysticism, just as they were in mainstream Egyptology itself, racialized fantasies of ultimate origins and ultimate truths were both means and end.

Indeed, the history of American Egyptomania is structured by a seemingly infinite list of assumptions and conclusions that seem to some altogether fantastic: the colonization of both North and South America by the ancient Egyptians, the construction of the pyramids of the Yucatán Peninsula by escapees from Atlantis, the erection of the mounds of the Ohio River valley by a mysterious race of beings who were parents to both Egypt and Atlantis. Of course, this tradition has continued well past the end of the nineteenth century, and, indeed, one could make the argument that for the level of cultural capital it has been able to maintain professional Egyptology owes as much to what it considers the fantastic tradition as it does to its more controlled rhythm of decades of slow excavation punctuated by periodic Eurekas. That is to say that the history of American interest in ancient Egypt is in large part one of the constant management of culturally disruptive revelations: whether scientific or revealed, orthodox or heterodox, any baseline interest in what is now professional Egyptology must derive at least in part from the fantasies that make up the bulk of American Egyptomania. Professional Egyptology, in other words, is in the business of constant debunking.

This is a critical point. For, throughout the nineteenth century, the same devices of debunking or labeling as pseudoscience or religious fables were used by mainstream Egyptology to deride any attempt to link the history of North Africa to the rest of the African continent. That is, the very suggestion of what today is referred to as "the blackness of ancient Egypt" was in fact the primary proving ground for the technologies of professionalized Egyptological debunking, and any claims against what has recently been revisited as "the Aryan model" of Egyptian civilization necessarily had to be made under the sign of heresy.[71] From the beginning, access to ancient Egypt as a secular artifact—in the form of travels abroad, lavishly illustrated folio volumes, or training in ancient languages—was the privilege of privilege, and this rather obvious fact was no more lost on European American spiritualists than it was on African American intellectuals. In this context, claims to an objective and apolitical "truth" rang as hollowly for one group as for the other. Just as spiritualism itself was a community marked by whiteness, in the interest of this field which was notoriously nonconformist, the political hammer of "scientific objectivity" took on a brighter sheen when wielded by a degree in classical languages.[72]

The first dynamics of modern scientific counterclaiming arose in nineteenth-century Egyptology, and they operated along two closely related fronts: that of the question of racialization and that of the question of what counted as the proper study of Egypt itself. Were, for example, the boundaries of Egyptology marked by the quest for a chronological origin beyond 4004 B.C.? Or for a Nubian or Ethiopian connection to ancient Egypt? Or for the people who built the Mayan pyramids? Or for the literal settlers known elsewhere as Ham, Shem, and Japheth? Or, as would become popular later, for a race of aliens who arrived from another planet? At any given point during the nineteenth century, any one of these questions—or their local versions—could seem as likely or unlikely to a given respondent as the next. This discursive and antagonistic structure not only produced a dynamic in which the earliest heterodoxes were racially charged ones, but in fact produced an endemic tendency in the history of Egyptomania that is quite possibly unique.

What would become Egyptology had, after all, made a name for itself in just this mode of heretical and heterodoxical challenges—to Christian chronology, to theology in general—which it nevertheless constantly resisted when it came to the issue of race. The charge of "the blackness of ancient Egypt" became the central model for challenging the privilege represented by those who would become professional Egyptologists—and whose immediate progenitors in the nineteenth century were doctors, politicians, and chaired professors—and the highly fraught, strikingly racialized, and constantly embattled structure of American interest in things ancient Egyptian would eventually produce New Age iconography as clearly as it would Elizabeth Taylor's Cleopatra and Tamara Dobson's Cleopatra Jones.[73] Indeed, not only were the boundaries between what counted as so-called Egyptology and so-called Egyptomania extremely hard and even impossible to draw, but the relationship between the two is cause for a singularly important point: as much as from the tensions between representations of ancient or modern blackness and whiteness and the subsequent development of modern racialization, American Egyptomania derived from the tensions between intimately related discourses that would develop into professional Egyptology and those that would remain somewhat divergent.

What was at stake, then, in the development of nineteenth-century rationalism was not just the construction of rationalism as a single system, whether of explanations or definitions. Rather, what was at stake was the relative validity of *competing* systems of rationalism; if nothing else, the multiple efforts made to codify the idiomatic structures of Christian chronology as a response to the threats posed to them by early Egyptology are testimony to this. But the rise of rationalism in the nineteenth century was not merely limited to the systems of explanation that would later develop into what might be loosely referred to as mainstream science; at every turn, claimants for the validity of a given rationalized system were engaged in constant turf wars, the boundaries of which were often blurry and quick to change. "Science" necessarily developed in tandem with "pseudoscience," their equivocating dynamics of mutual self-definition perfectly mirrored in each other.

In a space like that of Egyptomania, we can see this competition most strikingly. Rationalism, after all, played a central role in virtually all of its most important discourses: linguistics, chronology, archaeology, biology. And every one of these discourses was structured by a relationship to its arch-nemesis, often claiming territorial rights to precisely the same terrain and almost always understanding its position as the besieged one: monogenesis, polygenesis, secular history, sacred history, abolitionism, antiabolitionism. *What counted as* a valid frame of reference for an emergent system of rationalist discourse was always already a structuring concern, and more than a few rational systems cohered around a desire for representational capital in an overcrowded rationalist marketplace. With all of their highly elaborate rationalized structures, and with all of their manifest contempt for other systems, divergent branches of Egyptomania such as spiritualism and professional Egyptology are perfect examples of this dynamic—no less clearly than are the relationships between black and white Egyptomaniacs.


## Pyramids of Atlantis

This same set of territorial disputes—the same scandals that produced ethnology, archaeology, and Egyptology, that is, the chronological scandals of radical antiquity—also found expressive form in speculative scientific fantasies like those of Minnesotan Ignatius Donnelly. "The pyramid," wrote Donnelly in 1882, "is one of the marvelous features of that problem which confronts us everywhere, and which is insoluble without Atlantis."[74] In his *Atlantis: The Antediluvian World*, Donnelly provided a list of connections between ancient Egypt and ancient America:

4. The great similarity between the Egyptian civilization and that of the American nation.
5. The fact that the Egyptians claimed to be *red* men.
. . .
7. The presence of pyramids in Egypt and America.[75]

America, for Donnelly, was a colony of Atlantis. So was Egypt. So, in fact, was much of the rest of the world. "Atlantis," Donnelly wrote in cadences only too familiar in the history of Egyptology, "was the region where man first rose from a state of barbarism to civilization."[76] In Donnelly's narrative, "kindred races, with the same arts, and speaking the same tongue in an early age of the world, separated in Atlantis and went east and west— the one to repeat the civilization of the mother country along the shore of the Mediterranean Sea . . . while the other emigration advanced up the Amazon, and created mighty nations upon its headwaters in the valleys of the Andes and on the shores of the Pacific."[77] "Even the obelisks of Egypt," he wrote, "have their counterpart in America."[78]

Donnelly's Egypt is in what one might call the Atlantean mode, or perhaps his Atlantis is in the Egyptian mode. In this figuration, Egypt and Atlantis slide into one another; they both occupy the space between the mythic and the historical, between the sacred and the secular. Atlantis, after all, was the "*antediluvian* world," a figure poised precisely on the space of the Noachian deluge as inescapably biblical and yet sharply secularized. The very site of charges of "hoax" and "pseudoscience," archaeological melodramas like those of the story of Atlantis drew on the very manias they at times so desperately wanted to rationalize for their very logic and appeal. They networked the material and the fantastic, the biblical and the secular, the teleological and the apocalyptic. When the discovery of ancient Egypt became the discovery of ancient*ness* in general, Atlantis became the Egypt *of* Egypt, the archaeological fantasy of the archaeological.

With the help of America, then, Atlantis becomes Egypt in the apocalyptic mode. As the sign of both inexplicable origin and inexplicable apocalypse, Atlantis provided a crucial link between most of the variant modes of nineteenth-century ancient historiography: sacred, secular, rationalist, speculative, moralistic, romantic, prophetic. In fact, in Donnelly's formulation, the flood of Noah was actually the destruction of Atlantis: "An event," he describes with a classic apocalyptic shape, "which in a few hours destroyed, amid horrible convulsions, an entire country, with all its vast population—that population the ancestors of the great races of both continents, and they themselves the custodians of the civilization of their age. . . . Either the Deluge record of the Bible is altogether fabulous, or it relates to some land other than Europe, Asia, Africa, or Australia, some land that *was* destroyed by water. It is not fabulous; and the land it refers to is not Europe, Asia, Africa, or Australia—but Atlantis."[79] The sign of the apocalypse is thus what most securely sutures Atlantis to Egypt.

In true Egyptomanic form, however, even the sign of apocalypse is incomplete, deferred, merely an invitation to revisit the site of disaster in the hope of finding treasures forever buried. Once destroyed and lost to the ages, the sign of Atlantis, like Egypt, returns as one of inevitable rediscovery: "There now lies beneath the waters of the Atlantic, covered, doubtless, by hundreds of feet of volcanic débris, an amount of gold and silver exceeding many times that brought to Europe from Peru, Mexico, and Central America since the time of Columbus; a treasure which, if brought to light, would revolutionize the financial values of the world."[80] This colonialist fantasy—generated, by Donnelly, from the point of view of a colony that is itself establishing colonies—returns to and relies on the sign of origin, of parentage, of a tremulous and anxious vision of empire. But always the signs of desire are marked by those of mourning. "And how mighty must have been the parent nation," Donnelly laments, "of which this Egypt was a colony!" Elegies for Atlantis, elegies for Egypt.

## "The Whole Question of the Future"

There was, then, a recognizable formula for nineteenth-century American images of apocalypse: a great civilization rises from a status of insignificant colony to achieve a height of culture, either slides into weakness or spirals into decadence, and crumbles with a mighty tremble into the cataclysmic dust. This formula was based on, and repeatedly revealed to be, the sign of ancient Egypt. Indeed, the only indispensible requirement of apocalypse can be said to be a figure of this dust, otherwise known as the *trace*. Ruins, remnants, fragments of texts and their meanings, impenetrable mysteries and degraded racial types, origins, purities, and the hunt for the original man: these are signs, in their always already disappearing presence, of the always already reappearing absence of that which has left its mark only to vanish from sight and that which has vanished only to leave its mark. Like the synecdoche of apocalypse it was, these traces were everywhere shaped into the sign of ancient Egypt.

The problem with Greece and Rome as signs of apocalypse was that their respective slides and spirals were too well documented to allow for facile generalizations regarding their collapse—and even overdocumented by such efforts as Thomas Cole's four-part painting *The Course of Empire* of the 1830s.[81] Likewise, there was a similar problem with Atlantis, that other great signifier of advanced civilization lost in distant time to a mysterious apocalypse, even if merely reversed. Atlantis was too loosely documented, too easily dismissed, and of course too invisible both to archaeology and to the Grand Tour to provide material for sustained scholarly treatments. "We will not speak of the ancient island of Atalantis," admitted Josiah Nott, "that probably antedates all the nations of antiquity to which we have alluded. . . . All the civilization of antiquity sprung from a mighty race that once inhabited this island, which disappeared beneath the waters of the Atlantic, long before the names Hebrew or Chaldean were known."[82] The functionality of ancient Egypt was thus twofold and immediately obvious: on the one hand, it occupied the space between the representational validity of its more evident historiographic relatives in the locatable and specifically more recent Mediterranean, as well as the representational robustness of its more mythic cousin lost somewhere in the more distant Atlantic; on the other hand, the lack of clear documentation of either its origin or its end lent itself smoothly to mythologization. But it fulfilled—even revolutionized—an additional requirement for visions of nineteenth-century national apocalypse. It provided an opportunity for the introduction of race.

Race, in fact, was the best thing to happen to images of apocalypse since the book of Revelation. "It was for the most awful crime that man can commit in the sight of God," one self-appointed prophet wrote in 1867, "of which the punishment is on earth." God "now destroys by fire, not by water, but by fire, men, women and children, old and young, for the crime of miscegenating of *Adam's race with the negroes*."[83] Needless to say, contemporary accounts like these bore a great deal of resemblance to historical accounts of the fate of ancient Egypt. "Let me impress it with vivid letters upon the mind of the reader," A. Hoyle Lester wrote of Negroes and Egyptians, respectively, "that this degraded race was instrumental in hastening the decline and fall of this proud and illustrious people."[84] Miscegenation was the ultimate commonality between Egypt and America, just as was race itself. "Here again are the first symptoms of sexual intercommunication since the deluge between the high-born and ignoble races," Lester thundered, "which utterly debased the original Egyptian, and brought upon this beautiful, this lovely country, the prophetic vengeance of an incensed Jehovah."[85]

Miscengenation became apocalypse in the valleys of American Egyptomania. As the infamous John Van Evrie wrote in the "Historical Outline" to his 1875 *White Supremacy and Negro Subordination:* "Caucasian tribes or communities entered the valley of the Nile possibly before the delta of the lower country was sufficiently hardened to admit of cultivation. . . . These early adventurers conquered the aboriginal population, subjected them to their control, compelled them to labor for them, built magnificent cities, temples, palaces, founded a mighty Empire and advanced, to a certain extent, in civilization. But wealth and luxury, with their effeminate consequences . . . and, worst of all, interunion and affiliation with the conquered races, tempted purer and hardier branches of the race to invade them."[86] In completing the formula, Van Evrie went on to write of this "conquest, then the erection of a mighty Empire, followed by a grand civilization," followed by "effeminacy, affiliation with the subject races, debauchment and debility inviting a new conquest by pure Caucasians," which "in their turn, g[o] through the same round of glory and decay, of conquest and degradation."[87] The signs of race and the inevitable gravity of teleological historiography were both the means and the end for American Egyptomania.

Race became the sign of apocalypse, for many Afrocentrists as well as many Aryanists, as it became the sign of race mixing: the mark of the scarcely containable, frantically identifiable, always immanent irruption that was nevertheless somehow always barely avoided in its full apocalyptic opulence. Miscengenation was the signifier of racialization par excellence—indeed, the only such signifier that made any kind of operative sense in the oppositional dynamics of nineteenth-century nationalist rhetoric—and as such was much more critical to its political deployment than any invocation of purity could ever be. "This is the question," wrote Van Evrie, "the whole question of the future." The northern states

> now rule the south by military force, and by the same force have torn four millions of negroes from their normal condition, and are striving

to "reconstruct" American society on a Mongrel basis. . . . The Northern States have overthrown society in the South, and the simple problem
before this generation is the mode of social restoration—will it be done
through the common sense and reason of the people, or through civil
war, national bankruptcy, years of anarchy, and universal misery? . . . We
will return to the Constitution and the "Union as it was;" and every man,
and woman too, in this broad land must accept the simple but stupendous truth of white supremacy and negro subordination, or consent to
have it forced upon them by years of social anarchy, horror, and misery![88]

Race, like race mixing, race baiting, and race-based slavery, were as much
a part of the inheritance of American Egyptomania as the iconography of
the Great Pyramid.

The signs of race, like the signs of Egypt, were, however, radically structured by the impossibility of a purity that they declared themselves to signify, even as they warned of an apocalypse that they could never fully produce, even as they inscribed as their horizon a purity that their very iteration
forever deferred. "Just emancipated as they are from slavery," wrote Fontaine of an obvious group of people,

> and all the depressing influences of the ignorance, superstition, and
> hereditary barbarism of four thousand years, if they presume to grasp
> the reins of power and *to govern the white people* of America, who have been
> steadily advancing in all the arts and sciences, and improving in all the
> wisdom and refinement of Christian civilization for eighteen centuries,
> it then requires no inspired prophet to tell them that, in less than fifty
> years, from this date, a group of them in any of the cities of the United
> States will be as great a curiosity to the white people of that day as a gang
> of wild Indians are now to the children of a New-England village; and
> in the next century the whole black race will have faded from our shores
> like the shadow of a dark cloud which will be seen no more.[89]

The signs of race were made into the signs of immanent apocalypse, and
the prima facie evidence for the veracity of this equation was produced from
ancient Egypt.

But Egypt was well accustomed to the signs of the apocalypse. Indeed,
it was instrumental in drawing them into shape: as a mighty civilization
lost to the sands of time, its massive stone structures buried, the bodies
of its inhabitants crumbling to dust, an indispensable feature of American Egyptomania was the presentation of Egypt as tragically, inexplicably,

apocalyptically flawed. That the categories of biological racialization early Egyptologists were instrumental in constructing lent themselves so readily to narratives of national disaster is testimony to the communal ontologies of savagery, civilization, and decline that race science and early Egyptology shared. Likewise, that twinned visions of Egyptian and American empire could so easily accommodate the racialized dualities of amalgamationist discourse is as much a mark of the frantic operations of racialism in general as the matching obelisks outside the Streets of Cairo at the World's Columbian Exposition or Paschal Randolph's invocation of the metanymnic relationships between the United States and Egypt.

Nineteenth-century American Egyptomania encouraged speculative fantasies of race, nation, history, and civilization and produced a range of figures of doubled doubleness like no other cultural formation in the nation's history; that it could be used to communicate the terrors of a racialized apocalypse which, in its continual rediscoveries and permanent impermanence, dispelled the very fears it was intended to invoke, should come as no surprise. Surviving the end of the world was a daily routine. "I went down to Egypt, I camped upon de groun'," went the spiritual recorded by James Weldon Johnson after the close of the century, in language reminiscent of both an exodus from and a return to Egypt. "At de soundin' of de trumpet de Holy Ghost came down."

> An when de seals were opened, the voice said, "Come an' see,"
> I went an' stood a-looking to see de mystery.[90]

CHAPTER ONE

# "A Veritable

# He-Nigger after All"

EGYPT, ETHNOLOGY,

AND THE CRISES

OF HISTORY

During the first week of June 1850, a large crowd gathered at the Tremont Temple in Boston, Massachusetts. They had come to see a series of public lectures on many things related to ancient Egypt: its history, its customs, its geography, its monuments, and, in particular, as was the title of the course of the lectures, "The Art of Mummification among the Ancient Egyptians." The lectures took three days, held on Monday, Wednesday, and Friday, were attended by a wide range of spectators—scientists, housewives, businessmen, medical doctors, schoolchildren, historians, and dilettantes from many fields—and were dramatically interconnected by a central device. A mummy, recently acquired from Egypt, was to be unwrapped, a little at a time, over the course of the three days, and was to be used as both a centerpiece for the performance and a springboard for the relation of any number of facts and comments about ancient Egypt in general. On Monday, the sarcophagus was opened and its hieroglyphs translated, on Wednesday the outer linen was removed and a lecture given on the material process of mummification, and so forth. "Enquire of these parched and shriveled lips," the lecturer intoned, "what were their owner's vocal articulations. . . . Or ask this scorched though gilded hand, to trace in hieroglyphics upon papyrus paper the memoirs of a lady. . . . The gentle owner of this exquisite foot danced in girlish gladness to the sounds of harps which were struck long ere David sang." [1]

This lecturer—star speaker, procurer of the mummy, and notorious showman in his own right—was George Robins Gliddon. Gliddon was British born, a former U.S. vice consul for Cairo, and an avid amateur Egyptologist; he had organized the Tremont event almost single-handedly, as much as a tribute to himself as anything else, and so his place on center stage at the week's culminating moment was not only to be expected but was also intended to confirm his status as America's leading authority in the field of Egyptology. This chapter will have more to say on Gliddon, but for the time being it should be noted that it was only with Gliddon as one half of a dual centerpiece—Gliddon and his mummy—that the Tremont Temple show garnered the rather phenomenal excited attention that it did.

For the early part of the summer preceding the lectures of early June, Boston was gripped by *mummy fever*: as news of Gliddon's intended performance spread, many different sectors of Boston society built up an enthusiastic riff on the upcoming visit to the city by Gliddon and his "Egyptian Princess." Costume balls were held with Egyptian themes, rapturous poems were written to local newspapers, and the first fashionable topic of the summer had been found. And it was quite specifically a fashion of gender: what was advertised as the mummy of a *priestess* quickly became for those participating in the fad a *princess*, and this royal fantasy of the undressing of a Near Eastern princess long dead, before a crowd of two thousand, by her owner and possessor was, behaviorally speaking at least, not at all separate from the intellectualized endorsement that accounted for much of its public acceptance. "It was the dawn of paleopathology," writes Bob Brier of such public unwrappings, but it was also somewhat later in the day for the kind of Orientalist ambivalences on which Gliddon's event was so obviously based. [2]

The unwrapping process was accompanied by the inclusion of several guest speakers, attendees with seats of honor; at appropriate times, scientists from all over the United States would step forward and lecture on their various specialties — religion, anatomy, linguistics, and so on — and so this Boston lecture had a performative dynamic that borrowed from the institutionalized behaviors of professional academics. Given, however, the popularized appeal and the show's bodily centerpiece, the week's events were also highly reminiscent of those that took place in the "lecture rooms" of showmen such as P. T. Barnum. Barnum himself had displayed Egyptian mummies and their sarcophagi as early as the 1830s, but this Boston lecture was funded by all the intellectual capital its star speaker could muster, and as such it was framed as somewhat anxiously separate from the even more popularized displays of exotic artifacts to which it was nevertheless explicitly akin.

Gliddon was capitalizing on the successes of both similar events staged by others in England and Europe as well as earlier, similar lectures of his own, and they had all partaken equally of the combination of scholarly and public endorsement that characterized the Boston event. "The subject of Egyptian Antiquities has excited for some time past, and is still exciting," explained the editor of the published version of Gliddon's lecture for unwrapping, "but in this country, the excitement is pretty much confined within the narrow circle of Egyptian scholars themselves. . . . Mr. Gliddon's labours, however . . . have completely reversed this state of things: the public has been excited to a very unusual degree."[3]

On Friday, though, on the day of the final lecture, with a crowd of two thousand in attendance, with some of the most famous scientists in America looking on, and with members of the press eagerly awaiting the end of their story, as Gliddon removed the final bandages, reached in, and pulled the mummy out of its case for all the hall to see, a sharp gasp went up from the crowd: the mummy was that of a man. The crowd burst into laughter, the press had a field day, and Gliddon was more or less run out of town. Even at the moment, as one newspaper account had it of two of the more famous scientists participating, Jacob Bigelow and Louis Agassiz, "Dr. Bigelow blushed, and Professor Agassiz put his hands in his pockets."[4] Gliddon blamed his embarrassing mistake alternately on the illegibility of the hieroglyphic inscription on the mummy case or the bumbling of the workers at "the mummification establishment" in Egypt, thousands of years prior, who might not have been as attentive to issues of gender identification as he was. Either way, even though his supporters liked to claim that Gliddon's reputation as an Egyptian scholar was undamaged, most of the popularized images of him after the first week of June 1850 were one-sidedly satirical and expectedly merciless.

It would be almost four years before Gliddon regained the popular respect he obviously craved, and, not coincidentally, it would be through a concerted attempt at controlling the epistemological instability that had so embarrassingly attended his Boston performance. His definitional concerns in his later life, though, would be much more specific regarding their anxieties; they would treat gender in a much more occluded and erasable way, as a virtually forgotten and intentionally forgettable footnote in a long history of the production, reproduction, and decline of peoples, nations, and empires. His epistemologies after 1850 would concern themselves almost exclusively with issues of race.

Indeed, Gliddon's interest in utilizing his Egyptological lectures as a platform for discussing issues of race was by no means absent from the days of the Tremont event. "In this man's skull," he had exclaimed over another, less ambivalently male, mummy, during an earlier unrolling, "we behold one of ourselves—a Caucasian, a pure white-man; notwithstanding the bitumen which has blackened the skin."[5] In point of fact, Gliddon's career to this point had in every way been associated with the rise of race science, as it would be for the rest of his life, and his American lectures were as famous for their raciological conclusions as they were for their highly crafted, if at times unintentional, drama. "Are anatomical laws so false," Gliddon would ask while unwrapping his mummies, "that a people with such physiognomical and osteological characteristics—a people whose mighty deeds are still erect in stone . . . should not possess a development of head and volume of brain commensurate with the grandeur of their work?" Displaying his Egyptian skulls onstage, he would ask rhetorically: "Could a people gifted with such facial angles, elevation of forehead, smooth hair and aristocratic noses as these, fail to be great men and women?"[6]

Gliddon's Boston event was one in a long line of moments partaking of links between nineteenth-century American Egyptology and the rise of racialized science, and it is with these links that the rest of this chapter will be concerned. Yet it is also crucial to remember that Gliddon's efforts were by no means going unnoticed by the very group he was attempting to analyze out of the history of the Nile Valley. By the end of the month of Gliddon's Boston debacle, the African American abolitionist newspaper *The North Star* ran this article:

### WERE THE THEBANS NEGROES.

There has been a wonderful fuss over a mummy at Boston lately. It is described as very ancient, and was supposed to be a Princess or Priestess of Thebes, in her glory. — Great parade and ceremony has been made as to the unrolling of the mummy. It has been done with much care in regard to highly excited literary taste in Boston, and in regard to the science of mummy-making, as well as the presumption that jewels, or manuscripts, might be found entombed in this relic of mortality.

Before the unrolling of the antiquated thing, we had many literary strictures and lectures from the learned, in Boston and about, in regard to the genealogy of the Thebans, of whom the mummy was supposed to be a royal relic. One important point was, to make out, that the Thebans, were a different race from the poor black creatures that mope now among the ruins of the city of a hundred gates. Oh! no. It would be bad taste enough to be paying great respect to the corpse of a nigger, if it be royal. We were assured therefore, by the learned doctors, that the Thebans were not Africans, but a nobler race, and had none of the particularities of niggerdom. Although this did not quite agree with Heroditus, and their contemporary historians, nevertheless the learned were sure it must be so.

Well, the poor old mummy, was at length stripped of its swaddling clothes, and disembowled, and furnished evidence of little else than that it was a veritable "he-nigger" after all. A humbling relic enough of Theban royalty, learning, and renown.[7]

## "A Fearful Crisis Must Come, Sooner or Later"

In 1854, Gliddon and an Alabama medical doctor named Josiah Clark Nott published in Philadelphia *Types of Mankind; or, Ethnological Researches, Based upon the Ancient Monuments, Paintings, Sculptures, and Crania of Races, and upon their Natural, Geographical, Philological, and Biblical History.* Over 700 pages long and drawing on the work of dozens of leading scholars, *Types of Mankind* took developments in the fields of phrenology, craniometry, comparative anatomy, and other biological and natural sciences, presented them in collaboration with developments in the newly burgeoning field of Egyptology, and produced what is still considered the signature work of what would quickly come to be known as the American School of Ethnology. "Ethnology demands to know," wrote Nott, "what was the primitive organic structure of each race?—what such race's moral and physical character?—how far a race may have been, or may become, modified by the combined action of time and moral and physical causes?—and what position in the social scale Providence has assigned to each type of man?"[8] The critical phrase here is *organic structure*; *Types of Mankind* and the tradition it represents mark the initial consolidation of an extended appeal to *biology* in American racialized discourse and the presentation of the notion of biological racial types. Married to the notion of biological racialization was what was an equally strong selling point for many nineteenth-century naturalists and one that was seen as inseparable from its other innovations: the contributions the volume made to the defense of slavery. Offered in support of this project, as both proof and conclusion, were contemporaneous developments coming from the study of ancient Egypt.

*Types of Mankind* is infamous today for being the representative text of the American School and thus for many the best example of racist science the Western tradition has to offer. It was a watershed event in the history of American culture; it was the signature text of the American School, and Nott and Gliddon were its self-appointed messiahs. "Here we see the white and black races together," Nott had written two years before the publication of *Types of Mankind*, "under circumstances which cannot last always. A fearful crisis must come, sooner or later."[9] Like Gliddon, Nott had lectured and published actively on the issue of biological racialization before 1854, but the appearance of *Types of Mankind* was widely recognized as the fulfillment of a promise repeatedly made by the field of ethnology since its inception: a particularly American reply to a particularly American question. "The time must come," Nott prophesied, "when the blacks will be worse than useless to us. What then?"[10] Answering himself with a voice as urgent as it was self-assured, Nott foretold destruction, and the American School thundered its biological politics: "*Emancipation* must follow, which, from the lights before us, is but another name for extermination."[11] The argument was straightforward: "The numberless attempts by the Caucasian race, during several thousand years, to bring the Mongol, Malay, Indian, and Negro, under the same religion, laws, manners, customs, etc., have failed, and must continue to fail, unless the science of Ethnography can strike out some new and more practical plan of operation. So utterly fruit-less have been the attempts of the philanthropist, that we might well pause and ask whether we are not warring against the immutable laws of Nature, by endeavoring to elevate the intellectual condition of the dark, to that of the fair races."[12] Nott and Gliddon were key figures in the establishment of an objectivist racialized discourse whose most explicit agenda was the stabilization of theories that could provide the conceptual support for in-stitutionalized American slavery. *Types of Mankind* was at times both cause and effect of that agenda.

What ethnology owed to prewar institutionalized slavery was a system of control that was as attentive to epistemology as it was. The very same contingencies that the American slave system had to negotiate every day — "lazy, shiftless Negroes," biblical controversies over the justifications for slavery, and children of slave mothers who could pass as white—were the basis for the interests of ethnological science, and of this branch of natural history in general. The American School was the high-water mark for racialized naturalism in America: as widely influential—and as widely controversial—as any science before or since, it occupies a foundational moment for conceptions of human biological diversity, drawing on de-veloping notions of scientific objectivity, secular knowledge, and factual impartiality even as it declared its relevance from a place of social up-heaval, political controversy, and public implications. Its members were as fiercely committed to its application as a social solution as they were to the demands of its intellectual labors, and the particular strategy of staging social arguments through claims of objective observations that made the American School so famous would be as important to its effects as any single truth claim that emerged from its ranks.

The interdisciplinary structure of *Types of Mankind* was as responsible for its success as its authors, and in its collaborative logic can be seen the alliances of proslavery science; as the product of a violently racist medical doctor and a popularizer of Egyptology, *Types* did more in the half cen-tury it was in print to promote theories of both biological racialization and racialized Egyptology than any other single text in either of its fields. Nott and Gliddon were explicitly proslavery race theorists, and to the Ameri-can School belongs the dubious honor of the simultaneous introduction of a systematic biologization of human cultural diversity and the point-edly political application of that system. Only rarely, however, if ever, is note taken of the centrality of contemporaneous discoveries in the Nile

Valley for both the shape of the ethnological argument in general and the structure of *Types of Mankind* in particular. The text is structured primarily through a discussion of ancient Egyptians.

## "The Climate of Egypt Will
## Never Change a Caucasian into a Negro"

"The truth of these observations is sustained by all past history, backed by every monument," wrote Nott and Gliddon in *Types of Mankind*:

> Much as the success of the infant colony at Liberia is to be desired by every true philanthropist, it is with regret that, whilst wishing well to the Negroes, we cannot divest our minds of melancholy forebodings. . . . The Negro races possess about nine cubic inches less of brain than the Teuton; and, unless there were really some facts in history, something beyond bare hypotheses, to teach us how these deficient inches could be artificially added, it would seem that the Negroes . . . must remain substantially in that same benighted state wherein Nature has placed them, and in which they have stood, according to Egyptian monuments, for at least 5000 years.[13]

It is no accident that this passage is at once one of truth, Liberia, brain size, race, and Egypt. It is also no accident that in it history runs into the future, Teutonism leads to enlightenment, and ancient Egyptian monuments stand judgment over it all. The connections between the issues of this passage, and the habits of thought and writing that constitute those connections, relied on such equations: race was a matter of truth, civilization was a matter of cranial capacity, and Egypt, properly understood and represented, was the ultimate authority of the ages.

Indeed, the increasingly rarefied discourses on which this passage draws were as much a matter of *making* these connections as of their consequent rarification; the conjunction of craniometry, natural history, ancient history, and contemporary politics that produced this passage also produced the field from which it comes, ethnology. "The authors esteem it a very high privilege that 'Types of Mankind' should be the first work to remove all doubts upon the type of the earliest monumental Egyptians," Nott and Gliddon wrote. "A powerful and civilized race may be conquered, may become adulterated in blood; yet the type, when so widely spread, as in and around Egypt, has never been obliterated, can never be washed out. . . . History abundantly proves that human language may become greatly corrupted by exotic admixture — nay, even extinguished; but physiology demonstrates that a type will survive tongues, writings, religions, customs, manners, monuments, traditions, and history itself." [14] In America, the scientific construction of race *begins* with the question of ancient Egypt and vice versa: the question of the race of the ancient Egyptians inaugurates the field of American Egyptology. [15]

It has been virtually forgotten that the bodily scientistic discourses of racialized difference that arose in America in the 1840s and 1850s did so primarily through the mobilization of the discourses of the history and archaeological significance of ancient Egypt and vice versa. "The academic account of Egypt was not simply influenced and changed because of increasing racism and racialism," writes Robert J. C. Young, "but actually provided the key to the arguments and constituted the proof of racial theory itself." [16] The rise of American *Egyptology* was thus coincident and thoroughly imbricated with the rise of American *Ethnology*, and so there is a historiographic specificity: the rise of American Egyptology did not crest until the 1840s and 1850s — that is, until the period of tension marking the decades immediately preceding the Civil War. From their earliest appearances in nineteenth-century America, images and discourses of and about ancient or Pharaonic Egypt were scandalously racialized — and thus established their basis for continuing to be so even to this day — and can be traced back to the racialized tensions within American cultures concentrated around the institutionalized systems of African slavery. The critical contention was succinctly presented by a contributor to *Types of Mankind*: "Negroes were numerous in Egypt. Their social position, in ancient times, was the same that it is now; that of servants or slaves." [17]

The European traditions of discursive racialization and the development of racialized sciences are ones that have been recounted in any number of studies, as has the rise of the American School. [18] My interest here is not necessarily to rework these previous studies but more specifically to show some of the ways in which the rise of American ethnology was coincident and interactive with the rise of American Egyptology; with proliferating discourses of race-based slavery, mostly in the United States; and with the ways in which both theological and secular discourses about pre-Darwinian practices of history, historiography, and chronology were uneasily and vigorously mapped onto discourses about and practices of biology, racial capability, racial typology, institutionalized political and social agency, and "civilization." "Egypt, as the earliest civilization, developed in Africa," writes Young, "clearly represented the major stumbling-block to the claim for the permanent inferiority of the black race which, it was alleged, had never created or produced anything whatsoever of value."[19]

The scientific and social interest in ancient Egypt for Americans in the nineteenth century was directly related to the tensions, concerns, and anxieties over the institutionalized uses of Africans and their descendants as the foundation of an entire economic and social system in the United States. Within the history of American opinions concerning ancient Egypt is contained the history of American opinions concerning race and racial identity and vice versa. Throughout the nineteenth century, arguments about race—and in particular racial *origin*—were made on the basis of arguments about ancient Egypt. And, equally importantly, claims about ancient Egypt were made in the service of claims about the nature of race. Throughout nineteenth-century America, a tightly interwoven set of questions and answers about race, racial origin, Egypt, and Egyptian history was constitutive of the formation of *both* racial politics and attitudes *and* professional and popular Egyptology. Egypt thus became a semiotically folded space: a primary place of legitimation for both secular and theological accounts of the history of "man" and a primary place of legitimation for both secular and theological accounts of the history of races. American Egyptology was founded on anxiety about human origin.

The most famous formulation of this anxiety is the debate in the nineteenth century between monogeny and polygeny, and ancient Egypt figured crucially in the exchanges of that debate. "It is now generally conceded," wrote Nott, "that there exist no data by which we can approximate the date of man's first appearance upon earth. . . . We turn, unshackled by prejudice, to the monumental records of Egypt as our best guide."[20] As Nott put it in a letter to J. B. D. De Bow in 1849: "Having passed our childhood and manhood in daily intercourse with the white and black races, it is but natural that you and I should have become deeply impressed not only by the physical but also by the moral and intellectual differences which exist between them: nor is it less natural that a doubt as to their common origin should suggest itself to our minds."[21] The debate over "multiple origins," as it was usually termed in the nineteenth century, had as its stakes both an authoritative chronology and an authoritative biology. "The grand problem," wrote Nott, "is that which involves the *common origin* of races; for upon [it] hang[s] not only certain religious dogmas, but the more practical question of the equality and perfectibility of races."[22]

> Twenty-five years of unceasing professional intercourse with these races, and study of their diseases, anatomy, and physiology, a careful perusal of all the leading works published in the French and English languages on the Natural History of Man, from Camper and Blumenbach down to the present day, and an examination of the earliest known records of nations, both written and monumental, have not only served to strengthen this doubt in my mind, but have ripened it into a firm conviction that the Almighty in his wisdom has peopled our vast planet from many distinct centres, instead of one, and with races or species originally and radically distinct.[23]

The production of a racialized history was thus the production of race *as* history, of history as that of races. "Looking back over the world's history," Nott and Gliddon wrote, "it will be seen that human progress has arisen mainly from the war of races."[24]

Initially, then, Western Egyptology can be seen as not so much a search for or explanation of the origins of the world or of "man," but a complication of and challenge to existing models of origin. Its intersection and interaction with somewhat more developed discourses of origin and origination—that is, with what was becoming ethnology—provided the space for the production of texts such as *Types of Mankind*. In America, at least, the rise of racialized science was precisely coincident with the development of narratives of comparative natural history, and the currency and stakes of this exchange were, among other things, chronological. "We come now to the great question of *Chronology*," pronounced Nott, "which may be regarded as the touchstone of history."[25] Nott and Gliddon wrote that "the Egyptian, Negro, several White, and sundry Yellow races, ha[ve] existed, in their present forms, for at least 4000 years; and . . . it beho[oves] the statesman to lay aside all current speculations about the origin and perfectibility of races, and to deal, in political argument, with the simple facts as they stand."[26]

For American Egyptology, this chronological prize was crucially encoded. If Egyptologists were right, and the biblical chronology *was* rendered obsolete by the dating and deciphering of the monuments of ancient Egypt, then that only cleared the way for the more important revelation:

that even given this huge expanse of prebiblical past—and in fact on the authority of it—the races of mankind known by racial theorists in the nineteenth century *had not changed*, even in the slightest, for all those thousands of years. "Nowhere on the face of the globe," claims *Types of Mankind*, "do we find a greater diversity, or more strongly marked types, than on the monuments of Egypt, antedating the Christian era more than 3000 years." [27] The American School issued its challenge to Christian chronology plainly: "We are told, in the book of Genesis, that the whole human race was destroyed by the deluge, except Noah and his family, which event took place, according to the Hebrew text, but two thousand three hundred and forty-eight years before Christ, and according to the Septuagint, three thousand two hundred and forty-six years; and, from one of these dates, the repeopling of the whole earth commenced. . . . Can any one ask for further argument to prove that these dates are wholly untenable, when it is so clear that Egypt, India, and China, and probably America, contained immense populations, with organized governments, and were greatly advanced in civilization, even as far back as the spurious Septuagint date for the deluge? when, too, it is remembered that the tombs of America, the catacombs and monuments of Egypt—the earliest history known to all of us nations, show the types of men to have been as distinct, and even more so, than the adulterated races of the present day?" [28] Thus the title of Nott and Gliddon's book; thus races today are the same as races in ancient Egypt and hence are *permanent* "types of mankind"; thus Negroes have been and eternally will be slaves: "The monuments of Egypt prove, that *Negro* races have not, during 4000 years at least, been able to make one solitary step, in Negro-Land; the modern experiences of the United States and the West Indies confirms the teachings of monuments and of history; and our remarks . . . hereafter, seem to render fugacious all probability of a brighter future for these organically-inferior types." [29] Earlier in his career, Gliddon had been less equivocal: "The climate of Egypt will never change a Caucasian into a Negro, a black into a white man." [30]

For nineteenth-century students of the Bible, whether clergy or not, debates about race centered around issues of divine creation and competing interpretations of certain passages in the book of Genesis. This was also the territory traveled by scientists and historians; even after Darwin, issues concerning biological or historical origin were heavily indebted to accounts found in the Bible. So virtually every American biologist, naturalist, or ancient historian working in the nineteenth century, either dur-

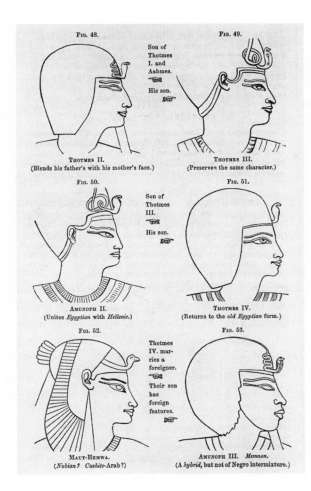

FIG. 48.

THOTMES II.
(Blends his father's with his mother's face.)

Son of
Thotmes
I. and
Aahmes.

His son.

FIG. 49.

THOTMES III.
(Preserves the same character.)

FIG. 50.

AMUNOPH II.
(Unites *Egyptian* with *Hellenic*.)

Son of
Thotmes
III.

His son.

FIG. 51.

THOTMES IV.
(Returns to the *old Egyptian* form.)

FIG. 52.

MAUT-HEMWA.
(*Nubian? Cushite-*Arab?)

Thotmes
IV. mar-
ries a
foreigner.

Their son
has
foreign
features.

FIG. 53.

AMUNOPH III. *Memnon.*
(A *hybrid*, but not of Negro intermixture.)

"The Caucasian Types Carried through Egyptian Monuments." (From Josiah Clark Nott and George Robins Gliddon, *Types of Mankind.* Philadelphia: Lippincott, Grambo, 1854, figs. 48–53, p. 146. Library of Congress.)

ing the peak of race-based African slavery or after Emancipation, had to answer what was by all rights a very tricky question: were the physical, social, economic, and geographical differences that operated to such widespread effect in the Western Hemisphere threatened by the Bible's account of a single human origin, or not? In the opinion of Nott and Gliddon, the answer was clearly yes: "To Egyptology, beyond all question, belongs the honor of dissipating those chronological fables of past generations, continued belief in which . . . implies simply the credulity of ignorance. . . . Scientific truth, exemplified in the annals of Astronomy, Geology, Chronology, Geographical distribution of animals, &c., has literally fought its way inch by inch through false theology. The last grand battle between science and dogmatism, on the primitive origin of races, has now commenced. It requires no prophetic eye to foresee that science must again, and finally, triumph."[31] The single most cathected point of intersection for these concerns, both secular and sacred, political and scientific, was ancient Egypt.

## "Them Critters Is of African Descent True as Preachin"

Virtually every American text produced in the middle to late nineteenth century with an interest in human history and ethnology contains at least a brief consideration of the color or racialized "type" of the ancient Egyptians. "Only illiterate people imagine that the people of Northern Africa were negroes," wrote a Virginia minister in 1891, using the pseudonym "Caucasian": "The Egyptians, Carthagenians and Moors were powerful and civilized nations, and exterminated or enslaved the negro populations of their respective territories. They were all Caucasians; and to suppose that Hannibal, Cleopatra, Saladin, St. Augustine, Cyprian, Tertullian, and others of distinguished fame, were negroes because born in Africa, is as absurd as to suppose that the descendants of modern Europeans settled in America are Indians."[32] Some writers framed the question in terms of whiteness, others in terms of blackness; some proceeded by asserting the obvious objectivity of their beliefs, others by challenging the absurdity of the beliefs of their intellectual or political opponents. But with a rapidity that seemed to its adherents like a promise redeemed, and to its critics like a threat made good, certain rhetorical moves regarding racialized types, human origin, and human capabilities were rehearsed over and over again and, like many developments in nineteenth-century science, were quickly sedimented. "The Caucasian is the only historical race," wrote one white ethnologist in 1866, "and is the only one capable of those mental manifestations which have a permanent impression behind. It is the only race that can be said to leave a history. . . . The excavations of Champolion and others demonstrate the specific character of the negro race four thousand years ago, with as absolute and unmistakable certainty as it is now actually demonstrated to the external sense of the present generation."[33] The colonialist archaeological discoveries in Egypt produced chronological possibilities that were addressed by scholars both sacred and secular, in ethnology and

Egyptology, and, with the ontological ramifications of these possibilities carefully and frantically racialized as they were, a history of the development of one of these fields carries with it a history of the development of another.

For some writers, the question of the race of the ancient Egyptians was of importance vital enough to base an entire career around. In *Types of Mankind*, Nott and Gliddon devote most of their chapter "Egypt and Egyptians," in which they call Egypt "the last geographical link in African Ethnology" and "the mother of arts and sciences,"[34] to defending against any claims that the ancient Egyptians—by which they mean both the pharaohs and the individuated "autocthonic" race of which they were a part—were "Negroid" and, more generally, against any claim that they were anything but "autocthonic." "In the broad field and long duration of Negro life," they wrote, "not a single civilization, spontaneous or borrowed, has existed, to adorn its gloomy past. The ancient kingdom of Meroë has often been pointed out as an exception, but this is now proven to be the work of Pharaonic Egyptians, and not of Negro races."[35] More or less professionalized American scientistic discourses of racialization in the nineteenth century were precisely those which were configured by and through this intersection of ethnology and Egyptology—and, just as importantly, vice versa. Along these battle lines were placed questions of the color of the ancient Egyptians.

American ethnology developed in part out of an anxiety about just these questions. "For many centuries prior to the present," rages *Types of Mankind*, "the Egyptians were reputed to be *Negroes*, and Egyptian civilization was believed to have descended the Nile from *Ethiopia!*"[36] Early in its history, one foundational figure documented his concern:

> NOTE.—On the *Supposed Affinity between the Egyptians and Negroes.*—I trust I shall be excused for offering, in this place, a few brief remarks in reference to an opinion which, however much at variance with multiplied facts, has still some strenuous advocates: I allude to that hypothesis which classes the ancient Egyptians with the Negro race. Among the advocates of this opinion was Volney, the celebrated traveller. He looked upon the *Sphinx*, and hastily inferred from its flat features and bushy hair, that the Egyptians were real Negroes: yet these circumstances have no weight when we recur to the fact, that the Budhists of Asia . . . represent their principal god with Negro features and hair, and often sculptured in black marble; yet among the three hundred millions who worship Budha,

there is not, perhaps, a solitary Negro nation. The Egyptians borrowed many of their mythological rites from their southern neighbors . . . but such facts are no proofs of the affiliation of races. . . . There is no absolute proof, moreover, that the Sphinx represented an Egyptian deity: it may have been a shrine of the Negro population of Egypt, who, as traffickers, servants, and slaves, were a very numerous body.[37]

Even Gliddon himself was at times visibly nervous: "It has been the fashion to quote the Sphinx, as an evidence of the Negro tendencies of the ancient Egyptians. They take his *wig* for curly hair—and as the nose is off, of course it is *flat*. . . . But even if the face (which I fully admit) has a strong African cast, it is an almost solitary example, against 10,000 that *are not African*."[38] How surprised would Gliddon's unwrapped mummies be, he asked his audiences, "could we recall them to life, to learn that we moderns have actually speculated in learned works, whether their countrymen were Africans or even Negroes . . . or their hair actually wool!"[39]

What is important here is not just that Nott, Gliddon, and their fellow researchers are making it such a point to disagree with the claims of the "pro-Negro" position, and not just the ways in which they do so (the Sphinx is wearing a wig, Buddha is represented as a Negro but has no Negro worshipers), but that it is called "the fashion" in the early decades of the nineteenth century to be sympathetic toward claims of blackness for the ancient Egyptians. Much is implied in these remarks. Historical documentation notwithstanding (the balance of these "strenuous advocates" are not named), early American Egyptologists certainly believed that the proposal of a "supposed affinity between the Egyptians and Negroes" was an organized and insistent threat. *Types of Mankind*, for example, asserts that "did archaeological science now solely rely, as before Champollion's day, upon the concurrent testimony of early Greek writers, we should be compelled to conclude that the Egyptians, previously to the Christian era, were literally *Negroes*. . . . Although new facts supersede the necessity for recurring to such past disputations. . . . it must be conceded that Negroes, at no time within the reach even of monumental history, have inhabited any part of Egypt, save as captives."[40] "From the poetic age of Homer," wrote Gliddon, casting a historical eye, "down to the sentimentalism of the present age, it has been fashionable, to take much for granted on Egyptian subjects, of which a sober and practical investigation of the facts would at once have exposed the fallacy. . . . I deem it requisite only to allude to the prevalent, but erroneous notion of the African origin of the ancient Egyptians."[41]

Even as the first studies were being conducted and the first texts were being written, ethnological scholarship was profoundly concerned not only with orienting itself around these questions but also, and just as importantly, with establishing the *danger* of such claims. "We may safely assert," wrote Gliddon, "so far, then, as the record, scriptural, historical, and monumental, will afford us an insight into the early progress of the human race in Egypt . . . that history . . . will not support the superannuated, but untenable doctrine, that civilization originated in Ethiopia, and consequently among an African people, and was by them brought down the Nile to enlighten the less-polished, and therefore inferior, Caucasian children of Noah . . . or that we, who trace back to Egypt the origin of every art and science known to antiquity, have to thank the sable Negro . . . for the first gleams of knowledge and invention."[42] In the tightly knit community of scholars whose research led to the development of institutionalized Egyptology, much theoretical and practical work was directed toward and targeted at discrediting any effort to suggest a strong connection between ancient Egypt and "black" Africa. "For civilization, that never came *northward* out of benighted Africa," Gliddon wrote in 1842, "*could* not spring from Negroes, and *never did*."[43]

In fact, this association—between the American School and American racism—was sufficiently well known during its midcentury height to even inspire parody. "An old lady at the Museum a day or so ago," reported the *Chicago Times* in 1863, "coming suddenly upon a case containing two Egyptian mummies was extremely horrified at their exhibition without clothing of any kind." She

> remark[ed] to the young girl who accompanied her,
> "Sairy them critters is of African descent true as preachin, and that accounts for their not being buried like white folks and Christians."
> "These are mummies, madam," remarked a gentleman who stood nearby, endeavoring to control his inclination to laugh heartily at the old lady's speech.
> "Well," returned she with renewed indignation, "I don't keer whose mummies they be, its a tarnal shame to have human beings dug up and made a show of, even if they be niggers. But its just like them poky southerners to beat their colored brothers to death and then stick them in the ground with nary stitch of clothing on to hide their nakedness."[44]

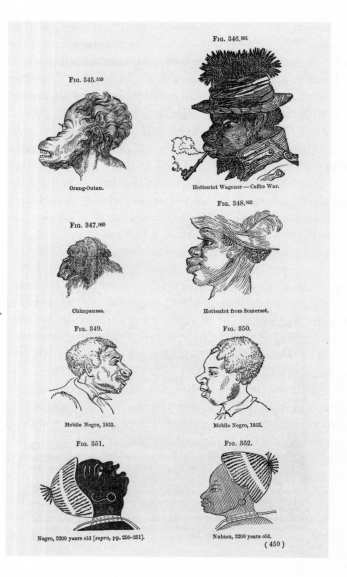

Fig. 345.559

Orang-Outan.

Fig. 346.561

Hottentot Wagoner — Caffre War.

Fig. 347.560

Chimpanzee.

Fig. 348.562

Hottentot from Somerset.

Fig. 349.

Mobile Negro, 1853.

Fig. 350.

Mobile Negro, 1853.

Fig. 351.

Negro, 3200 years old [*supra*, pp. 250–251].

Fig. 352.

Nubian, 3200 years old.

( 459 )

"Negro Types." (From Josiah Clark Nott and George Robins Gliddon, *Types of Mankind*. Philadelphia: Lippincott, Grambo, 1854, figs. 345–52, p. 459. Library of Congress.)

In other words, nineteenth-century American Egyptology was always in something of a constant panic over what would later come to be called Afrocentricity.

## "A Slave of Slaves Shall He Be to His Brothers"

One of the most characteristic upshots of this period in American history—which, by the way, is also a period in the history of positivism—is that painfully contemporary social debates were being waged in and through more or less professionalized discourses of chronology: of biblical history; ancient, secular history; of natural history. And for those participating in one of these debates a point through which almost everyone had to pass was the point at which these discourses were perhaps most closely related or most carefully teased apart: the ninth and tenth books of Genesis:

> And the sons of Noah, that went forth of the ark, were Shem, and Ham, and Japheth: and Ham is the father of Canaan. These are the three sons of Noah: and of them was the whole earth overspread. And Noah began to be a husbandman, and he planted a vineyard: and he drank of the wine, and was drunken; and he was uncovered within his tent. And Ham, the father of Canaan, saw the nakedness of his father, and told his two brethren without. And Shem and Japheth took a garment, and laid it upon both their shoulders, and went backward, and covered the nakedness of their father; and their faces were backward, and they saw not their father's nakedness. And Noah awoke from his wine, and knew what his younger son had done unto him. And he said,
> Cursed be Canaan;
> a servant of servants shall he be unto his brethren.
> And he said,
> Blessed be the Lord God of Shem;
> and Canaan shall be his servant.
> God shall enlarge Japheth,
> and he shall dwell in the tents of Shem;
> and Canaan shall be his servant.[45]

The Curse of Noah and the Table of Nations which follow it in Genesis 10 became, for many embroiled in ethnological debates, a typically Old

Testament example of unity and diversity, of origination and repetition, but one that in America had enormous implications for the politics of race-based slavery. "The son of Noah, Ham, may not have been black," wrote Edward Fontaine in a defensive tone typical of the embattled positions of proslavery biblical ethnology, "but all of his descendants who continued, generation after generation, to dwell in the hot and dry regions watered by the Nile, north of Khartoum, must have gradually been made so by the atmosphere. . . . The ancestors of these tribes seem to have degenerated into . . . miserable wretches . . . and were enslaved by the ancient Egyptians as they are by the modern occupants of the Black-land, whence they originally migrated." [46]

According to this shared narrative, Noah, the carrier of history and the point of beginning anew, produced a unified family that famously dispersed over the earth, each son generating a different nation—and "race"—from whole cloth, each one becoming a patriarch who resembled his father as much as each other and yet not at all. That both the traditional and nontraditional interpretations of this book of the Bible included accounts that were for nineteenth-century Americans already racialized, and that these accounts were also already of geography and genealogy, further ensured—and indeed produced—the importance of this text for discourses of ethnology. "To get rid of the responsibility of brotherhood to the Negro," wrote Edward Wilmot Blyden in an obvious swipe at the American School, "an American professor, in an elaborate work, claims for the tropical African a pre-Adamite origin, and ignores his relation with Ham. His arguments, however, are, as yet, beneath the level of scientific criticism." [47]

Much of this importance was based on the importance of ancient Egypt. Because it was either Ham or Canaan who received the curse, and because it was Mizraim, the son of Canaan, who went south and was said in one tradition to have founded Egypt, the coextant tradition of interpreting, in one way or another, the curse of slavery as a curse of color—one of many traditions of interpreting Ham as the founder of the black "race"—provided, in relation, the means for a particularly fraught set of discursive negotiations. [48] "This speculative view is so far applicable to Egypt," wrote Gliddon, "that Mizraim, who may have acquired the most fertile soil of the earth as a grant from Providence, was not an outcast from the patriarchal family: while, being of the same blood with Noah himself, he was in physical conformation a Caucasian." [49]

Like many of his antiblack colleagues, Gliddon saw only too well the radical implications of this African Trojan horse: if, by whatever means, Negroes could be understood to have been the original inhabitants of the Nile Valley, then problack forces would have an obvious beachhead in the war over Western history. "So the Greeks got their letters from a Hamite," wrote African American naturalist theologian Harvey Johnson in 1889, "whether Phoenician or Egyptian, and the Hamites not only taught the Greeks their letters, but the present governing and prevailing mother languages of the earth are Hamitic in their origin."[50] Even worse for the advocates of the American School, this beachhead would be biblically sanctioned, and thus they found themselves defending themselves against both unorthodox ethnologists and orthodox Christians. "Canaan," thus argued Gliddon nervously,

> was not *physically* changed in consequence of the *curse*. He ever remained a *white* man, as did, and do, all his many descendants. No scriptural production can be found, that would support an hypothesis so absurd, as that, in consequence of the curse, Canaan was transmuted into a negro. . . . If then with the curse branded on Canaan, and on his whole posterity, the Almighty did not see fit to change his skin, his hair, bones, or any portion of his physical structure, how unjust, how baseless is that theory (unsupported by a line in Scripture, and in diametrical opposition to monumental and historical testimony), which would make Canaan's immediate progenitor, Ham, the father of the Negroes! or his apparently blameless brother, Mizraim, an Ethiopian![51]

The cost, then, of the biblical justification for black slavery was the loss of a white Egypt. Faced with this choice, the American School chose Egypt.

The importance of the story of Ham and Canaan was what most often tied the secular and sacred accounts to one another, the value that tended to calibrate the narrative economy of racialized origination. "The woolly-haired negroes who were the earliest occupants of Egypt . . . were not necessarily degraded savages," concluded Fontaine. "Cut off from all intercourse with the most favored nations for many ages, any race will be liable to sink into the darkest and deepest barbarism."[52] Likewise, this was quite regularly the space in which the microdynamics of differentiation were played out, as multiplying accounts of multiplying versions of these narrative objectivisms—accounts that were, almost by definition, mutually exclusive—were used to distinguish, even as they were used to refer, one from and to another.[53] Like their ancient proxies, ostensibly polarized nineteenth-century Americans found themselves locked in an intimate embrace.

## "You Will Find Yourself in Africa, By-and-By"

In 1854, Frederick Douglass presented a piece called "The Claims of the Negro Ethnologically Considered" and wrote specifically in the context of the American School: "I think I have never seen a single picture in an American work, designed to give an idea of the mental endowments of the Negro, which did any thing like justice to the subject; nay, that was not infamously distorted." Douglass insisted that "the heads of A. Crummel, Henry H. Garnet . . . M. R. Delany . . . and hundreds of others . . . are all better formed, and indicate the presence of intellect more than any pictures I have seen in such works."[54] In the clarity with which Douglass presents the politics of the powers of visibility, his "The Claims of the Negro" is an early example of the infamy the American School had quickly and effectively gained. But Douglass's lecture also gestures toward a much larger, much more significant aspect of the argument being made here. For all of the recent work done on the American School, and even its connections to early Egyptology, what the 1854 "Claims" points to is a still underrecognized feature of the ethnological controversies of the nineteenth century: the extent to which the developments in white Egyptology were being directly engaged, and even shaped and directed, by African Americans.

There is no question, of course, that scholarship on African American constructions of ancient Egypt has been at least as voluminous and significant as parallel studies of white attitudes, if not more so: whether studied as Afrocentrism, Egyptocentrism, Ethiopianism, or any number of similar scholarly subsets, research concerning African American cultural innovations regarding ancient African history is an indispensible part of this study and is treated frequently and at length throughout this book.[55] Yet I am here insisting that attention be paid to a dynamic of *interaction* between black historians of Africa and white. "We need not resort to any long drawn arguments to defend negro-Ethnography against the Notts and Gliddons of our day," confidently wrote black nationalist, race theorist, and future Episcopal Bishop of Haiti James Theodore Holly in 1859. "Let them prove, if they can, to the full satisfaction of their narrow souls and gangrened hearts, that the black faced, woolly haired, thick lipped and flat nosed Egyptians of ancient times did not belong to the same branch of the human family that those negroes do, who have been the victims of the African Slave-trade for the past four centuries."[56] It is a central claim of this chapter that what characterized nineteenth-century American ethno-Egyptology was not so much an alliance between ethnology and Egyptology and the interests of the white proslavery factions that were responsible for their popularity but rather a radically dialogic relationship between those factions and widespread African American antislavery forces which challenged them at every turn. "Let them prove by the subtlest refinement of reasoning," dared Holly, "that those ancient darkies were pure white men."[57]

"Ham was the first African," wrote no less visible a figure than Henry Highland Garnet in 1848, in what by midcentury was an extremely common claim. "Egypt was settled from an immediate descendant from Ham. . . . Yet in the face of this historical evidence, there are those who affirm that the ancient Egyptians were not of the pure African stock."[58] What is worth noticing about Garnet's claim is not only its place in the long tradition of Afrocentric theorizing but, more importantly, its obvious role in the ongoing argument between Afrocentrists and those who British abolitionist Wilson Armistead sarcastically called in the same year "the enlightened Negrophobists of America."[59] "The gigantic statue of the Sphinx has the peculiar features of the children of Ham," Garnet asserted, clearly one of the causes for the anxious defenses of the Sphinx by the American School quoted above.[60] Garnet's assertions about the visibility of the "pure African stock" of the Egyptians, made after the publication of Samuel George Morton's *Crania Aegyptiaca* and *Crania Americana* but before the publication of *Types of Mankind*, indicate not only how prolifically black historians and race theorists produced arguments during this period but also just how dialogic, interactive, and ongoing these arguments were. "These intellectual resurrectionists dig through a mountain of such evidence," wrote Garnet, "and declare that these people were not negroes."[61]

From the carefully unnamed but nevertheless influential "strenuous advocates" of the African model of Egyptian origin that so unnerved Morton, Nott, and Gliddon—who despite their best efforts would have been readily identifiable, then as now, as figures like Garnet and William Wells Brown, whose 1863 *The Black Man, His Antecedents, His Genius, and His Achievements*, like Garnet, presented similar observations concerning the Sphinx—to formalized countertracts like Douglass's "The Claims of the Negro" and countless interventions into antiblack accounts lodged by black naturalists, intellectuals, and community theologians such as David Dorr, Paschal Beverly Randolph, and Harvey Johnson, African Americans across the country ran a constant and varied campaign of anti-antiblack ethno-Egyptological countertheorizing. "The image of the negro," countercharged Brown, continuing the argument with the American School almost ten years after the publication of Types of Mankind and during the height of the Civil War, was "engraved upon the monuments of Egypt, not as a bondman, but as the master of art." [62]

Far from being quiescent or uninformed objects of white Egyptological theories, African Americans, drawing on the incredibly rich traditions of both "folk" and professional theorizations of race, racial origin, and the figure of ancient Africa, were as invested in the ongoing developments within white Egyptology as white Egyptologists were about what panicked them. "The newspapers are reporting the Hon. Fred Douglass as having said," one antiblack polygenist relayed in 1887, "after his return from his foreign travels, that his investigations in Egypt satisfied him that the ancient Egyptians were not negroes. Happy Egyptians!" [63] This heated, often violent, largely underrecognized dynamic was, more than almost any other single factor, responsible for the racialized legacy of American Egyptology. [64]

The list of historians of color working throughout the nineteenth century is not a list which is regularly cited in discussions of nineteenth-century Egyptology, but the development of professional Egyptology and African American historiography shared much in the way of cultural context: James W. C. Pennington, Alexander Crummel, Edward Wilmot Blyden, William Wells Brown, Drusilla Dunjee Houston, Martin Delany, W. E. B. Du Bois. However, while the rise of American Egyptology is relatively well-documented, the rise of black writers of history is not. The history of one, though, carries within it the history of the other. The pressures brought to bear on early Egyptologists by African American historians and other historians of the African diaspora profoundly shaped both fields, even though one was coalescing and the other was more diffuse. "Whatever the claims the American School of Ethnology may lay to Sappho, Euclid, St. Cyprian, or Terentius," wrote Thomas Hamilton, editor and publisher of The Anglo-African Magazine, in the opening pages of his first issue in 1859, "they must yield to the negro an undoubted share in Pushkin, the Negro-Russian poet, in Placido, the Negro-Spanish poet, and in Dumas, the Negro-Celtic Historian, Dramatist, and Romancer." [65] Black activists and intellectuals understood how quickly claims about "Negro nature" in the ancient world were being imported for use into the nineteenth century, and they insisted on disproving ethnological claims on the grounds both of the past and of the present. The history of this relationship is therefore somewhat spotty at best, but its implications are broad indeed.

In his 1855 *My Bondage and My Freedom*, Douglass makes a rather glancing reference to a text in this history, in the middle of a discussion of his mother:

> But to return, or rather, to begin. My knowledge of my mother is very scanty, but very distinct. Her personal appearance and bearing are ineffaceably stamped upon my memory. She was tall, and finely proportioned; of deep black, glossy complexion; had regular features, and, among the other slaves, was remarkably sedate in her manners. There is in "*Prichard's Natural History of Man*," the head of a figure—on page 157—the features of which so resemble those of my mother, that I often recur to it with something of the feeling which I suppose others experience when looking upon the features of dear departed ones.[66]

The text to which Douglass refers is British ethnologist James Cowles Prichard's *The Natural History of Man: Comprising Inquiries into the Modifying Influence of Physical and Moral Agencies on the Different Tribes of the Human Family*. First published in 1843, the *Natural History* was one of the final installments in what had become Prichard's life's work—an explanation of what he called "the nature and causes of the physical diversities which characterize different races of men"—and on which he had been publishing since 1813 under the title *Researches into the Physical History of Mankind*. Prichard is perhaps best known not only as a seminal figure in early ethnology from any country but also as an early, and isolated, advocate of the theory that all humankind in fact originated in Africa or, as he put it, that "the primitive stock of men were Negroes." Prichard's career was, however, also marked by a series of compromises due to pressures over this point, and by the time he published the text to which Douglass refers—1843—all traces of this claim had either been reversed or erased.[67]

All of this might at first seem more an ironic subtext to Douglass's narrative than an explicit reference, though, as the adult Douglass of 1855 finds himself forced to refer to an illustration in a British ethnological treatise for a visual memory of the mother from whom the slave-child Douglass was so early and brutally separated. And, indeed, Douglass's fetishistic and talismanic reliance on Prichard's *Natural History* as a family photo album does seem to be of a piece with the complicated series of maternal replacements to which he would look all his life. "The mother is still a mystery," writes Michael Chaney, "and her image does not bespeak her face. . . . Instead, her image speaks to and against the ethnographers who have captured her in their pages."[68] This pattern of maternity and erasure is made all the more poignant for its direct role in the plainly racialized system of nineteenth-century ethnology, but Douglass seems to be aware of a more radical analogy as well: he was torn from his mother even as her image was torn from history.

My interest in this brief moment in Douglass's narrative, however, is not strictly in the passage itself. Rather, it is in another representation of this moment, in what could still be considered part of the text itself. The introduction to the original 1855 edition of *My Bondage and My Freedom* was written by a figure who concerns the argument being made here more directly: James McCune Smith. Smith was the first African American in history to receive a medical degree, and his introduction to *My Bondage and My Freedom* concludes with an extended consideration of contemporaneous developments in the related fields of ethnology and Egyptology and uses the moment of Douglass's reference to Prichard's *Natural History* as his centerpiece. Referring to Douglass's reference to the figure that reminds him of the face of his mother, Smith writes that "The head alluded to is copied from the statue of Ramses the Great, an Egyptian king of the nineteenth dynasty. The authors of the *Types of Mankind* give a side view of the same on page 148, remarking that the profile, 'like Napoleon's, is superbly European!' The nearness of its resemblance to Mr. Douglass's mother, rests upon the evidence of his memory, and judging from his almost marvelous feats of recollection of forms and outlines recorded in his book, this testimony may be admitted."[69]

Smith uses Douglass's brief reference to his mother's face as an opportunity to draw attention to the simultaneous placement in Douglass's narrative and Nott and Gliddon's *Types of Mankind* of an image supposedly modeled on that of Rameses the Great and from that to make a protracted argument regarding race, biology, and their relationship to early Egyptology. "The friends of the 'Caucasus,' " Smith writes, "will forgive me for reminding them that the term 'Caucasian' is dropped by recent writers on Ethnology, for the people about Mount Caucasus are, and have ever been, Mongols. The great 'white race' now seek paternity . . . in Arabia."[70] Smith

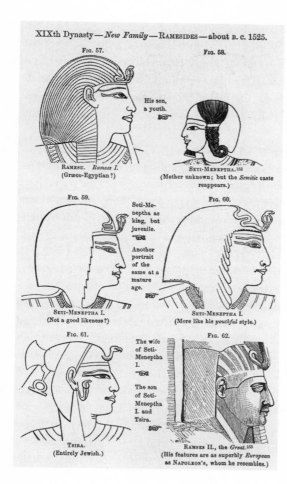

XIXth Dynasty — *New Family* — RAMESIDES — about B. C. 1525.

FIG. 57.

RAMESU.   *Ramses I.*
(Græco-Egyptian?)

FIG. 58.

His son,
a youth.

SETI-MENEPTHA.152
(Mother unknown; but the *Semitic* caste
reappears.)

FIG. 59.

Seti-Me-
neptha as
king, but
juvenile.

Another
portrait
of the
same at a
mature
age.

SETI-MENEPTHA I.
(Not a good likeness?)

FIG. 60.

SETI-MENEPTHA I.
(More like his *youthful* style.)

FIG. 61.

The wife
of Seti-
Meneptha
I.

The son
of Seti-
Meneptha
I. and
Tsira.

TSIRA.
(Entirely Jewish.)

FIG. 62.

RAMSES II., the *Great*.153
(His features are as superbly *European*
as NAPOLEON'S, whom he resembles.)

"The Caucasian Types Carried through Egyptian Monuments." (From Josiah Clark Nott and George Robins Gliddon, *Types of Mankind*. Philadelphia: Lippincott, Grambo, 1854, figs. 57–62, p. 148. Library of Congress.)

then takes his allusion regarding the racial impurity of whiteness one step further. "For his energy, perseverance, eloquence, invective, sagacity, and wide sympathy," he writes, Douglass "is indebted to his negro blood. . . . The versatility of talent which he wields . . . would seem to be the result of the grafting of the Anglo-saxon on good, original, negro stock."[71]

This type of argument, of course, was commonly used by defenders of slavery, but in reverse: slaves were either improved through their biological amalgamation with whites or, as white supremacist John Van Evrie had it, "in the case of mulattoism, where a monstrous violation of the physical integrity of the races is involved, nature interposes and forbids it to live."[72]

Abolitionists, too, would commonly understand race mixing to be positive for one race only—Africans—but here Smith is inverting the binary opposition, suggesting that it is in fact the Anglo-Saxon blood that benefits from intermixture with the African, and as a case in point he offers the ancient Egyptians: "If the friends of 'Caucasus' choose to claim, for that region, what remains after this analysis—to wit: combination—they are welcome to it." [73]

Smith's argument enacts an explicit reversal of what was by 1855 a clearly delineated series of connections regarding race and biological inferiority, and as a final coup de grace he drives home a point that would have hit proslavery polygenists in the tenderest spot of all: "Keep on, gentlemen; you will find yourselves in Africa, by-and-by. The Egyptians, like the Americans, were a *mixed race*, with some negro blood circling around the throne, as well as in the mudhovels." [74] What Smith's comments mark is a theoretical compromise: the notion of the ancient Egyptians as "a mixed race" is appearing here, alongside the development of the notion of "race" in general and the politics of slavery in particular. It is still somewhat common to hear this reference to the Egyptians as a mixed race, but it consolidated in the radically polarized racializations of early Egyptology as an explicitly contingent negotiation with Nott, Gliddon, Afrocentric Egyptologists, and the proslavery politics of the American School.

As we have seen, Douglass himself had weighed into the controversies surrounding the American School in his "The Claims of the Negro" the year before, but Smith is additionally interesting for a very particular reason: he was a trained medical doctor. By and large, African American participants in ethnological debates were either independent intellectuals, full-time abolitionists, or religious leaders. Smith, however, gained recognition for the extent to which he could engage the rapidly territorializing discursive formations that were mobilized by the American School. "When the natural ability of the negro was assailed, some years ago, in New York," wrote William Wells Brown in 1863, "Dr. Smith came forward, as the representative of the black man, and his essays on the comparative anatomy of the races . . . completely vindicated the character of the negro, and placed the author among the most logical and scientific writers in the country." [75] The son of "a self-emancipated bond-woman" and a slave freed by the state of New York, Smith, after being refused a full medical education in the United States traveled to Scotland to train at the University of Glasgow and in 1837 became the first African American ever to receive a medical degree.[76] Returning to New York the next year, Smith was a high-profile advocate of abolitionist causes, but what his career more specifically marks is the rapid logic with which training in medicine meant a necessary versatility in the accelerating developments of race theory. As his comments in My Bondage and My Freedom indicate, it also marks a clear sense of the strategic importance for all of these fields of the role of Egyptology. He also marks a moment of innovation and connection for the next, much more famous, African American medical doctor to rise to prominence in the interwoven nineteenth-century politics of race: Martin Delany.

## "The Beginning and Origin of Races"

The black nationalist novelist, activist, explorer, politician, and military leader Martin Robison Delany was perhaps most actively and prominently involved in ethnological debates in the decade before the Civil War, when in the spring of 1851 he lectured on the abolitionist circuit on racialized comparative anatomy and physiognomy. His personal interests in natural history both pre- and postdate the 1850s, however, and the extent to which his engagement with ethnology and narratives of ancient history spanned his career is testimony to the long and resilient life racialized science had throughout the nineteenth century and the continually potent role it had through its relationship with Egyptology. Delany is particularly important for the extent to which he represents several different modes of black Egyptomania, both before and after the Civil War. A typically multifaceted black activist, Delany's efforts to fashion an Afrocentric black masculinity spanned his serialized 1862 novel Blake, his emigrationist travels to West Africa, his grassroots organizing, and his international political actions. Again and again his efforts returned to the signs and wonders of ancient Egypt.

This is especially visible in Delany's short but seminal 1853 Origin and Objects of Ancient Freemasonry, in which the Egyptomanic beliefs of a black Freemason, the biblical historiography of a Christian abolitionist, and the secular agenda of an antiracist activist are networked in an explicitly political history of Prince Hall Masonry. Prince Hall, writes Maurice Wallace, "was intent upon securing New England's enslaved and free men of color a meaningful place in two of the most crucial spheres of masculine authentication in colonial American culture, Freemasonry and the military," and explains Hall's "profound iconicity as the talismanic hero of African American Masonic history" even after his death in 1807.[77] This iconicity was realized by Delany and other Prince Hall Masons not least because of its reliance on the similar iconicity of an Afrocentric Egypt. "To Africa is the world indebted for its knowledge of the mysteries of Ancient Freemasonry," Delany declares. "Truly, if the African race have no legitimate claims to Masonry, then it is illegitimate to all the rest of mankind."[78]

Delany's short text is long on ambition, proposing to give a history not just of Freemasonry but of the history of humanity. "The three great stages of man's existence," Delany explains, framing them as those represented by the biblical figures of Adam, Noah, and Solomon, are "all . . . impressively typified, in the cardinal degrees of Masonry."[79] Most important to Delany's Masonic history of the world, however, is Moses, because of his highly charged role as both Egyptian and Hebrew, as both master and slave. Moses "was said to have been learned in all the wisdom of the Egyptians," Delany argues, responding to white Masons who were attempting to exclude African Americans from membership in any branch of Freemasonry, "and was not only descendent of those who had been slaves, but of *slave parents, and himself, at the time* that he was so *taught* and *instructed* in this wisdom, *was a slave!*"[80] That the politics of 1850s America were of crucial importance to Delany could not be avoided in his message. "Are not we as Masons, and the world of mankind," Delany asks, signifying on the *free* in *freemasonry*, "to him the Egyptian *slave*—may I not add, the *fugitive* slave— indebted for a transmission to us of the Masonic Records?"[81]

Delany's most explicit vision is one of radical monogeny, in which various modes of human historiography are yoked together and pointedly realigned, along a pattern of absolute African origin, and laid atop a map of the politics of American slavery. This is a vision of world history that, like the physical layout of the Masonic lodge room itself, is made of concentric layers of origin and effect: "In the earliest period of the Egyptian and Ethiopian dynasties, the institution of Masonry was first established. . . . Being a people of a high order of intellect, and subject to erudite and profound thought, the Egyptians and Ethiopians were the first who came to the conclusion that man was created in the similitude of God. . . . To convince man of the importance of his own being and impress him with a proper sense of his duty to his Creator . . . [and] also impress him with a sense of his duty and obligations to society and the laws intended for his government . . . was the beautiful fabric of Masonry established."[82]

Africa produced Egypt, Egypt produced Masonic knowledge, and Masonic knowledge produced the world. "Had Moses or the Israelites never lived in Africa," Delany asserts, "the mysteries of the wise men of the East never would have been handed down to us."[83] The implications of this narrative for early black nationalism are impossible to miss. Even the structure of *The Origins and Objects of Ancient Freemasonry* replicates a Masonic ritual: the pamphlet gradually initiates its reader into its world of wisdom, and at its end a secret is suddenly revealed. "Must I hesitate to tell the world that, as applied to Masonry, the word—Eureka—was first exclaimed in Africa?" Delany asks dramatically in his final sentences. "But—there! I have revealed the Masonic *secret*, and *must stop!*"[84]

Delany's *Origins and Objects* is important not merely because it offers an early example of the kind of cultural leverage black Masons were able to gain from the Egyptomanic iconography of nineteenth-century freemasonry but also for the extent to which it represents the highly centralized vision of this brand of black Egyptomania: Egypt, as a sign of Africa, is the sign of ultimate origin, both historical and cultural, not just for black people but for the entire world. Indeed, like so much black self-fashioning conducted in the hotly contested arena of ancient historiography, Prince Hall Masonry offers a wealth of examples of what Wilson Jeremiah Moses has termed the "vindicationist" mode of black national history.[85] "There is hardly a more original experiment in the social (re)production of the black masculine ideal than in the ritual formalizations of identity and ideality in African American Freemasonry," writes Wallace. "A uniquely black male subculture often overlooked, African American Freemasonry illustrates, in microcosm, the broader dialectics of African American male identity construction."[86] Thus, Delany's title remarks on itself: Egypt is meant to serve as the origin of black identity, and serves as its object instead.

Yet the correlational dynamics between black and white freemasonries, with their overlapping identifications with a sacralized and mystified Egypt on one hand and their flatly segregated histories of members and member spaces on the other, points to just the kind of interactive dialogics between black and white Egyptomanias with which this chapter is most concerned. "Although both black and white Freemasons have shared certain narratives of Masonic history for centuries," Wallace explains, "only those histories authored by black Freemasons record the ancestral Egyptians as black."[87] This is hardly surprising, of course, given the polarizing politics of American Egyptomania, but what is worth further note is the extent to which racialization as such, as an explicit strategy for combating racism, was claimed by black Masons. "No such racialized genealogy has ever come to be espoused by white Freemasons," Wallace recounts. "That fact hardly matters to their Prince Hall fraters, however, who hold that white Freemasons owe their Masonic inheritance to the genius of the black man as well—this is the Prince Hall myth of pride."[88]

In the relational histories of white and black Masons—at once convergent and yet divergent—we can see how the signs of ancient Egypt were enlisted in the negotiation of modern American politics—specifically those based on race—and allowed black Americans to articulate an intimate relationship with their white counterparts while simultaneously worrying its waters. When Hall lobbied for his first African Lodge during the early days of the American Revolution—both endorsing notions of American nationalism and opposing those of American racism, relying on one set of structures of American identity while rebuffing another—and when he did so explicitly under the signs of ancient Egypt, he enacted a typically complicated example of the uses to which Egyptian imagery could be put to use in America. But, perhaps most importantly, he marked his moment in the long dialectic that offers so many opportunities for familiar exchanges between black and white over the icons of ancient Egypt, the long American call and response. In this regard especially, the lessons of black freemasonry are incredibly succinct: "We profess to be both men and Masons," Delany wrote, "and challenge the world to try us, prove us, and disprove us, if they can."[89]

This structure of Egyptomanic origin, historiographic alignment, and political resistance reached its fullest elaboration in 1879, when at the age of sixty-seven and only five years before his death Delany published his *Principia of Ethnology*, a singular intervention into the imbricated and politically fraught fields, discourses, and traditions under discussion here: Egyptology, ethnology, race theory, biology, and nascent Afrocentricity.[90] Indeed, the subtitle of this treatise, *The Origin of Races and Color, with an Archaeological Compendium of Ethiopian and Egyptian Civilization, from Years of Careful Examination and Inquiry*, marks the strong similarities it has with *Types of Mankind* and registers the extent to which the "Afrocentric" and "Negrophobic" positions were in dialogue and the extent to which they relied on many of the same assumptions. "This is a subject of very great interest to social science," wrote Delany, "which has as yet not been satisfactorily treated. . . . The Singular and Plural theories of the Creation or Origin of Man, have been fully examined and duly considered, accepting the Mosaic or Bible Record, as our basis, without an allusion to the Development theory. The theory of Champollion, Nott, Gliddon, and others, of the Three Creations of Man—one black, the second yellow, and the last white—we discard, and shall not combat as a theory, only as it shall be refuted in the general deductions of this treatise." [91] Race theory and Egyptology were explicitly shaped through this relationship—between "Champollion, Nott, Gliddon, and others"—as much as they were shaped by novel discoveries in the field of archaeology, and the terms and problematics of inquiry that structure Egyptological research have from their inception been intimately political.

As with most ethnographic writers supporting the biblical chronology, Delany explicitly accepts the tradition that Ham, father of Canaan and grandfather of Mizraim, called Egypt, was black: "That Shem was of the same complexion as Noah, his father and mother—the Adamic complexion—there is no doubt in our mind. And that Ham the second son was swarthy in complexion, we have as little doubt. Indeed, we believe it is generally conceded by scholars, though disputed by some, that the word Ham means 'dark,' 'swarthy,' 'sable.' And it has always been conceded and never, as we know of, seriously disputed, that Japheth was white." [92] Likewise, Delany in a relatively straightforward way accepts the entire racialized tripartite division of the sons of Noah: "There is to us another fact of as little doubt; that is, that these three sons of Noah all differed in complexion, and proportionate numbers of the people—their dependents in and about the city and around the Tower—also differed as did the three sons in complexion. And these different complexions in the people, at that early period, when races were unknown, would have no more been noticed as a mark of distinction, than the variation in the color of the hair of those that are white, mark them among themselves as distinct peoples." [93] For Delany, though, the sons of Noah were merely different in *complexion*—these individual complexions being somehow stabilized in their progeny. But, as we will see, the "origin of races" was for Delany a product of the moment of the Tower of Babel, and this emerges as one of the most critical innovations in Delany's anti-antiblack raciology. As recounted in the chapter of Genesis that immediately follows the Table of Nations, God produced linguistic differentiation among the Tower builders, all, of course, descendants

of Noah and still merely, however conveniently for God, differently complected. The centerpiece of the *Principia of Ethnology* is the Tower. It, rather
than the Deluge, is the site of the origin of races.

At the beginning of his extended argument concerning "the origin of
races and color" proper, Delany recounts the biblical story of the Tower of
Babel. Contained within his gloss is not only a relatively traditional account
of the motivation of God, and not only a somewhat controversial account
of the agenda behind that motivation, but also what for Delany becomes
a theory of the dynamics of culture itself. "Man could best contribute" to
the promotion of God's glory, Delany writes,

> by development and improvement in a higher civilization. Could this be
> done be confining himself to a limited space in one quarter of the earth,
> rearing up a building whose top may reach unto heaven? Certainly not;
> because as the people were all one, and as "like begets like," the ac-
> quired manners, habits, customs and desires of these Tower builders,
> who would have been taught and schooled into their descendants, to the
> neglect of all other employments and industries, confining themselves
> to comparatively limited spaces, caring nothing for the requirements of
> community . . . lest they be "scattered abroad, upon the face of the whole
> earth." Here, just what God designed in the creation of man, these de-
> scendants of Noah desired to prevent.
>
> The progress of civilization, was God's requirement at the hands of
> man. How could this be brought about, seeing that the people were
> all one, "speaking one tongue," gathered together and settled in one
> place? . . . By this method then, of an All-wise Creator, the people lost
> interest as communities in each other, and were thereby compelled to
> separate.[94]

In its configuration before the construction of the Tower, Delany proposes,
humankind was growing stagnant, complacent, and even inbred. Given
this situation, the effectively undifferentiated mass of postdiluvian humanity was something which amounted to a mass of defiant heresy. God
solved this problem, then, by the separation of humankind into distinct
communities along the admittedly preexisting lines of differing complexion, but with *language*, not color, providing the only significant workable
distinction.

For Delany, God's treatment of the Tower builders was not so much a
punishment as a mandate, not reprimand but revelation, and the directive
implicit in diversification was equally one of "progress" as of linguistics.

Moreover, since the Tower of Babel was built after the differently complected sons of Noah repeopled the earth in their chromatically differentiated way, the linguistic distinctions introduced by God were the very distinctions that allowed for cultural differentiation, all in keeping with His plan. "Is it to be supposed that God wrought a special miracle, by changing for the occasion the external physical characteristics of at least two divisions of the people?" Delany asks.

> He did not. This was not His method. He has a better and even wiser method than a miracle. . . . The division was brought about by the confusion of tongues, so as to settle and harmonize the people, instead of distracting and discouraging them. . . . Hence, when the confusion took place, their eyes became open to their difference in complexion with each other, as a division, each preferring those of their kind with whom they went, thus permanently uniting their destiny. . . . And this confusion of tongues, and scattering abroad in the earth, were the beginning and origin of races.[95]

What is at stake for Delany is a wholesale revolution in the theory of culture, positioned against the proslavery theories of the Egyptology of the American School. The Tower, in the *Principia of Ethnology*, will thus emerge as a critical agent in this revolution. But, like Delany's vision of "race" and ethnology, it is far from its whiter self.

The moment of Babel is a moment of *liberation* for Delany, but this is only a step, however critical, in his overall project. From his discussion of biblical history, through his study of human anatomy, *Principia of Ethnology* goes from being a study of "*The Origin of Races and Color*" to a study of "The Progress of Races" (the title of chapter 8) and finally to an extended account of what, in the title of chapter 9, becomes the "Progress of the Black Race": "The African branch of this family is that which was the earliest developed, taking the first strides in the progress of the highest civilization know[n] to the world, and for this cause, if for no other, it may be regarded as the oldest race of man, having, doubtless, centuries prior to the others, reared imperishable monuments of their superior attainments."[96] The sons of Ham—the curse on Canaan is never so much as mentioned in the *Principia*—become the kings and gods of antiquity. And to write this genealogy, in a series of sweeping equations Delany wrenches into alignment all of the discourses and timelines he has up to this point been alternating between, making biblical, ethnological, and Egyptological chronologies coincide, all fixed through a lens of historiographically masculinized racial elevation:

> Ham, the head, first prince and ruler of Egypt, in the course of time dies of old age, leaving the rule to Mizraim, when the old king, Ham, is at once deified and worshipped as a god, under the name of *Jupiter Ammon*. . . . He is also consecrated with the royal dynastic title of Rameses I. Mizraim in turn when passing away, was also worshipped as a god . . . taking the royal title Rameses II. . . . These two great princes [Mizraim and Cush] acted in concert . . . in the erection of the pyramids—a style of architectural monuments with which they were familiar, having themselves taken part in the construction of the Tower of Babel. . . . The three principal Pyramids, no doubt, were originally erected for and dedicated to these three great princes, father and two sons.[97]

The pyramids of Egypt were based on the model of the Tower of Babel; the son of Ham, Mizraim, was also Jupiter Ammon and Rameses I; Mizraim's brother, Cush, founded Ethiopia, and together they founded Western civilization: Delany is taking the very categories for political biologization in use by the American School and only too explicitly placing them under the sign of revision.

Delany makes not only the political implications of these categories the subject of his problematic but the very process of their construction as well. Step by step he constructs the history at stake, leading his readers through what is at once ancient history (Noah was followed by the Tower and the Tower was followed by Egypt) and the process of writing that history (Mizraim was also Rameses I), rendering the process of writing ancient history equivalent to the politics of its construction. Moreover, he is in effect reestablishing these categories as categories with prior authority: as Delany knew only too well, the American School had had to negotiate its proslavery historical narratives in the context of Herodotus and Volney, along with innumerable—but, by the American School, erased—previously existing claims to the African roots of Egypt. Delany is enacting a return to the days before the American School, using the ethnology of the American School to provide him with the means to do so.[98]

As Delany makes clear, crucial to this series of equations is the role of Ethiopia. In Delany's account, he makes the most of the intimacy between these two spaces—at once geographic and conceptual, factual and political, national and racial:

The reign of [Mizraim] in succession to his father is said to have been magnificent in the extreme, and conjointly with his brother Cush, a matchless prince in the adjoining kingdom, Ethiopia, it is believed was commenced an international policy, these invaluable intellectual blessings to the human race, the propagation of the science of letters. . . . These two great princes acted in concert for the mutual benefit of both countries, in . . . the enlargement and architectural improvement of their common countries and principal cities, as Meroe in Ethiopia and Thebes in Egypt, pushed forward with an energy and determination unsurpassed, if equalled, in the history of man.[99]

Thus, the blackness of Ethiopia is precisely the touch of that which Delany wants to give his portrait of ancient Egypt and that which antiblack historians wanted and still want to avoid. Egypt and Ethiopia are as important in their proximity as they are destabilizing, potent as a unit because of the narrowness of their separation. It is not accidental that Delany chooses Egypt and Ethiopia as the joint site for what he knew were radical and revolutionary claims. Indeed, it was *because* they were seen to be radical and revolutionary that he makes his claims in the way he does. Because the history of Egypt was being marked by others as either a biologically or culturally "white" history and because Egypt was being colored as a white land, Delany both makes his revolutionary claims and, through them, enacts their politics of contradistinction. In other words, Delany is helping to provide a point of stabilized contest in the contingencies of whiteness and blackness, helping to script the dialogic politics of race.

## The Blacker the Berry

From this point, *Principia of Ethnology* now becomes a study of the close relation between the two nations, an account of the influences, similarities, and debts owed Ethiopia as a result of its "invaluable intellectual blessings to the human race." As Delany implies, though, this narrative of color is at once geohistoriographic and biophysiological. Moreover, it is one with a tragic ending: "Our subject is the 'Origin of Races and Color,' and our present theme, the 'Progress of the African Race'; hence we shall closely confine ourselves to what pertains to the original settlers, Ham and his sons, without regard to their successors who centuries after, succeeded them, in the persons of the descendants of Shem and Japheth, to usurp their places and imitate their greatness."[100] Before Delany moves into this register, though, and before he segues into the black nationalist program that organizes the rest of the volume, he has had to establish what exactly constitutes blackness itself, the place from which the color of the pharaohs of color comes.

In the standard ethnological appeal to biology, it was most common for that biology to be one of surfaces, of external appearance, of aesthetics. Indeed, it was because "black" as an ontological property was so radically unstable in nineteenth-century America that "Negroid" was presented by the American School as a more tenable concept. Given just the situation of which Nott, Gliddon, Van Evrie, and their supporters were so critical— "Every race," they wrote, "at the present time, is more or less mixed"[101]— black skins were notoriously polychromatic. Craniometry, phrenology, and ethnological anatomy as sciences were concerned to produce a notion of the essence that lay underneath the skin but was no less biological. For Delany, however, this move toward stabilization, toward a confidence of vision, is the opposite of the account he generated in *Principia of Ethnology*. For Delany, this move to the body is quite literally *into* the body. "The rete mucosum or middle structure of the skin," he writes, "now becomes the most important subject of investigation, the 'opening of the second seal' of the great mystery of the revelation of color, answering the question, 'When and How did the negro race begin?' In this again, rete mucosum, the coloring matter which gives complexion to all races in general and every individual in particular, lies."[102] Aside from his use of New Testament rhetoric, what characterizes the middle section of Delany's book is his mobilization of discourses of biology and natural history. He in fact interrupts his historiographic narrative of Noah and his sons and the linguistic development of civilization with a narrative that is limited to a very precise biologicism and circumscribes this *as* an interruption by then resuming his prior biblical/historical account. This telescopic ellipsis in Delany's discursive architecture channels biblical and natural history quite literally through the body—specifically, a racially and anatomically comparative body—and places a politically radical physiological unity within this channel, a unity that, for polygenists like Nott and Gliddon, would be all the more destabilizing. In addition, for a monogenist, in following chapter 5, "The Family of Noah," these chapters on anatomy and biology occur just at the point at which in any number of other studies the discussion of "the origin of races" would have turned to the Curse of Canaan for the justification of theories of racial inferiority.

After a brief appeal to "the laws of nature," which involves enlisting "our present familiarity with the spectroscope" as an actor and rehearsing an account of "the properties of the sun, as transmitted through the rays," Delany begins his narrative (re)production of the body as infinitesimally biological, explaining that "the human body is covered by a structure composed of three distinct parts: the cuticle or external surface; the rete mucosum, middle or intermediate structure, and the cutis vera or true skin, underlying the other two, covering the whole surface of the fleshy parts or muscular system, called the hide in slaughtered animals." [103] The skin of the body is splayed in Delany's narrative, rendered transparent, even microscopic, and in Delany's Christian naturalism the agency of God functions through its chemical managers: "The rete mucosum is a colorless jelly-like substance, composed of infintesimal cells like a sponge or honey-comb. . . . The cells of the rete mucosum are filled with limpid fluid, and whatever the complexion of an individual or race, the coloring matter is deposited in the cells of the rete mucosum, mixed with the limpid fluid. This is deposited there by the process of elaboration and selection in animal chemistry, a function simply of physiology." [104] Delany's move is thus toward radical similarity, radical unity, along two orbits: "This coloring matter in the Caucasian or white race is rouge as we shall term it, the essential properties which give redness to the rose. . . . Thus the color of the blackest African is produced by identically the same coloring matter that gives the 'ruby cheeks and ruby lips' to the fairest and most delicately beautiful white lady." [105]

In sharp contrast to many of the other uses of physiological discourses —the craniometry and comparative anatomy of Samuel George Morton being the most relevant here—Delany's biology situates the body between logics of visibility, enacting at both ends a naturalistic politics of contradiction. The body is not what it appears to be, in either case: "It will at once be observed, that the cuticle or external surface being transparent, the rete mucosum next below it being also colorless, and the surface of the cutis vera underlying all being white, that all human beings by nature are first white, at some period of existence, whether born white or not." [106] The black body is twice not black: neither visibly—that is, the skin you see is not the true skin, the cutis vera—nor epistemologically—that is, there is no dualistic opposition between "black" and "white." Delany continues this logic of visibility even further, along its second orbit, that of "the redness of the rose" — that is, toward the comparison of human life and nonhuman life — and in radical sympathy with some of the same discourses of comparative biology that forty years before were first used to establish the African as inferior:

> For illustration, to prove that concentrated rouge or concrete redness is black, take blood caught in a vessel, let it cool and dry up by evaporation of the liquid part; when condensed in a solid mass it becomes perfectly black, more so than the blackest human being ever seen. Look . . . at . . . fruits, black-berries, black-cherries, poke-berries and the like. . . .
> Take now this clot of dried blood, and these fruits, macerate them in water and you have not a black, but an assuredly red solution. Compare these deep red fruits called black with the color of the blackest person in complexion, and there will be the most remarkable contrast between the fruit and the skin.[107]

Delany's alliance is thus to the negotiation of difference *and* sameness: given the physiological account, "black" people are "identically the same" as "white" people, even as there is "the most remarkable contrast between the ["black"] fruit and the [black] skin." By the same token, comparative biology functions according to a similar logic, of negotiation no less than visibility, as comparative idioms in general establish difference *through* sameness: the *variety* of species across the globe may be seen from their *uniformity* in distribution, or, through the discourses of objectivism, the same laws — be they of racial capability or, in the case of comparative natural history, of geographic boundaries — apply to all nature, whether black people or black berries.

In many ways, Delany's problack/pro-Hamitic model of the development of civilization already distinguishes *Principia of Ethnology* as a remarkable text in nineteenth-century histories of Africa, and, if it is mentioned in a modern survey of early black nationalism or black historiography it is almost exclusively in this context.[108] What further marks Delany's monograph, though, is the arrangement and deployment by an African American of exactly those discourses that had been used by European Americans for the construction of the field of white supremacist ethnology — biology and comparative anatomy — *in collaboration with* his black nationalist history, a history that itself drew on the same discourses white ethnology had in common with Egyptology. Moreover, the discursive choices Delany makes within the fields of biology and anatomy—his strategies for accounting for the physical "origin of races and color"—mark him and *Principia of Ethnology* as unique in the history of American science. Delany occupies discourses and utilizes moves that other racial and historical theorists used before and after him, but never has this particular combination appeared in another text.

Consider the passage quoted above: "all human beings by nature are first white, whether born white or not."[109] That a foundational figure in black nationalism, and one as radical and militant as Delany no less, should claim this is enough to give remarkable pause. For my purposes here, it marks primarily the extent to which traditions of African American Egyptology are also an intervention in the notion of "race" itself, and one that here intrudes into all the discursive territory used by white Egyptologists to establish the validity of what Martin Bernal has called, in the most recent of what has become a long line of scandals, "the Aryan model of classical civilization."[110] It is also an example of the extremely complicated and radically contingent process by which ancient history is written, influenced by a variety of pressures, and framed for a variety of audiences and according to a variety of traditions. "The principle of reality," writes historian and theorist of science Bruno Latour, "is other people."[111]

In this context, it becomes very difficult—indeed, impossible—to decide what counts in these foundational years as epistemologically "pure" race theory or epistemologically "pure" Egyptology, even as the politics of *making* these distinctions would structure the field in years to come and as much as the politics of their imbrication was responsible for their origin. The politics of establishing these epistemologies—of "black," "white," "Caucasian," "Negro," and even "Egypt" itself—shaped the problematics of both racialized science and Egyptology, even as they shaped debates about slavery and its aftermath. Definitions of "race," like those of "white," "black," "Egypt," and "the West" signify whatever they do for a given person at a given moment not in spite of disbelief, but because of it.


## "We Are Face to Face with the African at Last"

The Egyptology of Nott and Gliddon was one of race, chronology, and biblical controversy. Highly controversial, it was nevertheless extremely efficacious; more and more specialized, it was also famously popular. The complicated and increasingly rarefied debates in which *Types of Mankind* was intervening combined and drew on—even as they teased apart and territorialized—enfolded assumptions about natural, secular, and sacred history; racial origin and racial capability; and the cultural power of a given transcendent episteme. The epistemic claim to final truth would bear either the label "biblical" or "scientific," which was itself a binarism being developed within the pointedly controversial space of Western Egyptology: "It is now generally conceded that there exist no data by which we can approximate the date of man's first appearance upon earth; and, for aught we yet know, it may be thousands or millions of years beyond our reach. The spurious systems, of Archbishop Usher on the Hebrew Text, and of Dr. Hales on the Septuagint, being entirely broken down, we turn, unshackled by prejudice, to the monumental records of Egypt as our best guide."[112] To claim epistemic truth was to claim destruction of one's enemies. "We now stand upon the ruins of creations," proclaimed Nott, "the beginning of which was myriads of years before Adam and Eve walked together in the garden of Eden."[113]

What can be seen here, then, from this genealogy of discourses of scientific racialization, is scientific factuality being constructed before our eyes. Delany's ideas on the layers of skin were influenced in large part by James Prichard's *Physical History of Man*, the book that so reminded Frederick Douglass of his mother and James McCune Smith of the politics of Egyptology—and was also excerpted at some length in the June 1827 issue of the antislavery *African Observer*[114]—but they were also ideas addressed by Nott and Gliddon, and they were found in an American political context as early as 1781, when they were used by Thomas Jefferson in his *Notes on the State of Virginia*.[115] The discourses that configure Prichard's text, then, having drawn on biological theories already in circulation, were disseminated across a range of social and political contexts, with very different applications and thus very different effects—and only one effect among many comes from the mobilization of more or less coherent accounts of "truth." Seen as not nearly scientific enough by some, as rather too scientific by others, as too concerned with surfaces or too concerned with depth, as a constitutive part of biological essentialism or necessary for its downfall, it is the very multiplicity of competing claims that allows proclamations of truth to take hold. Ways of thinking about race are being negotiated in and through the very political contexts that constitute their effectiveness in the first place, from the level of the international slave trade to the level of the layers of the skin.

Thus, what we have in evidence is a dialogic network of contingent relationships, a situation in which what counts as scientific or true or even relevant varies widely, not only from text to text and writer to writer but also, and perhaps most importantly, according to the social and political upshot a given set of evidence has, or which is seen by a given audience and from within a given tradition to have. Indeed, the fluidity, connectibility, and negotiability of any one of the numerous discourses that helped comprise, support, or problematize American ethnology are illustrations of discursive dynamics not limited to ethnology, which are radically resistant to any further binary distinctions between "science" and "pseudoscience," however well-meaning such distinctions might be. Moreover, the specificity of certain ethnological moments helps to render legible the tensions in texts that to twenty-first-century eyes—whether problack or antiblack, progressive or conservative, Aryanist or Afrocentrist—may seem self-evident, nonsensical, allegedly obviously allied, or allegedly obviously irreconcilable. These differences, in other words, are based on proximity.[116]

The network of nineteenth-century American science was constantly negotiated on the contested field of teleological narrativity: naturalistic discourses of origination, chronology, and struggle—or theological ones of creation, genealogy, and prophecy—were increasingly and unevenly mapped onto methodological practices of biology, a developing colonialist archaeology, and human medicine. And in terms of a conceptual logic that privileges the radically contingent development of discourse in general—to which this study is a blatant adherent and for which this period of American ethnology is such a useful example—what is especially important to recognize is that these contingent dynamics were (and are) made in the name of contingency's reported refutations: objectivism, determinism, essentialism, positivism. Indeed, nineteenth-century American Egyptology provides both much of the raw material for understanding the history of the construction of many ostensible binarisms and an excellent model for their radical dissolution: irreducibly political claims regarding historical "absolutes" made in the name of an apolitical positivism—even if, as in recent years, that positivism is seen to be in the service of an antiracist objectivity[117]—are laid across the backs of the legacies of racialized essences and the bodies that bear them.

Afrocentric Egyptology has always been an interrogation into the very structure of racial identity, and historians in this tradition have always been acutely aware of how claims—especially epistemological ones—about Egypt and Egyptians are crucial to the consolidation of white identity. The architecture of white identity, historicized with teleological shape and apocalyptic warnings, is precisely what was fashioned in the twinned fields of ethnology and Egyptology. This was especially the case in the nineteenth century, as Delany and his intellectual colleagues could see the alliances white Egyptology had with the forces of proslavery. Physicians such as Smith and Delany, abolitionists such as Douglass and Brown, and race theorists such as Nott and Gliddon understood the extent to which arguments about Egypt were being made through biology and vice versa. They also understood how quickly and firmly arguments with this structure became sedimented and black-boxed and how appeals to authority were also appeals to whiteness and the authoritativeness that whiteness brings.

Traditions of black and white Egyptology were thus in some sense always separate, even as they were always inextricably linked. Arguments coming from white Egyptologists have long been viewed with mistrust in black quarters, just as black Egyptology has been a regular site of debunking for white Egyptology. This is the long legacy of the anxiety of proximity. "The coarse garb of the slave concealed the Negro himself," wrote one white ethnologist near the century's end, in language eerily recalling that of the unwrapping of mummies and under the title An Appeal to Pharaoh. "We stripped him of his rags, and clothed him with the robe of citizenship. Some of us have since stripped him of his robe—after his brief masquerade in it. We are face to face with the African at last." [118]

# CHAPTER TWO

# The Egyptian Moment

### RACIAL RUPTURES AND

### THE ARCHAEOLOGICAL

### IMAGINARY

On November 26, 1922, the British archaeologist Howard Carter made a small hole in the second of a series of sealed doorways in a sunken passageway in the Valley of the Kings near Qurna, Upper Egypt, and produced for the twentieth century the materials for the making of modern Egyptomania. The discovery of the tomb of Tut-ankh-Amen has since become the stuff of legend, of course, but it is a legend that has a number of predecessors, and in fact the world of 1922 was fashioning for itself experiences that had been tailored many times before. Never in the same way twice, though: Europe and England had been rediscovering ancient Egypt routinely for hundreds of years, as had the United States since its very inception, but every episode in what has become a long history of repetitions has its own shape, its own context, its own maniacal intensity.

Carter was to write of this intensity in his published account of his discovery:

> Let me try and tell the story of it all. It will not be easy, for the dramatic suddenness of the initial discovery left me in a dazed condition, and the months that have followed have been so crowded with incident that I have hardly had time to think. . . . I suppose most excavators would confess to a feeling of awe—embarrassment almost—when they break into a chamber closed and sealed by pious hands so many centuries ago. . . . The exhilaration of discovery, the fever of suspense, the almost overmastering impulse, born of curiosity, to break down seals and lift the lids of boxes . . . the strained expectancy—why not confess it?—of the treasure-seeker. Did these thoughts actually pass through our minds at the time, or have I imagined them since? I cannot tell.[1]

Published a year after the initial find, Carter's narrative is just that—a narrative—and, its author's doubts notwithstanding, it partakes of highly developed narrative techniques that were in use well before its composition. *The Tomb of Tut.ankh.Amen, Discovered by the Late Earl of Carnarvon and Howard Carter* was the result of modifications made to Carter's field journal, and the changes from diary to book are telling. The texts below present two different versions of arguably the most famous scene from the entire Tut dig, a fame that resulted in no small measure from the narrative shape in which it appeared in Carter's book. From the opening word to the pacing to the imagery to the closure—or lack thereof—of the anecdote, Carter's sense of suspense and narrative control renders archaeology as adventure tale.

The text on the left is from Carter's journal, and that on the right is the passage that appears in *The Tomb of Tut.ankh.Amen*:

| | |
|---|---|
| Feverishly we cleared away the remaining last scraps of rubbish on the floor of the passage before the doorway . . . in which, after making preliminary notes, we made a tiny breach in the top left hand corner. . . . Darkness and the iron testing-rod told us there was an empty space. . . . Candles were procured. . . . I widened the breach and . . . looked in . . . it was sometime before one could see; the hot | Slowly, desperately slowly it seemed to us as we watched, the remains of passage debris that encumbered the lower part of the doorway were removed, until at last we had the whole door clear before us. The decisive moment had arrived. With trembling hands I made a tiny breach in the upper left hand corner. Darkness and blank space, as far as an iron testing-rod could reach, showed |

air escaping caused the candle to flicker, but as soon as one's eyes became accustomed to the glimmer of light, the interior of the chamber gradually loomed . . . with its strange and wonderful medley of extraordinary and beautiful objects. Lord Carnarvon said to me "Can you see anything?" I replied to him, "Yes, it is wonderful." I then with precaution made the hole sufficiently large for both of us to see. With the light of an electric torch as well as an additional candle, we looked in. Our sensations and astonishment are difficult to describe. . . . The first impressions suggested the property-room of an opera of a vanished civilization. . . . We closed the hole, locked the wooden grill which had been placed upon the first doorway; we mounted our donkeys and returned home contemplating what we had seen. (Howard Carter, Diary, Sunday, November 26, 1922)

that whatever lay beyond was empty, and not filled like the passage we had just cleared. Candle tests were applied as a precaution against possible foul gases, and then, widening the hole a little, I inserted the candle and peered in, Lord Carnarvon, Lady Evelyn and Callender standing anxiously beside me to hear the verdict. At first I could see nothing, the hot air escaping from the chamber causing the flame to flicker, but presently, as my eyes grew accustomed to the light, details of the room within emerged slowly from the mist, strange animals, statues, and gold—everywhere the glint of gold. For the moment—an eternity it must have seemed to the others standing by—I was struck dumb with amazement, and when Lord Carnarvon, unable to stand the suspense any longer, inquired anxiously, "Can you see anything?" it was all I could do to get out the words, "Yes, wonderful things." Then widening the hole a little further, so that we both could see, we inserted an electric torch. (Howard Carter, The Tomb of Tut.Ankh.Amen, 1923)

Mary Louise Pratt has discussed what she understands to be the three main modes of narration in the long tradition of European explorationist discovery scenes—that of the esthetic, that of density of meaning, and that of mastery between seer and seen—and certainly Carter's scene partakes of all three, presenting something of an ultimate Egyptomanic version of what Pratt calls the "monarch-of-all-I-survey scene." "Thus the scene is deictically ordered," she writes, "and is static." [2] Yet Carter's vision is strikingly and constitutionally unstable. It depends not on stasis but on uneasy and uncertain actions: the straining of optic nerves, the lighting of dark spaces, the penetration of hidden places. Indeed, what Pratt would call Carter's "rhetoric of presence" is fundamentally structured by the operations of absence, by gaps in the representation of presence that are at once ones of text, identity, and the represented space. The relationships suggested by these operations—of presences and absences, stabilities and instabilities, barriers and holes and boundaries and gaps and continuities and their discontents—are, perhaps too much like those that so entranced Carter, what this chapter will be driven to explore.

Both of these passages are used to conclude sections—a diary entry and a book chapter, respectively—and the shift from one to the other is largely one of narrative suspense.[3] The stylistic changes produced during the composition of The Tomb of Tut.ankh.Amen—including among other things the cliffhanging break and the delayed, reflective renewal—relate memoirs like Carter's to dramatic principles taken directly from popular fictions of many kinds, with histories stretching back through the past century. The scene of discovery at the heart of the legend of King Tut is nothing, after all, if not culturally effective storytelling. "While the ordeal required to make the discovery is unforgettably concrete," Pratt writes, "the 'discovery' itself . . . has no existence of its own. It only gets 'made' for real after the traveler (or other survivor) returns home, and brings it into being through texts."[4] As Carter himself admits, he thus presents a moment of discovery as also a moment of return; his twentieth-century narrative generously partakes of the colonialist dramas of Egyptian exploration of the eighteenth and nineteenth centuries of which he is so nervously aware and to which he provides an unquiet link.

This type of agitated relationship was to serve as a similar kind of unstable nucleus in America. Related, of course, to their British equivalents—Richard Burton and John Hamilton Speke, Samuel White Baker, Amelia Edwards, Carter himself, even the earlier Italian narratives of Giovanni Belzoni—African, Egyptian, and Orientalist travel narratives were big business in the United States.[5] By the winter of 1838, writes Malini Johar Schueller, American travelers to Egypt were more numerous than those from any other country save England, and this surge in tourist traffic resulted in a constant stream of travel narratives; thirty-four of the forty-nine American travel works published between 1823 and 1843 were based on voyages to Asia, the Near East, and the Middle East. "The popularity of books on

Oriental travel," writes Schueller, is "indicative of a cultural intimacy with the Orient and an eagerness to embrace things Oriental that energized and popularized literary Orientalist works."[6]

These works form as much a history of texts documenting a fascination with Egypt as a history of genre, and this is by no means accidental. "No one was better at the monarch-of-all-I-survey scene than the string of British explorers who spent the 1860s looking for the source of the Nile," Pratt argues, and certainly this indicates the importance of international imperial exchanges to the history of American Egyptomania.[7] So I return to Carter's cliffhanger: the precise moment of discovery is also the moment of delay, of deferral. The moment of breach is the moment of containment. For Carter, and for many of his stylistic antecedents, the episodic epiphany is the defining principle of the archaeological imagination, and hereafter I will be most concerned with the implications of this figure, which is at once a presence and an absence, an assertion and a fear, an intrusion and a retreat.

## The Racial Rupture

This is the way this chapter will work. Having introduced the figure of a sort of Egyptomanic puncture, I will now turn my attention to its cultural implications. Specifically, I am interested in what I am here calling the racial rupture: a punctiform figure—be it hole, opening, container, veil, or any other such often interchangeable device of intrusion and release—that acts as both barrier and entrance to spaces, zones, or states of being that are represented as both dangerous and irresistible to agents of imperial power and operates as a sign of that power's instabilities. I will examine a range of texts that feature various modes of the imperialist adventure romance; typically feature narratives of hidden lands, lost cities, concealed cultures, and buried treasures; and as a result produce tropes of breached barriers and explosive secrets as frantically racialized. The racial rupture appears in virtually all of the most famous forms of colonialist narrative culture— exploration, expedition, discovery, conquest, and of course inevitable destruction—and I take its pointedly racialized placement as a sure symptom of its importance to the structures of racialized identity. An obvious metonym of the whole of the colonial project—or at least a crucial tool for the construction of an important stage of its multifold operations—it represents the narrative mechanisms by which imperialism is crafted into a single moment or drawn as a single swift step. The long, hot journey to the door in Upper Egypt is at once also a resting at the door to the Other. As Carter's shaky puncture so deftly shows, what marks the racial rupture is its symbolic brevity: it can produce an artifact, a relic, or a terrible curse, and it can conceal a mystery, a treasure, or a whole lost world, yet it is marked as a liminal barrier that is crossed only at great cost to the agents of empire who do.

More specifically, though, I am interested in the tradition of what are known variously as lost race or hollow earth novels. An understudied tradition to be sure, its combinations of racist imagery, imperial anxiety, and popular appeal are matched only by its reliance on the figure of the racial rupture, and this profoundly productive relationship—which produces, I argue, the very legibility of Carter's twice-scripted story—is made possible by the structures of modern Egyptomania. In short, I read the lost race/hollow earth tradition as one of the major carriers of the impulses of nineteenth-century American Egyptomania, and the figure of the racial rupture as the surest sign of that fact. Indeed, the repeating figure of the racial rupture—especially in its dual role as a sign both of segregation and of inevitable contamination—can be said to uneasily link some of literary culture's most familiar faces with bodies of work that are often suggestibly ignored. Fascinated fears of interior space, scientific controversies involving time and cultural origins, overtly raced narratives of savages and civilizations, colonialist melodramas that return again and again to Africa and the signs of Africa, mysterious punctures that serve as passageways between that which is known and that which is not: all of these figures could be said to describe equally the traditions of the lost race or hollow earth novel and the traditions of American Egyptomania.

The nineteenth-century narrative tradition of lost races and secret interior worlds has, of course, its canonized authors—H. Rider Haggard, Jules Verne, H. G. Wells, Edgar Rice Burroughs—but is especially important, for many reasons, in terms of Edgar Allan Poe, and so in this chapter I discuss several of Poe's works. Yet what is especially interesting about the racial rupture is how, quite characteristically, it is both connective and disruptive—in this case for canons and the histories of canons: the imperialist fantasies of African adventure, the rationalist ones of scientific archaeology, the chronological ones of speculative fiction. Thus its importance in the context of Poe, for in Poe the links between the lost race/hollow earth novel and American Egyptomania are particularly clear. His 1838 *Narrative of Arthur Gordon Pym* is unusually concerned with such interconnections, and it is a text that occupies the center, as it were, of this chapter.

The trope of the racial rupture—which appears in the final words of *Pym*—appears elsewhere in Poe, however, and before discussing *Pym* I will first analyze its role in several of Poe's shorter works. What will become obvious, though, is that I am not especially interested in Poe or *Pym* exclusively but rather in resituating both in a much larger context of outrageously raced narratives—narratives that take as their organizing impulses the contradictions of the colonialist expedition and, through epistemological holes much like the ones they feature, pass frantically between both genres and the histories of genres. The figure of an opening in the earth's crust located in the polar seas—which I take to be a sign of racialized fear directly produced by the discourses of American Egyptomania—recurs throughout the nineteenth century, both predating and postdating Poe, and with its shape I will be frequently concerned.

Too much importance cannot be attributed to Poe in the history of the lost race novel, yet too little scholarly attention has been paid to this connection. For reasons that are probably clear, academic treatment of Poe has traditionally contextualized his work more in terms of, for example, the international Gothic or the American Renaissance than in terms of the pulp fiction novels of lost races and the hollow earth. And while certainly Poe has had his share of convoluted and conflicted critical receptions it is only recently that he has even been able to be resituated in a context of nineteenth-century American race relations—much less in a context of popular fantastic fiction.[8] Poe's *Pym*, suspended as it is between the conventions of the psychoanalytic Gothic and ethnological lost race novel, marks such a split: between the directions of academic criticism on the one hand and the productivity of the popular racial imaginary on the other. Yet the lost race novel owes much to Poe, even as it occupies a central place in the landscape of nineteenth-century American racialization. In it is present a combination of racialized anxiety; pre-, post-, and actively Darwinian biological and social theory; explorationist adventure; and civilizationist commentary that appears nowhere else in as clear a form. No doubt the rococo stylings of late-nineteenth-century hollow earth novels may cause contemporary readers to roll their eyes, but their heterogeneous blend of racialized fantasy, accounts of biological origin, ambivalent adventurers, and apocalyptic imagery—all recounted through the structuring device of a terrestrial rupture—place them in a clear genealogy with Poe and what I call his Egyptian mode.

As if in a tale by Poe, in a heady admixture of elements of race theory, speculative science, and colonialist melodrama, the terms of nineteenth-century hollow earth theory are most clearly codified. "The central idea contained in the following work," wrote William Lyon in 1875, "is that this globe is constructed in the form of a hollow sphere, with a shell some thirty to forty miles in thickness, and that the interior surface which is a beautiful world in a more highly developed condition than the exterior, is accessible by a circuitous and spirally formed aperture that may be found in the un-explored open Polar Sea."[9] Lyon's *The Hollow Globe*, which bears a strong resemblance to early Egyptology's speculative scientism, has pronounced similarities to the works of Poe. Lyon's treatise, avowedly nonfiction, is presented as having been told to him by "a strange gentleman [who] made his appearance in the office" and describes an unpredictable mix of poli-tics and scientism: it is antislavery and anti-Catholic, and in addition to being explicitly colonialist it also puts forth the theory that the moon was constructed by the earth's inhabitants at some point in the distant past.[10] This combination of race science, politics, and theories of Manifest Des-tiny should be enough to help situate its author: Lyon's text forms a link between the speculative interiority of discourses like Egyptology and the speculative interiority of the hollow earth tradition.

The trope of the hollow earth presents a dense and intricate network of assumptions concerning race, region, and the biological and earth sci-ences that shares much with the fields that feed Egyptomania. Writers of treatises on hollow earth theories frequently emerged from the same mix of preprofessional science, imperial nationalism, speculatory imagination, and racialized anxiety that produced early Egyptology, and many of the same structures interpolate both. Of particular interest to me, however—as well as to the conventions of the lost race form—are how dependent this trope is on the figure of the racial rupture. Narratives of the colonial expedition, like those of colonial identities themselves, depend almost en-tirely on the eventual confrontation of the boundary that segregates Self and Other—and thus depend equally on dramas of its collapse. The racial rupture is such an obvious metonym for the concentric circles of colonial-ist identity that it cannot help but appear in a wide range of forms, but nowhere else does its combination of race theory, speculative possibility, and expeditionary anxiety appear as plainly as in the lost race fictions of the hollow earth.

As will become clear, I will at times take some extreme liberties of my own with the metaphorics of the punctiform figure, yet they are all intended to return to the signs of race and ancient Egypt. The relationship this figure has with the figure of ancient Egypt will, I hope, become clear enough; as Carter's twinned texts demonstrate, the racial rupture played a critical role in the discourses of colonialism and nineteenth-century Egyptology. Yet I imagine that some disagreements will converge on my treatment of the figure of the breach, and so I offer some preliminary clarification. I understand this trope of the puncture to be racialized not merely because it allows access in and out of such blatantly racialized spaces—interior or otherwise hidden worlds populated by races of perfect whiteness and races of savage blackness—but also because it is a figure of *collapse*, of a radical instability between binaries of black and white, of the unsustainability of the ethnological fantasy. It is in a way a figure of racialization itself: a sign of the inevitable and inescapable ruptures in systems of rationalized hierarchy. In Poe, the figure of the rupture is of course manifestly deconstructive, whether in terms of language or racial identity; later, in other years with other authors, it becomes more naturalized, less disruptive to the texts that feature it, more one term among many than one that disturbs the rest. But this does not, I believe, lessen the importance of the racialized legacy of the figure of the breach. Rather, it seems to me that it makes it all the more appropriate for analysis: what better subject of desedimentation than a figure of sediment itself?

## The Egyptian Moment

What I wish to describe is what I will call *the Egyptian moment*: a crisis in chronology and of the colonial imagination. This crisis underwrites the cultural production of at least four intertwined literary genres in nineteenth-century literary history, three of which appeared in America during the initial period of Egyptological excavation in the early 1800s and all of which partake of the uneasy fascination with archaeology and the distant past that constituted the nineteenth century's own version of Egyptomania. The first three of these—utopian fiction, speculative fiction, and what is variously called the ethnographic narrative, adventure story, or expeditionary tale—separate as these genres might or might not be today—were by no means distinct in the early nineteenth century. And, while the travel tale predated and influenced both utopian fiction and early science fiction, these latter two did not emerge in the United States until the second decade after the onset of modern archaeology.[11] The fourth genre—the detective story—emerged from the same cluster of early-nineteenth-century cultural concerns: the twinned emergence of imperialism and scientific rationalism; the development of several allied systems of thought, including linguistics, ethnology, and comparative anatomy; the rise of racialization; and many other corresponding effects resulting from what some historians have loosely and imprecisely analyzed as the transition from the Enlightenment to the Age of Science.

The Egyptian moment functions as a watershed moment in narratives of *analysis*: linguists and archaeologists are seen as twinned characters in a drama of analytic rationality, piecing together the scattered evidence of what was both a civilization of death and a dead civilization, as crucial players on a field of lost secrets, buried answers, and hidden mysteries. "The analyst," it is reported in what is so often thought of as the very first detective tale, "is fond of enigmas, of conundrums, of hieroglyphics."[12] As the nineteenth century wears on, the imperial adventurousness of the Egyptological travel narrative comes to share the stage with a figure that becomes equally dramatic, one that is equally concerned with excavation but is significantly different: the Egyptologist is now the scientist, the scholar, the savant, the detective. "Considering Poe's frequent admiring references to Champollion," writes John Irwin, "it is tempting to speculate that one of the models for the character of Dupin . . . was Champollion."[13] These unambiguous references to Egypt in what are narratives of either detection or adventure mark the type of radical interrelatedness of discourses and practices I am here calling the Egyptian moment.[14]

There is an *archaeologic* to these motions, these movements of uncovering, excavating, deciphering, analyzing. These generically intertwined narratives dramatize over and over again the instant or the process of discovery, the exact moment or the careful achievement of breakthrough, the precise shape of the archaeological or analytical epiphany. Often the most crucial figure is that of the rupture: whether the literal one of a stone wall, the visual one of an eruption in an optical field, the economic one of instant wealth, or the conceptual one of entering another time or another culture or of deciphering a set of clues, some moment of secular revelation is one of the benchmarks of the archaeologic form. But this revelation is never wholly pure, never without cost, and the rips and tears in bodies, spaces, or texts that rely on the figure of the archaeologic rupture make this clear. The Egyptian moment can refer either to this extended period in imperial cultural history or to the precise point in a text when the dangerous implications of the archaeological imperative are rendered their most clear or metaphorical, but scenes of such explosive archaeologic and the cultural moment that produced them exist as concentric circles waiting to be discovered.

And yet neither the adventurer, the archaeologist, nor the detective can ever arrest their impulses to penetrate; like so many other binary systems, the twinned figures of rationality and irrationality, of wreckage and reconstruction, so common to such archaeologics, are based on their necessary confusion. Sometimes immediate, sometimes almost infinitely protracted, the racial rupture is the sign of a bifurcated fascination with a particular kind of danger made literal—the danger of the collapse of systems of separation, the danger of epistemological miscegenation. The Egyptian moment presents itself as an epistemological threat: to time, space, rationality, identity. The Egyptian moment marks the crisis of the racial rupture, with its initial overtones of colonial invasion and imperial power and its later ones of cryptography and detection, and traces the sutures of narratives of discovery and utopia to narratives of translation and the future.

Melodramas of archaeological entrance—of passage, puncture, and imperial panic—and their racialized implications are what the next section will be concerned to describe. Related to what Pratt has thematized as arrival scenes in explorationist writings,[15] representations of the racial rupture are without question similar framing devices, but unlike arrival scenes they are also explicitly and recurrently marked as scenes of disruption as well as cohesion, of instability as well as stability. This paradoxical status is just what I wish to draw attention to, especially as it figures as a foundational moment in raced narratives of exoticized exploration: rupture scenes are paradigmatically contradictory in ways that are succinct and explicit and not available in most other expeditionary narratives, and as such I read them as figures of racialization. More to the point, I read them as figures of American racial identity: manifestly contradictory, anxious, and unstable, operating both to conceal and reveal, to admit and deny, to open and close. That the Egyptian moment proceeds by such a visibly fitful process indicates not only the centrality of such scenes of racialized discovery to its frantic logic, and not only the centrality of such instability to the ideological project of American race making, but the importance of such unstable operations to the whole of the colonial project and the Afro-Egyptian dramas that were its narrative treasures.

## "Dat Sabage Kind ob Style"

At the climax of Edgar Allan Poe's 1843 short story "The Gold-Bug," Poe's unnamed narrator, his friend William Legrand, and Legrand's officially manumitted but nevertheless pointedly servile elderly ex-slave Jupiter all stand around a recently excavated pit under a tree growing on a barren section of coast of extreme southern South Carolina and gaze upon an open chest containing an immense treasure of gold and jewels, which they have just uncovered. "I shall not pretend to describe the feelings with which I gazed," Poe's narrator recounts. "Amazement was, of course, predominant." He also takes stock of his friend: "Legrand appeared exhausted with excitement, and spoke very few words." The narrator's description then turns to the ex-slave: "Jupiter's countenance wore, for some minutes, as deadly a pallor as it is possible, in the nature of things, for any negro's visage to assume. He seemed stupefied — thunderstricken. Presently he fell upon his knees in the pit, and burying his naked arms up to the elbows in gold, let them there remain, as if enjoying the luxury of a bath."[16] That the narrative climax of this tale of treasure seeking should rely so crucially on the overly stereotyped excesses of a stock racist character in antebellum American fiction would not, perhaps, be quite as noticeable in this scene if it were not in this story that we have one of the very few prolonged appearances of a black character contained in all of Poe's works. Nor would it be quite so striking if it were not for the soliloquy Jupiter delivers to himself immediately after his plunge, his arms still buried in gold: " 'And all dis cum ob de goole-bug! de putty goole-bug! the poor little goole-bug, what I boosed in dat sabage kind ob style! Aint you shamed ob yourself, nigger? — answer me dat!' "[17]

The scene of the two white men standing on the edge of the treasure-filled pit carefully containing their excitement and their words while the servile black man unleashes both of his within it, performing in "dat sabage kind ob style," is a scene of quadrilateral desire—between the three men and the pit—with a relatively routine kind of racist structure. The black character, in his animalism, acts unconditionally on an impulse that the white characters are also feeling but are too cerebral or civilized to give in to. The servile status of Jupiter is a sign by which the white characters can experience, if vicariously, unrestrained libido, while simultaneously and literally controlling it completely. The scene depends on Jupiter's frenzy while also enacting a racialized distance from it—a distance made literal by the image of the pit—and so the white characters are allowed to partake both of whiteness and of blackness while still remaining somehow both and neither, balanced on the brink of the pit.

For a number of Poe scholars, though, "The Gold-Bug" is important not for the scene of geologic revelation that reveals the buried treasure but for what occurs in the pages afterward, in the scene of cryptographic revelation in which Legrand reveals how he discovered the instructions that resulted in the corollary discovery.[18] The intellectual excavation—occurring first in the story's "real" time but revealed secondly in the story's narration—is thus for many readers the more significant of what are twinned discoveries, the linguistic—or, as Poe calls it at one point, the *hieroglyphical*—superseding the physical. There is good reason for this, of course, especially given Poe's famous interests in language in general and cryptograms in particular, and so much attention is paid by Poe in his story to the hieroglyphical logistics of Legrand's excavation that one could hardly expect otherwise.

Critically, however, the scene that takes place immediately after the discovery of the treasure also has a structure that recalls the words of Toni Morrison, writing, not incidentally, in part of another piece by Poe: "Because they appear almost always in conjunction with representations of black or Africanist people who are dead, impotent, or under complete control . . . images of . . . whiteness seem to function as both antidote for and mediation on the shadow that is companion to this whiteness—a dark and abiding presence that moves the hearts and texts of American literature with fear and longing."[19] When Morrison writes that "no early American writer is more important to the concept of American Africanism than Poe," she is for me indicating the importance of scenes like that around the unearthed treasure chest in "The Gold-Bug."[20] So "The Gold-Bug" and the twinned machinery of semiotic and geologic exhumation that structures it are justifiably famous, for more reasons, no doubt, than I can enumerate here, but for me it stands as an extremely important "x" that itself marks the spot of the explicit linkage of a scene of linguistic translation with a scene of geologic, racialized excavation on the shores of America.[21]

Without question, Poe owes much of his anxious cultural theorizing to highly attenuated American dramas of race. Indeed, this aspect of Poe's work is a high-water mark of nineteenth-century American racial anxiety, phrased in a language that is explorationist, excavational, and archaeological. Yet what makes Poe additionally important is how he draws enormous and repeated attention to the process or figure of *transition*, to the stages or devices of passage from one epistemological field to the next—so much so that, quite famously, the boundaries in Poe are themselves so blurred as to be radically unstable, the status of the ontologies themselves the subject of the narrative. His famous blurred boundaries between waking and sleeping or his representations of drug-induced apprehension can, in fact, be said to be an effect of his attention to the shape of the archaeological imaginary. Poe's career-long treatment of the expeditionary tale is a wholesale theorization of the genre and its ideological and epistemological assumptions. Bedloe dies, maelstroms swallow, manuscripts are found in bottles, Pym faces his ambiguous fate. Poe is a theorist of the anxieties of Manifest Destiny.

And so it is with Poe's multilayered signs of terrestrial rupture—of excavation, of hieroglyphical translation, of an archaeologic that changes everything except the racialized hierarchies that first brought it into being —that I linger over here. Specifically, I am concerned with that scene of terrible excitement that in "The Gold-Bug" leaves the figure of blackness shouting at itself and the two figures of whiteness unable to speak. What particularly interests me, though, is not so much the relationship between the two white men and the nominally "free" black man. Rather, what interests me here is their relationship, as a racially configured triangle, to the *pit*. This newly excavated earthen hole contains enough wealth to reverse the fallen fortunes of Legrand, the search for it causes the narrator and Jupiter both to fear for Legrand's sanity, and the scene of racialized excess enacted on its edge and in its depths is overwhelmingly concerned with dual configurations of seen and unseen, said and unsaid, containment and removal, submerging and surfacing, inhibition and exhibition. In short, what interests me is the scene of excavation as the scene of *mania*, and what the figure of a servile black man burying his naked arms up to the elbows in gold on the slave-heavy coast outside nineteenth-century Charleston, South Carolina, can tell us about it.

### "I Was Not a White Man, Compared with Him"

Poe built his initial reputation on the exploitation of the blurriness of the line between the ostensibly accurate travel narrative and the suasively suspect "supernatural" voyage, a tone that signals the onset of his Egyptian mode. His first published story, the 1833 "MS. Found in a Bottle" is ostensibly an expeditionary tale, but it has to it more than a touch of the *underworldly*, of the sign of rupture. In it, a restless, difficult, prodigious young man books passage on a ship sailing from Java, finds himself stranded by the effects of a hurricane, and is later picked up by a sinister black ship. This ship sails as far south as the pole, and disappears, with the narrator, into an apocalyptic whirlpool. The last paragraph of "MS." ends with this descent: "Oh, horror upon horror! — the ice opens suddenly to the right, and to the left, and we are whirling dizzily, in immense concentric circles, round and round the borders of a gigantic ampitheatre, the summit whose walls is lost in the darkness and the distance. But little time will be left me to ponder upon my destiny! The circles grow rapidly small — we are plunging madly within the grasp of the whirlpool — and amid a roaring, and bellowing, and thundering of ocean and tempest, the ship is quivering — oh God! and — going down!"[22] Poe's inauguration of his own Egyptian moment begins with the beginning of his career.[23]

The final sentences feature a reference to what is today a little-known work of early American fiction, the first full-length work of American speculative fiction, John Cleves Symmes's 1820 *Symzonia: A Voyage of Discovery. Symzonia* was the first American science fiction novel, and, as we will see, it provided Poe with a narrative trope and dramatic image that he used in at least two other major works, the 1841 "A Descent into the Maelström" and the 1838 *Narrative of Arthur Gordon Pym*. But as forgotten as he is today, especially when considered in light of his relationship to Poe, Symmes can in fact be said to have supplied a central trope and image to Western speculative fiction as a whole: the Symmes Hole. Symmes's legacy extends from a place in his own *Symzonia* to Verne's *Journey to the Center of the Earth* and Edgar Rice Burroughs's novels of Pellucidar, and from the archaeologically inflected movements of the colonial fantastic to the lost race and hollow earth novels of the rest of the century. The anxieties on which he drew—those of colonialist discovery, geology, the rise and fall of civilizations, preevolutionary race theory, and earthly interiority—are foundational anxieties for the Egyptian moment.

TO ALL THE WORLD!

I declare the earth is hollow and habitable within; containing a number of solid concentrick spheres, one within the other, and that it is open at the poles 12 or 16 degrees; I pledge my life in support of this truth, and am ready to explore the hollow, if the world will support and aid me in the undertaking.

(Signed) Jn. Cleves Symmes
of Ohio, late Captain of Infantry.[24]

Symmes's pseudonymously published *Symzonia* is the earliest known utopian tale written and published in America; it is part scientific treatise, part travel narrative, part adventure story, part picaresque novel, part utopian philosophy, and part dystopian morality tale. It is a utopia but also what today we would call "science fiction"; it is carefully rendered as a sea voyage, but the voyage is just as fantastic as one to the moon. Ostensibly written by one "Adam Seaborn," the novel chronicles the journey of a sea captain who, "avail[ing] himself of all the lights and facilities afforded by the sublime theory of an internal world, published by John Cleve Symmes," sails through a hole in the South Pole—the Symmes Hole—and discovers a fabulous ancient city within the center of the earth. "In the year 1817," the novel opens, "I projected a voyage of discovery, in the hope of finding a passage to a new and untried world." [25] Like all utopian narratives, *Symzonia* exists in as syncretic a form as those with which it was networked, and it is from within this network of images of colonialism, race theory, and earthly penetration that the hollow earth emerges.[26]

Symmes was a former army captain and amateur scientist from Ohio who published his theory of the hollow earth separately, in 1826, as *Symmes Theory of Concentric Spheres: Demonstrating That the Earth is Hollow, Habitable Within, and Widely Open at the Poles*.[27] He spent most of his adult life after leaving the military attempting to publicize his theories and prove them. In 1818, he had printed in St. Louis his "Circular Number 1," in which he declared more concisely that "the earth is hollow and habitable within; containing a number of solid concentrick spheres, one within the other" and "pledge[d] my life in support of this truth." He also presented himself in the guise of an adventurer, "ready to explore the hollow, if the world will support and aid me in the undertaking."[28] After something of a limited locally-based grassroots campaign, during which he gave various public lectures—aided socially, no doubt, by his membership in one of Cincinnati's most famous and powerful first families—petitions and memorials based on Symmes's theories began to reach Congress. In a variety of ways, and with more than a few delays, support gradually built to a final point in 1838 when Charles Wilkes set sail from Hampton Roads, Virginia, in command of the five ships of the United States South Seas Exploring Expedition, which just over two years later would, ironically, officially "discover" Antarctica.[29]

Symzonia's configuration of generic characteristics neatly iterates an American popular polylogic, and the text marks the beginning of the American utopian-fantastic tradition with a rhetoric that is explicitly colonial. The "voyage of Columbus was but an excursion on a fish pond, and his discoveries, compared with mine, were but trifles," Seaborn rhapsodizes. "His was the discovery of a continent, mine of a new World!"[30] It also describes a form that is anxiously ethnographic: on reaching the world within the hollow earth, Seaborn discovers a race of people who are whiter than he is. "The sootiest African does not differ more from us in darkness of skin and grossness of features," writes Symmes, "than this man did from me in fairness of complexion and delicacy of form."[31] In a moment strikingly reminiscent of the gestures of dressing and undressing that were such an important part of the erotics of racial identification, Seaborn reveals his own flesh in a stage show of ethnographic striptease: "I shoved up the sleeve of my coat, to show them, by the inside of my arm (which was always excluded from the sun), that I was a white man. I am considered fair for an American, and my skin was always in my own country thought to be one of the finest and whitest. But when one of the internals placed his arm, always exposed to the weather, by the side of mine, the difference was truly mortifying. I was not a white man, compared with him."[32] In the interior of Symmes's explorable world, he confronts a perfect ethnographic specimen. Seaborn's encounters with the natives of the internal world, however, invert his place in the schemes of European racialized hierarchies. His specimen, therefore, and his apprehension of it are structured not only by a shock to his racialized expectations but by a shock of perfect inversion—which turns, perfectly, on an axis of black and white. Some years later, when Edgar Allan Poe returned to the image of the concentric Symmes Hole, he would also return to this drama of inverted black and white.

The structure of *Symzonia* is a concise example of the Egyptian moment. The speculatory tradition describes a movement that, given this network of exploratory narrative, dystopian commentary, and internal concealment, while possessing a heritage more than a century old could be understood in the nineteenth century as archaeological in shape, and *Symzonia* is built around a logic of interiority, configured by the signs of passage, puncture, and racialized anxiety. *Symzonia* chronicles a voyage to the heart of darkness made spherical. The earth *itself* is the object of the voyage of expedition; it is *given* interiority as a means by which the colonialist adventure and its panicky denotations can remain infinitely in play. Passage into the interior of the earth will yield the shift in epistemology that is so much a part of the speculative or expeditionary voyage; the earth is now the secret, racialized space, holding entombed treasures and the bodies that surround them.

The earth in *Symzonia*, in other words, is structured by the sign of Egypt. Egypt is the doubled sign of the archaeological: at once a sign of the unknown but also of the fantastic, of the potential and speculative—that is, of a space that is unimaginable and yet, under the imperial racialized gaze, infinitely knowable, imaginable to an infinite degree. The Symmes Hole is as much a rupture into deep time as Carter's hole in Tut's tomb: it is a puncture into a medium of containment that holds something both terrible and grand, both sought after and unattainable. It marks the space between two epistemologically distinct and mutually exclusive zones, the potential relationship between which would result in the disruption that the rupture both contains and only suggests. The logic of the Egyptian mode both reveals and denies. The inevitable rejection of the traveler from utopia is thus the structural equivalent of the Curse of Tut's Tomb. Utopia is found only to be lost again; the treasure is found but at too high a cost. The colonialist voyage imagined new worlds in many places, but the shock of the new that was old, and of the explosive interior penetrated place, has its epicenter in the racialized masculinized adventure fantasies of American Egyptomania.[33]

It should hardly be a surprise, then, that the image of a rupture in both the earth's surface and the exploratory expedition structures a range of texts written across Poe's career. It is spotted from a balloon by Hans Pfall, it opens at the close of "MS. Found in a Bottle," it is made hydrologic in "A Descent into the Maelström," and, given its manic power and plainly related imagery, it also appears as the terrestrial rupture in "The Gold-Bug." Moreover, given its fluidity as a structuring device, the matrix of racialized anxiety and penetrated spaces here theorized as the racial rupture could even admit familiarity with the expeditionary puncture of "A Tale of the Ragged Mountains" and the animalistic one of "Murders in the Rue Morgue."[34] But what is important for me here is how easily the figure of the rupture lent itself to racialized fantasies of all kinds: the geologic, chronologic, hydrologic, or archaeologic rupture becomes, in Poe and forever after, a racial rupture—a rupture in whiteness, which, as in *The Narrative of Arthur Gordon Pym*, becomes whiteness itself. "The heart of darkness revolves around a vortex of fear," writes Pratt, and in the context of Poe and his racialized vortexes her language could not be more appropriate.[35]

The racial rupture—whether it be Symmes Hole, maelstrom, or archaeological pit—is the space of crisis par excellence for the binaries it draws into focus: inner and outer, safe and dangerous, known and unknown, placid and violent, black and white, perfectly content and almost irresistibly attractive. In other words, the racial rupture reveals the logic of the Egyptian mode: radically epistemologically unstable, marking a division between two more stable states even as it blurs the very line that it draws between them, configured by the twinned effects of rationalism and terror and produced by their structural interrelatedness. From Seaborn's expedition to Jupiter's plunge to what Poe's sailor from within the maelstrom describes as "lines of horridly black and beetling cliff, whose character of gloom was but the more forcibly illustrated by the surf which reared high up against its white and ghastly crest, howling and shrieking for ever,"[36] the rupture describes a space that is both unstable and patently irresistable. "After a little while," Poe's sailor admits in words reminiscent of Legrand, "I became possessed with the keenest curiosity about the whirl itself. I positively felt a *wish* to explore its depths."[37]

This dangerous fascination, this obsessive magnetism that is both potentially self-destructive and somehow inevitable, is, then, a mania. Like that portrayed at the edge of the excavational pit on the South Carolina coast of "The Gold-Bug," it is the mania produced by the melodrama of the binaries of inside and outside and black and white, shaped into the expeditionary voyage, poised on the edge of a rupture, and experienced by Howard Carter at the door of the tomb of Tut-ankh-Amen. It lies at the center of a range of raced adventure tales remarkable for, among other things, their formulaic repetition. It reveals the instabilities of American racialization but only at terrible cost: lost ships, lost sailors, fractured bodies, fragmented texts, mountainous funnels of devouring blackness, and unrepresentable ruptures of cavernous whiteness. The costs of approaching nineteenth-century racial ruptures are equivalent only to the regularity with which they are paid.

## "Where a Chasm Threw Itself Open to Receive Us"

The figure of the racial rupture was written both into the center and altogether out of the text of Poe's 1838 *Narrative of Arthur Gordon Pym*. That this is important to my reading here should be readily apparent; in the series of recent revisions of Poe's literary output, *Pym* has emerged as a central text, especially in terms of understanding his attitudes regarding the cultural politics of race.[38] Moreover, as should be equally familiar to any reader of *Pym*, the importance of its collusion of racialized anxieties and Egyptian imagery claim for the story a place of obvious importance to my argument here. "Insofar as *Pym* is indeed the most powerful racial allegory of the antebellum period, and insofar as the mainspring of its tension is 'a crisis of color,' " argues Stephen Dougherty, citing Sidney Kaplan and Joan Dayan, "the specter of Egypt was bound to rear its head in one form or another."[39]

And while obviously my study is interested in placing *Pym* in something of a privileged place as well, it is also my concern to show how the imagery that structures it—particularly in the form of the racially fraught, punctiform rupture—traverses Poe's career and was in no way limited to *Pym*. Indeed, the image of the colonialist expedition was from its earliest representation in the American utopian-speculative tradition radically unstable and subject to inversion. The inversions that occur in *Pym* thus echo the primary inversion of Symmes, one no less of geography than of ethnology: the appearance of radical whiteness in the midst of expected blackness. A journey to the most extreme reaches of southernness produces the most extreme reaches of whiteness.

As is well known, Poe's *Pym* was an ambitious intervention into the thick tradition of seafaring adventure narratives of the eighteenth and nineteenth centuries, and at its most explicit it is a rewriting of a colonialist adventure tale—specifically, that of the South Polar expedition. The whole of chapter 16, in fact, is a history of expeditions to the pole: James Cook is presented, as is the American Benjamin Morrell, along with Russian and other British expeditions, with the effect of producing "feelings," Pym writes, "of most intense interest . . . of pushing boldly to the southward."[40] Indeed, the American connotations of southernness are not to be missed; they are at once geographical and radically ethnological, of temperature and direction and race. "As Poe's most-often-historicized work," writes Teresa Goddu, "*Pym* reveals how a racial reading of Poe depends on the cipher of the South."[41] The tale famously "ends" with an excursion onto a southern island populated by "natives," cartoonish "savages" of thoroughgoing blackness, violently racist and outrageously overwritten. "*Pym*'s pursuits deliver to the 'eye of science' not only the news of a temperate and productive zone," writes Dana Nelson, "but several 'natural' proofs of racial hierarchy as well."[42] In other words, *Pym* presents the textual embodiment of all the central anxieties of American ethnology.[43]

The decrease in temperature south of Tierra del Fuego and the appearance of ice floes in the farther southern longitudes was, of course, well known to Cook and Morrell and other eighteenth-century explorers, to say nothing of Ferdinand Magellan, Francis Drake, and the numerous seagoers who predated the colonial period.[44] In ethnology, though, the drive was toward rationalist *racialization of cartographic* space: races constantly *darkened* as they moved south. With quite a lot depending on this one abstraction—American ethnology, after all, was nothing if not a system with designs on absolutist principles—the *directionality of color* was an axiom of racial typology. With the rise of ethnology, then, and its cartographic racialization, representations of extreme southernness were placed in a bind: to account for "southern" races in a patently "northern" climate. Insofar as the South Pole was seen to be the most unlikely place for a region of cold—or, at least as according to the geographical logic of early ethnology, the least likely *region* to produce northern *races*—the last thing a colonialist direction could imagine was a return to the north.

Antarctica and the South Polar region were thus mirror images of Egypt itself and the surrounding geography of the continent of Africa. Both were configured by antinomies between black and white; both were seen as wastelands, uninhabitable by Europeans. Both were examples of extreme geologic conditions; both were monotonies, one of ice and one of sand. Even as Pym, like Wilkes, ends up in the icy wasteland of polar floes, he has a premonitory dream much earlier, in yet another extreme condition, deprived of food and water in the hold of the *Grampus*: "Deserts, limitless, and of the most forlorn and awe-inspiring character, spread themselves before me. . . . The scene changed; and I stood, naked and alone, amid the burning sand-plains of Zahara."[45] This epistemological vacillation, then, is precisely what structures the end of *Pym*: a trip to the south is a journey into the north, and once arriving there it is a journey back again. Hot, cold, hot, black, white, black: *Pym* turns on the axes of these extremes.

Ethnological antinomies thus structure Poe's utmost south.[46] The south is *so* utmost that black and white implode and collapse into one another; the racialized distinctions that produce the region of the ethnological south are the very terms by which *Pym* cannot conclude itself. What makes the south so utmost is the fact that the binaries *invert*, producing, as an effect, both an inversion of color and one of nature. And so *Pym* ends with the cardinal mark of the Egyptian moment: the sign of the liminal boundary, the boundary about to be breached. Yet the moment of breach is forever, radically, deferred. The rupture in the sea is never completely attained, its denial producing a rupture in the text. Just as Carter's chapter concluded with the breaching of Tut's tomb, Poe's narrative does *not* conclude with the deferral of the breach. That both narratives' ends take place under the sign of Egyptian hieroglyphics indicates how eerily precursive *Pym*'s journey was. Adventure tale, anxieties of containment, translation, and, of course, radically racialized ethnology: *Pym* consists of virtually all the discourses that made up American Egyptomania.

Poe choreographs the end of *Pym* through a meditation on the cultural politics of American Egyptomania that in its symbolism is almost operatic: by placing set pieces of black and white binaries around a protracted drama of impossible interpretation. Its final pages are filled with illustrations based on hieroglyphics—or runes or Hebrew or Coptic or Ethiopian letters—found in a scene of ethnological archaeology, and are overwhelmingly concerned with the link between ancient languages and racial identity, that is, with the decipherability of the signs of black and white. The figures Poe provides are both maps and alphabetic analogues, signs that are at once cartographic and architectural. Moreover, they are also signs of the racialized body itself. "It is more than probable," Pym writes, "that the opinion of Peters was correct, and that the hieroglyphical appearance was really the work of art, and intended as the representation of a human form. . . . The upper range is evidently the Arabic verbal root 'To be white,' whence all the inflections of brilliancy and whiteness. The lower range is not so immediately perspicuous. The characters are somewhat broken and disjointed; nevertheless, it cannot be doubted that, in their perfect state, they formed the full Egyptian word, 'The region of the south.' "[47]

That Poe makes sure to destabilize the racialized identity of ancient Egypt—through his inclusion of the possible Ethiopian etymology of his Egyptian hieroglyphs, foreclosing any attempts to securely claim the Egyptian markings as partaking only of whiteness—further illustrates the extent to which *Pym* describes the link between nineteenth-century Egyptology and the instability of nineteenth-century racial identity. References to Count Volney's proto-Afrocentric position regarding the racial identities of the ancient Egyptians had become commonplace by 1838, as had a much wider range of complexity regarding the connections between "blackness" and Egyptian symbolism than is usually recognized. The works of James Cowles Prichard had already arrived with controversy in the United States, and African Americans had been making inroads into claims of the whiteness of Egyptian civilization for at least ten years. And regardless of whatever claims might be made concerning Poe's personal views regarding slavery as an institution, it is clear that he understood only too well the threat that such connections between blackness and ancient Egypt represented to white identity, to white racial typologies, to whiteness as such.

When Poe segues his depictions of savages into depictions of mysterious languages, which are both represented in—or as—racialized archaeological space, there seems to be no more streamlined summary of the anxious logic of American Egyptomania. As signs of language, race, and the archaeological space itself, *Pym*'s hieroglyphics are radically difficult to decipher. At a moment clearly intended to rescript the central climax of the archetypal adventure tale—the ultimate Egyptian moment of discovery, translation, revelation, ultimate origin and ultimate truth—Pym finds not only an indecipherable Egyptian hieroglyph but a radically heterogeneous one as well. Instead of finding a single source—of history, language, or racial identity—Pym instead finds multiple sources; instead of finding an answer, he finds only more questions. From its rewriting of the terms of the colonial fantastic to its overwriting of the biological implications of the burgeoning discourses of ethnology and the monumental encounters with hieroglyphical inscriptions that are explicitly named as Egyptian, *Pym* moves in full intertextuality with American Egyptomania.

Poe, it seems, is working not with a system of transparent metaphoricity but rather at the very edges of its racialized limits. He writes an ethnological adventure story that turns itself on its head, concluding with a scene of radical disruption. His tale is one of terror—racialized terror, to be sure—but it is also an investigation into the terms of the representations of terror. "Race" as a sign is overdetermined in Pym, but this applies to "white" as well as to "black." Even as they preclude conclusion, the binaries themselves are what conclude the motion of the tale. The expedition is unable to sustain its own preconditions:

> March 22d.—The darkness had materially increased, relieved only by the glare of the water thrown back from the white curtain before us. Many gigantic and pallidly white birds flew continuously now from beyond the veil, and their scream was the eternal Tekeli-li! as they retreated from our vision. Hereupon Nu-Nu stirred in the bottom of the boat; but upon touching him, we found his spirit departed. And now we rushed into the embraces of the cataract, where a chasm threw itself open to receive us. But there arose in our pathway a shrouded human figure, very far larger in its proportions than any dweller among men. And the hue of the skin of the figure was of the perfect whiteness of the snow.[48]

Poe is deconstructing the attempt to stabilize white racial identity through colonial quests in, and archaeological claims on, ancient Egypt. An unstable sign of both the fascinations and the fears of the archaeological imaginary, the fissural imagery that closes Pym is as literal a rupture in the binary structures of self and text and racialization as exist in nineteenth-century European American literature.[49]

## "What Bunglers Those Egyptians of Ours on the Exterior Globe Were, After All"

This trope of a puncture in the surface of the earth was remarkably widespread throughout the nineteenth century. It occupied a range of literary and cultural traditions—or, better, it demonstrates the interconnectedness with which so many ostensibly separate literary or artistic genres operated—but as a figure it was almost always racialized. Sometimes the puncture was on dry land, sometimes in the sea; sometimes it was symbolic, a distant metaphor of disruption; sometimes it was functional, a literalized portal. Most often, the crater in the earth's crust did in fact have a utilitarian purpose—whether for the revelation of riches or as a passageway into another land or another time—and it was in this utility that its use became radically racialized. Especially given their function in systems of binary opposition like those operating in Poe, punctiform figures like the Symmes Hole are remarkably fungible.

The genealogy of this trope is quite interdisciplinary and international: at least from the journeys into the underworld of Dante and Odysseus, representations of passageways between exterior and interior habitations of the earth—however hellish—have played a major role in Western thought about subterranean space.[50] Indeed, as Richard Hamblyn reminds us, equations between representations of the earth's interior and the temperaments of those people living in regions of high geologic—especially volcanic—activity were a crucial feature of the development of early geology. "The Italian landscape and people had themselves been continually figured by northern Europeans as eruptive and unpredictable," Hamblyn writes. "William Hamilton, for instance, referred to the inhabitants of Naples as a 'tumultuous and impatient mob' that was ready to 'set fire' to public buildings as was Vesuvius itself."[51] Even more than reminding us of the way early racist thought was characterized by geographical determinism, however, the role of early vulcanology in the rise of nineteenth-century scientific thought also demonstrates how consistently connections were made between punctures in the earth and social and cultural disruptions.[52]

Most importantly, however, what links punctiform figures like the volcano and the vortex in nineteenth-century speculative or utopian fiction, apart from the obvious, if inverted, similarities of both function and form, is their status as signs of scientistic speculation. Too much cannot be said about the role speculation—especially racialized speculation—played in nineteenth-century Egyptomania nor about the extent to which early fantastic fiction grew out of this same impulse. As Lyon's *Hollow Globe* indicates, the interest in origin in general—cultural, geographical, historical, biological—is what motivated both nineteenth-century Egyptology and nineteenth-century speculative fiction. Poe understood this well enough to deconstruct the connection in *Pym*, and yet in its racial allegoricism, its hollow earth imagery, and its hieroglyphical, Egyptomaniacal inscriptions *Pym* presented nineteenth-century American culture with a combination of images that would prove central to the colonial fantastic. In particular, *Pym* illustrates the link between the lost race novel and American Egyptomania.

To be sure, the lost race tradition presents what might politely be thought of as the challenge of democracy: violently racist, aggressively xenophobic, even hard to read and often badly written, its authors found in the form a productive outlet for their visions of racialized utopia that today seems hard to stomach or to justify in reprintings. But it must be said that the utopian-fantastic tradition out of which these distinctly racist fantasies arose, even in its most "acceptable" forms—Haggard, Verne, Burroughs, Wells—was deeply intertwined with a much more widespread racialization than is merely contained within their covers. Likewise, the scientific constructions of racialized hierarchies that so dominated mainstream Egyptology at the beginning of the twentieth century—to say nothing of the popularized Darwinism with which, along with Egyptology, the lost race novels were so obviously in dialogue—were hardly less violent than those more fantastic ones found in the pulpy visions of lost races, vanished civilizations, and inverted worlds. Indeed, the social shock of radical racialization—stark dichotomies of black and white supported by rediscovered ruins and signs from the ancient past—is what the lost race novels most insisted on preserving. In so doing, they most naggingly remind their cultural cousin Egyptology of how close they once were. "We had expected to surprise the natives," wrote W. J. Shaw in the 1888 *Cresten, Queen of the Toltus*; "they had surprised us."[53]

It is thus striking—though, given the intimacies the lost race novel has with its cousin Egyptomania, not surprising—how often explicit Egyptian imagery appears throughout the tradition. Beginning with the hieroglyphical inscriptions that confront Pym and reappearing in such famous forms as Haggard's *She* and *The Ivory Child* or in such forgotten ones as Verne's *The Sphinx of the Ice*, a paradigmatic investment in the imagery of Egyptomania structures the entire lost race/hollow earth tradition. In Shaw's *Cresten*, for example, an adventurer, like Hans Pfall, floats over the polar cap in a balloon and spies an opening in the earth's crust; he then discovers a lost civilization, and, like so many of Poe's characters, narrates his story through a second narrator:

It appears from his narrative that if the unfortunate Arctic explorer, Captain Hall, had been enabled to advance even 100 miles beyond where he could see with his glass, that the land had put off its mantle of snow, he would have been rounding the earth's verge, and have fairly entered upon a land of eternal day, peopled by peculiar and hitherto unheard-of races. He locates the kingdom of that most remarkable woman, Cresten, Queen of the Toltus, on the interior of the globe, upon the Asiatic side and north of the 55th parallel. . . . I have not the shadow of a doubt that, had this narration not been made to me, I should have gone to my grave without having learned how man and all other animals originated; where the white races came from; when the Deluge occurred, and what caused it.[54]

Unfortunate explorers followed by endlessly intrepid others, unexpected discoveries of lost civilizations which explain the history of the world and especially the origin of the races: in 1888, Shaw was writing words that, with only a few substitutions, could have been taken directly from texts on Egyptology almost a century before.

The lost race/hollow earth tradition preserved the combination of racialized hypothesizing, adventurous melodrama, and speculational interiority first presented by American Egyptomania but which had been suppressed by professionalized specialization over the intervening years. Indeed, while the force of the fantastic—the mysterious, dangerous, liminal, and terrifying—was never fully hollowed out of professional Egyptology, lost race/hollow earth novels seized on the elements of the speculative long associated with the signs and wonders of ancient Egypt and continually presented them in what was, for better or worse, a radically democratized form. Authors of lost race/hollow earth novels—many of them publishing privately, their personas often associated with the figure of the crackpot maniac so frequently reworked as the hero of such pieces—formed, like the spiritualists and theosophists whose texts theirs at times closely resemble, a kind of group of amateur Egyptologists. That the racialized constructions found in both branches of this family tree were at times so similar is testimony to their kinship; that one pushes toward institutionalized authority and the other toward literary iconoclasm clearly is as well.

This combination of race theory and Egyptian adventure tale that was so critical to Egyptology's early development can easily be seen in Shaw's novel. Once inside the hollow earth, *Cresten*'s crucial plot device is the awakening of a king long thought dead yet preserved in the earth and suddenly reanimated: "Lying half embedded in the clay, as within a mould in which it had been cast," Shaw's explorer discovers,

> was a human being. . . . I stripped the outer coat at the waist from the body and began chafing the flesh to promote circulation of the blood. . . . The Queen of Knowledge, however, proposed something more expeditious than my antiquated modes. [She] placed in the palm of his hand that mysterious ball which had such a marvellous effect upon the nervous system. Instantly there was a quiver throughout the whole organ-

ism, and I could feel beneath my other hand that rested on his breast his lungs begin to expand. A single respiration proclaimed returning life — that is, if he could be supposed ever to have been dead. I perceived that the blood began to flow through the arteries and veins and give color to that transparent skin which the Queen's race inherited from Nordroff's wife, the Queen of the Toltus.[55]

Even if the figure of royal reanimation was not in itself enough to invoke scenes of Egyptian mummies, Shaw makes the connection perfectly clear. "Was he not the affianced husband of the Queen 547 years ago or thereabouts?" Shaw's narrator asks. "Then I suddenly remembered having read of seeds being taken from the sarcophagus that enclosed an Egyptian mummy within which they had remained some thousands of years without destroying the vital germ, so that when they were planted they grew."[56] Later Shaw has his hero cement the connection between the signs of the hollow earth and the signs of ancient Egypt. "When we had approached within a few hundred yards of the outer walls of the city, the sight of it filled me with awe," remembers the narrator, in a flatly formulaic moment. "I stood awe-struck before this revelation of an antiquity, compared with which that of the Pyramids of Egypt is but yesterday. . . . I longed to enter this monument of an antiquity for the human race that I had never dreamed of."[57] Shaw is recycling one of the central figures of Egyptomania: concentric circles of exploration, excavation, reanimation, racialization, and extreme antiquity, and a desire to plunge into their center.

Much of the action in the second half of *Cresten*, in fact, involves the search for the process by which the ancient inhabitants of the underground world built their immense city, and thus leads almost inevitably to the sign of Egypt. "How they quarried and cut this hard material, and elevated such huge blocks to their lofty position," Shaw has his narrator wonder, "is as interesting a mystery as how a race called the Egyptians, on the exterior of the globe, built the pyramids."[58] The very antiquity Egypt invokes is then used as the sign by which to denigrate Egypt, particularly as regards a line of teleological progress, but not without reference to the evidently inescapable fantasy of accurately identifying what the ancient Egyptians actually looked like. "Why, what bunglers those Egyptians of ours on the exterior globe were, after all," the narrator exclaims. "Their shrunken, dark, leathery product shows them to have been novices at the business of embalming; and yet our moderns have not found out how they did it. If they had only known this mode of antediluvian pickling, what a much better idea we should have of the personal appearance of the builders of the pyramids."[59] Recalling the Egyptological lectures of George Robins Gliddon, one of the most portable products of Shaw's narrative is speculative shock. Along with his speculative relatives in other fields, and clearly recalling the ethnological scandals of early Egyptology, Shaw is enacting ontological reversals along the lines of race, chronology, and human origin.

Images of extreme antiquity, antediluvian races, and the powers and dangers of excavational interiority: it is these that so effectively communicated the threat of early Egyptology, and it is these that Shaw intentionally recalls. "Although a believer always in the great antiquity of the human race," the narrator assures us, "I had, nevertheless, assumed that it had ever been barbarous in the remote past, and that the Hindoo and Egyptian civilizations had been the first evolved out of that barbarism."[60] Yet in this Egyptological mode of imperial excavation Shaw's narrative reveals the unexpected, and that which changes everything. "But here was this antediluvian palace," the narrator admits, "vastly superior to any grand work of art that even our modern times had produced, which quite upset my notions, and along with them, the theories of our scientists."[61]

Like its ethnological and para-Darwinian forebears, this racialized archaeological expedition produces not only embalmed kings but explanations for the origins of races and civilizations. Shaw's character's search leads to more embalmed blue-eyed men, encased in sarcophagi and dating from before Noah's flood, and which, therefore, reverse all of his previous conceptions regarding the history of humanity. "There is no doubt in my mind," the narrator affirms, "that the city was built by antediluvians. . . . You must imagine the strange sensations I experienced while thus standing face to face with the contemporaries of Noah."[62] That Shaw is clearly reworking the ethnographic debates of racialized Egyptology from some forty years earlier is clear enough; that the terms of pre- and post-Darwinian evolutionary speculation had changed so little should be as well.

## "These Black Demons Have Come through the Crevice, and They Must Be Driven Back"

As many scholars have noted, the narrative and imaginative possibilities offered by the speculative tradition could be particularly attractive to women writers and presented them with what Val Gough calls the "appropriat[ion] for feminist ends the trope of role reversal found in early science fiction" and "an ironic revision of narratives of exploration which, by privileging male physical prowess and action, reinforced heterosexist gender stereotypes."[63] Indeed, nineteenth-century speculative writings can easily be seen as being undertaken largely under the sign of early feminism: from Mary Shelley to Jane Loudon to Charlotte Perkins Gilman, visionary constructions of antipatriarchal gender roles stand out as a hallmark of the tradition. So clearly adapted for feminist causes, in fact, was the speculative form that by the turn of the century there was a wide range of parodies of the gender role–reversing novel including Mrs. J. Wood's 1882 *Pantaletta: A Romance of Sheheland*, the works of John DeMorgan, and Frank Cowan's 1880s *Revi-Lona*.[64] Cowan's novel, one of the most elaborate of this antitradition, includes a concise summary of the features of the genre by way of burlesque:

> This book has been written in a plain, straight-forward and truthful manner, to tell how a big and brawny man, with many of the vices of his sex and years and a few of the virtues, went from the backwoods of Pennsylvania to the South Pole of the Earth and found, in a volcanic or hot-water wilderness, an isolated oasis of tropic warmth and rare fertility, containing strange survivals from a bygone geologic age, and inhabited by a remnant of a former continental people, enlightened, white-skinned and of surpassing beauty, but voiceless — a perfect but petticoated paradise, where big and beautiful women ruled and little and learned men obeyed in a marvelous communisitic government; . . . and how, by reason of his superior proportions as a man . . . he at first willy-nilly and afterward, in despite of all his efforts to the contrary, disorganized the perfect commonwealth, destroyed the pure and happy people and annihilated the lovely land, with all its natural and artificial wonders.[65]

"A perfect but petticoated paradise" of the "enlightened [and] white-skinned . . . where big and beautiful women ruled and little and learned men obeyed" in a socialist utopia hidden at the South Pole until the figure of colonialist masculinity brings about its destruction: by the 1880s it was a prominent enough tendency of the speculative form to link utopianism and feminism to feature it with parodic ease.

Equally prominent, however, is the extent to which many of these white women writers rescripted and reinscribed nineteenth-century ethnological hierarchies of race. As Amy Kaplan and Jean Pfaelzer have noted, frequently visions of antipatriarchal imaginary spaces are also visions of Anglo-Saxon racial purity. "Utopians prefer blondes," writes Pfaelzer in her introduction to Mary E. Bradley Lane's 1880s feminist polar hole/lost race/hollow earth novel Mizora, in which all the women are blonde and all the people of color have been eliminated, but this is not particularly surprising considering the ethnological origins of speculative fiction.[66] In ways obviously related to the historical narratives of Sarah Josepha Hale—not to mention the more general forms of racial segregation operating within the white feminist circles out of which Hale and early speculative women writers developed their political identities—what the tradition of white women's nineteenth-century speculative fiction often shows is naturalized hierarchies of race used as explicit support for challenges to denaturalized hierarchies of gender.[67] The radically racialized adventure narratives of eighteenth- and nineteenth-century Europe and America so deconstructed by Poe presented speculative writers with tropes of inversion and epistemological reversal that were often used to great effect in terms of gender roles, but, in sharp contrast, the racial ideologies of the colonial fantastic were left reinforced and all the stronger.

This mode of speculative fiction—in which both the implicit movements and the explicit imagery of American Egyptomania are preserved and re-presented, and against which are obviously mapped late-century politics of race and gender—can perhaps best be seen in Lillian Frances Mentor's 1897 The Day of Resis. A hollow earth adventure in which a white American woman travels to Africa and discovers a lost civilization underneath Zanzibar, Mentor's novel makes it clear from the outset that it is self-consciously aware of its literary heritage. "Works, which for the average woman held no attraction, aroused in her the liveliest interest," Mentor writes of her heroine. "Her enthusiasm had reached such a pitch that but one course seemed open to her, namely, to experience the adventurers which had made the names of Baker, Grant, Speke, Livingstone and Stanley famous."[68]

With her adventurous female lead and overt references to the myth of the British African explorer, Mentor begins her work by announcing her intentions to rewrite the plot of the masculine quest; carefully, though, Mentor's novel places its main character squarely in turn of the century controversies over women's roles with an ambivalent combination of pluckiness and patriarchy. "There was nothing of the so-called New Woman about her,"

Mentor writes; "far from it; she was a womanly woman with a great sympathetic heart and kindly nature."[69] Over the course of the novel, though, its genealogy will become clear: opening with a fragmentary manuscript à la Poe and Haggard, Mentor's Enola Cameron will engage in a colonialist adventure as fiercely racist as anything in the tradition, and will, in her staging of her characters' escapades, rely on the three-part structure of white heroes, black enemies, and ancient Egyptians.

"She had so long made a study of Africa and its dark secrets," Mentor writes of Cameron, "that nothing pertaining to it seemed strange to her."[70] The Day of Resis baldly represents Africa in the most violent of racialized ways and throughout its pages enthusiastically engages in what Valentin Mudimbe has called "the reification of the 'primitive.' "[71] "For centuries Africa has been known as the Dark Continent," says Cameron. "Africa is synonymous with mystery and darkness. . . . Africa is to-day a mystery which, it seems, will never be penetrated."[72] In fact, Mentor's Africa is in many ways so unremarkable in its stereotypical racism that there would be little to distinguish it from its other versions which are not, as Mudimbe writes, "epistemologically inventive."[73] Yet the lost race/hollow earth speculative tradition allows for a kind of epistemological innovation, which Mentor exploits. Like the hierarchical inventions of the American School of Ethnology, Mentor's Dark Continent is populated by two different types of Africans: shamelessly reified savages, contemporaneously immediate yet forever primitive, and pointedly civilized nobles, ancient and lost yet rediscovered under the earth's surface.

The Day of Resis features an ancient Egyptian civilization still living under the lands of East Africa. After first discovering some curiously preserved mummies and later being confronted by seven-foot-tall bronze-skinned men riding a herd of zebras, Mentor's band of adventurers are introduced to an underground society ruled by a monarch, whose members are identified by the resident linguist as direct descendants of the ancient Egyptians. "Mr. Bruce," writes Mentor, "who had carefully studied a piece of papyrus upon which the King had inscribed some characters . . . declared the characters to be Egyptian hieroglyphics. . . . All these convinced him that the strange people around him had originally come from Egypt, but it must have been thousands of years before."[74] And, as with the ethnological narratives that were its predecessors, this is a journey into both earth and time:

"One would think," said Harry, "that we had been taken from the world of hurry and bustle which we so recently knew, and set back two or three thousand years into this ancient city."

"Yes," said Mr. Bruce, "one could easily imagine from the beauty of the city, the stateliness and courtesy of the people, and the delights of the feast, that we have dropped into something supernatural."[75]

Mentor's hollow earth is archaeological, raciological, and speculative, in terms of both biology and chronology. In other words, it is built on the foundation of American Egyptomania.

There is, of course, a scene of explication, itself a version of the Egyptian moment: through the introduction of the character of a high priest, and incorporating both biblical and secular history, Mentor's Americans learn that these hollow earth Egyptians — now called Onians — are descendants of a group contemporaneous with Moses who escaped Egypt during the time of the plagues. In fact, Mentor recuperates the paganism of her ancient Egyptians by portraying them as proto-Christian — or at least Jewish: "Many Egyptians in the vicinity of Goshen, the dwelling place of the Israelites, had accepted the religion of that people," explains the priest, "and seeing no end to the plagues which were scouring this country, they gathered together and determined to emigrate to some distant land where they could live in peace and happiness, and without fear of molestation from their idolatrous countrymen."[76] Mentor's Egyptians discovered the world inside the earth through a cave in a mountainside and have lived peacefully (and, presumably, kosher) and in hope of the appearance of Christ—about which they of course have heard nothing—in their utopia ever since. "I have fitted to the opening in the mountain a stone turning on pivots and opening on a secret spring, of which I alone know the secret," discloses the priest, and "none of my countrymen to-day are aware of the existence of an outside world."[77]

Mentor's hollow earth ancient Egyptians are soon threatened, however, by the sudden appearance of a barbarous "negro" tribe, who have accidentally discovered the underground world through a volcanic breach. "Suddenly all pulled up their steeds as of one accord," reads the chapter titled "A Black Surprise." "Ahead of them was a camp-fire, and about it, dancing and throwing their arms in the air, were a hundred naked black Africans. The scene was a weird one, and the whole thing was such a complete surprise to our friends, that they could do nothing but stare in open-mouthed wonderment. The negroes were naked, with the exception of a cloth about the loins. . . . The dance was wild and the yells, which broke from the large mouths of the men, were terrible."[78] Mentor pits her heroic white Americans against Africa's savage black inhabitants; at stake is the survival of ancient Egypt.

The Americans rouse the otherwise peaceful Onians to fierce battle, and the savagery of the Africans is confirmed through the justification for their slaughter. "The Onians looked at the King and his white companions," Mentor writes, "as if wondering if they had been led to this point by a lie, to fight these black animals, for none of them realized that these black, shiny-skinned and nude beings were human."[79] The entire battle sequence, in fact, is so violently racist and so suggestive of the tenor of 1890s American race relations that it seems to function openly as a mouthpiece for the Ku Klux Klan. "Men," shouts the leader of the Onians to his troops, "yonder horde of black demons are here to take your country, to take your lives, but worse, to take your wives, mothers, brothers, and sisters. They are here to destroy our land, to devastate our fields of grain and fruit, to steal and kill our animals, to destroy our beautiful city. . . . They know no law, they have no religion, they care nothing for the lives of others. . . . Will you not fight for country, home, loved ones, and for the right? These demons have come through the crevice which we were this day to commence closing, and they must be driven back."[80]

The white adventurers encounter the savage race of Negroes in an obvious allegory of post-Reconstruction American politics, framed as militant nationalism and with its historical narratives provided by popular Egyptology: an ancient noble civilization is threatened by savage, naked, black Africans, who live just outside its gates. "The men looked at each other in astonishment," Mentor writes of her Egyptians in a moment of allegorical property rights indignation. "They could not realize at first that such a state of affairs could possibly exist, as there being the remotest possibility of their being driven from this land, which was theirs by right of inheritage and possession."[81] Mentor even includes a scene in which the white Americans are temporarily blackened by soot, in an explicit invocation of blackface minstrelsy: " 'But where have you been?' " asks Cameron of the men returning from battle. " 'Your faces and garments are as black as the skin of the negroes which have just been killed.' . . . It was true, they had been so long exposed to the smoke of the crater that they had become perfectly black, and it might have been this which made the negroes laugh so when they saw them approaching. They had seen the white skins before and they must have thought that it was a ruse to fool them, in thus blacking their faces."[82] The implied metaphorics of a perceived threat to nineteenth-century Egyptology by 1890s Afrocentrism are not to missed, either: innocent white explorers discover ancient Egypt only to find it almost overrun by Negroes.

Indeed, the naked allegoricism of the scene—contemporary white Americans rousing ancient Egyptians to war against savage black Africans in defense of their land, culture, and civilization—is matched only by the one-sidedness of the victory. "The Onians," writes Mentor, "remembering the death of their companions, became as Bruce had said they would, regular fighting machines. . . . The negroes, overpowered and almost crazed with fear at the slaughter going on among their people, forgot all about fighting or even defending themselves. . . . The Onians . . . had fallen on to the flanks of the negroes, and such was their fearful onslaught, and so fast were these hacked and mutilated bodies piled up, that it looked as if the awful carnage would not cease, until every black carcass was heaped up in one fearful mass of reeking and quivering flesh."[83] This is more than mere colonialist adventure tale. It is a Reconstruction lynching fantasy written into Egyptomanic epic.

If for nothing else, the study of nineteenth-century American Egyptomania owes to works like Mentor's *Day of Resis* a debt for their racist violence: carefully speculative yet provocatively literal, fantasies of lost Egyptians saved from black Africans by heroic white Americans scripted a response to threats to "civilization" as epic as genocide. The terms of such early science fiction occupy the terrain of American race relations like an invading army; saving Egypt from Africa was a matter of the very survival of whiteness. That the ancient Egyptians of the hollow earth were ultimately so willing to fight on the side of whiteness was, no doubt, the only thing that saved them from sharing their new enemies' fate. "Turn on them," the leader of Mentor's Onians shouts as he orders his noble Egyptians against the savage Africans, "cut them, chop them, beat them, hammer their foul bodies into the earth, slash them until not a piece large enough is left to feed a jackal. On to them."[84]

That the literary figure of the punctiform rupture in the earth's surface characteristically takes place in a racially fraught, epistemologically unstable space marked by the machineries of colonial imperialism would have been clear to Howard Carter. The patriarchal imperatives so obviously suggested by the overtly phallic imagery of masculine adventurers penetrating interior spaces inhabited by terrifying inversions of power, identity, and social roles would have been equally clear to Lillian Mentor. Yet in the extended moment they both describe there is a distinct sense that the signs of ancient Egypt are both means and end; Mentor saves her hidden Egypt from black Africa in order to have it rediscovered yet again twenty years later by Carter, but these cooperative dynamics of the burial and excavation of Egyptomanic whiteness had already been in play for at least a century. Likewise, the alliances between patriarchy and imperialism taking place during the long tick of the Egyptian moment were by no means the only ones so enabled; as Mentor's blatantly racist parable of American nationalism shows, the heteronormative narratives of Egyptological exploration articulated by Carter and his antecedents could be unwound, but in the interests of such an attempt an even more reinforced racial taxonomy was a powerful ally. "The blacks look and see the awful enemy coming straight for them," writes Mentor climactically, "on which their murderous hatchets could have no effect."[85]

Thus, the reassurance of apocalypse: adventurers escape as disaster comes to those who dawdle, the rupture reseals itself regularly, the chasm closes like a comfort. And perhaps this is what the figure of the racial rupture reveals most clearly—that in order for the rupture to take shape, in order for the sign of disruption to cohere, it must rely on some supportive framework that is in itself not disrupted, not challenged even by its proximity to the rupture, but is left even stronger, more reinforced, by virtue of the force of the disruption being directed elsewhere. Binaries can, after all, be most easily overturned in the interests of other binaries. The collapse of the passageway between self and other or inner and outer or black and white in the lost race/hollow earth tradition occurs as predictably as its initial formation, as a rupture of the rupture; the formulas of expeditionary tales and speculative fiction bleed into one another as often as they congeal, the treasures and terrors produced by the archaeologics of American Egyptomania disappear as regularly as they return. "On the negroes ran," writes Mentor in her moment of Egyptomanic apocalypse, "and the Onians sped after them. The negroes had now reached the crevice, and were fighting for a foothold on the ledge. Some of them were successful, but most of them were forced over the side, falling into the yawning abyss below."[86]

# CHAPTER THREE

# The Curse of the Mummy

## RACE, REANIMATION, AND

## THE EGYPTIAN REVIVAL

Hark from de tomb a doleful soun'
My ears hear a tender cry.
A livin' man come through the groun'
Whar we may shortly lie.[1]

During the course of Charles T. White's 1830s blackface minstrelsy farce *The Virginny Mummy*, the character Captain Rifle, in order to gain entrance to the home of his beloved, plots to fool her legal guardian, Dr. Galen, into believing he has a mummy for sale. Galen, a pompous scientist and crackpot inventor, has created a new formula, an elixir to revive the dead called the "Compound Extract of Live Forever," and wants to give it the most strenuous test possible: the revivification of an ancient Egyptian mummy. "Now, if I can only resuscitate life that has been extinct for 8,000 years," Galen pronounces, "the world shall begin all anew."[2] Rifle thus devises a plan: he will convince his slave Ginger Blue to masquerade as a mummy. Posing as an Egyptian merchant recently arrived in America, Rifle will present Galen with a counterfeit sarcophagus, within which Ginger will lie still, and while the scientist is busy examining the merchandise Rifle will woo his intended. The plan all hinges on the acting abilities of Ginger, though, so Rifle attempts to explain the plan to his slave:

> Rifle. Here, Ginger, is a silver dollar for you. How long can you hold your tongue without speaking?
> Ginger. Well, I guess I can hold my tongue 'till I git about tired.
> Rifle. Can you shut your mouth—not speak without I told you?
> Ginger. Yes. . . .
> Rifle. I want you now to make folks believe you are a mummy.
> Ginger. Whose mommy?
> Rifle. You don't understand. I said mummy not mommy. A mummy is a dead man, preserved in spices, and put into a coffin, then deposited in a tomb, and never moulders away.
> Ginger. And so you want to fix me up dat way! 'Massa, de wedder am too hot; I wouldn't keep from now till Sunday.
> Rifle. I want you only to have the appearance of it, to make people think you are a mummy, when you are only Ginger Blue.
> Ginger. Well, did you eber hear de like? You are too dam smart for dis nigger.
> Rifle. Come along after me to my room, where I will dress and paint you, and give you a lesson how to keep silence. . . .
> Ginger. Neber mind dat. I'll swear black is white. I is a mummy.[3]

The rest of the play, predictably, involves the series of comic reactions to Ginger/the mummy when, after he and Rifle achieve entry into Galen's home, he cannot keep still or silent. He scares the Irish handyman who attempts to take one of his toes for a souvenir; he drinks the scientist's elixir, thinking it liquor and then believing it to be poison; he bites the finger of his master's betrothed; and finally, after several such gags, he leaps out of his coffinlike sarcophagus and disrupts the entire experiment.[4]

Ginger Blue is a standard blackface coon, an ignorant and unmanageable buffoon, alternately impetuous and scared, hopping between disposability and dangerousness. But several aspects of The Virginny Mummy are immediately striking. First, there is the drama of authenticity which structures the action: a white man playing a black man playing an ancient Egyptian mummy meant to be inspected for its fitness by another white man is an obvious enough example of what Eric Lott calls "a complex affair of manly mimicry," [5] but White emphasizes the theme of counterfeits onstage even further by introducing another, "real" mummy and a mummy dealer, who threaten to expose the fakes:

> *O'Leary.* Here's a gentleman that has brought another of those pickled mummies, or whatever you call 'em.
> *Galen.* Show him in. I'll try the experiment on all they bring. Now, if I fail on this mummy, I shall be sure to hit it on the other. . . .
> *Ginger.* Oder mummy! Oder mummy! How do you do! Oh, you don't talk like a Virginny mummy.[6]

Moreover, at the center of White's masquerade is a highly self-conscious reference to the very act of blacking up. "I will dress you and paint you," Rifle says to his actor, and soon it becomes clear that this has involved further darkening Ginger's skin. "I'm afraid I won't be able to hit the dark shades of the face," worries a supporting character who is attempting to paint the mummy's portrait. "How confoundly it smells of shoe blacking!" [7]

Second, what is remarkable about this otherwise routine bit of racialized theater is the extent to which it seems to anticipate one of the standard narrative tropes that would forever after be associated with the figure of the mummy: the uncontrollable awakening. Played for comic effect in *The Virginny Mummy*, and there related on one hand to similar blackface plotlines involving ungovernable coons and on the other to similar scenes involving the humiliation of authority figures, especially scientific or medical ones,[8] the uncontrollability of the ancient Egyptian mummy assumed long dead and harmless would become very nearly its one primary characteristic, a principal, indispensable aspect of its representation, from its earliest appearances to the present day. And, third, as is so plain in *The Virginny Mummy*, and as we will see more fully in the sections that follow, it is by no means incidental that the chaotic dynamic introduced and represented by the mummy derives almost entirely from an anxiety about race.


## "Statue of Flesh, Come Prithee Tell Us!"

The trope of the mummy—and it is as much a trope as a character, with the figure of the mummy almost always being equated with the narrative arc it represents—appears consistently throughout the nineteenth century. Its earliest incarnations are usually in newsprint, as exoticized or dramatically enhanced stories that document the beginnings of the Orientalist industry in America: newspaper accounts of mummies shipped in from Egypt, popularized scientific blurbs reporting unwrappings, press releases advertising P. T. Barnum's latest displays. But in these early representations the mummy is more inert artifact than anything else, yet another fossilized remain of a past civilization; during the first two decades of the nineteenth century, mummies were an especially visible part of early American exhibition culture, but they were placed alongside other motionless curiosities such as dinosaur bones and Native American artifacts, with very little distinction in status.[9] Many of the first mummies that toured the United States were in fact accompanied by a short piece by English poet Horace Smith, who, like Percy Shelley, had previously written a sonnet on Ozymandias in full elegaic mode: "In Egypt's sandy silence, all alone, / Stands a gigantic Leg, which far off throws / The only shadow that the Desert knows. . . . The city's gone! / Naught but the leg remaining to disclose / The sight of that forgotten Babylon."[10] The traditions of representing the antiques of ancient Egypt that early-nineteenth-century America inherited from England were of just this type; the Ozymandias of Shelley and Smith and the Cheops of Byron are paradigmatically exanimate, signs of life long gone and specifically beyond any hope of return.[11]

The cause for these early representations of the mummy as submissive, docile, and altogether impotent stemmed almost entirely from its status as a medical object. Seen most famously in the history of the mummy long associated with the "Ether Dome" in Boston's Massachusetts General Hospital, virtually every mummy that entered the United States before 1840 was at some point presented as an object of medical curiosity.[12] Early Egyptological investigations invariably had an anatomical flavor, producing documents from surgeons and doctors set firmly in the idioms of early autopsies: minute details recounting sizes, weights, colors, procedures, and the remaining range of concerns of early anatomists fill the pages of the authoritative accounts accompanying America's first mummies.

These explorations were, however, by no means separate from the socially entangled spaces of early American medicine, and so even in their beginnings mummies were oddly ambivalent objects; medical reports were presented alongside doggerel verse, often these medical specimens were displayed in highly sensationalized contexts—the museums of Barnum and Peale were only the most respectable — and the host of racialized controversies attending comparative anatomy were present from the start. "The mummy at Roxbury, in the vicinity of Boston," reported Dr. John Collins Warren of Massachusetts General on investigation of his hospital's ancient celebrity in 1823, "has a fine confirmation of head. . . . The forehead is elevated and large, the jaws filled with fine teeth, not prominent, and the head altogether is the European or Caucasian form." [13] From the national tours of these mummies to the professions of their handlers, the role of mummies in early-nineteenth-century America was to serve as a link between representations of ancient bodily practices and modern ones, with all of the complexities that entailed. By effect if not design, mummies began entering the country not so much as historical objects as bodily ones, and their status as objects of interest was framed very quickly and thoroughly as materials for unwrapping, inspection, and dissection by the newly burgeoning American medical community.

With extreme rapidity, however, the figure of the mummy changed in America. By the 1830s, the Egyptian mummy was becoming more and more associated with a particular kind of either literal or symbolic revenge, with themes of reprisal, retribution, and retaliation. "Beware of the Mummy's Curse," wrote Louisa May Alcott in 1869, by which time the trope had become ingrained; "the curse that had bided its time for ages was fulfilled at last." [14] Throughout the nineteenth century, the ancient Egyptian mummy appears primarily as a sign of *reanimation*, of the terrors of death disavowed. "Oh! No mortal could support the horror of that countenance," cries the century's most famous instigator of bodily reanimation, "a mummy again endued with animation could not be so hideous as that wretch." [15] With its close Gothic relatives, Frankenstein's monster and the vampire, the mummy is part of a sort of great trinity of nineteenth-century reanimational terrors. "The danger of monsters lies in their tendency to stabilize bias into bodily form," writes Judith Halberstam of the family of Frankenstein's monster, "but monsters are always in motion." [16] In the figure of the mummy, this repetitive volatility becomes its primary sign.

During the first decades of the nineteenth century, the mummy underwent its most important transformation: from an inert artifact of lost ancient splendor to a reanimated agent of disruptive modern terror. "Statue of flesh, come prithee tell us!" wrote Philadelphian John Fanning Watson around 1830, addressing the mummy that had visited his city, with an uncanny prediction for its future behaviors. "Since in the world of spirits, thou hast illuminated what thou hast seen, what strange adventures number'd." [17] The associations of mummification with an aged, prostrate, and withered desiccation beyond repair remained a feature of its imagery throughout the century, but what the literature reveals is this tradition operating in a minor mode. Like the other most famous products of Western Egyptomania—Cleopatra, the Sphinx, pyramids, and obelisks—mummies had been part of the cultural consumption of Egypt since well before 1800, but, with the confluence of the particular anxieties related to the nineteenth century, the mummy slipped its yoke and began to run amok.

## The Curse of the Mammy

The mummy has several factors to thank for its graduation into the ranks of the terrible—among them the rise of the biological sciences and the methods of dissection and surgical investigation they helped to codify—but additional conditions shaped the figure of the mummy into something qualitatively different from the reanimated constructions of Shelley or Stoker. Principal among these is the sign of excavation: the mummy is covered in layers of excavational drama, becoming the very sign of exhumation, of disinterment, of unearthing. More elaborate than the grave-robbing controversies of Shelley's Edinburgh and more literalized than the self-reanimations of Stoker's successors, the dramas of archaeological discovery that came to attend the figure of the mummy in the 1800s were one of the primary channels through which the many fears of unearthing were realized. The enclosures and disclosures that so typically describe the rhythms of plots involving mummies—tombs, sarcophagi, and bandages; adventurers, archaeologists, and scientists—relate the Gothic and the Egyptian in a family of surfacing terrors that would eventually result in the ascendant placement of the mummy—of the sign of Egypt—as the decisive sign of the fear of irruptive revelation.[18]

In a little-known short story by Alcott, these sympathies between archaeological violation and mummified vengeance had allied sufficiently to be abstracted a step beyond the anthropomorphic. In January 1869, she published "Lost in a Pyramid, or The Mummy's Curse," and her tale demonstrates the extent to which authors by midcentury had become accustomed to the automatic relays between mummies and revenge and had begun taking liberties with, as well as capitalizing on, the trope.[19] In the story, a young woman listens to a tale told by her cousin and fiancé of an adventure he had in a pyramid. "While in Egypt," the fiancé recounts, "I went one day with my guide and Professor Niles, to explore the Cheops. Niles had a mania for antiquities of all sorts."[20] The pair eventually becomes lost in the pyramid, the situation becomes desperate, and the fiancé decides to light a fire, whose smoke will act as a signal for help. Short on flammables, however, he frantically seizes on a nearby mummy case for firewood. "Reaching up," he says, "I pulled it down, believing it to be empty, but as it fell, it burst open, and out rolled a mummy."[21] He attempts to save the mummy from the conflagration, but is forced to burn it anyway: " 'Burn that!' commanded the professor, pointing to the mummy. . . . A dull blaze sprung up, and a heavy smoke rose from the burning mummy. . . . My brain grew dizzy, [and] I lost consciousness."[22] As a result of this violation, the fiancé incurs the wrath of the mummy. The adventuring pair is rescued from the pyramid, but "among his spoils," he explains, the professor found "this inscription [which] said that the mummy we had so ungallantly burned was that of a famous sorceress who bequeathed her curse to whoever should disturb her rest. . . . I sometimes wonder if I am to share the curse."[23]

This curse, it turns out, is quite promiscuous; before the story ends, both the young woman, her fiancé, and the professor will have been affected. But it is in the actual mechanics of the curse that Alcott plays openly and self-consciously with the trope: it is not the mummy itself that wreaks it vengeance, but another sign of reanimation, the mummy once removed. The "seeds of some unknown Egyptian plant," which were rescued by the fiancé from the mummy's belongings, become a source of interest to the young woman and the agent of her destruction. "I have a queer feeling about the matter," the fiancé says, but against his wishes she secretly plants them and so invites the curse. The flower that grows from the seeds is revealed to contain a highly toxic contact poison, and the woman, who wishes to wear the flower on her wedding day, exposes herself to it. After completing the ceremony but before consummating the marriage, the new bride sinks into a coma, from which she never recovers. "There, gleaming spectrally on her bosom, was the evil blossom," Alcott writes. "No recognition in the eyes, no word upon the lips, no motion of the hand—only the faint breath, the fluttering pulse, and wide-opened eyes, betrayed that she was alive."[24] The fiancé is horrified but never remarries, discovers that his professor friend has also succumbed to the poisons of reanimated Egypt, and spends the rest of his life caring for his comatose wife. "He died in great agony," a note informs him of the professor, "raving of mummies, pyramids, serpents, and some fatal curse which had fallen upon him." [25]

The woman herself becomes a mummy, a horrifyingly liminal figure between life and death. She is also a symbol of repetition: in choosing to willfully ignore the warnings of her fiancé, she repeats his violation of the mummy's body, which was itself a repetition of his original defilement of the mummy's tomb. In fact, Alcott draws even further attention to the sympathies between the identity of the woman and the identity of the mummy: they are both women. "Come and help me unroll this," the professor says to the fiancé while still in the pyramid. "This is a woman, and we may find something rare and precious here." [26] The two men undress the Egyptian woman, and in doing so discover the container that holds the seeds—literally—of the mummy's curse: "All the bandages but one were cut off at last, and a small head laid bare, round which still hung great plaits of what had once been luxuriant hair. The shriveled hands were folded on the breast, and clasped in them lay that gold box." [27] Alcott makes it a point to construct a parallel between the stricken figure of the poisoned bride and the withered figure of the mummy, just as she makes the connection between female sexual violation and male homosocial adventuring; "the young face" of the new husband's wife, "so lovely an hour ago, lay before him aged and blighted by the baleful influence of the plant which had drunk up her life," when, helping to unroll the mummy, he "wonder[ed] as I worked, if this dark, ugly thing had ever been a lovely, soft-eyed Egyptian girl." [28]

Both women are thus defined by their violations by men—one by fiery destruction following an archaeological penetration, the other by marriage. Even the flower itself is an obvious symbol of hypersexualized danger. "There, standing in the sunshine, was the unknown plant," writes Alcott. "Almost rank in their luxuriance were the vivid green leaves on the slender purple stems, and rising from the midst, one ghostly-white flower, shaped like the head of a hooded snake, with scarlet stamens like forked tongues, and on the petals glittered spots like dew." [29] Moreover, it is a pronounced feature of both the young woman and the poisonous flower that they are both characterized by excessive whiteness: "the three scarlet grains lying in the white hand" of the bride-to-be are structurally repeated at the moment of the discovery of the comatose bride, "the evil blossom gleaming spectrally on her bosom, its white petals spotted now with flecks of scarlet, vivid as drops of newly spilt blood." [30] By 1869, the conventions of the reanimational horror story have become familiar enough to Alcott that she can not only equate them with other narrative conventions but can abstract them to the point of a set of pointedly interchangeable free-floating signifiers, structured along the lines of masculine violation, feminine revenge, and the overarching curse of heteronormative whiteness. That in the midst of this deconstructive play the mummy herself retains her uncanny power is testimony to the longevity she continues to have.

Second, what attenuates the figure of the mummy to the sign of resurrected terror is the crisis of chronology that underwrites it. The chronological controversies discussed in chapter one were so inseparable from the signs of ancient Egypt that the anthropomorphic figure of the mummy, especially in its retributional mode, could not help but become their most succinct representative. Indeed, this characteristic of the trope of the mummy is so pervasive throughout its history that, regardless of the relative levels of panic associated with a given appearance—regardless of whether the mummy is enclosed, domesticated, tame, and forever asleep, or whether it is on the loose, destructive, and running wild—it is always a reminder of the scandalous mathematical and philosophical clashes between biblical and secular chronologies that were introduced, sustained, and continually invoked by developments in Egyptology.

The curse of the mummy is thus, to some extent, always a trace of the racialized ethnographic controversies that not only arose in the Nile Valley in the first half of the nineteenth century but also produced the very shape of modern Egyptology. The racially ambiguous mummy run amok is chronology unbound, scholarship unfettered from Christian traditions and become unpredictable, destructive, secular. The almost inseparable connection between the mummy and the very sign of secular rationalism that unearths it—the scientist, the scholar, the unwitting archaeologist— is a clear token of this genealogy, between the rise of secular science and the forces it unleashed. Like his literal counterparts, the fictional secular scientist excavating in the sands of Egypt acts as midwife to a power beyond his control and sets loose a destructive force composed of equal parts chronology and racialization. The mummy becomes not only the representative of antiquity as such but of its violation.

In other words, the logic of a barely balanced relationship between sacred chronology and secular time made Egypt into a sign of explosion. Egypt was the point of passage between the distant past and the distant future, the liminal stage between savagery and civilization, paganism and Christianity, so-called science and so-called superstition, Africa and Europe and black and white. It was the sign that organized the teleological fantasies of nineteenth-century chronologists and embodied the fears of what those fantasies repressed. Egypt was both the most monumental civilization in the history of the world for these chronologists, and the first; it was both the sign of the height of civilization and the most fledgling child in all of civilization's family, and thus its status was not only enormously unstable but *formatively so*, foundational in its instability. It inaugurated the linearity by which all previous times, civilizations, prehistories, or savageries could be called, literally, into line, yet it presented this chronological imperative alongside figures of chronological resistance such as the mummy; Egypt both led away from the anarchy of the distant past and directly to it. The mummy, as the century's preeminent sign of the ultimately unmanageable terms of these unstable relationships — and thus the agent of their destructive consequences — went from being Egypt's safest and most docile artifact to its most horrible and deadly.

Thus the perfect logic of a cartoon that appeared in an 1855 issue of *Punch*, "The Effects of a Hearty Dinner after Visiting the Antediluvian Department at the Crystal Palace."[31] After touring the 1855 prehistoric exhibit at the Crystal Palace, a dreamer is accosted by the literally nightmarish spectacle of a Pharaonic Egyptian riding a dinosaur. Though not an actual mummy, he is clearly a fraternal twin; he partakes of the same logic of reanimation, retribution, and chronological violation as does the mummy. The ancient Egyptian is the central figure in the cartoon's nightmare, placed as he is on the dinosaur on the dreamer's chest — but he is also one of three distinct terms of the ancient past, all come to haunt the postdiluvian sleeper.

The Egyptian, the dinosaurs, and the "Indian," gazing rather amazingly at himself in the modern mirror, are now a grand triumvirate of the threat of the ancient past: the undeniable antediluvian, the questionably contemporary "primitive" postdiluvian, and the figure that rides terrifying herd over them both. They are all signs of the ancient past, but they are also, each in a different way, signs of the radical instability of the very linear system that produces them as "ancient." The linear logic that gave the sleeper his antediluvian exhibit stridently insists that the ancient past is gone, but the exhibit also visits on him the fear that it is not. All three visitors are exactly that which will *not* disappear, even as the sign of the "modern" or the linear "now" demands that they do. The three signs of the past are only

"The Effects of a Hearty Dinner after Visiting the Antediluvian Department at the Crystal Palace." (*Punch* 28 [February 3, 1855]. *Punch* Cartoon Library.)

too cartoonishly the return of the repressed past, drawn chronologically. Extinct, in ruins, and unevolved: these are the three most critical terms for the construction of the trace of the past, for the diagrammatic anatomy of the detritus of the present. *Of course* the ancient Egyptian, reanimated and ruinous, appears in this nightmare. As the cartoon so clearly depicts, his is the figure that permits its appearance and organizes its terrifying effects.

Third among the reasons for the quick and lasting association between the figure of the mummy and the sign of reanimation — and not just with its appeals but with its terrors as well — comes from a source that will concern the bulk of the rest of this chapter: the rise of architectural revivalism in the United States. Specifically, the context for this shift is a period in American architectural history that served as literally the most visible manifestation of American Egyptomania in the nineteenth century: the Egyptian Revival. This primarily involved a set of controversies arising from the pressures of urbanization of the early nineteenth century, but its genealogy was quite multilayered and often unexpected; it involved newly developing theories of prison reform, controversies over Christian imagery for use in public cemeteries, arguments over slavery conducted through the medium of public architecture, and the signs of racialized antiquity being fashioned for a new republic. The rest of this chapter will be concerned with these issues.

Over the course of the nineteenth century, the mummy graduates from medical school, leaves home (or leaves the series of domestic spaces so intimately populated with gentlemanly scientists and their manly tools), and goes on to appear on the national stage of imperial architecture. There is no better single image of the conflicts I will discuss—between the signs of antiquity as inevitably white and those same signs resisting any claims to absolute whiteness, between the forced Christianization of a pagan iconography and the unwanted return of Christianity's pagan ancestor, between the ideals of Christian resurrection and the desire for penal containment, between the ancient past as a solution for young America and that past as a raging problem, all of which were being acted out on and through a field of images glaringly Egyptian—than that of the mummy's house.

What follows, then, is an argument in several stages. First, there is an analysis of a short story by Edgar Allan Poe, written precisely at the moment that the mummy goes from being a mute and helpless inanimate medical specimen to a figure that is something like its opposite, or its revenge: a figure of retribution, a reanimated Other. Next follows a brief history of the architectural context in which the mummy goes from being what is in Poe's story a figure of domestic terror, of private and professionalized reprisal, to one characterized quite explicitly by a discourse of publicness, of nationalized identity and epic revenge. The implications of this context fill the rest of the chapter: the connections between the Egyptian Revival, other forms of architectural revivalism, and national anxieties over social control, race, and race-based slavery.

### "I Am Heartily Sick of This Life, and of the Nineteenth Century in General"

In April 1845, Edgar Allan Poe published in the American Review a short story entitled "Some Words with a Mummy." Although it has been discussed in recent years by Malini Johar Schueller and Dana Nelson, it is still rarely read today.[32] However, Poe's story is nevertheless for me a particularly instructive instance of the ways in which the cultural anxieties centered around the specifically racialized questions raised by American Egyptomania found expression in the literature of the period and of the landscapes in which we still, to this day, find visions of Egypt. Clearly influenced by Jane Webb Loudon's 1827 *The Mummy!*, it is a story in which the figure of ancient Egypt is placed at anxious odds with the inhabitants of the nineteenth century and one in which Egypt is seen as a marker of the absolute, the eternal, and an authority to which *all* questions—social, scientific, trivial, and profound—can be referred. "Some Words with a Mummy" takes as its subject trends in 1840s American Egyptomania and uses them as a site for a meditation on what becomes the entire project of writing history as such. What is at stake in the story—the assumptions of science, the functions of authority, and the dynamics of certainty—are, even to this day, still foundational issues for thinking about Egypt.

Poe's story is a burlesque, a satire on science. Its narrator is a cartoonish dilettante, a man prone to self-indulgence and intellectual posturing, who tends to embarrass himself by his ignorance but nevertheless, for the duration of the story, keeps some intentionally distinguished company. As the story opens, the narrator, who remains anonymous throughout the text, is awakened from a drunken sleep by a summons from a friend, a "Doctor Ponnonner," to attend, immediately, a private examination of an Egyptian mummy recently uncovered from near Thebes. Rushing to the doctor's house, the narrator is greeted by a small group of scientists and experts on things Egyptian. The group intends to remove the mummy from its case, unwrap it, characterize it, analyze it, and dissect it. Interestingly enough, the specific motivations for performing these tests are left conspicuously unspecified; the narrator finds himself "in an ecstasy" over the mere prospect, as if it were blandly self-evident why he should be interested, and only later, when hard-pressed, does a justification emerge. Indeed, the question of "why" structures a major moment in the story, and its answer is given not by the narrator but by one of the other members of the assembled group, a man whose appearance in the piece, given its subject matter, might be considered almost mandatory: George Robins Gliddon.

"By good luck," the narrator informs us, "Mr. Gliddon formed one of our party."[33] Gliddon is, in fact, one of only two of the story's characters given a real-life name; the narrator is anonymous, and many of his named colleagues are given obvious pseudonyms. Meant to refer, no doubt, to contemporaneous scientists, physicians, and Egyptologists, these pseudonyms add to the comic atmosphere of the piece, but Gliddon, appearing by name, takes center stage. As might be expected, Gliddon acts as authority on Egyptology throughout the text, translating hieroglyphs and providing background information. His is the voice of the height of Egyptological knowledge, having "travelled and resided in Egypt," as one character says, "until one might imagine [him] to the manor born."[34] His role in the piece thus corresponds with his fame and celebrity in the world of Poe himself, representing not the undereducated enthusiasm of the narrator, nor the specialized but only partly related knowledges of the other men, but precisely the point at which American Egyptology could be said in 1845 to have come into its own.

All of this is important because of what Poe does with the figure of Gliddon, and through him with the field of Egyptology in general, and, in no mean stretch, with a belief in history as an object of empirical study as a whole. Gliddon and his training will be rendered a fool. He will come to stand in for a particular way of doing history in the nineteenth century, a particular way of imagining knowledge, and, more importantly, a particular way of imagining knowledge of the ancient world and ancient Egypt. He will be above all a figure of positivism, of the linear accumulation of facts leading to truth, of the authority of the present to pronounce knowledge of the past. Through his structural treatment of the characters in "Some Words with a Mummy," Poe will perform a radical skepticism of this figure of positivism, satirizing the project of science and scientific history as such. He will portray each of his experts as idiotic in turn, their ignorance of what they claim to know matched only by the strength of their beliefs in their certainty. But it is not, however, in the service of an *absolute* skepticism that Poe performs this satire; rather, he presents his readers and his foolish experts with a figure of something *more* authoritative than mere authorities, something that marks them as only empiricists. He imagines the past come into the present, as a figure of *absolute* authority, and casts this figure in the shape of the mummy.

On the arrival of the narrator to Ponnonner's home, the examination of the mummy begins in earnest. The characters engage in what by 1845 was a virtual stereotype of mummy unrollings: the group cuts into the mummy's outside sarcophagus, Gliddon translates the hieroglyphs, they open up the second case, and a third, and they prepare the specimen for dissection.

Finally removing the body of the mummy, they examine it in detail, but find, to their surprise, that certain things are missing. There are no incisions in the body, for example, "the usual openings through which the entrails are extracted." [35] And at this point the story takes its turn. "We were about to separate," the narrator recounts, "when some one suggested an experiment or two with the *Voltaic pile*. The application of electricity to a Mummy three or four thousand years old at the least, was an idea, if not very sage, still sufficiently original, and we all caught it at once. About one tenth in earnest and nine tenths in jest, we arranged a battery in the Doctor's study, and conveyed thither the Egyptian." [36] The party makes some incisions, applies some electricity, and after a few galvanic responses succeeds in bringing the mummy back to life. "Morally and physically—figuratively and literally," Poe writes, "was the effect electric. In the first place, the corpse opened its eyes and winked very rapidly for several minutes . . . in the second place, it sneezed; in the third, it sat upon end; in the fourth, it shook its fist in Doctor Ponnonner's face; in the fifth, turning to Messieurs Gliddon and Buckingham, it addressed them, in very capital Egyptian." [37]

The mummy sits up and looks around but behaves in a manner exactly opposite the way revived mummies have been behaving ever since. It does not grunt and growl and lurch about the room; rather, the mummy turns out to be a sort of more gentlemanly than thou polite proper gentleman. Really quite offended at his treatment at the hands of the assembled group, the first words out of his mouth—translated retrospectively by the narrator, courtesy of Gliddon—are a soliloquy not of inarticulate anger but of aristocratic indignation. "I must say, gentlemen," the mummy announces, "that I am as much surprised as I am mortified by your behavior. . . . What am I to think of . . . me [being] thus unhandsomely used?" [38] Gliddon himself is even singled out for the mummy's disdain, and Poe makes clear that the rise of Egyptology itself will be the subject of reanimated scorn. "Of Doctor Ponnonner nothing better was to be expected," the mummy sneers. "He is a poor little fat fool who *knows* no better. . . . But you, Mr. Gliddon . . . you, whom I have always been led to regard as the firm friend of the mummies—I really did anticipate more gentlemanly conduct from *you*." [39]

In keeping with the deadpan delivery that characterizes the tale throughout, no one in the room is particularly frightened by these events. "It was . . . the Mummy's exceedingly natural and matter-of-course air," the narrator explains, "that divested his words of the terrible." [40] The group is embarrassed, more than anything else, at the situation, especially as it is put forth

by the mummy. Moreover, the mummy immediately announces his familiarity with both the members of the group and their unwrapping projects
and makes it clear that, to his mind, the more like an Egyptologist someone is—Gliddon, the mummy points out, has "been so much among us
that you speak Egyptian fully as well, I think, as you write your mother-
tongue"—the less like an Egyptologist they should behave. The mummy is
offended at his treatment, and the scientists are duly ashamed. They find
him some clothes, sew up their incisions, and when he is made comfort-
able, "Mr. Gliddon gave him his arm, and led him to a chair by the fire,
while the Doctor rang the bell, and ordered a supply of cigars and wine."[41]

What follows is the bulk of the short story. It becomes a drawing
room drama of ideas, a series of exchanges between the scientists and the
mummy, an extended conversation on a variety of topics. It begins with the
question of why. Not being able to get a sufficient answer from anyone else
to his question—"What am I to think of being so unhandsomely used?"—
the mummy "turned, peevishly, to Mr. Gliddon, and, in a peremptory tone,
demanded in general terms what we all meant."[42] To answer this question,
Poe immediately stages an opposition between the body of the mummy and
the abstractions of science. "It will be readily understood," the narrator
recounts, "that Mr. Gliddon's discourse turned chiefly upon the vast benefits accruing to science from the unrolling and disemboweling of mummies; apologizing, upon this score for any disturbance that might have
been occasioned him, in particular, the individual Mummy."[43] In response
to this distinction, the mummy has "certain scruples of conscience," admits the narrator, "the nature of which I did not distinctly learn."[44] An
intimate opposition results, and drives the rest of the story.

This opposition quickly becomes written in much larger terms, however, when the conversation turns to matters of mutual interest between
the examiners and the examined—that is, to questions of ancient Egypt.
The scientists engage the mummy at first to have him explain what they
take to be the extraordinary circumstances that resulted in his revival. But
they find very quickly that they, not the mummy, will become the examined; in the course of the night's conversation, they find themselves explaining and defending the very opinions and convictions on which their
experiments were based. They find not only that they are mistaken about
some of the details of Egyptian culture they believe to be accurate—embalming was performed not with asphaltum but with mercury bichloride—

but that the entire collection of assumptions and conclusions they hold about ancient Egypt are, according to their guest, utterly false. One by one, the mummy provides the party with versions of his culture and his time that completely contradict the ones they currently have. The process of embalming, the life span of the ancients, the structure of Egyptian theology: the mummy serves as a corrective for what he announces to be the erroneous beliefs of the assembled representatives of authority on the world of ancient Egypt. "Ah!" the mummy exclaims after a while, "a deplorable condition of ignorance!"[45]

In the company of George Gliddon and the mummy, it does not take long for the conversation to turn to the subject of race. In the catalog of nineteenth-century follies that Poe's mummy provides, chief among them is the question of human origin. And indeed, the mummy takes the folly to be not only the conclusions of nineteenth-century natural science but in fact the very question as such. "The ideas you have suggested," the mummy says, "are to me utterly novel. During my time I never knew any one to entertain so singular a fancy as that the universe (or this world if you will have it so) ever had a beginning at all."[46] Poe does not, however, have his mummy endorse either the American School of polygeny or the Christian one of monogeny; rather, the mummy ridicules both schools, in fact collapsing them together and dismissing altogether the belief that humankind had one parent or set of parents and the belief that it had more than one: "I remember once, and once only, hearing something remotely hinted, by a man of many speculations, concerning the origin of the human race; and by this individual, the very word Adam (or Red Earth) which you make use of, was employed. He employed it, however, in a generical sense, with reference to the spontaneous germination from rank soil . . . of five vast hordes of men, simultaneously upspringing in five distinct and nearly equal divisions of the globe."[47] Poe has his mummy perform a correction on the field of nineteenth-century naturalism as a whole, treating the entirety of the achievements of Poe's positivist century as an immature joke. "It ridicules the political project that underwrites their use both of religion and science," Nelson writes, "their desire one way or another to establish their own preeminence (sanctified origins, heroic progress) and to evade any recognition of alternate human possibilities."[48] Poe's mummy wreaks his revenge not on bodies of flesh but on bodies of belief.

The mummy's role is that of an aristocrat, even a monarch, of history. Indeed, his title, "the Count," reveals as much. He acts as a sign under which *all* of nineteenth-century science and politics are to be placed. "The late-night unwrapping is a fraternal ceremony of professional, white manhood," Nelson explains, "a brotherly rehearsal of sameness and coherence in the ritualistic unveiling of otherness."[49] The mummy disrupts this fraternity not by intruding as an outsider but by admitting himself as an insider. "The symbolically hollowed mummy turns literal revenant," writes Nelson, "whose return severely interrupts the privileged invocation of white manhood."[50] The mummy's judgments are absolute, or, in Poe's farcical display, absolutized, relying on the errors about which Poe's scientists are so embarrassed to enact his historical revenge. His sneering condescension operates through a mechanism of inversion and according to a multilayered logic that is as much one of reversals as reanimation: as a specimen made peer, an abstraction made specific, a mute made to speak. Moreover, this sign—of the pronouncement of the past on the present, of the judgment of authority over the foolish, of the project of Egyptology— is even given a name. Early in the story, Gliddon translates the name of the mummy, and his name clearly functions in a way that pronounces judgment on the century into which he is so suddenly placed. The mummy's name is translated as *Allamistakeo*.[51]

Poe's mummy is a kind of time traveler, resting in suspended animation, entering a time centuries removed from his own. But by his very presence he is also a historical *policeman*, a figure of radical correction, a disciplinary presence that has to do little more than exist in order to shatter centuries of accumulated belief. He ridicules the designs of nineteenth-century scholarship through a kind of antipositivism; he is teleology put in reverse. And, as Poe makes clear, the force of this discipline has more than a superficial impact. The party is ashamed and embarrassed, yes, but for Poe's narrator the effect is much more devastating and widespread. After his words with a mummy, he returns home and is seized with a profound melancholy of historiographic proportions. "The truth is," the narrator writes at the end of his tale, "I am heartily sick of this life, and of the nineteenth century in general."[52] The story concludes in this mode, with the narrator's final abjection. The mummy performs for Poe's scientists a series of shameful revelations, both grand and mundane. Architecture, railroads, political systems—all are believed by Gliddon and company to be the pinnacle of progress, but all are shown by the mummy to be mere misguided shadows of the achievements of ancient Egypt. "And," Poe has

Allamistakeo remark, "as for Progress, it was at one time quite a nuisance, but it never progressed."[53]

In "Some Words with a Mummy," ancient Egypt and its representative are performing a policing function, and it is in this role that the discourses of American Egyptomania, especially the chronological ones, are placed again and again. "The mummy's arguments produce a radical historical revision of USAmerican conceptions of epistemology, time, and space," writes Schueller of Allamistakeo,[54] and too much cannot be said about the extent to which the mummy—in whatever form it appears—threatens historiography itself. The mummy attacks not so much the *inhabitants* of the present as the notion of the present *as such*, whatever accepted system of beliefs that allows the present to think of itself as different, distinct, and safe from the past. Throughout the nineteenth century, the figure of Egypt in its retributional mode is seen as a kind of slumbering giant of truth—and the mummy is the representation of this slumber made literal. Indeed, as the century wears on its subliminal terror becomes its main feature, becoming more and more pronounced, finally culminating in the Hollywood horror films of the 1930s and 1940s. It is awakened but definitely not controlled, summoned but regretted, the sign of its ancientness a sign of its dangerous virility. Egypt, in all of its temporal distance, is much too close for comfort, and this discomfort underwrites virtually its entire American history.

Poe's story uncannily forecasts an equation that would become standard by the beginning of the twentieth century but had already been plainly described in *The Virginny Mummy*: that between mummy and slave and between professor—whether he be collector, scientist, or charlatan—and master. Indeed, this relationship describes one of the central instabilities in the racial identities that emerged from nineteenth-century American fascinations with Egyptian mummies: to treat an imported African artifact as a kindred Caucasian or a sibling in the family of civilization, yet to do so in a way that relied only too plainly on the interpersonal *tableaux* of slavery, was to depend on and even make most important the possibilities for epistemological chaos. That "the imagined fraternity of white men" whose ranks so spawned the medical field and the popular stage as well as the slaveholding class relied on the public display of immobilized black bodies is one thing; that these bodies were at times claimed *not* to be Other but a type of Self is, it seems, quite another. At the very least, it makes legible the close kinship between the all-too-public anxieties over the racial identities of the supposedly docile African (if not Negro) bodies held captive onstage in the North and those over the notoriously restless Negro (if not African) bodies held captive offstage in the South.

## "A Sort of Knowing Original
## Preposterous Nightmare Look That's Rather Taking"

Of all of the varieties of what S. J. Wolfe and Robert Singerman call "mummy mania" in the nineteenth century[55]—whether the mummy is male or female, royal or priestly, accidentally discovered or intentionally unearthed—there is one primary characteristic they all share, without which the movements of the mummy's vengeance would have no motor. It involves the representation of the *breach*: of the precise moment of discovery, the moment at which the mummy is unearthed, or of the precise moment of reanimation, the moment at which the mummy is seen to rise from the dead, break its supposed bonds, escape from its tomb, sarcophagus, or examining table and begin its rampage, whether it be savage or genteel. And, indeed, the various terms of this breach are structurally identical, if supposedly opposed, and are always already set by the trope of the mummy itself, as the mummy invariably arrives for inspection contained in, if not by, something, whether it be the material device of bandages or, as in Poe's story, the social conventions of white fraternity. But it is my argument here that that figure of the mummy's containment—which is also the figure of the containment breached—can be traced back to something quite specific and framed as something quite precise. American Egyptomania was very particular about the connections between mummies and their original places of rest—the spaces that were originally breached and from which they were initially torn—and the damage wreaked by the ancient Egyptian bodies forced to emigrate to the United States inevitably recalled the damage first done to their ancient Egyptian homes: the tomb.

The mummy escapes only *from* something, and, in the fantastic visions of nineteenth-century America, the space most commonly associated with that original violation—which was to be repeated over and over again once the mummy arrived on foreign shores, like a trauma—was the tomb. "It is impossible to give any description sufficient to convey the smallest idea of those subterranean abodes, and their inhabitants," confessed the Italian adventurer Giovanni Belzoni, the most notorious and popular of early tomb raiders. "But what a place of rest! Surrounded by bodies, by heaps of mummies in all directions; which, previous to my being accustomed to the sight, impressed me with horror." [56] The protracted balancing act performed by these Egyptian funereal icons—forever at rest in their tombs and monuments yet forever torn from them and sent on cross-country tours—was described perfectly by the prurient delights available in accounts of architectural penetration. From the nonfiction narratives of Theodore Davis, Arthur Weigall, Amelia Edwards, and Belzoni to the fictional ones of Poe, Alcott, and Jane Loudon, nineteenth-century American readers were first introduced to what has become a stereotype of excavational drama: the discovery of an Egyptian tomb inevitably reveals an Egyptian mummy. "Poor soul," quipped Weigall, the British chief inspector of antiquities for Egypt and codiscoverer of an Egyptian tomb in the early twentieth century, "how she must have hated having an electric lamp blazing in her eyes after thirty-four centuries of darkness. . . . We have not yet examined her husband closely, but he stares solemnly at us all the time as we work and whistle and swear about the tomb." [57]

There is a radically architectural history to the figure of the mummy. The curse of the mummy, initiated by the dramatic device of the breach, never shed its architectural heritage. Nor would it want to: whether rendered grand or small, exploded in size to fill an opera stage or shrunken down to a Barnumesque sarcophagus, architecture and architectural imagery were some of Egyptomania's most durable and transportable products. Even the visual language of early cinema relied on the architectural materials provided by Egyptomania; "the immense range of attractions of Egypt for early cinema," writes Antonia Lant, were "central to cinema's desire to signal an evolving spatial language. . . . Filmmaking cultures were, like audiences and critics, steeped in Egypt's association with striking spatiality, be it of flatness, of strangeness, of layers, of emergence." [58] Painted backdrops, cheap props, generalized Orientalist motifs—the incredibly succinct imagery provided by the immediately recognizable architecture of ancient Egypt conveyed precisely the mix of noble grandeur and exoticized decadence so crucial to the recipe of mummified revenge. Indeed, what the visual projections of American Egyptomania recount is a history of extreme synecdoche; linen wrappings conveyed inner coffins, inner coffins conveyed outer sarcophagi, outer sarcophagi conveyed hidden antechambers, hidden antechambers conveyed buried Egyptian tombs. To breach one was to breach them all. That this violation was one of Western imperialism into "darker" lands—whether in the garb of science or profit or picaresque adventure—was of course much of the thrill; that the curse of the mummy was a narrative of racialized revenge was an open secret.

The mania for Egyptian architecture during this period was not, however, limited to stage sets and photographic panoramas. In fact, the architectural curiosities piqued by the narratives of archaeological adventuring and tomb exploration—which were already in fashion by the turn of the nineteenth century and already frequently associated with the display of their spoils, both mummified and otherwise—were presented with a large range of literalized satisfactions. Like its counterparts in Greece, Italy, and elsewhere, Egyptian architecture enjoyed an American revival during the nineteenth century, and, like those other styles, an interest in Egyptian forms occurred simultaneously with an expanded American presence abroad, both military and financial. As American interests were becoming more and more vested in countries outside Europe, America was undergoing a period of rapid urbanization, and the architectural developments that occurred during this period were of a piece with the often violent social conflicts that attended them. Egyptian architecture was to play an important part in the cultural politics of antebellum America, and even more importantly it would be particularly attuned to American anxieties over race.

The Egyptian Revival was one of a large number of competing architectural styles vying for prominence throughout the nineteenth century and was part of a larger movement in architectural fashion known as revivalism. Sometimes called eclecticism, American revivalism owed its material conditions of possibility to the explosion of urban building in the first decades of the 1800s, but it was also famously structured by what can be called a mode of historiographic visuality. The temples of ancient Greece, the buildings of ancient Italy, the ruins of ancient Egypt: revivalism was characterized by, among other things, a strong reliance on visual references to earlier architectural traditions. "How strange it is that in all the inventions of modern times architecture alone seems to admit of no improvement," one supporter rhapsodized; "every departure from the classical models of antiquity in this science is a departure from grace and beauty."[59] Architectural historian Vincent Scully writes that in such historiographical debates early American national identity was formed: "[a] new wave of classicism came along in time to house Lincoln's gigantic presence in a simplified temple. . . . It can be no accident that such a renewal of activity . . . took place during America's period of imperial adventure. . . . The United States was born out of it." [60]

Egypt's orbit within the motions of architectural revivalism, however, had a distinctly bifurcated trajectory. Egypt was frequently set both in narratives of classical ancient civilizations—that is, in direct relation to Greece and Rome—and in narratives of the exoticized East. "Egypt," writes Edward Said, "was the focal point of the relationships between Africa and Asia, between Europe and the East, between memory and actuality." [61] Indeed, the Egyptian Revival is, for this very reason, an uneasy figure standing between traditional neoclassicism and full-scale Orientalism. Egypt was thus a passageway in more ways than one: it acted as a marker for the approach of the distant past, as a revivalist traveler moved backward in time, and as a marker for passage into the distant Other. British landscape painter David Roberts marked just this combination of architecture, race, and chronology when he wrote from Cairo in 1838 of "splendid cities, once teeming with a busy population and embellished with . . . edifices, the wonder of the world, now deserted and lonely, or reduced by mismanagement and the barbarism of the Moslem creed, to a state as savage as the wild animals by which they are surrounded." [62] Architectural revivalism could thus be an extremely efficient shorthand for any number of colonialist justifications, and Orientalism returned again and again to metaphors of space, be they architectural or geographical. "Egypt's own destiny," writes Said, "was to be annexed, to Europe preferably." [63]

Much of the project of architectural revivalism was the construction of a set of essentialist connections between people and their buildings, and architectural styles were rendered with an ethnographic precision to rival any illustrator of the American School. Nineteenth-century revivalist architects were voracious in their considerations of nationalized or racialized styles of architecture, and the history of revivalism is characterized by continual comparisons between carefully delineated geographic—and what during this period were therefore ethnological—regions. Especially in its early days, revivalism depended on graphic resources taken from architectural studies published for those people who could not visit the source structures—the Parthenon, the Colosseum, the temple at Abu Simbel—and in the case of the Egyptian Revival these resources were indispensable. [64] Architects took great pride in establishing the authenticity of their designs, alluding to the temples and other structures from which they were derived.

Much of the dynamic of revivalist architecture, therefore, was a game of *citation*. Whether adhering or diverging, designing or critiquing, authenticity was and still is a primary stake in revivalist aesthetics, and thus there is an academic quality to revivalist design built along these lines of origin and derivation that is crucial to the intellectual funding of revivalist architects and their projects.

Importantly, though, what also characterized revivalist architecture in the United States was an opposite tendency, away from ostensible ethnographic accuracy and toward avowed and outright fantasy. Particularly pronounced in the works of architects who utilized "Oriental" styles — which in open dialogue with neoclassicism also laid claim to the Egyptian Revival — revivalism also tended toward a kind of freewheeling extravagance, with structures being built on larger and larger scales and with more and more elements borrowed, adapted, and combined with aspects of other revivalist styles. P. T. Barnum's Iranistan, Frederick Edwin Church's Olanna, the Longwood house of Natchez planter Haller Nutt: the architectural products of American Orientalism could be as fantastic as their literary, painterly, or sculptural counterparts, and for the Americans who were interested in constructing such structures the terms of their aesthetic visions were size, scale, scope, and idiosyncrasy.[65] As the century wore on, this syncretic tendency was seen more and more in structures built in the Greek, Roman, and Gothic styles, but it was seen earlier, for a longer period, much more often, and with much greater zeal in the Orientalist Revival.

The history of the Egyptian Revival is particularly instructive in this regard: throughout its history, the Egyptian style has been seen as particularly adaptable to some of the most extravagant and eccentric public architectural projects in the United States. Robert Mills's Washington Monument in Washington, D.C., originally designed in 1833 but not begun until 1848 and not completed until 1884, is perhaps the most recognizable example of the excesses encouraged by the dynamics of the Egyptian Revival, but even at 555 feet high it seems somehow less exorbitant when one considers Mills's original plan for the monument. "He envisaged a stepped pyramid 680 feet high surmounted by a 100-foot-high statue of Washington," recounts architectural historian Pamela Scott, with "colossal buttresses at each corner support[ing] 350-foot obelisks."

The body of the structure was pierced throughout by vaulted galleries on seven levels of decreasing height. The first stage had thirteen arched doorways on each face, representing the original union of states, with the names of each state in bronze letters on the voussoirs. The second stage had nine arched openings, each of which was to contain a 33-foot statue of a hero or statesman of the Revolution. This second level opened onto a 150-foot-wide balcony, or "terrace walk." The third level had seven arched entries and 6-foot-wide balconies; the fourth, five openings and 50-foot terraces; and the fifth, three arches. Statues of additional unspecified "worthies of the Revolution" would be contained on the third level, but Mills did not specify any sculpture for the next two stages. The sixth level consisted of a 40-foot-high pedestal for the statue of Washington, which was on the seventh level. The lower part of the pedestal was enriched with inscriptive panels recounting events in Washington's life, while each face of the upper part was decorated with a wreath encircling Washington's name. Visitors would walk or drive carriages up "inclined planes" on all four 1,000-foot sides to reach the summit.[66]

Mills's massive and fantastic Washington Pyramid had a number of antecedents—particularly the intentionally extreme utopian imaginings of French architects Etienne-Louis Boulée and Louis-François Cassas, friend of Napoleonic Egypt Expedition member Vivant Denon—but it was in the nineteenth-century United States that the combination of nationalist bravado and exoticized opulence so characteristic of revivalist architecture in its grand mode found a willing partner in the Egyptian style. As one commentor remarked in 1847 on a design proposed for the Washington Monument by another architect, rejected but strikingly similar to the final design by Mills: "a combination of obelisk, church steeple, and gas house chimney intended to look Egyptian, and five hundred feet high, is horribly ugly, but has a sort of knowing original preposterous nightmare look that's rather taking."[67]

I dwell on these aspects of the Egyptian Revival for a number of reasons. First and foremost, it is to gesture quickly toward distributions in the style that will not be treated at length in the discussions below but are nevertheless important to recognize at least in passing—those associated with nationalism and excess in particular. Second, it is to emphasize those aspects of the style that are all too often underplayed in architectural histories: those which arose from the politics of race. Indeed, while the eclectic mix of structures that make up the history of the Egyptian Revival is routinely noted, there is still, I believe, inattention to the social and political conflicts that produced that mix, and to the extent to which nineteenth-century anxieties over race, racial origin, and racial identity were carved in stone. What makes the Egyptian Revival important in this respect is that in many ways the eclecticism within the style did not want to resolve itself, for it was about a conspicuous heterogeneity of opinion regarding its various functions, a pronounced anxiety over its competing uses, a concerted opposition to itself. The Egyptian Revival in its American phase was a style that operated because of—not in spite of—a certain complexity of representation attending architectural representations of ancient Egypt, and this complexity was directly related to the complexity of positions associated with the racialized status of this liminal land.

In particular, I am referring to the plainly visible set of widespread associations the Egyptian style had for attitudes that were arguably nowhere near the noble nationalist or fraternal ideals often attributed to its version of neoclassicism. Well before the height of the Egyptian Revival, Egyptian motifs had become clearly associated with some of the most pronounced racialized fantasies of the nineteenth century: from the ethnological controversies of the American School to North African travel narratives and later projections of harems, dancing girls, and other erotic mysteries, the Orientalizing Egyptianisms of American popular culture were as much a factor in the reception of Egyptian imagery and had as many associational claims on the public that frequented public architecture as any supposed scholasticism or neoclassical idealism. "After passing through only one or two rooms of the building which he has fitted up in the styles of the dead races," one observer recounted in 1898 following a visit to a characteristically extravagant Egyptian Revival structure in Washington, D.C., "one feels as though he has just stepped either from a Roman drama or a novel of Bulwer Lytton." [68] It is these kinds of racialized anxieties that are illustrated by the excesses of the Egyptian style.

Certainly the terms of all nationalized neoclassical styles were in part those of size and scale, but very few architectural historians make any direct connections between, for example, the anxiety-ridden excesses of the Orientalist Revivals and the size of the Washington Monument. "There is something in this simple, majestic, obelisk to my mind eminently proper as commemorative of the character of Washington," intoned the congressman for the District of Columbia from the floor of the House of Representatives in 1874: "Strong and enduring, it cannot be more so than his fame; lofty and majestic, it cannot be more so than the motives which governed his life; higher than any like structures in the world, it cannot excel them by so much as he stands above all others in the spotless purity of his character."[69] Even—or perhaps especially—in the overwrought idioms of political rhetoric there is something in characterizations like this that betrays the ostensible associations of the Egyptian style with simplicity, majesty, and purity, not the least of which is the irony in the choice of wording; merely that the historical importance of George Washington intersected with the appropriateness of the Egyptian obelisk for a funerary monument hardly seems a sufficient explanation for the conspicuously overcompensational final design. The mammoth efforts to police the boundaries between the neoclassical—nationalized—designs of the Egyptian style and the Orientalist—racialized—connotations radiating off of Egyptian imagery everywhere else in America can be seen in every inch of the Washington Monument's 555 feet.[70]

The historicized anxieties regarding the placement of images of ancient Egypt—classically "near" or exotically "far"—were thus plainly racialized anxieties regarding the status of the inhabitants of Egypt: "black," "white," or "yellow"; Muslim, Christian, or Jew. The Egyptian Revival—especially in its nationalist mode—was thus a split sign: both of a potential ancestor of American civilization and the apprehensive ambivalence over that ancestor's family tree, both of imperial power and the fears of racial "contamination" that power inevitably invoked. Claiming ancient Egypt as an ascendant of America meant also inviting many unwelcome guests. This is, in fact, one of the keys to understanding the mysterious exoticism Egypt continues to have in the grand triumvirate of ancient civilizations. Only in counterpoint to the constructions of ancient Greece and ancient Rome did ancient Egypt become not positively politicized but exoticized, not modeled but scorned, not worshiped but feared. Much of what we will see was a widespread anxiety regarding ancient civilizations fixed on ancient Egypt, and with all of the uneasy fascination given to symbols of the repressed. The Egyptian Revival stood at the epicenter of a semiotic instability in the newly urbanizing nation.

Revivalist styles competed against one another for connotation, importance, and their very viability. Greek Revival buildings, for example, appeared not so much because they were intended to connote a connection with ancient Greece, "the cradle of democracy," or even the struggle for Greek independence, but more because they did so only in counterposition to other models of ancientness. Greece was democratic only when compared to Rome; Rome was grand only when compared to Egypt. The slaveholding

Greece of the neoclassical revival was a paragon of democracy and free-dom, but only *relatively* so, only insofar as it was represented as a society *not* based on slavery. Rome was a model for republicanism only insofar as it was not a model of decadence. Egypt was the land of wisdom only as long as it was not the land of oppression. Revivalism, then, is here seen as the very model of national anxiety: of the anxieties of national identity in general and of national historiographic anxiety in particular. Revivalist structures were constructed not as a means of expressing intended asso-ciations with the ancient past but as a means of attempting to control the unwanted associations that past always carried with it. Historicism was a police state.

Greece and Rome were benchmarks of the ease with which ancient civili-zations could be marketed as passing virtually untouched across the cen-turies, pressed into the service of postrevolutionary American nationalism, but Egypt was not. Greece was never terrifying when discovered; Rome never attacked wrapped in white decay. Moreover, the racialized contro-versies over the ancient past that surrounded ancient Egypt were in fact in-strumental in securing the status of the ancient pasts of Greece and Rome. Greece and Rome were, in a word, *whitened*: the most recurrent of villains in Rome only fed Christians to the lions, and Socrates never seemed to whip his slaves. Ancient Egypt violated the logic of this campaign of the whitening of history. Egypt was configured not only by discourses of radi-cal temporality—becoming, in effect, the sign of the ancient as such or at least the sign of the *edge* of the ancient—but it was also configured by that most disruptive of national discourses, race. The racialized controversies in which ancient Egypt figured so prominently interfered with any smooth transition from "the ancient past" to "the nineteenth century," whether it was shaped into a conflict between pagan and Christian or Negro and Cau-casian. As a result, Egypt became the sign of historiographic anxiety. As a result, out of Egypt came the curse of the mummy.

## "Both Buildings from
## Which One Does Not Escape with Ease"

This combination of revivalist aesthetics, social anxiety, ambivalent asso-ciationism, and police-state architecture was literalized in the first decades of the nineteenth century in a public building project that presented all of the constituent parts of the Egyptian Revival in stark exactness. In it was contained the uncontainable pressures that grew out of attempting to reconcile the warring iconographies of ancient solitude and modern urbanization, of unbreachable barriers and radical permeability, of limitless power and limitless vulnerability. This structure was intended to enclose and yet repeatedly erupted, was intended to connote justice and yet instantly conveyed horror; it was a deeply conflicted icon of both control and uncontrollability, Egyptian and explosive, just like the mummy. Even before its completion, the structures officially titled the New York City Halls of Justice and House of Detention had come to be referred to by the nickname with which they would immediately become much more widely known, and by which they are to this day still known: "the Tombs."

During the height of its popularity, the Egyptian Revival was most commonly associated in the nineteenth-century United States with two major types of structures: cemeteries and prisons. The nicknaming of the Halls of Justice "the Tombs" betrays a connection between these two types and indicates an ambivalence about the uses of the Egyptian Revival that will be the final focus of this chapter. The nickname marks a central feature of American Egyptomania: an interest in containment joined with a fear of escape, a desire for entombment combined with a fascination with excavation, a relief at interment mixed with a hope for resurrection. Thus when architectural historian James Stevens Curl writes of the almost exclusive uses of the American Egyptian Revival for the construction of cemeteries and prisons that "it is easy to see why, for both building types are those from which one does not escape with ease,"[71] he is being glib—but my interest instead is to show how deeply connected these two styles were, and how important their iconography was to the cultural logic of American Egyptomania.

Most famous to students of American literature for being the space in which Bartleby is finally interred in Herman Melville's 1853 "Bartleby the Scrivener," the New York Tombs were designed in 1835 and completed in 1838 by British-born architect John Haviland.[72] "Undoubtedly the most important Egyptian Revival monument in America," writes architectural historian Richard Carrott, the Halls of Justice were at the time America's premier penal complex: a combination courthouse and prison, the integrated structure was designed to consolidate and centralize the various stages of the penal system. Booking, arraignment, trial, sentencing, and imprisonment could all take place in one merged complex and thus maximize

"The Tombs," New York City Halls of Justice and House of
Detention, John Haviland, architect, 1835–38. J. Clement,
engraver. (From *The Century* 45:2 [December 1892]. Picture
Collection, Branch Libraries, New York Public Library,
Astor, Lenox, and Tilden Foundations.)

the efficiency of the penal process by allowing all the necessary phases to
take place in one space. The Halls of Justice were a major innovation in
nineteenth-century prison design; intended as a culminating statement in
what had been a full three decades of upheaval in European and American penal philosophy and resultant prison reforms, the complex was one
of the most high-profile public works projects in America's early history.
It was matched in size and significance only by its recent predecessors in
prison construction, and there was an enormous amount of interest in its

design. "The whole subject of prison architecture and prison discipline is one of deepest importance," wrote one interested architect. "It affords me peculiar pleasure to find that New York is awake to this matter."[73] It is thus of no small importance that the architectural style chosen for the complex would be that of the Egyptian Revival.[74]

By the late nineteenth century, popular opinion held that the choice of the Egyptian style for "the Tombs," as well as its nickname, originated with the publication of John Lloyd Stephens's *Incidents of Travel in Egypt, Arabia Petraea, and the Holy Land.* "When the Common Council determined to erect a new jail in 1833," one popular history of the Tombs explained in 1883,

> there was quite a dispute as to the order of architecture to be observed in its construction. About this time there was published a book entitled "Stevens' Travels." The author was John L. Stevens, Esq., of Hoboken, who had recently returned from an extended tour through Asia and the Holy Land. The book was full of interest, and contained many illustrations of the rare and curious things he had seen. Among these illustrations was one of an ancient Egyptian tomb, accompanied by a full and accurate description. The committee appointed by the Common Council to decide upon the necessary plans for the new prison were impressed with the idea of erecting a building whose general appearance and construction would correspond with the tomb described in Stevens' book. They accordingly made their report, recommending the construction of such a building, suggesting as a most fitting and appropriate name, "The Tombs." The report was adopted and work was begun at once.[75]

This bit of folk etymology, however, cannot possibly be true. As Carrott points out, the two volumes of Stephens's *Incidents of Travel* were first published in early 1837, and the designs for the complex were to be submitted by interested architects by February 1835.[76] Moreover, this representative bit of retrospective backstory is itself full of holes: Stephens (not Stevens) was originally born in Shrewsbury, New Jersey, and moved to Manhattan at the age of thirteen months. When not traveling, he resided almost exclusively in New York, he never visited Asia, and he seems never to have set foot in Hoboken. Yet the easy and almost automatic connection between these two landmarks in the history of American Egyptomania, both appearing in the late 1830s, is telling.[77]

Students of American architectural history have long recognized the confluence of prison architectural design and the Egyptian Revival. There were at least seven prisons built in the Egyptian style between 1808 and 1858, and while this number might seem small and while the style was not limited to the penal tradition, the concentrated appearance of so many large-scale structures usually fixes this aspect of the Egyptian revival for architectural historians. "The most significant group of buildings whose meaning relates to the idea of the Land of Wisdom and Mystery is that which comes under the heading of courthouses and prisons," writes Carrott. "It should be noted that in the earliest case in America the style was applied solely to a prison, later to a courthouse and prison complex, and eventually to a courthouse alone. Thus, the primary association is that of penal architecture."[78] Indeed, of the many misconceptions regarding the Egyptian Revival—including, for example, that it was never used as a domestic style[79]—one commonplace that is not inaccurate is that it came into a uniquely American prominence as a style appropriate for prisons. "The general appearance of the Egyptian style of architecture," wrote one influential architect, "is that of solemn grandeur amounting sometimes to sepulchral gloom. For this reason it is appropriate for cemeteries, prisons, &c.; and being adopted for these purposes, it is gradually gaining favor."[80]

In America, the iconography of ancient Egypt is a missing link of sorts, a central, if forgotten, mechanism in the establishment of what Michel Foucault calls the political technology of the body.[81] "The prison," writes Foucault, "through an administrative apparatus, will . . . be a machine for altering minds."[82] The period of social upheaval that produced the Tombs, the penal philosophy represented by Haviland, and the development of the Egyptian style which many felt to be its purest architectural completion, are landmarks in the histories of prison design, humanitarian reform, and the development of urban America, and they warrant a crucial place in Foucault's 1979 Discipline and Punish. "Then came the Philadelphia model," Foucault writes. "This was no doubt the most famous because it was associated in people's minds with the political innovations of the American system and also because it was not, like the others, doomed to immediate failure and abandonment; it was continuously re-examined and transformed right up to the great debates of the 1830s on penitentiary reform."[83] The Egyptian Revival provided the most ready visual vocabulary for this heady mix of bodies and ideologies housed as prisoners.[84]

The Philadelphia system, so famous in the history of prison reform, was also known as "the separate system." Prisoners were kept in complete isolation: on entering a prison in the separate system, they were stripped of their outside possessions, their heads were hooded, and they were led to their cells, in which they remained for the complete duration of their sentences.[85] Food was delivered through a hole in the door, and aside from visits from the prison chaplain, prisoners in the Pennsylvania system were kept in complete isolation. This system

> would cause the prisoner to pass his whole time in reflecting on his situation; and his thoughts, especially during the silent hours of the night, would be of such a nature, as not to be lost upon the most hardened criminal. . . . Left to himself, his own reflections will be melancholy and depressing; his evil propensities, instead of being confirmed by the unrestrained intercourse with his more wicked companions, will infallibly be checked; the good advice he may have received from pious parents, will recur to his mind with a force it perhaps never possessed before, and thus, instead of being more vicious, as at present, when emerging from prison, than when he entered it, will be chastened, and disposed to follow his trade, and to lead a regular and sober life.[86]

"In the Pennsylvanian prison," Foucault writes, "the only operations of correction were the conscience and the silent architecture that confronted it."[87] This was architectural didacticism turned social weapon, associationism ratcheted into individualized discipline.

Yet even if Haviland had not gone on to codify the Egyptian style for his prisons, the architecture of which was so crucial to the separate system, already the analogy is manifest to that other great Egyptian image: the tomb. "I see your cell as no more than a frightful sepulchre," Foucault quotes one warden as saying, "where, instead of worms, remorse and despair come to gnaw at you and turn your existence into a hell in anticipation."[88] This is the space of imprisonment *and* entombment, this combined space of secular rationalism and Christian apocalypse, this space of forced rebirth, this space not of justice but of terror. "It is true," another warden would tell arriving prisoners, "that while confined here you can have no intelligence concerning relatives or friends. . . . You are to be literally buried from the world."[89]

Like Christian death, however, this rationalist death was only temporary, a secondary, if structurally necessary, moment in the shape of the trajectory of the reborn. "By forming regular, temperate and industrious habits, learning a useful trade, yielding obedience to laws, subduing evil passions, and by receiving moral and religious instruction," the warden told his new inmates, "your case is far from being hopeless. Your sufferings during confinement will be greatly mitigated; you will return to your friends and to society with correct views and good resolutions, and then friends and society will receive you again with open arms."[90] He concluded by quoting Luke 15:24: "Like the compassionate father to his prodigal son, they will say of you, 'he was dead, and is alive again.' "[91] The separate system combined these two strategies, of isolation and divine solicitation. American disciplinary rationalism understood its end point to be Christian conversion. This is the space rendered wildly legible by the figure of ancient Egypt.

The operating logic in the separate system was one of corrective Christianity based on the architectural iconography of ancient Egypt. *Penitence* was the core of the penitentiary, rehabilitation as moral and physical entombment. "All our endeavors therefore ought to be directed toward the production of that state of mind," wrote James Mease, "which will cause a convict to concentrate his thoughts upon his forlorn condition, to abstract himself from the world, and to think of nothing except the suffering and the privations he endures, the result of his crimes. Such a state of mind . . . is only to be brought about . . . by complete mental and bodily insulation. . . . But neither this frame of mind, nor these reflections can take place, without a special interposition of Providence."[92] Through proper observation of the dictates of the separate system, isolation produced shame, shame produced penitence, and penitence produced Christianity. The Pennsylvania prisons were tools of God, even as they were also, as their name makes clear, machines of separation. "Society is improved by removing the law breaker," wrote a contributor to the *Journal of the Pennsylvania Prison Society*, "and the law breaker is much more in his place by separation from other law breakers. Hence advanced penology says, 'Separate System.' "[93] The radical analogy between the criminalized population, the singularized body of a given offender, and the prison cell was itself contained by the sign of ancient Egypt.

Neither all of the Pennsylvania prisons nor all of their philosophical descendants were designed in the Egyptian style, of course, but ancient Egypt provided the iconographic model sine qua non for the disciplinary logic of containment in America. It described both a space of incredible confinement and a space of incredible pressure. It drew on the iconography of the tomb as well as the monk's cell, but above all it declared the power of the state to *force* Christian conversion or rational repentance. "Conscience cannot sleep long in *solitude*," wrote another supporter of the theories that became the separate system. "The worst of men, when left for a while to themselves, are made prisoners by their own reflections. These reflections are the messengers of Heaven to bring them to repentance, and a sense of their duty. . . . To be delivered to a merciless overseer of a public work of any kind, or to be delivered to a sheriff for execution, are both light punishment compared to a wicked man being delivered by *solitude* and *confinement* to his own reflections."[94] The iconography of ancient Egypt, in the revivalist mode of nineteenth-century urban architecture, provided American disciplinary logic with its most effective vocabulary of terrifying constraint.

Especially visible in the architecture of the Egyptian prison, the sign of ancient Egypt was directly related to burgeoning images of nineteenth-century social unrest and the mechanisms of control. Images of Egypt were constituted in large part by a set of iconographic relays and discursive habits, which in their operation produced an idiomatic orientation around—a fascination with and a constant return to—dramas of enclosure, imprisonment, entombment, and burial. Likewise, they produced *escape*: as seen in the trope of the mummy, the drama of imprisonment was only as pressing as the power of that which was imprisoned. The disciplinary logic of the Egyptian prison, like so much of the rest of American Egyptomania, was configured by a frantic concern with strategies and dramas of containment. The iconography of the Egyptian Revival expressed in prison architecture contained the danger of unwanted American bodies; it in fact marked them *as* dangerous, and legitimized the strategy of separation. The Egyptian Revival was a monument to anxiety. Separation, containment, and the control of contagion: this was the origin of the Egyptian prison.

It is also, perhaps, the sign of the limit of Christian rationalism. The bodily control that American rationalism worked so hard to establish through prison reform would be, of course, ultimately superseded by the Christian resurrection, the moment when bodily control belonged only to God. The prison as machine of Christian morality, as site of judgment, atonement, and ultimate correction, inevitably begged comparison with the machine on which it was modeled, the machine of the ascension. That the iconography of imprisonment was so closely connected to that of the tomb is reason enough to show the figure of Egypt as central to the machinery of regulation. That Christian agendas like those promoted by prison reform would find expression in the images of pagan Egypt is enough to see how ambivalent the operations of that machinery were. The Egyptian style both referenced this Christian rationalism and, as a marker of resurrection that was almost, but not quite, Christian, described its instability.

## "The Dead Shall Be Raised"

In the early 1840s, Connecticut architect Henry Austin designed the gate for the Grove Street Cemetery in New Haven. Finished in 1848 and loosely based on the porticos of the Temples of Esne and Hermopolis Magna, the gate is a *distyle in antis*—a thick rectangle, sloping in on the sides, with a recessed opening and four pylons, two in recess and two up front. The two front columns are stylized papyrus stalks, sharp and angular, surmounted by a cavetto cornice, the centerpiece of which is a winged orb. There are torus moldings and a carefully busy "battered" surface to most of the masonry—and in general the gate is a typical example of Egyptian Revival architecture. What makes Grove Street important, however, is the stone banner just above the two front columns, between the top of the entranceway and the cornice. It is both perfectly smooth and the location of the following inscription: THE DEAD SHALL BE RAISED.[95] Stylistically, the inscription is something of a discontinuity in the overall design of the gate—and in fact it was probably added not by Austin but by the committee that hired him to design the gate—but it is also centrally placed, a primary feature of the structure.[96] The inscription is both at odds with the rest of the gate and explicitly contained by it, and, indeed, a pointed part of the whole effect is this relationship: the oddly modern words on the plainly ancient style.

The inscription itself comes from 1 Corinthians 15: "Behold, I show you a mystery; We shall not all sleep, but we shall all be changed, In a moment, in the twinkling of an eye, at the last trump: for the trumpet shall sound, and the dead shall be raised incorruptible, and we shall be changed."[97] Paul's first letter to the Corinthians is concerned, in this its penultimate chapter, with an explanation of Christian resurrection, and thus its relevance for the designers of a Christian cemetery gate would seem transparent. "For if the dead rise not," Paul writes, "then is not Christ raised: And if Christ be not raised, your faith is vain."[98] The problem itself raised by Grove Street, however, was not in the inscription per se, nor in the choice of

Entrance gate to Grove Street Cemetery, New Haven, Conn., ca. 1890, George R. Bradley, photographer. (Courtesy of the New Haven Colony Historical Society.)

an Egyptian style alone. Rather, it was in their juxtaposition. The aesthetics of the gate produce an uneven signification configured by the terms of death and resurrection. An overtly Christian reference crowns the overtly Egyptian Grove Street gate, and the uneasy relationship that produced the inscription was the central relationship in the dynamics of Egyptian Revival funerary design. A tension between Egyptian associations and Christian beliefs produced an anxiety over what was in fact the point of their most intimate contact—conceptions of the afterlife—and, as with the figure of the Christian criminal released after being reborn in the Egyptian prison, this tension would result in one of the most recurrent figures in American Egyptomania: the ambivalent anthropomorphic sign of the resurrected Egyptian inhabitant of the ancient tomb, the mummy.

The Grove Street gate was one of a series of American cemetery gates in the first half of the nineteenth century designed in the Egyptian style. Others appeared in Baltimore, Boston, Philadelphia, New Orleans, Farmington, Connecticut, Roxbury and Cambridge, Massachusetts, and many other cities.[99] The combination of ancient Egyptian iconography and funerary architecture—whether it produces a cemetery gate, a design motif, or a full-scale obelisk—is one of the most lasting and important aspects of nineteenth-century revivalist architecture and is today familiar to the point of ubiquity. Ubiquitous as this alliance might be, however, the inscription on the Grove Street gate indexes a history to that ubiquity that is, at the very least, one of extreme instability. Put more forcefully, that history is one of radical antagonism, violent repression, and an explosive fear of the body and bodily containment, and describes the architectural aesthetics of reanimational anxiety.

Egyptian Revival funerary architecture, especially in the decades before the Civil War, was structured by a central ambivalence. On one hand, there was what appeared to be an obvious appropriateness to the combination of Christian interment and Egyptian imagery, and the movement had its vocal supporters. "It is essentially the architecture of the grave," wrote a guidebook to one such cemetery in 1855. "Imposing and somber in form, and mysterious in its remote origin, it seems peculiarly adapted to the abode of the dead, and its enduring character contrasts strongly and strangely with the brief life of mortals." [100] In contradistinction to the cultural practices of ancient Greeks, ancient Egyptians very famously buried their dead, and the supporters of Egyptian cemetery designs used this awareness to stylize a connection to Christian custom. "Some of their sculptures and paintings," wrote one advocate of the style, "were undoubtedly symbolical of the resurrection of the soul, a dread of the final judgment, and a belief in Omnipotent justice." [101] The rising popularity of early Egyptology made such connections readily available and easily made. "Derived, as it is, from a land which is emphatically a monumental one," pronounced the dedicator of an Egyptian Revival cemetery gate in 1842, "and one that may be regarded as one vast cemetery, it cannot be considered as out of keeping with associations of a place of burial." [102]

On the other hand, however, the interfaith marriage of Christianity and Egyptology had its equally vocal opponents. "Egyptian architecture reminds us of the religion which called it into being," wrote architect James Gallier in the *North American Review* in 1836, "the most degraded and revolting paganism which ever existed. It is the architecture of embalmed cats and deified crocodiles." [103] Egyptian architecture, impressively ancient as it was, was also seen as pagan, pre-Christian, idolatrous, and blasphemous. "Solid, stupendous, and time-defying, we allow," Gallier wrote, "but associated in our minds with all that is disgusting and absurd in superstition. . . . It is very doubtful whether the Egyptian style is most appropriate to a Christian burial-place. It certainly has no connexion with our religion."[104] Even as the most famous Egyptian cemetery gates were being erected, concerned observers were waging a worried campaign of strict Christian interpretation. In its Revivalist incarnation in America, it was for many a gratuitously offensive endorsement of pagan associations, an architectural manifesto of anti-Christian sentiment. "In spite of the funerary tradition of Egyptian forms," writes Carrott understatedly, "the more specific expressions of the style in cemeteries drew forth growls of disapproval."[105]

This was all the more the case because of the conspicuous placement of Egyptian funerary designs at the gates of a critical feature in the Christian moral landscape: the cemetery, not the ultimate but the penultimate stop for a believer. "Now, there is certainly no place where it is more desirable that our religion should be present to the mind than the cemetery," wrote Gallier, "which might be regarded either as the end of all things . . . or, on the other hand, as the gateway to a glorious immortality, the passage to a brighter world, whose splendors beam even upon the dark chambers of the tomb."[106] As the site of the last earthly habitation before that final event which was so specifically referenced by the inscription at Grove Street, the housing of a Christian soul in a pagan tomb was for some a particularly painful insult—both to God and to His believers. "It is from the very brink of the grave . . . that Christianity speaks to us," Gallier concluded, "of victory over death, and a life to come. Surely, then, all that man places over the tomb should in a measure speak the same language."[107] When the Connecticut committee decided to add a Christian inscription to Austin's Egyptian gate in words that told of death and resurrection, they were attempting to do just that.

The kind of inscription found on the Grove Street gate and the tensions that it represented were not limited to Austin's design but were a characteristic feature of Egyptian Revival cemetery gates wherever they appeared. In Cambridge, the gate at Mount Auburn—designed in 1831 by Jacob Bigelow and the design to which Gallier was in fact responding—is inscribed:

> Then Shall the Dust Return
> To Earth as It Was
> And the Spirit Shall Return
> Unto God Who Gave It[108]

Likewise, in Roxbury, H. A. S. Dearborn's 1848 Egyptian Revival cemetery gate reads, on one side, "Though I Walk Through The Valley of The Shadow of Death I Will Fear No Evil," and on the other, "I am the Resurrection and the Life."[109] Even Robert Mills worried about having his Washington Monument evoke the "frivolity of Heathen superstition, as the gloom of Egyptian darkness."[110] So what we have is a visual record of the tension between the iconographic appeal of the Egyptian style and the Christian objection to it, an ambivalence carved in stone.

And there *was* appeal: for all of the Christian disapprovals, the Egyptian cemetery style was enormously popular. Its proliferation during the nineteenth century and subsequent naturalization—the ubiquity of which is so codified today—are testimony to that. "Its original examples are the monuments of remote ages," said one defender of the architecture of ancient Egypt, "of buried cities, and of peoples," and this alliance—one not so much of religion as of antiquity itself—would be the more lasting one.[111] It is of course ironic that the victory in this almost forgotten iconographic campaign would be so complete, but, like the objections to other pre-Christian styles, support for interpretive latitude often grew in the face of fundamentalism. Detractors had a relatively straightforward objection—one basic point about the opposition between Christianity and paganism—and very little effort was needed to grasp its significance. Apologists and advocates of the style, on the other hand, had their work cut out for them in the face of this Christian opposition, and many took to it with a vengeance.

The solution, as supporters of the Egyptian style saw it, was to convince their opponents that the very terms of their objections—an antiquity that predated Christianity—were in fact grounds for acceptance. "As regards monuments or designs of the Egyptian style, for places of Christian interment," C. W. Walter, a defender of Mount Auburn, acknowledged, "we are aware that an objection to them has been made, that they mark a period anterior to Christian civilization—a period of relative degradation and paganism." This very anterior status, however, was the key; ancient Egypt had been pagan, yes, "but it has ever been a pleasure with the thoughtful," Walter chided, "to look beyond the actual *appearance* of a figure, to the right development of its original idea."[112] In other words, pre-Christian Egyptian paganism was not *non*-Christian, but *proto*-Christian. "The now mythologized doctrines of Egypt, seem to have been the original source of others more ennobling," visitors to Mount Auburn were assured, "and hieroglyphic discoveries have traced, and are tracing them far beyond the era of the pyramids, to an unknown limit, but to a pure, sacred, and divine source." [113] Egypt, Walter and his allies argued, was in fact not the pagan enemy of all that was Christian and holy but rather its *parent*: "When the art of writing was unknown, the primeval Egyptians resorted to symbols and emblems to express their faith; and these, as correctly interpreted, certainly present many sublime ideas in connection with those great truths which in an after age constituted the doctrines of 'Christianity.' " [114] Monotheism was a useful, if unexpected, ally in nineteenth-century debates over the Egyptian Revival, and its scholasticism was pressed into immediate service. [115]

"Christianity" was now placed in quotation marks, a child historicized into its monotheistic family tree. Even the supposedly warring symbols of Egyptian religion and Christianity were domesticated, monotheistically familiarized. "The very *pyramidal shape*, of which the Egyptians were so fond," Walter assured his readers, "is believed to indicate an idea not disgraceful to a wholly Christian era." [116] Like the pyramids themselves, the famously familiar winged orb — like the one that originally was to grace the lintel of the door to Mills's Washington Monument — was made into a sign not of Christian *oppression* but of *Christianity*. "The 'winged globe,' which is carved on the gateway of Mount Auburn," asserted Walter, "is a most beautiful emblem of benign protection. In the form of a sun, with outstretched wings, it covers the facades of most Egyptian buildings, and was the primitive type of the divine wisdom — the universal Protector. We do not know of a more fitting emblem than this for the abode of the dead, which we may well suppose to be overshadowed with the protecting wings of Him who is the great author of our being — the 'giver of life and death.' " [117] God, it turns out, was as Egyptian as the Revival.

What resulted was what, depending on one's point of view, was either the Christianization of ancient Egypt or the Egyptianization of Christianity, and the most critical point of engagement was at the moment of resurrection. "I do not so much object to the obelisk, Egyptian though it may be, and savouring, as some think, of an idolatrous homage of the sun," wrote the author of an 1847 guidebook to Brooklyn's Greenwood Cemetery, "because its tall shaft with its pyramidical apex, losing itself in the air, and pointing to the sky, may seem to speak to the living of the heavenly home to which their departed friends have entered." [118] An alliance was created between the two terms along the lines of an antiquity seen to be more connective than divisive — and which, therefore, overrode what were seen to be mere differences in surfaces — but which was, most importantly, one that relied on the shared concept of reanimation. The guidebook to the Forest Hills cemetery in Roxbury presented the matter succinctly in 1855. "There is a difference of opinion as to the propriety of using, as is much the custom, the Egyptian architecture about our burial places," it said. "A relic of paganism, it is by some estimated out of place in a Christian cemetery. But," it went on, "nor is it without the symbols of immortality, which the purer faith of the Christian can well appropriate and associate with the more sacred and divine promises of the gospel." [119] Resurrection, reawakening, rebirth, reanimation: whatever the terminology used, campaigns on both sides of the Egyptian Revival controversies converged on concepts of an ambulatory afterlife.

Thus the striking equation made in 1883 by the amateur British Egyptologist Gerald Massey between the risen Christ and the risen mummy: "*It is in this image, as the actual mummy,*" wrote Massey, "*that the Christ of the Gospels rose again and reappeared.* When he 'stood in the midst of them' . . . and said 'Peace be unto you,' it was emphatically as the *corpus-christus,* or the mummy of the monuments." [120] Massey's vision of "The Child-Christ as an Egyptian Mummy" is more than just one of monotheistic familialism, and he insists on a precise bodily correspondence between these two signs of ancient resurrection. "Thus the preserver of men and savior of the world conforms to the image of the most perfectly preserved mummy of the Egyptians," he writes, "and the reappearance as a proof of immortality is in accordance with that of the mummy." [121] Massey's alignment of the figure of Christ and the figure of the mummy partook of the exact same logic that shaped the Egyptian Revival. In their ambivalent placements, carved like Christian totems on symbols of pagan belief, the biblical inscriptions on Egyptian Revival cemetery gates declare nothing so much as their anxiety over their combined status, each wanting to assert dominance over their prone antagonist even as they are nervously forced to acknowledge its disruptive power.

With all of their tensions and ambivalences intact and on display, the radical instabilities of the Egyptian Revival and the racialized controversies that forced it to rise are rendered their clearest by the fears of the loss of social control described by these spaces of bodily unrest. In their very negotiations, theorists of the revival made visible a critical — indeed, indispensable — space of common ground: what the guidebook to Forest Hills calls "the architecture of buried peoples," what the guidebook at Mount

Auburn called "a dread of the final judgment," and what the warden of Auburn Prison meant by telling his prisoners "he was dead, and is alive again." In this shared space of Egypt and America, of pagan and Christian, of containment and escape, of burial and resurrection, there is a pronounced thematic relay between the iconography of prisons and the iconography of cemeteries that is described by and traveled over by the figure of the mummy. There is an underlying terror to these nineteenth-century discourses of Christian resurrection, a terror that is rendered legible by their relation to Egyptomania. Egypt was a perfect fit: not only was its penal imagery drawn to shape the logic of containment, drawn to force a rationalist conversion, but, for Christians, there were some supple possibilities in Egyptian conceptions of the afterlife. In the structure of nineteenth-century American Egyptomania, prisons and cemeteries thus shared a relationship that was closely analogous, and anxiously so. Prisons were where one hoped the dead *would* come back to life. Cemeteries were where one hoped they did *not*.

These are the anxieties that are institutionalized in the fear of the mummy. The reanimated mummy is the figure of this terror par excellence; it is a body *not* contained by the tomb that is its prison. The mummy is located precisely at the intersection of these images and discourses of prisons, cemeteries, and the iconography of ancient Egypt, of the desires to contain, control, and rationalize, and the fears and fascinations of the failure to do so. Quite literally a return of the repressed of American Christian rationalism and the uncanny fear it embodies, the mummy appears precisely at the intersection of resistance to the logic of disciplinary imprisonment and uneasy fears of Christian resurrection. The mummy defies both the rationalist understandings of disciplinary imprisonment and the Christian understandings of the function of the cemetery, and its power was first put in motion by the iconography of its own origin. Its resurrection is a Christian one haunted by the limits of rationalism, its reanimation a secular one that lurches out of an ostensibly Christian tomb. The figure of an ancient Egyptian escaping from a Christian cemetery is an anxious refraction of the release of a Christian from an ancient Egyptian prison, and the social anxieties over the loss of control over the body of the prisoner once released from the ancient Egyptian prison were projected onto the disruptive figure of the ancient Egyptian mummy reanimated and run amok. The power of the mummy is a sign of the strength it took to escape from God, the Warden of Heaven.

This is the space the mummy crosses. A chronological space built around the logic of containment, a deeply ambivalent rationalism, a politically anxious historicism, and a radically unstable Christianity. The mummy arises as if it were a prisoner of the Tombs not affected by the pressures of disciplinary penitence, unaware of the distinction between the Egyptian afterlife and Christian resurrection. It uprises, this figure of Egypt, dragging itself back to the shores of America, wrapped in the costuming of American architectural revivalism, wrapped in the fraying strands of a decaying dirty whiteness. And that the image of reanimation — whether of a Christian reborn, a prisoner released, an oppressed population thought docile, or a decomposing monster thought long dead and buried — could be utilized for political ends by any number of interested parties, no matter how unlikely, would come as no surprise to Josiah Nott, racial theorist and proslavery activist. "Yes, the evil-doers are up and at work night and day," Nott wrote in the final paragraph of his 1851 *Essay on the Natural History of Mankind, Viewed in Connection with Negro Slavery,* "and it is time for us of the South to arouse from our long and chilling slumber. The spirit of Liberty, the spirit of Philanthropy, the spirit of Christianity, aye, and the ghosts of the murdered whites of St. Domingo rise up — shake their gory locks at you — and bid you, '*Sleep no more.*' "[122]

# CHAPTER FOUR

# Undressing Cleopatra

RACE, SEX, AND BODILY

INTERIORITY IN

NINETEENTH-CENTURY

AMERICAN EGYPTOMANIA

When African American lesbian sculptor Edmonia Lewis sent her large marble sculpture *The Death of Cleopatra* from Rome to Philadelphia to be shown at the Centennial International Exposition in 1876, she was staging a radical intervention. She was exhibiting her sculpture at a moment in nineteenth-century American history when the popularity of images of Cleopatra was at something of a cultural high, but clearly she had more on her mind than postbellum art fashions: she was intentionally entering into an exchange with the very notions of Cleopatra herself. In dialogue with both other contemporary American Cleopatras and the much wider range of Cleopatran images that had helped give birth to hers, Lewis's Cleopatra was both timely and historical, both a participation in a specific history and a highly visible critique of it. Not only a lesbian rewriting of the sexual politics that attended the midcentury obsession with Cleopatra and not only a racialized signification on the ethnological controversies that colored her white marble, Lewis's *Death of Cleopatra* is a primary example of the destabilizing maneuvers enacted by African Americans around representations of ancient Egypt.

As in her selection of subject, Lewis was extremely careful about her timing: she chose to sculpt and show her Cleopatra at a moment when one *other* Cleopatra had recently claimed for itself the lion's share of the attentions given to an already overcrowded Cleopatran marketplace, one that for a number of reasons would be the piece to which Lewis's sculpture would immediately be compared. This more famous piece was William Wetmore Story's monumental marble *Cleopatra*, begun in 1858 and completed in 1860, which was at the time something of a cultural phenomenon, especially in the upper-class educated white circles of New England of which Lewis was an ambivalent observer. Among other things, Story's *Cleopatra* had been presented and given a pivotal role in Nathaniel Hawthorne's 1860 novel *The Marble Faun,* and its portrayal functioned in ways not incidental to Lewis's decision: not only did Hawthorne base his novel featuring expatriate American women sculptors living in Rome before the Civil War on the very social circle of which Lewis herself was a member, and not only did he highlight the very issues of gender and gendered creativity and power that were so obviously of concern to a lesbian sculpting a figure of Cleopatra, but, perhaps most importantly, he also described the Cleopatra of his novel in a way that foregrounded the issue of race.

Both Story's sculpture and Hawthorne's treatment of it will receive greater attention below, but for now it should be enough to mark the intensity of this moment: at the Centennial Exhibition of 1876, Lewis was responding both to the famous and already allied representations of Cleopatra by Hawthorne and Story and to the related representations of the communities that supposedly produced that Cleopatra they engendered. Seizing the occasion of the American centennial, Lewis was commenting on both her immediate moment and the many like it that had preceded her and her Cleopatra; like almost all of the other makers of Cleopatran imagery, she understood that to portray the body of the infamous Egyptian queen was always already an act concerned with far more than aesthetics

Edmonia Lewis, *The Death of Cleopatra*, 1876. (Courtesy of Smithsonian American Art Museum, Gift of the Historical Society of Forest Park, Illinois.)

or history. In addition to Lewis's obvious interest in the specific moment of her exhibition, her *The Death of Cleopatra* was also an intervention into the more general dynamics of inner and outer, concealment and display, and veiling and unveiling that so widely structured nineteenth-century American signs of ancient Egypt. "The means and manner of her death," wrote one of Lewis's contemporaries of Cleopatra, "seemed to be involved in impenetrable mystery,"[1] and Lewis was reinscribing such language of layered and sexualized interiority as clearly as she was signifying on its politics of racialization.

Occupying and mobilizing as they did the spaces between representations of power, gender, sexuality, and race, what was at stake with images of Cleopatra in America throughout the nineteenth century were questions of epistemology: masculine or feminine, queen or whore, civilized or savage, Greek or Egyptian, white or black. In this context, Lewis's Cleopatra is oddly contradictory—sexually available yet beyond possessibility, obviously displayed yet apparently oblivious to her audience—and if nothing else her sculpture seems to feature these contradictions in ways that directly suggest those of her creator and her creator's context. Chief among these contradictory contexts are questions concerning Lewis's sexuality, and issues of sexual historiography—including among others the attribution of the label "lesbian" to a woman whose life largely predated the formation of that term and the various social structures it implies—will be a primary concern of this chapter.

Lewis's intervention—with its implications for material history, art history, literary history, and the politics of racial representation both before and after the Civil War—marks not only one of the most striking instances of cross-cultural intertextuality in nineteenth-century American arts and letters but also one of the most important moments in nineteenth-century American Egyptomania. From the eroticized displays of female nudes in American neoclassical sculptural traditions to the lesbian appropriations of those traditions, and from European American colonizations of the racialized figure of Cleopatra to African American resistances to them, Lewis and her sculpture stand as more than an isolated pair responding to a single event; as are those of this chapter, their eyes were on the larger history of the American Cleopatra.

# "Show Me the Veiled Figure"

The 1850s was a busy decade for the American Cleopatra. Beginning with a book-length study of her life in 1851 and encompassing at least three well-known dramatic poems; several additional smaller attempts at authoritative biographies; a high-profile issue of a premier art journal virtually dedicated to her which included articles, verses, and engravings; more than the usual retinue of references to her in periodicals and newspapers; and concluding with two of the century's most famous monumentalizations of her—one in marble and the other in the pages of a novel—the years at midcentury amply illustrate how marketable images of Cleopatra were in the nineteenth-century United States. And in this she was not lonely for upscale Egyptian company: Herman Melville's "Bartleby, the Scrivener" first appeared in 1853, as did the *Knickerbocker* cover article "Orientalism"; Nott and Gliddon's *Types of Mankind* was published at the peak of racialized Egyptological controversies in 1854, as was Frederick Douglass's reply to it—plus Gliddon had already been unrolling mummies for years; Bayard Taylor's two Egyptian travelogues arrived in 1854 and 1855, to be followed by David Dorr's *A Colored Man Round the World* in 1858; Edward Troye painted and displayed his five Holy Land paintings in the second half of the 1850s; John Banvard showed his panorama of the Holy Land continually during these ten years; and throughout the decade the monumental structures of the Egyptian Revival were at the height of their fashion. With "a mighty but vague impersonation of power, guilt, and grandeur," wrote one of her most influential nineteenth-century biographers, "Cleopatra stands before us a vivid reality combining with her historical and classical celebrity all the interest that poetry, romance, and the arts could throw around her."[2]

Even during this demonstrably vigorous phase of American Egyptomania, however, there was a precise and specific dialogicism to the appearances made by the most infamous of Egyptian queens. This is visible both in visual culture and in print: beginning with the British feminist Anna Jameson's famous *Memoirs of Celebrated Female Sovereigns*, which appeared in the United States in 1842, midcentury studies of Cleopatra usually appeared as biographies. "There have been five or six Cleopatras conspicuous in the dynasties of Egypt and Syria, either for their crimes or their misfortunes," wrote Jameson, "but Fame seems to acknowledge but one, and with her celebrity has filled the world. As a woman, she can scarcely be said to claim either our sympathy or our respect; as a sovereign, she neither achieved great exploits nor great conquests, nor left behind her any magnificent or enduring monuments of her power—but she has left behind a *name*, which still acts as a spell upon the fancy."[3] As its title implies, Jameson's account of Cleopatra appears as a chapter in her two-volume study of "Celebrated Female Sovereigns," and in this can be seen the first of many examples of the careful eyes which biographers of the queen kept on one another.

American historian Jacob Abbott published a more conventionally structured book-length biography, *The History of Cleopatra*, in 1851, but at least three other nineteenth-century biographers included their chronicles of Cleopatra in much larger collections of writings on famous or powerful women explicitly modeled after Jameson's *Memoirs* and explicitly aimed at a female readership: Sarah Josepha Hale's 1853 *Woman's Record*, Mary Cowden Clarke's 1857 *Well-Noted Women*, and Lydia Hoyt Farmer's 1887 *Girl's Book of Famous Queens*.[4] This approach was itself based on texts that in the nineteenth century were understood to be most authoritative accounts of the life and death of Cleopatra, the *Julius Caesar* and *Life of Antony* of Plutarch and Boccaccio's *De Claris Mulieribus* of 1362, which plainly served as a model for Jameson's collection and thus indirectly for those that followed it.[5] Indeed, this structure of indebtedness was usually written directly on the page; virtually all the nineteenth-century accounts borrow liberally from their earlier sources, at times quoting directly, but often loosely paraphrasing or even outright plagiarizing. Anecdotes from Plutarch's *Antony*, passages from Boccaccio's *De Claris*, scenes from Shakespeare's *Antony and Cleopatra*, even lines from their own contemporaries: Cleopatra's nineteenth-century biographers freely wove threads from a variety of sources in order to clothe—or unclothe—their queen.

The effect of these influences was that, along with what they at times understood to be unproblematic facts, these nineteenth-century writers could not help but base many of their conceptual structures on those of their source materials. But by no means did this result in a homogeneity of Cleopatran imagery in America; rather, it created a field of representational references from which individual authors could piece together a variety of associations. Cleopatra was perfectly suited for the conveyance of mixed messages. Certain issues, writes Mary Hamer, "continued to crystallize around the figure of Cleopatra and [were] variously inflected and renegotiated."[6] Having said this, however, for the American readers of her nineteenth-century biographies there was a more or less discernible canon of representational moments around which the images of Cleopatra were grouped; principal among these were her seduction of Caesar, her corruption of Antony, and her death by suicide.[7] "Cleopatra: The Queen, the Mistress, the Suicide," advertised her 1858 biography as its title; Cleopatra's life was now reduced to a three-part structure built on power, sex, and death.[8]

All three of these will be of concern to me here. Throughout this chapter, I will dwell on the details of the state of Cleopatra's wardrobe and the status of her undress during this period in American cultural history, and I will do so for a number of reasons: first, to refresh our memories as to the centrality of representations of Cleopatra in the midcentury cultural wars being fought over the appropriateness of the nude female form in the marketplace of nineteenth-century American artistic production; second, to clarify the extent to which the status of being partially clothed was a critical feature of the whole host of nineteenth-century productions of the Cleopatra image; third, crucially, to emphasize the extent to which that state of partial clothing was altogether framed both by the inheritance of Plutarch's story of Cleopatra's emergence from her secret hiding place before Caesar and by the long tradition of imagining that emergence as gradually involving fewer and fewer clothes; and, finally, to fully thematize what is the central concern of this chapter: that of the implications of this extended striptease, of these patterns of layering and interiority, of the cultural logic of inner and outer that they describe, of the relationship between revelation and rape and the ancient past, of chronology and gender and sexuality and race, of undressing Cleopatra.

Gradually, over the course of the nineteenth century, Cleopatra's emergence from the carpet becomes an archaeological striptease, as she eventually emerges not just from the folds of history, not just from the folds of her fabricked hiding place, but from the folds of all of her clothing as well, finally shorn of all protection and displayed as an offering to all who care to look. Even the epiphanic revelation of the figure of Cleopatra in Hawthorne's The Marble Faun is structured by a kind of collaborative striptease between art, artist, and audience:

> "My new statue!" said Kenyon. . . . "Here it is, under this veil." . . .
> "Be it so!" said Miriam. . . . "Show me the veiled figure. . . ."
> But, as Kenyon was about to take the cloth off the clay-model, she laid her hand on his arm.

"Tell me first what is the subject," said she. . . .

He drew away the cloth, that had served to keep the moisture of the clay-model from being exhaled. The sitting figure of a woman was seen. She was draped from head to foot in a costume, minutely and scrupulously studied from that of ancient Egypt, as revealed by the strange sculpture of that country, its coins, drawings, painted mummy-cases, and whatever other tokens have been dug out of its pyramids, graves, and catacombs. Even the stiff Egyptian head-dress was adhered to, but had been softened into a rich feminine adornment, without losing a particle of its truth.[9]

It is this bifurcated image—queen Cleopatra as slave under the gaze, part neoclassical ideal and part Orientalist abjection—that can be seen in the whiteness of her carved marble flesh, and in the marble folds of cloth sculpted to reveal it, one breast in and one breast out.

For twentieth-century scholars of the queen, however, this tradition of representation approaches a primal scene of historical distortion, especially and most importantly on the stage of her suicide; even though in the earliest and most authoritative accounts of her life she is explicitly rendered as fully and richly clothed at the moment of her death, Cleopatra forever after is quickly stripped bare. "Plutarch clearly states that the Egyptian queen dressed herself for death," writes Lucy Hughes-Hallett, "donning her crown and all her royal robes. . . . It is all the more remarkable, then, that of the scores of representations of Cleopatra's death in painting and sculpture the overwhelming majority show her more or less naked."[10] As demonstrated by the most recent analyses and the collections of images that reinforce them, the cohesion of this iconography is one of the primary stories in the life of Cleopatra.[11] This insistent stripping has long been one of the hallmarks of Cleopatran imagery, and it is my argument here that such historical liberties played an important role in the constructions of race, gender, and sexuality in nineteenth-century America.

In addition to refreshing our memories as to some of the central visual issues at stake in the cultural life of the American Cleopatra, however, I also rehearse the details of what are probably, to most viewers, a familiar set of images for three further reasons. The first is to signal the complicated range of cultural responses to such a regularly sexualized image as Cleopatra's breasts. Apart from the odalisque, which was also closely associated with the trope of Cleopatra, the juxtaposition of bared breasts and serpentine death was the clearest and most common indicator that an artist was creating a Cleopatra. As Hughes-Hallett summarizes: "Cleopatra, nude or at best in *déshabillé*, exposes her upper torso to the viewer, while an asp writhes across her milk-white breasts to bury its fangs in her nipple."[12] As virtually every recent study of the iconography of the queen indicates, this anachronistic image produced the final, if irregular, consolidation of Cleopatran iconography. "It is not difficult to see how a primary commitment to constituting the image of Cleopatra as the site of the most pleasurable looking at a woman might produce this bare-breasted queen," writes Hamer. "The visibility of the breasts indicates the satisfaction of the look of knowledge that penetrates below the surface to the true nature of things. . . . To show it exposed is to indicate that the eye has mastered the knowledge of woman."[13]

Hamer's language here is telling; her equation of nudity with an epistemology of knowledge — specifically gendered, acutely sexualized — has implications for this entire chapter. "Between the threat and the domination of the unknown," writes Inderpal Grewal, "transparency, as the visibility of what lay underneath, or the matching of surface with depth, became an important cause of beauty in the nineteenth century. . . . The desire for transparency was clearly visible in conceptualizations of women, in which the supposed opacity of female nature was to be understood."[14] Obviously there are connections to the widespread cultural legitimacy associated with what Anne McClintock has called the "anxious vision mark[ing] one aspect . . . of a recurrent doubling in male imperial discourse," but where my analysis will eventually take us is to some much more specifically institutionalized forms of what Michel Foucault calls the combination of "the privileges of a pure gaze . . . and those of a gaze equipped with a whole logical armature": the medical table, the anatomical chart, the operating theater, the speculum.[15]

Second, I mark these moments of historical continuity to emphasize that throughout her long life as an icon, central to representations of Cleopatra was a highly visible and self-conscious tradition of willful reframing in regard to the so-called "facts" of her life. Whether stripping her naked or applying the asp to her nipple or painting her as an eighteenth-century British noblewoman, a pronounced willingness to generously manipulate the iconography of Cleopatra marks her entire history. Moreover, as we will see, this iconographic flexibility places her at the center of a certain type of representational praxis that valued such appropriability, especially in a woman. The appropriations of Cleopatra seen in the nineteenth century were at no point unfamiliar to her; far from it. But while it does seem clear that this is the case, it is also my claim that the ease with which Cleopatran imagery was so freely interpreted in the nineteenth century did not by any means release representations of the Egyptian queen from tension, conflict, or the possibilities of political scandal; quite the opposite. That Cleopatra was prone to be seen as a bit of a slut—even in regard to her own imagery—made her perfect for inclusion in the explosive debates over her character that so concerned the nineteenth century. Plainly visible, whether clothed or unclothed, the body of Cleopatra was a battlefield.

Third, all of this is to reaffirm what has been obvious for almost two hundred years: that there was a pronounced sexualization of the tropes of dressing and undressing associated with traditions of neoclassical representation—not merely in the "surface" sense of the erotics of the displays of naked marble flesh but also in the more comprehensive sense of a widespread politics of gender and sexuality. But it is also my assertion that in addition to this sexualization there was an inescapable politics of race at work as well. Specifically, I read the cultural logics of drapery and disrobing as a primary site for the elaboration of discourses of interiority in the nineteenth century: as a form of theoretical investigation into what lies within; into what, if anything, was contained within the folds of flesh and its metaphors; and where, if anywhere, a critical gaze might be arrested. Perhaps, like the sexual elements of such interest in neoclassical figuration, this is obvious enough; but that this logic of interiority was irreducibly imbricated with contemporaneous constructions of race, gender, and sexuality perhaps is not. Such a logic was based on the tensions and exchanges between connotations of whiteness and connotations of blackness and was thus as much an erotics of racialized display as of anything else. "Thus perished the famous Cleopatra," Farmer would write at the close of her biography, in language drawn equally from that of feminist empowerment, moralistic disdain, and racialized fantasy, "whose marvellous attractions and enchanting fascinations of beauty and unequalled display of pomp and royal magnificence make parts of her story to read like the wonderful tales of the Arabian Nights, but whose selfish ambition, treachery, and sins shrouded her last terrible end in the impenetrable blackness of hopeless despair."[16] Whiteness and blackness are veiled and unveiled, just like Cleopatra's breasts; they are signs of abjection, empowerment, disgust, and allurement, just like Cleopatra.

And that Cleopatra was undressed during one of the most complicated moments in the long history of models of surface and depth should be increasingly clear: dramas of interiority were one of the watershed developments of the nineteenth century. "It is surely subjectivity and interiority which are the notions latest acquired by the human mind,"[17] wrote William James at the end of the century, and it is in part the argument of this book that the network of cultural attitudes and productions here grouped under the heading of American Egyptomania existed in an intimate and critical relationship with equally widespread technologies of interiority. "The gaze plunges into the space that it has given itself the task of traversing," writes Foucault of the rise of pathological anatomy at the turn of the nineteenth century. "The medical gaze must therefore travel along a path that had not so far been opened to it: vertically from the symptomatic surface to the tissual surface; in depth, plunging from the manifest to the hidden."[18]

More to the point, that the overlapping iconographies of Orientalism and Egyptomania occupied critical roles in these dramas should be at least provisionally clear. "In the Westerner's view," writes Malini Johar Schueller, summarizing a certain reading of Edward Said, "the Orient always invites penetration and insemination."[19] And even though much of the hope of this chapter is that it draws some critical attention to the implicit heteronormativity that attends the history of much of the theorization of such structures of interiority—"such metaphors for the West's appropriation of the East are at least implicitly heterosexual," writes Joseph A. Boone, and "Said's failure to account for homoerotic elements in Orientalist pursuits is a telling omission"[20]—it is nevertheless my contention that in figures like Edmonia Lewis, if not in the structures of Egyptomania in general, the shapes of racialized interiority refract across sexualities even as they do across themselves. From narratives of descents into Egyptian tombs to the rise of biology and its interiorized investigations, stagings of the slow unraveling of layer after layer of the wrappings of mummies, and the relationship race science had to the field of gynecology, what Egyptomania offers to the study of the cultural history of the nineteenth century is a framework for understanding the connections between these divergent manifestations of interiority and of the combinations of fascination and panic that were their hallmark.

What follows, then, in the rest of this chapter, is an argument about the American Cleopatra and the ways in which in the nineteenth century she operated as a multilayered sign of social danger and cultural transgression, primarily through her construction as a figure of racial ambiguity and sexual deviance. More specifically, I am interested here in the ways in which the figure of Cleopatra worked, on the one hand, as a radically disruptive and irreducibly irruptive figure, a highly visible and hotly contested prize for warring epistemologies, and, on the other, as an oddly regulatory one as well, a figure that derived an enormous amount of directive power from the very rebellious role that might otherwise be understood to counter-mand such a stable state of affairs. In other words, it was because the figure of Cleopatra was so unstable that it found itself having such remarkable stability in the fickle fashions of nineteenth-century American culture; be-cause she was so dangerous, she found herself curiously safe. Safe from what, of course, is a crucial question—and safety is a relative thing; though her life as an American icon was marked by some of the most violent social struggles of the nineteenth century, she was, put most plainly, safe from all but her own hand.

As should be suspected, the argument of this chapter is somewhat pro-tracted and the company it keeps often quite mixed. Overall, however, there is a pronounced concern to understand the trope of undressing as racialized, in a number of ways—primarily as a site for the negotiation of racial identity—and throughout my argument I give continual attention to the ways in which the tropes of veiling and unveiling map against those of racial identification, both in the sense of self-identification and in the sense of detection of the Other. Indeed, the erotics of detecting any num-ber of things on or about Cleopatra were critical to her continuing fame as a figure of wonder and warning, and it is with the overlapping glances of sexual ambivalence and ethnographic anxiety that this chapter is most concerned. The ongoing roles for the nineteenth-century American Cleo-patra were alternately those of criminal, role model, cautionary tale, and case study, and throughout her lifetime she proved enormously useful as a hybridized sign of provocative interiority—enigmatic mystery, *vagina den-tata*, veiled Orientalism, gynecological specimen. The racial identity of the American Cleopatra was concealed and revealed as often as her breasts; in her status as a figure of racial ambiguity, social deviation, and sexual inversion, Cleopatra is regularly examined, repetitively pathologized, and repeatedly undressed.

## "You Are Looking, My Dear Friend, on an *African* Queen"

The entire history of the figure of Cleopatra in nineteenth-century American culture is shot through with racialized controversy. Claims, counterclaims, and other territorial disputes were lodged throughout the century over the racial identity of Egypt's most famous queen. "Was Cleopatra a negress?" asked an outraged ethnologist in 1868. "Impossible! The refined, delicate, beautiful and fascinating Queen of Egypt a black negress? If so, is it not passing strange and unnatural that she should have captivated and held in thrall the noble, literary, and *epicurean* Mark Antony—a descendant of Japheth? Impossible! Were all the great, the rich and noble of Egypt, negroes? The millions of mummies lately exhumed and exposed to view 'give the lie to the base slander.' " [21] This tract—a proslavery scientific treatise deeply embroiled in the Egyptological debates of the 1850s and 1860s—was unusual neither in its conclusions nor in the terms of its assumptions. "Cleopatra was, as you know, a Greek by blood," wrote an angry art patron in 1890; "although an Egyptian queen, she was not of the Egyptian race. . . . While she may have worn royal Egyptian robes, she herself, physically, must have possessed all the characteristics of the Aryan— at least a *white* skin, and, possibly, blue eyes and golden hair." [22]

In 1887, Lydia Hoyt Farmer asked the question that forever seemed to be on everyone's mind: "Why is Cleopatra so fair of skin, though an Egyptian by birth?" Her answer drew on the virtually automatic associations among aesthetic convention, civilizationist historiography, and hierarchical race theory which the very terms of her question had already secured: "Though Egypt was her birthplace, Grecian blood flows through her veins, and whitens her skin, lightens the dusky shadows in her hair, and gives the brown shadings to her lustrous eyes. Grecian culture gives her voice its oft-narrated magic charm of melting sweetness; and a spark of Grecian genius quickens her powers of mind, and gives her the enchanting fascination of brilliant wit, and a native aptitude of acquiring knowledge, and all the polite arts and sciences." [23] In short, in this mode of Cleopatran representation, all of her traits American race theory associated with whiteness—art, science, knowledge, wit, and, pointedly, "culture" itself—were indebted to Cleopatra's "Grecian blood"; all of those it associated with something else were not. "Cleopatra was by birth an Egyptian; by ancestry and descent she was a Greek," wrote Abbott in a passage Farmer made it a point to quote.

"Thus, while Alexandria and the delta of the Nile formed the scene of the most important events and incidents of her history, it was the blood of Macedon which flowed in her veins. Her character and action are marked by the genius, the courage, the originality, and the impulsiveness pertaining to the stock from which she sprung." [24]

The implications are clear: if Cleopatra was not claimed as directly descended from members of the "higher" racial categories developed during the nineteenth century, then the rest of her mythology would be implicated as well. Her role as a black seductress would malign all those seduced by her, and her status as an archetype of Egyptian civilization would impugn all that which was said to have been descended from it. "Thus, day by day, as Egyptology advances," wrote George Robins Gliddon in 1857, proceeding from the assumption that the original, racially inferior inhabitants of Egypt were inevitably conquered later by superior Caucasians and Greeks, "we discover that many of the scientific, theological, and philosophical notions attributed to the simple and practical denizens of the Nile, are the posterior creations of Graeco-Judaico-Roman intellects at Alexandria." [25] The angry art patron was more direct in his demands: "give us the Queen in all the splendor of Aryan beauty!" [26]

Yet the interrelation and radical interdependency of two terms—race and sexuality—would remain a central and unresolved aspect of Cleopatra's mythology, for her defenders as well as for her accusers, throughout the century. "It was no pretty Greek beauty that worked such havoc with such men as those," wrote Edward Everett Hale in 1861. "The little jet of Greek blood, which Ptolemy brought into this dynasty three centuries ago, is only the smallest fraction of this Egyptian's life. . . . A line of Egyptian mothers for ten generations have made her wholly Egyptian—in this raring hot blood of hers; in this passionate temper; and in the whole quality, even, of her mind." [27] Farmer presented the same view, only pointedly reversed in its racial politics. "The agile litheness of the Greek is combined with the oriental voluptuous indolence of the Egyptian," Farmer wrote, "which combination explains the otherwise unaccountable allurements of face and form which history, romance, and poetry have accorded her." [28] The nineteenth-century American Cleopatra thus appears immediately as a sign of that most characteristic of her country's ongoing anxieties: racial ambivalence.

This, then, emerged as the central problematic of Cleopatran interpretation: in her whiteness, she would tend to be associated with purity and taintlessness, yet in her famous role as sexual predator and oversexed seductress she would tend to invoke racist images of the wantonness and licentiousness of nonwhite women and especially all the sexualized stereotypes of African American women under slavery. For African Americans, then, Cleopatra presented a particular problem: to admit her to the family of black Americans without qualification would be to invite imputations of the very sexual stereotypes antiracist activists were desperately trying to avoid. This problematic was recognized by both black and white Americans; rarely were African Americans or other problack artists of any color given the opportunity to represent the sexually predatory Cleopatra with even the slightest hint of blackness, and only a few would take it. "I will barely allude to the beautiful Cleopatra," wrote the redoubtable black nationalist Henry Highland Garnet in the pages of The North Star in 1848, "who swayed and captivated the heart of Anthony." [29]

Garnet's delicate skirting of the question of the role of Cleopatra in African American history was almost typical of black intellectuals of the period. Reticent, perhaps, of wholeheartedly embracing as an African a figure who was unavoidably linked with her rampant sexuality, Garnet instead conspicuously juxtaposes Cleopatra with another famous African queen, Sheba, and publicly affirms Cleopatra's racial heritage while deftly sidestepping the issue of black sexuality. "Solomon's most favored queen," Garnet writes, "was the beautiful sable daughter of one of the Pharaohs of Egypt. . . . Solomon was a poet, and pure love awakened the sweetest melody in his soul." [30] Such idealized things could hardly be said about Cleopatra, and, as Garnet's hesitance to do so suggests, few nineteenth-century black artists wanted to run the risk of undressing Cleopatra. The exception would be Edmonia Lewis, and her choice to leave Cleopatra exhausted and dead, and even she would surprise her viewers with her depiction of Cleopatra's race.

At her every appearance in black arts and letters, evidence is present of the ambivalence Cleopatra had for nineteenth-century African Americans, and her identity is shaped by these conflicting desires of embracing her blackness while distancing her sexuality. "Dr. Lord's 'Great Women' opens with 'Cleopatra,' a very interesting sketch," wrote Charlotte Forten Grimké somewhat delicately in 1888 of a review of the very sculpture to which Lewis had responded ten years earlier. "He has taken great pains to inform us that she had no Negro blood & that Story has made a mistake in giving to his statue the African features. If I may venture to criticise—there seems to me a little too much repetition in these lectures of Dr. Lord's."[31] Likewise, Anna Julia Cooper's portrayal of Edmonia Lewis partakes of the same mix of racialized pride and sexualized ambivalence that framed the sculptor's most famous piece. "From her studio in Rome Edmonia Lewis the colored sculptress continues to increase the debt of the world to her," Cooper wrote in 1892, using the language of late-century propriety, "by her graceful thoughts in the chaste marble."[32] With the mixed-race status she regularly claimed in her nineteenth-century American imaginings, Cleopatra was thus for black folks much less related to the sprawlingly eroticized nudes of Hiram Powers and international Orientalism and much more kin to the most famous of nineteenth-century American mulatta suicides, William Wells Brown's Clotel. "Why does she die?" Robert Reid-Pharr asks of Clotel, and while obviously no one then or now could seriously maintain that the body of Cleopatra was "pristine" or that it partook of many of the other logics of sexual purity Brown embodied in Clotel, fewer, I think, would disagree with Reid-Pharr's final conclusion, or its applicability to the dilemma of Edmonia Lewis. "The mulatto's dead body [w]as the site of calamity," Reid-Pharr writes. "The promise of America is finished, dead at the feet of constantly warring and inevitably homicidal racial combatants."[33]

White folks, meanwhile, were only too eager to look for the signs of the black Cleopatra, and to make them into the signs of sex: "So she sits there," wrote Hale of Story's *Cleopatra*; "not a pretty girl, with a girl's form and features, but a woman,—who has done all this and been all this,—with a woman's figure and woman's beauty. And do you remember,—that she is an African woman? . . . You are looking, my dear friend, on an *African* queen."[34] As Hale makes clear, it was this Africanness to which both William Wetmore Story and Nathaniel Hawthorne owed the notoriety of their midcentury Cleopatras. "The face was a miraculous success," writes Hawthorne in the chapter of *The Marble Faun* entitled "Cleopatra." "The sculptor had not shunned to give the full Nubian lips, and other characteristics of the Egyptian physiognomy. His courage and integrity had been abundantly rewarded; for Cleopatra's beauty shone out richer, warmer, more triumphantly, beyond comparison, than if, shrinking timidly from the truth, he had chosen the tame Grecian type. . . . In a word, all Cleopatra—fierce, voluptuous, passionate, tender, wicked, terrible, and full of poisonous and rapturous enchantment—was kneaded into what, only a week or two before, had been a lump of wet clay from the Tiber."[35]

The mutually beneficial relationship among Hawthorne, Story, and the statue they both created in the late 1850s and early 1860s was a crucial one in the history of the nineteenth-century American Cleopatra. "The Cleopatra," wrote Henry James of Story's sculpture, "ranks as one of the happy children, creatures of inspiration and prosperity," and, forty years later, it was even "a little uncertain" to one critic "whether it was Story or Hawthorne who made the Cleopatra."[36] Joy Kasson explains the appeal: "In the subject of the meditative queen, the powerful woman rendered powerless, Story had a fruitful theme, one he would pursue throughout his career. . . . The melancholy Cleopatra is the dark lady tamed, constrained, neutralized."[37]

The figure of Cleopatra was in fact something of a life's work for Story, and his career offers a case study in her profitability. Story would sculpt monumental marble figures of Cleopatra a total of three times during his working life, carve at least four copies of two of them, write his most famous poem about her, and write another, less known but equally telling, poem about an artist who becomes erotically involved with a model posing for his painting of Cleopatra.[38] Hawthorne and Story seized on the racially charged scandals they both knew—or no doubt at least hoped—would converge on them as a result of their de facto collaboration; the attention paid to Story's Cleopatra traveled precisely along what he was finding to be the enormously generative intersecting lines of race and sexuality, and Hawthorne's presentation of his sculpted Egyptian queen cannily featured just those aspects that were guaranteed to capitalize on them. Cleopatra was to be for Hawthorne and Story the best kind of Negro of all: almost nude, almost white, almost tamed, almost irresistible, almost punished, almost dead, completely silent, and very much for sale.

Given the nexus of interests and attitudes toward powerful women so dominant in the expatriate circles of American artists in Rome, it is perhaps not surprising that at the center of Hawthorne's novel should sit Cleopatra. Countless commentators have engaged Hawthorne's use in The Marble Faun of the characters of Miriam and Hilda, of what Charles Swann calls "that old nineteenth-century chestnut, dark and blonde heroines,"[39] but it is Inderpal Grewal, especially, who points to the role such a binary division played in the nineteenth-century metaphysics of race.[40] Hawthorne's inclusion of Story's Cleopatra is as revealing as anything provided during this period relative to these metaphysics of race: in a novel structured around

William Wetmore Story, *Cleopatra*, 1858. (Courtesy of Los Angeles County Museum of Art, Gift of Mr. and Mrs. Henry M. Bateman.)

the dynamics of the white lady and the dark lady, Cleopatra is both white and black, a "Nubian queen" sculpted in white marble and an African type rendered so delicately that today she barely passes as black.

Miriam's relation to Cleopatra in the novel makes explicit their shared status as racially liminal figures, if not their status as sexually dangerous and powerful. "Kenyon sculpts his Cleopatra in a 'repose of despair,' but Miriam is that despairing Cleopatra," writes Nancy Bentley, "like that statue, an aesthetic object representing tragic 'womanhood.' "[41] Indeed, Miriam exists in the same racialized no-man's-land that Cleopatra herself often did, oscillating visibly between various categories of antique racial types: Jewish, Oriental, African, white. "It was said, for example," wrote Hawthorne in one of the novel's most famous passages, "that Miriam was the daughter and heiress of a great Jewish banker (an idea perhaps suggested by a certain rich Oriental character in her face). Another story hinted that she was a German princess. . . . According to a third statement, she was the offspring of a Southern American planter, who had given her an elaborate education and endowed her with his wealth; but the one burning drop of African blood in her veins so affected her with a sense of ignominy, that she relinquished all, and fled her country."[42] This language of the sexually charged racially suspect ambivalently erotic object was familiar to the American Cleopatra. "*The Marble Faun* is a *discordia concors* of race and fable," writes Bentley, and more than either Miriam or the faun itself it is Hawthorne's Cleopatra who represents these discordant elements trapped in one body.[43]

Hawthorne's inclusion of Story's *Cleopatra* reveals not only the extent to which his white lady/dark lady novel is indebted to an imperialist metaphysics of race but, more, the extent to which such a metaphysics relied on a third term to calibrate the other two—one that is both white *and* black, and yet neither.[44] "The mulatto's body operates not as the refutation of racial distinctiveness but as its proof," writes Reid-Pharr. "She was the true hybrid, the third subject whose presence refracted the purity of her antecedents, the black and the white."[45] And in the sexual politics of *The Marble Faun* this term is critical in stabilizing the sexual limits of the two "ladies" as well—whether white, black, neither, or both, the figure of Cleopatra had a sexual identity that proscribed an erotic boundary over which neither Miriam nor Hilda would ever dare cross. "A marvellous repose . . . was diffused throughout the figure," writes Hawthorne of the statue of Cleopatra. "But still there was a great, smouldering furnace, deep down in the woman's heart. The repose, no doubt, was as complete as if she were never to stir hand or foot again; and yet, such was the creature's latent energy and fierceness, she might spring upon you like a tigress, and stop the very breath that you were not drawing, midway in your throat."[46] Thus Cleopatra sits like an erotic sentinel in the racialized metaphorics of Hawthorne's light and dark, marking a racial and sexual extreme that his nineteenth-century Americans could always point to in fascinated relief.[47]

It was precisely this racialized scandal that marked Story's sculpture itself. "I have often wondered why so learned and classical a man as Story should have given to his queen, in his famous statue, such thick lips and African features," complained American art critic John Lord in 1886. "There was nothing African about her."[48] And to be sure, Story was too invested in the blackness of his *Cleopatra*—among other things, for the celebrity it brought him in what was after all a busy season for Cleopatras—to let anyone forget it. "You make it out," Story raged back, "that even in my sculpture I take at 2nd hand and blunder into imagining Cleopatra an Egyptian. . . . You might, had you not set it down in your mind that I was an ignoramus, have supposed that I had some reason to believe Cleop. to be Egyptian before I undertook to make her so."[49] Clearly, Story is used to such criticism and directs his anger not only toward defending his own beliefs but toward attacking what he considers to be the rehearsed repetition of a baseless identification of Cleopatra as Greek. "Pray may I ask you," he sarcastically implores, "when you do fault me for making Cleopatra an Egyptian—what you suppose her to have been? You will answer I doubt not, very glibly, as you do in this Review that she was a Greek & one of the Ptolemies. Do you know that the legitimate branch of the Ptolemies was extinct when her father was taken to the Throne from Syria? Who was his mother—for the matter of that is it even clear who was his father—Who again was the mother of Cleopatra—was she not an Egyptian? I should recommend you to clear up your mind on this question before you attack others for ignorance."[50] Story places his Cleopatra at the center of ethnological controversies and understands one to be undifferentiated from the other.

And thus the cultural logic of the figure of ancient Egypt: one foot in the world of Greco-Roman neoclassicism, one foot in Orientalized Africa. Thus an ancient Egyptian queen appears in the landscape of nineteenth-century Rome. And, in point of fact, it is critical to remember that Hawthorne's Cleopatra is not at all historicized in her presentation, not a historical reference to a political or even sexual alliance between Egypt and Rome or between Antony or Caesar and the queen. Rather, she functions, in her Nubian way, to illustrate the essential differences between "the Egyptian physiognomy" and "the tame Grecian type." "You have the same old story of Africa," pronounced Hale of this Cleopatra, "always outwitted by Asia, always outfought by Europe. . . . She is not a Greek but an Egyptian; and if you will consent that Egypt shall typify Africa for you, you may make this the symbol of Africa's despair."[51] She is an ahistorical animalistic essence, transported to Kenyon's studio in spite of history, not because of it.[52]

Admittedly, however, the Africanness of the African queen was often distinctly indistinct. The racial codes of nineteenth-century American aesthetics were such that very little effort was in fact needed to suggest African character, Negro physiognomy, or black identity. "It is something of a surprise," writes Hamer of her reaction to reading *The Marble Faun* in the 1990s, "to find that the race assigned to Cleopatra is to be understood as Nubian."[53] And, while quaint, Hamer's bewilderment at the eagerness of nineteenth-century viewers "to look out for and interpret the signs of race" is nevertheless indicative of something important: the ease with which even a hint of blackness was seen as a scandal for Cleopatra. "The difficulty," notes Reid-Pharr, "is one of perception. The mulatto in America, no matter how cultured or 'white,' might always be returned to a black default status."[54] Rarely if ever was Cleopatra represented with the racial signifiers associated with "full-blooded negroid" types associated with related visual fields such as ethnology—and, indeed, the conventions of neoclassical sculptural traditions precluded it almost entirely—yet, as a sign of racial instability, sexual promiscuity, and possible miscegenation, she was always under suspicion.

And with suspicion came an avalanche of evidence. Even the merest hint of scandalous "Africanness" was enough to provide nineteenth-century Americans with the opportunity to pour out their racialized fantasies onto the body of Cleopatra. "The contemporaries of Cleopatra could not make this statue," wrote Hale. "Nor has any age till ours considered this constant tragedy of Africa: slave either of Asia's wisdom or of Europe's force."[55] What made Story's first Cleopatra and its appearance in *The Marble Faun* so racially marked, then, were not merely her racial markings. It was not a sudden and shocking innovation into the traditions of nineteenth-century Cleopatran representation. Quite the opposite; rather, it was the overt representation of what had been salaciously hinted at and suggestively gossiped about for years and what, when first presented, allowed for the immediate projection of a whole range of nineteenth-century American racialized fantasies and stereotypes. This 1860 *Cleopatra* was the moment when Cleopatra first came out of the racialized closet.

## Cleopatra: Plantation Mistress

To put it mildly, representations of Cleopatra—as seductress, compulsive spender, or monstrous mother—placed the Egyptian queen at the epicenter of nineteenth-century arguments over "female nature" and American women's roles. Hamer writes of how the figure of Cleopatra was used both in first-century Rome and in Renaissance Europe as a way of symbolizing the dangers of social upheaval—specifically, of those involving changes in the roles and status of women during these periods—and in ways strikingly similar, in the middle of the nineteenth century, the American Cleopatra appears as a figure of gender trouble. "The figure of Cleopatra VII," writes Hamer, "combining in one person a challenge to the public rule of the male and the domestic control of the husband, could not be anything but problematic."[56] This "problem" was named with none too fine a point by Jacob Abbott. "There is a law of nature, in the form of an instinct universal in the race," wrote Abbott while discussing Cleopatra and Antony, "imperiously enjoining that the connection of the sexes shall consist of the union of one man with one woman, and that woman his wife, and very sternly prohibiting every other."[57]

Still, however, what marks nineteenth-century America's queen as distinct from earlier aspects is the rise of Cleopatra as a signifier of race. As a figure of racialized controversy, she would emerge over the century as a figure of dangerously ambivalent and embattled racial status, her earlier dangerousnesses folding over and over again into her newer role as a sign of racial upheaval. To be sure, Cleopatra's ascension to the throne of racial instability was of a piece with the rise of racialization in general—she could hardly have been denigrated as a "mulatta," as she is in Charlotte Brontë's 1853 *Vilette*, before that term carried the charge it did only in the nineteenth century—but it is nevertheless crucial to mark these transitions as mutually supported. Moreover, it is also crucial to understand the rise of racialization as something like a revolution in representations of Cleopatra; other discourses that had so long been attendant to her dangerous ambiguities found their most powerful ally in centuries. What before had been "merely" sexual—assuming such a thing ever existed—could now be understood as racial as well; Cleopatra was not merely a seductress but now an Orientalized one, and the traditions of Otherness that almost four hundred years earlier had informed Boccaccio's use of the phrase "scortum orientalium regum," "the whore of the Oriental kings," were given new life.

The impact of racialization on American representations of Cleopatra was so far-reaching that it became, in effect, the dominant discourse in the tradition. Discussions regarding the physical appearance of the Egyptian queen no longer merely had to include a consideration of her family, national, or ethnic background as a subset of a larger discussion; rather, such concerns leapt immediately to the fore, and questions of Cleopatra's beauty—and therefore, of course, of her sexual magnetism—had to deal with the question of her race *first* and not later. Preracial fascinations with the body and life of Cleopatra set the stage for the radically racialized nineteenth century and converged on a figure already well known for her openness to scandal. So transformative was the arrival of racialization to older traditions of Cleopatran interpretation that they produced Cleopatra as one of the most visible examples of the irreducibly interrelated networks of race, gender, and sexuality to emerge in the nineteenth century.

So fraught with conflict was her shifting status as absolutely white or absolutely not, in fact, that not only would Cleopatra herself often appear as racially unstable but equally often the stains of racial controversy would spill over onto anybody who stood nearby. Consider the figure of Apollodorus, a critical figure in a critical scene in the life of the queen to be discussed at greater length in a moment. "Cleopatra," wrote Plutarch, took "only one of her friends with her, Apollodorus the Sicilian. . . . Apollodorus . . . carried [her] indoors to Caesar."[58] In the earliest of accounts, the figure by whose physical power Cleopatra gains entry into Caesar's presence is a Sicilian and a friend: τῶν φίλων Ἀπολλόδωρον τὸν Σικελιώτην, Plutarch's original Greek reads, "her friend Apollodorus the Sicilian."[59] Likewise, "the incident is quaintly related in North's Plutarch," writes the British Mary Clarke in her 1857 account of Cleopatra published in the United States, quoting her countryman Sir Thomas North's translation of the original Greek: "she, only taking Apollodorus of all her friends . . . laid herself down upon a mattress . . . which Apollodorus, her friend, tied and bound up together like a bundle."[60] Clarke is rewriting Anna Jameson's earlier version, however, in which Cleopatra "procured the assistance of a chamberlain named Apollodorus,"[61] and, by 1851 Jacob Abbott was writing that "the man on whom she principally relied in this hazardous expedition was a domestic named Apollodorus."[62] Sarah Hale, in her 1853 version, cements the sediment: "she caused herself to be tied up in her bedding and carried to Caesar's apartment," Hale writes of Cleopatra, "on the back of one of her slaves."[63]

By 1887, Apollodorus is monumentally a Negro. In an illustration in Farmer's *The Girl's Book of Famous Queens*, "Cleopatra Carried into Caesar's Palace," Cleopatra's slave is almost entirely the subject of the engraving, his body as animalistic as the stone lions between his legs. Visibly racist traditions of representing black physiognomy are so much a figure of the character that his grotesquely rendered body massively fills the frame; Cleopatra is almost hard to find, hidden in shadow yet borne along in her whiteness. Farmer's Apollodorus is a racialized grotesque, what Leonard Cassuto has called "the anomalous embodiment of cultural anxiety" and partaking of "a peculiar disruptive power . . . a mixture of signals that intrudes upon the desired order of the world."[64] Abbott had even made it a point to deemphasize the effort required by Apollodorus to carry his burden—"Cleopatra was at this time about twenty-one years of age," he wrote, "but she was of a slender and graceful form, and the burden was, consequently, not very heavy"[65]—and in his text's illustration of this same famous scene the emphasis is on anything but bodiliness: "Cleopatra Entering the Palace of Caesar" primarily presents architecture, like an image from Denon's *Description de l'Egypt*, and the two stealthy figures are intentionally dwarfed by the buildings that surround them.[66] In Farmer's illustration, however, Cleopatra's body has virtually disappeared from view in quite another way; almost all that remains of the journey toward her unrolling is the body of her slave. "Cleopatra never walks," writes Hughes-Hallett, "but is carried from place to place in a litter borne by naked Nubians."[67] Cleopatra's Sicilian friend has become her Negro slave.

Farmer's 1887 presentations of Cleopatra—*The Book of Famous Queens* and *The Girl's Book of Famous Queens*—are important for this if for no other reason: they clearly mark the moment at which Reconstruction fantasies of white plantation mistresses being safely attended by willing black slaves have permanently altered the iconography of the Egyptian queen. "Nineteenth-century Cleopatras are surrounded by black retainers," writes Hughes-Hallett, "living reminders that they come from the passionate

"Cleopatra Carried into Caesar's Palace." (From Lydia Hoyt
Farmer, *The Girl's Book of Famous Queens*. New York: Thomas Y.
Crowell, 1887. McCormick Library of Special Collections,
Northwestern University Library.)

"Cleopatra Entering the Palace of Caesar." (From Jacob Abbott, *The History of Cleopatra, Queen of Egypt*. New York: Harper and Brothers, 1851. Rare Book and Special Collections Division, Library of Congress.)

south."[68] This racial division of labor is quite literally on display in another of Farmer's illustrations in the *The Girl's Book of Famous Queens*, "Cleopatra Embarking on the Cydnus," in which the famous scene of the queen sailing down the Nile to meet Mark Antony becomes as much a portrait of slave labor as of Cleopatra's lassitude or Egyptian opulence — and, indeed, these three things are by now completely inseparable. "Her attendant maidens on this fairy-like barge stand round her like dusky figures cut from bronze," Farmer wordpaints in *The Book of Famous Queens*, "but her fair face and limbs gleam with pale ivory-tints."[69] What Hamer analyzes as "Cleopatra: Housewife" becomes in the radically racialized nineteenth century "Cleopatra: Plantation Mistress," with all of the ambivalences, contradictions, fears, and fantasies such a conflicted domestic scene suggests.[70]

Thus Cleopatra emerged not merely as a sign of racialization but as a sign of racialized panic. Attempts to control the racialized image of Cleopatra were attempts to control the racialized instabilities in play in America that both led up to and away from the Civil War. The marked inability of anyone to successfully control this uncontrollable figure should be significant enough. Like the fears of amalgamation Reconstruction fantasies of happy plantation darkies were designed to allay, Cleopatra's racialization fit neatly into preexisting and ongoing narratives of Cleopatran panic more generally. What was before domestic, political, economic, or sexual panic was now also racial panic, and, like the image of Cleopatra herself, the possibility of controlling all of these panicky signifiers at once was too tempting to resist. If Cleopatra could be shown as a white plantation mistress surrounded by nubile black slaves and yet still interested only in Roman rulers, then, as a sign of whiteness—if not of womanhood itself—she could be rehabilitated. If she could be shown to be an Orientalist despot, profligate and promiscuous, then, as a sign of both racial Otherness and monstrous womanhood, she could be punished. Either way, racialization had done its work, and Cleopatra had served her purpose. "Her death," wrote one proslavery southerner, "commends her more than all her life!"[71] Thus her enormous wealth as a figure of hybridity, as racially, sexually, or otherwise mixed: like the layered and secluded mysteries she was often seen to represent, her greatest value lay in her continuing status as an enigma, as a ghost in the phallocentric machine, as a racialized Rosetta Stone, as a permanent problem.

## "The Sex Needs a Good Many Veils"

"Take me with triumph and power," Story has his Egyptian queen snarl sexily in his 1864 poetic counterpart poem "Cleopatra," "As a warrior storms a fortress!"[72] This is the sexualized queen unleashed, and, unlike the delicate racial coding used by Story for his marble sculpture, no subtlety is needed for this Orientalist Cleopatra:

> Come to my arms, my hero,
> The shadows of twilight grow,
> And the tiger's ancient fierceness
> In my veins begins to flow. . . .
> Come, as you came in the desert,
> Ere we were women and men,
> When the tiger passions were in us,
> And love as you loved me then![73]

"Remarkable for its oriental strength and voluptuousness of passion," one reviewer called the poem, this Cleopatra of Story's has much in common with the long tradition of American Orientalist fantasies to which she owes her shape.[74] The Cleopatra of Story's poem is a classic racist construct, another veritable cartoon of Orientalist imaginings. She lounges restlessly with her handmaiden, daydreaming sexual fantasies in which she is at first filled with a romantic lassitude but in which she then suddenly imagines herself as a jungle tiger, violently killing other animals and violently mating with other tigers. "We grappled and struggled together," Story's Cleopatra recounts, "For his love like his rage was rude; / And his teeth in the swelling folds of my neck / At times, in our play, drew blood."[75] Hypersexualized, voracious, and animalistic, she is simultaneously vulnerable, capricious, and whiny. She is both sadistic and masochistic, alternately marked by bloodlust and laziness; she is at once a child and a man-eater.

Hughes-Hallett writes of a tripartite division of exoticized nineteenth-century European Cleopatras, and a similar three-part structure applies to American ones as well. Cleopatra could be white, a signifier of beauty, assaulted by charges of blackness and in need of defense against them; she could be black, a mixed race mulatta with "full Nubian lips," clearly American in her politics and features, faint enough traces though her Negroness might have; or she could be Oriental, in the most significant sense of the word, decadent and powerful, a voluptuous seductress who both kept slaves and was a slave—to her lusts, to her passions, to her whims, to herself.[76] "Fierce in a tyrannous freedom," Story's versified Cleopatra says, "I knew but the law of my moods."[77] There is no question that often these three overlapped, unevenly, irregularly, unpredictably—but they did so effectively, or at least effectively enough to keep Cleopatra continually circulating in a racialized whirlpool of unanticipated effects. And, given her reputation for impulsiveness and capriciousness, her unpredictable racial identity seemed somehow to suit her.

This was especially the case given the ways in which, possibly even more so than now, nineteenth-century observers understood the scandals associated with the racially and sexually charged imagery of Orientalist aesthetics. "Perhaps nowhere else are the sexual politics of colonial narrative so explicitly thematized as in those voyages to the Near East recorded or imagined by Western men," writes Joseph Boone. "The geopolitical realities of the Arabic Orient become a psychic screen on which to project fantasies of illicit sexuality and unbridled excess."[78] The racially prurient logic of colonialist representations allowed for the sexually graphic displays of nonwhite flesh in ways aggressively policed in other aesthetic arenas. "The sex needs a good many veils," wrote American art critic Earl Shinn of the French Orientalist master Jean-Léon Gérôme, "and he has rent away a good many in his time. What is left of woman after all the mystery is gone is perhaps less seductive than schoolboys believe."[79] What was equally clear to nineteenth-century viewers, however, was how closely such strategies of fleshly display related Orientalism to neoclassicism. "Gérôme has been entirely consistent in his painted discourses on women," Shinn wrote, "whether he makes Greek women like Almehs or Almehs like Greek statues,"[80] and such politics of sanctioned nudity—proper if Greek, improper if not—inevitably led to blurry boundaries and frequent border crossings. This is what makes the figure of Cleopatra so important for this land: she was a doubled figure, part neoclassical legend, part Orientalist archetype, and if represented nude she stood directly in the middle of the crossroads of nineteenth-century racialized eroticism.

Representing Cleopatra as nude could be sanctioned either on the grounds of neoclassical aesthetic authority, as seen in the marble busts of Cleopatra done by midcentury Americans, or under the sign of racy Orientalist excess, as in the large-scale paintings done by late-century Europeans. The most savvy of nineteenth-century artists—like Story and Gérôme—exploited just this opportunity. "Sculptors were not unaware that female nudes sold better than male nudes," writes William L. Vance, "or that busts with both breasts on view sold better than those even partially draped."[81] And particularly at midcentury the case for representing female figures with one foot in the sanctioned realm of neoclassicism and another in the titillating districts of Orientalism was made even more easily. Seen most famously in the case of Hiram Powers's *The Greek Slave*—a sculpture to which all the American artists living in Rome owed many opportunities—the added associations of abjection, romantic racialization, and liberal sentimentalism that came from invoking American slavery allowed for even further opportunism regarding images of suffering or enslaved women.[82] Story's Cleopatra "is as beautiful as creative genius and the pure white marble can make this sovereign and queen," wrote one observer,[83] and in such praise one can hear both the admiration for Story for classicizing Cleopatra and the delight with Cleopatra for remaining Oriental.

Moreover, Cleopatra's ambivalent racial status made her a perfect model

for the racially fraught idioms of Orientalist imagery. As several scholars have noted, Orientalist painting utilized two major strategies of racial
representation, especially in terms of female objectification or erotic display.[84] The first relied on the ethnographic portraiture of carefully rendered
"Oriental" types, often stripped bare and colored with the palette of the
mixed or multiracial Other: brown, tan, honey, beige. The importance of
chromatic typology was not lost on many, and the history of this mode of
representation is one of acute slippage between Orientalized people and
Oriental things. "Oh, what harmony in blacks!" wrote Frederick Arthur
Bridgman, the student of Gérôme who became the most important American Orientalist painter of the nineteenth century, in his 1889 memoir *Winters in Algeria*, of the colors both of a pile of old charcoal and of the man who
sold it: "How various they were on the greasy jars and cans. . . . And the
dealer, what was he like? A sickly and dusty-complexioned Moslem of the
lower class, crouching in a narrow alcove, and snoozing all day long."[85]

After the aesthetics of multiracial muddiness, the second mode of Orientalist representation relied on the dynamics of contrast: starkly white
bodies placed next to deeply black bodies, both often nude and almost
always erotically charged. Given the corresponding rise of Cleopatra's identity as white plantation mistress, it should go without saying that figures
of the former type—the bronze, the cinnamon, the olive, the tawny—were
rarely represented in positions of power, even corrupt ones; figures of ambiguous racial status are working as peasants, lounging as idlers, stoned
on opium, or sold as slaves. When rendered in white, however, Orientalized women are frequently being served by blacker ones, even if both are
in a harem; the relative hierarchy of mutual enslavement still followed the
lines of racialized science. And, as the popularity of Bridgman attests,
this racialized fantasy of a binary color scheme could be given any number of American connotations, ranging from mistrelsy to maternity.[86] Both
modes of erotic exoticism, however, regardless of their color wheels, had
more in common than not: both partook of the stereotypes of Orientalist
decadence, of indulgence, slavery, and sex.

Cleopatra was readily available for employment in both these modes.
Whether carefully colored as Shakespeare's "Tawny front," or given faint
"Negroid" features carved in tinted marble, Cleopatra in her mixed mode
could appear as a fantasy of Orientalist abjection but elevated to a position
of power never achieved by her sandy sisters. And whether fetishistically
"snowy" or genealogically secured, Cleopatra in her pure Anglo-Saxon

mode could be as surrounded by savage blackness as the most cartoonish plantation mistress yet endowed with all the dangerous, punishable sexuality forbidden to members of the cult of true womanhood.[87] So even in her whitest or most deracialized forms, Cleopatra is still stained by racialized spillage, every attempt to distance her from claims of blackness demonstrating her intimacy with them. Either way, she was constructed as something that was always partly white yet always partly not. She could be whiteness contaminated or blackness elevated, but one could not function without the other. Whether surrounded by slaves covered in leopard skins or half-naked harem girls colored as carefully as their clothes, whether defended by Nubians or nervous reminders of her Greek lineage, the figure of Cleopatra in the nineteenth century is always a sign of racialized anxiety.

## "See, Cleopatra! Bared"

Like her warring racial identities of black and white, a dialectic of drapery and flesh attends the figure of Cleopatra throughout her history. Indeed, the cultural politics surrounding the erotic display of white marble female "flesh" usually associated with the desires and anxieties of the nineteenth-century American art market was a central feature of all representations of Cleopatra in the United States. "See, Cleopatra! bared," wrote English poet and intimate of Story Robert Browning in 1872, in one of the most frequently quoted examples of nineteenth-century Cleopatran undressing:

> The entire and sinuous wealth
> O' the shining shape; each orb of indolent ripe health,
> Captured, just where it finds a fellow-orb as fine
> I' the body.
> Yet, o'er that white and wonder, a soul's predominance
> I' the head so high and haught—except one thievish glance,
> From back of oblong eye, intent to count the slain.[88]

Obviously, Browning is most interested here in what admittedly is a critical feature of Cleopatran imagery throughout her history: her breasts. "The dramatic possibilities of the subject" of Cleopatra's death, writes Hamer, "made it a favoured theme . . . especially as it provided an ideal opportunity to show a voluptuous young woman with her breasts bared."[89]

And breasts there were. "The white breast / Lay half revealed," wrote William Gilmore Simms in his 1853 poem "The Death of Cleopatra," and in doing so presented his version of that which became as close as anything to being an indispensable part of the political anatomy of the Cleopatran body:

> Oh! to behold,
> With eye still piercing to the sweet recess,
> Where rose each gentle slope, that seem'd to swell
> Beneath mine eye, as conscious of my gaze,
> And throbbing with emotion soft as strange,
> Of love akin to fear![90]

"The Cleopatra is practically a dressed heroine," wrote Henry James of Story's first Egyptian queen, and, even though "Story, obviously, at all events, loved the nude," James is forced to admit that "drapery, that is, folds and dispositions of stuff and applications . . . became a positive and necessary part of his scheme from the moment that scene was romantic," and in this tradition of partially clothing, partially exposing Cleopatra's breasts is the American reworking of a crucial overall feature of representations of the Egyptian queen from European traditions.[91] Especially important in the *ateliers* of the French Orientalists, but highly visible in the efforts of the Americans as well, a central trait of the arc of these representations was the overarching concern with stripping Cleopatra completely nude.

At international exhibitions like the Centennial Exposition at which Edmonia Lewis would display her Cleopatra with one breast exposed, viewers could see this visual dialogue play out before, as it were, their very eyes: in addition to Lewis's sculpture, the American sculptor Margaret Foley bared her Cleopatran bust's bust, the British painter V. C. Prinsep had the breasts of the Cleopatra in his *The Death of Cleopatra* fully covered by way of layered togas, and the Italian sculptor Enrico Braga carved his Cleopatra completely topless and virtually naked. "The persistent vision of woman's transformability," writes Kasson, "suggests a nightmarish world where good and evil, safe and dangerous, domestic and demonic, prove indistinguishable,"[92] and the panicky American transformations of Cleopatra from dressed to undressed and back to dressed again put the erotic metaphorics of transgressive transformability front and center.

This last pose, that of Cleopatra standing not so much nude as stripped,

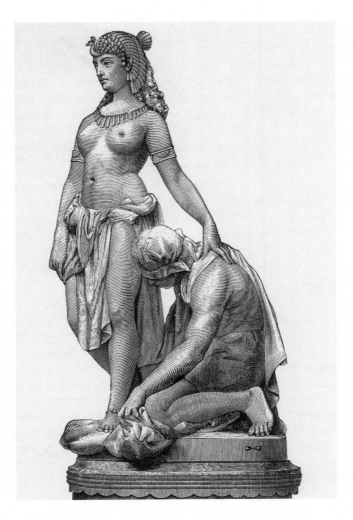

Enrico Braga, *Cleopatra*. (From Edward Strahan [Earl Shinn],
*The Masterpieces of the Centennial International Exposition, Illustrated.*
Vol. 1: *Fine Art.* Philadelphia: Gebbie and Barrie, 1876. Library of
Congress.)

is of critical importance to my argument here. Most famously painted by Gérôme in his 1866 *Cleopatra and Caesar*, this pose is one that haunts the figure of Cleopatra throughout the nineteenth century. Sometimes titled *Cleopatra before Caesar*, Gérôme's image is based, ostensibly, on one of the most familiar representations of Cleopatra in her history, presented originally by Plutarch and discussed above: that of Cleopatra, with the help of Apollodorus, having smuggled herself past the posted Roman guard, being unrolled from her hiding place of either rugs or a carpet or bedding before Julius Caesar. "The stout slave clears the drapery with a single gesture," narrated Shinn in 1881, "and crouches motionless, Cleopatra trusting her balance to his support with one royal knuckle, knowing that her chattel will not stir until released." [93]

Fifteen years before Gérôme's painting, Jacob Abbott, the American Cleopatran biographer, had narrated the same scene somewhat differently: "When it was unrolled, and Cleopatra came out to view," he wrote, "Caesar was perfectly charmed with the spectacle."

> In fact, the various conflicting emotions which she could not but feel under such circumstances as these, imparted a double interest to her beautiful and expressive face, and to her naturally bewitching manners. She was excited by the adventure through which she had passed, and yet pleased with her narrow escape from its dangers. The curiosity and interest which she felt on the one hand, in respect to the great personage into whose presence she had been thus strangely ushered, was very strong; but then, on the other, it was chastened and subdued by that feeling of timidity which, in new and unexpected situations like these, and under a consciousness of being the object of eager observation to the other sex, is inseparable from the nature of woman. [94]

Almost a century and a half later, Hughes-Hallett narrates it like this: "A gauzy skirt is split over each thigh to reveal her legs as high as her jewelled girdle. Her belly is bare, and her breasts are displayed by a sort of harness, which titillates by reversing expectation, proffering that which it might be expected to conceal. Caesar, seated at his ease, looks up from his writing as though coolly estimating whether this visitor is sufficiently diverting to justify the interruption to his work." [95]

The queen stands, powerful and yet vulnerable, hidden and yet revealed, next to her slave, before the eyes of the men. "The queen is charming and chaste," wrote the famous Maxime du Camp of the image, "despite being half nude and revealing her young breasts."[96] In none of the classical versions of this story is any mention made of the clothes of Cleopatra, but by 1866 Gérôme had transformed the scene of unrolling into a scene of undressing. Gérôme extended the logic of the unwrapping to the body of Cleopatra. "It is so Eastern," Shinn writes, "so despotic."[97] No longer is Cleopatra content to merely issue forth from a rug carried by her Sicilian friend; now she emerges topless from the bundle carried by her swarthy slave.

"I have always thought that Gérôme found his one true inspiration when he designed the figure of the queen," wrote Shinn in another moment of rhapsodic support, "especially in the nonchalance with which she leans upon the shoulder of the crouching slave, as upon a table or shelf, keeping him rigidly in the painfullest attitude with the weight of her royal finger, maintaining her own risky balance by her confidence in this support, and carelessly aware that unless she releases him her chattel will not stir."[98] Obviously recalling the elevation of Cleopatra to the status of plantation mistress some years earlier, such extended attention to both the body of the slave and his relationship to Cleopatra in the Reconstruction days of the 1880s spoke to some particularly American concerns. In 1876, Shinn wrote of Braga's marble adaptation of this scene, displayed like the Cleopatra of Lewis, at the Centennial Exposition in Philadelphia: "the slave, who parts the drapery, so supple, and submissive; the girl, standing, and leaning on his shoulder as on a piece of furniture, already so queenly, confident, and regal."[99] Morever, in his original vision of the scene, Gérôme reversed its gender politics as well, in a way also uncannily appropriate for American interests: Cleopatra is no longer the agent of her own actions, penetrating the offices of an invading general, but rather she is herself penetrated, unwrapped, her clothes disappearing, and she is forced to stand as a slave before a purchaser. "Cleopatra's pose is haughty," Hughes-Hallett writes, "but no amount of disdain can disguise the fact that the basic situation is that of a brothel, or of one of the slave markets which were stock subjects for Orientalist painters. . . . In Gérôme's painting the crouching attendant, swarthy and almost naked, pushes the carpet aside, as though unwrapping his wares for a critical customer."[100]

Indeed, this slippage—between the erotics of Cleopatra and the erotics of slavery—was a prominent theme in nineteenth-century commentaries on the Egyptian queen. "But no genius was equal to the task of thwarting the woman who had already made slaves of two Caesars," wrote Julia

J. C. Armytage, engraver, "Cleopatra before Caesar," after Jean-Léon Gérôme,
*Cleopatra and Caesar*. (From Edward Strahan [Earl Shinn], *Gérome: A Collection of the
Works of J. L. Gérome in One Hundred Photogravures*. New York: Samuel L. Hall, 1881,
vol. 10, plate 6. McCormick Library of Special Collections, Northwestern
University Library.)

Wiggin King,[101] and over and over again in nineteenth-century American visions of Cleopatra we find the erotics of inversion couched in the language of slavery. "This insolence is so right, so Eastern, so tropical, and so luckily invented," Shinn concludes. "You feel that for a mere masculine Roman, escape is impossible."[102] Cleopatra is produced in all her mastery but is still offered to Caesar like a slave. Emergent from her layers of cloth like an excavated artifact, her part-neoclassical, part-Orientalist fleshliness is as much part of the logic of stratified revelation as the rug from which she emerges. "The pose of the group . . . hits the moral character of the situation so justly that the picture is unforgettable," writes Shinn, "with the half-nude, tightly-strapped Egyptian figure of Cleopatra balanced on its forefinger upon the muscular bronze shoulder of Apollodoros, like the lid of a trap on its spring."[103] The undressed Cleopatra is revealed.

## Cleopatra in a Cakewalk

To be sure, many of Cleopatra's nineteenth-century biographers—especially those who were women—strenuously objected to the canonization of the unclad imagery that was so widely associated with the figure of the Egyptian queen. "Why both poets and artists should paint the Queen as applying the asp to her bosom," declares King before supplying a translation of the relevant portion of Life of Antony, "after the declaration of Plutarch to the contrary, we leave for them to explain. . . . This, it would seem, should be conclusive evidence that the asp was not introduced beneath the vestments of the bosom, as artists and poets have painted."[104] Similarly, albeit less polemically, Hale recounted that Cleopatra died fully clothed: "She had an asp, a small serpent, whose bite is said to induce a kind of lethargy and death without pain, brought to her in a basket of figs; and the guards who were sent to secure her person, found her lying dead on a couch, dressed in her royal robes, with one of her women dead at her feet, and the other expiring."[105] Even Farmer, by far one of the most liberal American borrowers of outside material, was careful to choose a source that clothed Cleopatra, even—or especially—if in doing so she made the Egyptian queen seem like the very model of proper Victorian manners. "When Cleopatra returned to her apartments after this sad ceremony," Farmer recounts of the moments following Antony's death, "she appeared more composed than usual. After taking a bath, she arrayed herself with all her queenly magnificence; and having ordered a sumptuous repast, served with the customary splendor, she partook of it with seeming calmness."[106] Cleopatra's remarkable reserve extends in Farmer's account to include the version of the queen's suicide, which, as for King, features her arm and not her breast and thus allows her to perform a most ladylike and decorous death: "After Cleopatra had examined the figs, she laid down upon her couch, and soon after appeared to have fallen asleep. The poison from the bite of the asp, which had been carefully hidden amongst the figs, and which had stung her upon the arm, which she held to it for that purpose, immediately reached her heart, and killed her almost instantly, and without seeming pain."[107] When Simms's Cleopatra dies, she is an erotic nest of heaving breasts and serpentine slithering. When Farmer's Cleopatra dies, she retires to her fainting couch.

The context in which women writers like Hale, King, and Farmer were writing was one dominated by male writers like Jacob Abbott and William Wetmore Story, of course, and too much emphasis cannot be placed on the extent to which the ladylike makeovers for Cleopatra were staged against the more prevalent, titillating, patriarchal, and frankly more famous versions of her career as one of uncontrolled debauchery. And yet, while their historical corrections do at times also favor the accounts in the earliest sources, what we see are these women writers engaged in a campaign of antipatriarchal sartorial redressing that relies on concepts of purity and chastity taken directly from the cult of true womanhood. Indeed, the extent to which Cleopatra is clothed in these texts is the extent to which she can be said to be white. Or at the very least she is undergoing a process of whitening; given the pronounced association in male-authored texts and male-created images of Cleopatra with Orientalist decadence, what we see in the efforts of women like Hale and King is a pronounced campaign of demure distancing from any associations with unladylike behavior. For these women, Cleopatra is no impenetrable erotic mystery, unpredictable and unfathomable; she is a confused and heartsick young woman given to overindulgence in love as well as in other things. She is also, therefore, no Orientalist tigress, no mixed race mulatta contaminating Greco-Roman purity; she is a composed queen suitable for admission to the ranks of any royal white family. She does not sprawl naked on a couch covered in animal skins; like any decent lady, she dresses for death.

Perhaps the most apt example of this comes from 1858, when a steel engraving based on an Italian painting was featured as the frontispiece to the *Cosmopolitan Art Journal*, with copies "to be awarded as a premium to subscribers." [108] This frontispiece was an engraving by John Rogers of "Cleo-patra Applying the Asp," itself a copy of one of the many *Cleopatras* painted by the Italian master Guido Reni in the 1630s. "The original, by the old master Guido," applauds King, "bears the same relation to Art that Shake-speare's creation does to the drama." [109] In Rogers's copy, Reni's queen has been significantly reworked, although the critical features of the asp and the breast are prominently displayed. A somewhat Elizabethan white lady — her social status sited by her elaborate outfit and her bouquet of fresh flowers — almost completely otherwise covered by a richly embroidered and heavily draperied gown, reclines in a chair, delicately peels aside her lacy top, and daintily applies an oddly horizontal asp to her breast, more for a kiss, it seems, than a bite. "Happily illustrat[ing] the moment and the event," King cheers, "the artist of the splendid painting of 'Cleopatra ap-plying the Asp' has sought to tell [it] upon the canvas." [110] No doubt King's pleasure was caused by the clarity of Rogers's iconography: Cleopatra's breast is delicately bared, her eyes are turned heavenward, and the asp is virtually suckling at her nipple. She is rich, white, and constructed of both an immediate and a historical play of chastity and pornography, piety and blasphemy, drapery and flesh.[111]

This gendered politics of claiming the white Cleopatra applies equally clearly to an underread novel from 1877, Elizabeth Stuart Phelps's *The Story of Avis*. The novelized parable of a woman artist trapped by domesticity and heteronormativity, *Avis* provides one of the more striking moments of Cleopatran territorialism of the last quarter of the nineteenth century. The plot follows the plight of Avis in her protracted struggle to negotiate the conflicting demands of her suffocating bourgeois lifestyle and her artistic creativity. "In *Avis* marriage stifles creativity," writes Carol Farley Kessler. "Although Phelps shows us a sensuous and sensual young woman in the opening chapters, sexual expression brings her not pleasure but pain. . . . For the female artist, the way becomes strewn with obstacles. Wifehood, homemaking, and motherhood . . . use all energy, all time." [112] A talented New England painter, Avis unwillingly sacrifices her artistic career in favor of support for her professor husband's, and throughout Phelps's novel she vacillates metaphorically between her activities as mother and house-wife and her efforts to complete a single symbolic painting. The painting in question is that of the Sphinx: romantic and windswept and obviously reminiscent of that of Elihu Vedder.[113] "Avis's use of the Sphinx highlights her own gender and racial biases," writes Deborah Barker, "but the image of the Sphinx also represents Avis's own liminal position as a woman artist."[114]

At one of the novel's final breaking points, however, Avis, distraught over her dilemma, swallows a glassful of an opiate liqueur and hallucinates a parade of powerful women, all of whom are understood to be white. "Cleopatra was there," writes Phelps, "and Godiva, Aphrodite and St. Elizabeth, Ariadne and Esther, Helen and Jeanne d'Arc, and the Magdelene, Sappho, and Cornelia—a motley company. These moved on solemnly, and gave way to a silent army of the unknown. They swept before her in file, in procession, in groups. . . . Each, in turn, these figures passed on, and vanished in an expanse of imperfectly-defined color like a cloud, which for some moments she found without form and void to her."[115] This is a litany of Anglo-Saxon womanhood, in full racial regalia, massing in the service of upper-class white feminism and linking their own status, power, and racial identity with that of Avis. Clearly reminiscent of the text collections of Jameson, Hale, Clarke, and Farmer, this is woman's history as white history and white history as linear history. Like the imperialist project with which Amy Kaplan identifies Hale's domesticity, Avis's resistance to that same domesticity is also predicated on the colonization of the Other.[116] "She saw a low, unclouded Eastern sky," Phelps writes of Avis's opium-induced Orientalist hallucination, "fire to the horizon's rim; sand and sun; the infinite desert; a caravan departing, faint as a forgotten hope. . . . In the foreground the sphinx, the great sphinx, restored. The mutilated face patiently took on the forms and the hues of life; the wide eyes met her own; the dumb lips parted; the solemn brow unbent. The riddle of ages whispered to her. The mystery of womanhood stood before her, and said, 'Speak for me.'"[117]

Phelps's Avis needs for her racial identity to be capable of expanding into history, backward as well as forward—and vice versa; Avis's historical identity, as a woman as well as a feminist, is dependent on her ability to enlist the signs of race. Indeed, Avis's imaginary allies seem less like a community of comrades than an army of whiteness, less like sisters in struggle than a platoon of privilege. And at the head of the line is Cleopatra. Her presence in Phelps's hallucination of white womanhood secures this epiphany of linear harmony, providing the terms of antiquity that at once legitimize Avis's struggles beyond the merely modern and protect against any possible encroachment from the monstrous mulatta. This is Cleopatra in whiteface, Cleopatra in a cakewalk.

# Cleopatra's Gynecologist

"The story of Cleopatra is a story of crime," wrote Abbott in 1851, and in this phrase is condensed much of the transgressive metaphoricity of the figure of Cleopatra: "It is a narrative of the course and the consequences of unlawful love." [118] Cleopatra's cultural violations are for Abbott so sweeping that she is a form of crime unto herself, her infractions only expressible as violations of the very notion of law itself—and, characteristically, this construction of "Cleopatra as crime" revolves constantly around sex and sexual power. "In her strange and romantic history," Abbott wrote, "we see this passion portrayed with the most complete and graphic fidelity in all its influences and effects; its uncontrollable impulses, its intoxicating joys, its reckless and mad career, and the dreadful remorse and ultimate despair and ruin in which it always and inevitably ends." [119] Hamer writes succinctly of Cleopatra's crimes: "Cleopatra's beauty, her drive, and the amplitude of her resources are all registered, but only to be categorized as forms of transgression. The law which they transgress is the Law of the Father, and it is this, which empowers only men at the expense of women, that is invoked how to define how Cleopatra has transgressed." [120] In Abbott's hands, Cleopatra is shaped into one of the most portable versions of her own myth: a scandalously attractive, libidinously ungovernable, politically powerful lead character in a sociosexual cautionary tale marketed for and consumed by antebellum American audiences.

At the very least, this midcentury association of Cleopatra with crime anticipates later constructions of female sexuality as dangerous, transgressive, inverted, and pathological. "As early as 1850," writes Marylynne Diggs, "medical science had begun discussing the implications of what Frederick Hollick called 'doubtful or double sex': the presence of sexual 'monstrosities' who, he determined, were females with masculine characteristics." [121] These formulations fit Cleopatra perfectly. "That which breaks over the barriers that God and nature have marked out for it, tends to make woman masculine and bold to indurate all her sensibilities," Abbott warned. "Cleopatra was beginning to experience these effects." [122] Indeed, Abbott makes it clear that the violations of which he considers Cleopatra guilty are those of gender roles. "We can not soften the picture which is exhibited to our view in the history of this celebrated family," he announces while discussing Cleopatra's father's line, "by regarding the mother of Auletes, in the masculine and merciless traits and principles which she displayed so energetically throughout her terrible career, as an exception to the general character of the princesses who appeared from time to time in the line." [123] This is essentialism enlisting all the allies it can find—biology, family history, geography, culture—and producing, for its troubles, a clinical case study of Cleopatran pathology.

As one of the most famous examples of female power run sexually amok and necessarily to suicide, Cleopatra emerges in the middle of the nineteenth century as a virtual case study in either gender inversion, hysteria, nymphomania, or all three. "Cleopatra was given up to history as a woman tarnished by crimes, yet endowed with many virtues," wrote King, "sagacious in all things, save in the want of control over her voluptuous passion." [124] Indeed, the language that describes Cleopatra during this period runs in uncanny parallel to that of newly emerging sexual pathologies, and often there seems to be no difference between the two. "The natural tendency of nymphomania is to insanity and death," wrote gynecologist G. W. Simpson in 1875. "Females sometimes become passionately attached to an object," wrote Boston obstetrician Horatio Storer in 1871, "and this passion may advance even to nymphomania or monomania." [125] This passage could have been pulled from any number of biographies of Cleopatra as easily as from the treatise on female reproductive pathology in which it actually appears. "If a woman once has her nature turned in such a direction, her embraces are unending, and it is impossible to satisfy her desires." [126]

Clearly reminiscent of the Orientalized fantasies of Cleopatra as sexually insatiable and driven ultimately to suicide, nineteenth-century gynecologists developed a language of what Diggs identifies as "abnormal gender identity and sexual ambiguity," but it was one that often relied on imagery equally at home in sexually charged ethnology. "The child has now become a maiden," wrote Storer. "Immediately the emotions, desires, and passions that, though latent, have been gradually foreshadowing themselves, are now established . . . like the smouldering fires of a volcano, ready to burst forth at any exciting moment." [127] Indeed, Cleopatra's optional status as a mixed race abnormality allowed her even greater connotative purchase on the wildly proliferating discourses of sexual pathology derived from the imagery and investigations of nonwhite women, especially those with which she already had enormous familiarity—slaves and tragic mulattas. "I am a hybrid," Diggs quotes one late-century text's sexually transgressive heroine as confessing. "Sometimes I think I am a monster, and the worst of it is, I certainly take pleasure in it."[128] As one of the most infamous icons of uncontrolled sexual passion in nineteenth-century American culture, and as one equally famous for her racially flexible cultural identity, Cleopatra cast a shadow across many a speculum.[129]

In wide-ranging ways, images of Cleopatra were floating signifiers of sexual resistance, seized on and fought over as sites of potentially explosive identification. This was especially true regarding the construction of that most inverted and pathological of the later century's medical identities, lesbianism. "Even before the middle of the nineteenth century," Diggs explains, "a broad spectrum of discourses, including the scientific discourses not directly related to sexuality and subjectivity, were constructing relationships between women in terms of sexual pathology,"[130] and these developments had first been explored during the same period as the rise of American Egyptomania. The groundwork for such connections between homoerotic desire and pathological criminality—for the complex rise, in fact, of lesbianism "as such," what Lisa Duggan calls "a terrifyingly difficult birth"—was laid earlier in the century by the study of sexually transgressive figures like Cleopatra.

"By 1892," writes Duggan, "there was a developing medical literature on same sex love and its relation to crime and insanity produced by American doctors who adapted the theories of Krafft-Ebing and other Europeans,"[131] and Cleopatra would by the end of the century have proved herself a valuable asset for both those whose agenda was pathology, and those whose agenda was to resist. "[D]iscourses of lesbian resistance also emerged in the late nineteenth century," Diggs writes, "elucidating the beginnings of lesbian identity politics in U.S. culture. Far from a presexological world in which women's intimacies were encouraged by a culture that perceived women to be innocent of sexuality, the nineteenth century was a period of contentious struggle over the definition and representation of lesbian sexuality—a struggle in which writers . . . were, by the 1850s, active participants."[132] Marked both as sexually transgressive and as ethnographically available for anatomical investigation, Cleopatra occupied a crucial role in the emergence of nineteenth-century concepts of the pathological. Moreover, this role derived not only from her status *as* pathological but also from her role as resistant *to* pathologization; the insistence with which Cleopatran imagery often spilled over patriarchal dams was not only all too familiar to the agents of pathology operating in the interests of that very same patriarchy but it was because of such insistence that she would be a subject for lesbian sculptors like Edmonia Lewis.

The depth of the water into which Lewis willingly waded was marked further by the intimacies shared by the cultural contexts that produced early gynecology and other discourses of sexual pathology and the ones that produced scientific racialization. "It is all science," wrote race theorist Josiah Nott in 1848; "exploring a woman and a mound are pretty much the same."[133] When Nott wrote these words, not only was he articulating the interdependency discourses of archaeology had in relation to those of other kinds of interiority—in particular bodily interiority, specifically and strenuously gendered female—but he was also articulating the implication of racialized science in that relationship. And surely that Nott's remark was made almost casually is what carries much of its force; as Dana Nelson has written, "Professional gynecology in its early days promised to stabilize a whole range of social, economic, and political samenesses and differences between white men, by rerouting those anxious negotiations to a mapping of female difference."[134] This rerouting was made possible by the network of associations between differential modes of bodily interiority, of which racial and gynecological were intimate bedfellows. The mixed race Cleopatra and the intense interest in her dying suicidal body clearly prefigure what Diggs calls "the medical construction of lesbians as somatically monstrous."[135] It is thus this multilayered operating table that is prepared for inspection: as a problematic specimen of biological racialization, as a well-known case study in sexual aberration, and, in the name of access to female nature, as a figure repeatedly subjected to constant dressings and undressings, Cleopatra presents herself.[136]

Cleopatra's status as a European, Anglo-Saxon, or Caucasian type—secured through constant battles in the fields of visual and literary representation—produced her as white, but her status as a case study in sexual pathology produced her as something else. Erotically radical, antimatrimonial, patriarchally uncontrollable, and politically powerful yet constantly embattled, doomed to tragedy, and ultimately suicidal: it is easy to see why any number of nineteenth-century parties affected by the approach of what Eve Kosofsky Sedgwick called in 1990 "the now chronic modern crisis of homo/heterosexual definition" found in images of Cleopatra fertile and fecund ground for potential action, whether hegemonic or resistant.[137] This is thus precisely what makes the antiheteronormative interventions of Edmonia Lewis and her circle of sexually transgressive colleagues so crucial to my argument here. Producing Cleopatra as sexually pathological allowed her to be represented as externally white but internally black; thus a young black woman on the frontlines of the early battles over the emergence of modern lesbian identity choosing to exhibit a sculpture of Cleopatra at the exposition marking her country's centennial should come as no surprise.

### "The Hour for Applause Has Come to Edmonia Lewis"

Obscured for years, the figure of Mary Edmonia Lewis is now much better known to historians of American and African American art. Born to a free black father and a mother of mixed African American and Chippewa background in Greenbush, New Jersey, in either July 1844 or July 1845, Lewis was raised with her older brother Samuel until she was nine, when, both of their parents having died, they were raised by their mother's two Mississauga sisters and their families near Niagara Falls, making and selling tourist trade Chippewa crafts before Lewis was sent to an abolitionist Baptist school at the age of about thirteen, from where she went on to Ohio two years later to attend Oberlin College.[138] At Oberlin, Lewis became entangled in a high-profile sexual scandal involving two young white women — also students — which was only resolved through a widely publicized courtroom drama in 1862 involving the intervention of the most famous black lawyer in America at that time, founder of the Howard Law School and Oberlin graduate John Mercer Langston.[139] Though acquitted of any wrongdoing, the taint of the scandal eventually forced Lewis to leave Oberlin before graduating, and so she moved to Boston in 1864, where she began to pursue a career as a sculptor full time. "Until I was twelve years old I led this wandering life, fishing and swimming and making moccasins," Lewis somewhat cagily explained in 1866. "I was then sent to school . . . but was declared to be wild—they could do nothing with me. . . . From this school I was sent to another, at Oberlin, in Ohio, where I remained for four years, and then I thought of returning to wild life again; but my love of sculpture forbade it."[140]

Through an extremely savvy combination of racialized self-fashioning and abolitionist networking, Lewis positioned herself as a neoclassical

Studio portrait of sculptor Edmonia Lewis, ca. 1876,
H. Rocher, photographer. (From Photographs and
Prints Division, Schomburg Center for Research in
Black Culture, New York Public Library, Astor, Lenox,
and Tilden Foundations.)

sculptor of antislavery themes once in Boston, and, through the sale of
plaster busts of Colonel Robert Gould Shaw, eventually raised the funds
to finance a move to Italy in 1865. "Some friends recommended me to
go to England," Lewis recounted, "but I thought it better first to study
in Rome." [141] Among these "friends" were William Lloyd Garrison, Lydia
Maria Child, the sculptor Edward Brackett, and the Boston contingent of
what would later become the Roman circle of Charlotte Cushman and Har-

riet Hosmer, and thus Lewis's career is marked by a rapid rise into the circles of some of the most prominent New England liberals of the nineteenth century.[142]

Yet even before Lewis left for Europe a pattern seemed to be in place, begun at Oberlin and carried into Boston, one of simultaneous exoticization and infantilization by her white peers and patrons. Eager to appear liberal in their support of a struggling black artist like Lewis, white abolitionists were at the same time deeply ambivalent about how to feel about someone who seemed so intent on maintaining some distinctly nonconformist and less than ladylike ways. This pattern is perhaps best exemplified by Child: "I hope the artists in general will be able to so far divest themselves of American prejudice as to give Edmonia a fair chance to make for herself such a position as she may prove herself entitled to," Child wrote carefully in a letter to an Italian contact in 1865. "Of course, any attempt to force her or any one else, above the level of their nature will prove unavailing; but assuredly all obstructions ought to be removed. Considering her antecedents, I think she has done wonderfully well, thus far; and I sympathize, as you do, in her energetic efforts to rise above depressing circumstances."[143] At other times, Child was less guarded in her racialized condescension. Frustrated after repeated attempts on her part to successfully instruct Lewis as to what she believed to be a mature management of monetary issues, Child wrote, exasperatedly, "How could it be otherwise, when her childhood was spent with poor Negroes, and her youth with wild Indians?"[144] Not at all unusual, of course, in the upper-class white abolitionist circles of New England, and even less unusual for Lydia Maria Child, these comments serve as an index of the patronizing attitudes that must surely have accompanied Lewis to her new home in Rome.[145] "The hour for applause has come to Edmonia Lewis," wrote Laura Curtis Bullard in the most often reprinted account of Lewis in her adult life. "All honor to the brave little African girl, who has earned her own way to fame and to independence!"[146]

Once in Italy, Lewis quickly found herself enmeshed in the social circle of white expatriate American women sculptors living in Rome, now recognized as representing an important moment in lesbian history and called by Henry James in his biography of Story "the white, marmorean flock." "Apropos of your Poems," Story wrote to James Russell Lowell in 1853, "you are creating at this time a furore in 28 Corso, Wood's harem (scarem) as I call it—among the emancipated females who dwell there in heavenly unity." [147] This homoerotic and homosocial circle revolved around the actress turned patron of the arts, Cushman, and the best known of the practicing "sculptresses," Hosmer. It also included many of their colleagues, peers, friends, romantic interests, and longtime partners. "The undercurrent of homoerotic energy" that flowed around Cushman, Lisa Merrill writes, "also served as a source of female creativity and strength and was to be an enabling force in their own artistic pursuits. . . . None of the independent women in Charlotte's company felt compelled to reenact in Rome the middle-class conventions of feminine decorum and deportment they left at home. . . . In this privileged, holiday-like climate, where members of the expatriate community entertained themselves and one another, there was a good deal of social freedom as well as artistic exploration." [148] Though less visible in her romantic relationships with other women than Cushman and Hosmer, whose relationship involved competition over the affections of British actress Matilda Hays, and though largely dismissed by James in his characterization of the "flock"—even erased, given James's colorless choice of phrase—Lewis was an integral, if exoticized, member of this group. "One of the sisterhood, if I am not mistaken," wrote James condescendingly, "was a negress, whose color, picturesquely contrasting with that of her plastic material, was the pleading agent of her fame." [149]

Not incidentally, then, many of the details of Lewis's life are still unclear, from her early life on, and even though it is clear that Lewis never married, that she adopted "mannish" attire for much of her adult life, and that she chose to be identified with the homosocial "white, marmorean flock" centered at 28 Corso, verifiable conclusions regarding any aspect of her personal history—much less her sexuality—are notoriously difficult to secure. Yet, as always, there are traces of Lewis's loves: her relationship with Adeline T. Howard, the free black woman with whom Lewis rather inexplicably moved from her well-established and advancing professional life in Boston to Richmond to live while Howard—a future principal in Washington, D.C.—taught freed slaves in 1865; her relationship in Rome with Adelia Gales, the painter who accompanied Lewis on her trip to Naples with Frederick Douglass and his second wife in 1887; her life with Hosmer and Cushman and their circle, of course; and even the early scandal at Oberlin, for which homophobia as well as racism seems clearly to have played a major, if closeted, role. [150] Indeed, even after every other member of the circle had left Italy, Lewis remained a citizen of Rome until her death—but it was unquestionably with the sculpture and exhibition of her 1876 *The Death of Cleopatra*, shown at the Philadelphia Exposition in obvious open dialogue with Story, Hawthorne, and any number of other artists of the racially and sexually scandalous queen, that Lewis would become most famously associated.

Lewis's *The Death of Cleopatra* is a carefully composed, dramatically imagined, five-foot-high sculpture of the Egyptian queen, depicting Cleopatra not before or during her suicide but afterward, her seated body slumped against a pillow laid against the hard heavy back of a carved marble throne, her head lolling to the left, both eyes closed, right breast bared, the asp still in her hand. Her dress is voluminous yet carefully restrained, a simple one-piece full-length gown embroidered on the hem with a plain floral pattern and belted by a single thin cord; on her feet are historically accurate open-toed sandals; on her slack head sits a headdress crowned by an ornamental vulture. Her throne is decorated with griffins, imitation hieroglyphs, and the title of the statue, written in English, and two sphinxes act as side columns and armrests. But certainly much of the effect of the piece derives from Cleopatra's conspicuously exposed breast; with her subject's head turned toward the left side of her body, away from the bared breast on her right, Lewis has constructed a tense interplay between the primary visual elements of the high-waisted upper torso of her Egyptian queen. "The composition of Lewis's Cleopatra is surprisingly vertical," writes Kirsten Buick, "with dynamism arising from a set of tensions put into play within the statue."[151] Yet this suggestively taut relationship is offset by an overall limpness diffused throughout the body and the apparent indifference Cleopatra now has either to the viewer or herself. "She appears," Buick writes, "as if she were about to slip from her seat onto the floor."[152] This, then, is Lewis's signature work: a racially ambiguous, sexually transgressive, powerful yet tragic figure, with an African past and an American future, who seems exhausted to death.[153]

Predictably enough, Lewis did in fact enter into the ethnographic controversies over Cleopatra—although her manner of entry was not, perhaps, nearly as predictable. "Story gave his Cleopatra Nubian features," wrote William J. Clark in 1878. "The Cleopatra of Gould suggests Greek lineage. Miss Lewis, on the other hand, has [given] her Cleopatra an aquiline nose and prominent chin of the Roman type."[154] As Clark indicates, surprisingly, Lewis chose to represent Cleopatra, according to the finely tuned visual codes of nineteenth-century racial typology, as neither African nor Greek but in a much less common third way, as Roman. Moreover, she appears to have done so with all the intentions of being as physiognomically accurate as possible; as Marilyn Richardson indicates, Lewis, living in Rome, had access to several of the items then as now believed to most accurately represent the historical Cleopatra.[155] Yet Story and Foley also had access to these items—as did countless others—and they still chose to sculpt their Cleopatras along quite different racialized lines. For Clark, these differences can be chalked up not to conflicting ideas about the race of Cleopatra but to divergent styles of American sculpture: "This was not a beautiful work," he writes of Lewis's Cleopatra, "but it was a very original and striking one. . . . This Cleopatra more nearly resembled the real heroine of history than either of the others." [156]

So once again the politics of warring truths structured the debates in American Egyptomania. Lewis, so regularly exoticized both as "wild Indian" and as "negress sculptress" and whom, as a result, would have been considered by many to be the most likely to represent Cleopatra in her most African of forms, chooses instead to stage what in 1876 would count as an archival reconstruction of the Egyptian queen. Especially because Story himself had already cleared the way for such a "Nubian" precedent, Lewis, it might seem, could easily have continued along the path so laid out; it would have been considered a safe one, even, given Story's abolitionist framing of his Negro queen. Yet Lewis opted for what amounted to both an artistic and a political trumping of the white sculptors, both male and female, so drawn to the exoticized depictions of the raced Cleopatra; the black woman did not sculpt her African queen as black. It was an unanticipated move, and it confounded expectations. Lewis was not merely debating the race of the American Cleopatra; she was also critiquing the American politics of the raced Cleopatra. Even the public reception of Lewis's statue centered rather unexpectedly on the race of the sculptor, not on the race of the sculpture. "She has the proud spirit of her Indian ancestor," wrote Bullard, "and if she has more of the African in her personal appearance, she has more of the Indian in her character." [157] What could easily have been dismissed as merely a political statement—merely a black work of art by a black art worker, what Buick calls "a tautological reading of the relationship between Lewis and her art" [158]—was instead celebrated for its achievements and heralded as one of the true triumphs of the exhibit.

Thus, while the silences and covert winks that attend Lewis's biography are important in part because of how distinctly they represent the tendency in the nineteenth century for celebrities of color—especially women, such as the equally complicated Adah Isaacs Menken, who was sometimes known as "Cleopatra in a crinoline"—to intentionally complicate the matter of their personal histories when asked to provide them for public consumption, it is also crucial to understand the role of the ambiguity of origins in relation to Lewis's Cleopatra. As we have seen, Cleopatra was known as much for the debates regarding her personal genealogy as for the details of her adult life, and to nineteenth-century audiences the two were virtually inseparable. The multilayered significance of Cleopatra in terms of her sign as a figure of ambivalent origin—historically, culturally, symbolically, biologically—would not be lost on her sculptor. Lewis, a multiracial nonwhite lesbian expatriate already well known both for her busts of famous white abolitionists like John Brown and for her deracinated ideal sculptures of nonwhite subjects, sculpted, in Rome, at the height of the vogue for neoclassical figuration, a classical figure infamous, among other reasons, for the controversies surrounding her racial identity, her eyes closed in an ambiguous death, her one bared breast left ready for inspection.

## "In Her Queer Egyptian Style"

Cleopatra had a jazz band
In her castle on the Nile
Every night she gave a jazz dance
In her queer Egyptian style[159]

It is of course crucial to place Lewis in the context of Cushman and Hosmer, of Boston marriages and other homosocial intimacies playing out in Rome in the last half of the nineteenth century. "As the very humanity of persons of color was being violently debated on the battlefield of the United States Civil War," writes Merrill, "Cushman, Stebbins, and Hosmer welcomed Lewis into their growing social circle."[160] Yet even Merrill's account of a kind of lesbian Roman holiday applies only irregularly to Lewis. "In Rome Lewis had no real friends," counter Romare Bearden and Harry Henderson, "and she did not fit into the jealous, emotional hothouse of the Cushman villa."[161] Certainly there is much to frown about in this quick dismissal of the Cushman circle, but there is nevertheless more than an element of truth to this characterization, and in any case, in ways clearly reminiscent of her relationship with Child, Lewis and her white colleagues seem to have had their fair share of difficulties. "Edmonia is very much of an aboriginal," bitched fellow sculptor Anne Whitney to her longtime partner Adeline Manning in no uncertain terms in 1864, "spiteful, vengeful, a little cunning and not altogether scrupulous about the truth when dealing with those she doesn't love; open, kind and liberal as day with those she does—I like her in spite of her faults and will help her all I can—I wish she were a little less of an aborigine about the ordering of her wigwam." [162]

But it is equally crucial to recognize how visibly sculptural self-fashioning was to these artists: virtually all of the most famous members of "the white marmorean flock" were at some point concerned with creating images like that of Cleopatra. The representation of regal, powerful, tragically doomed, and epistemologically disruptive women was a central creative project for this group of artists, and it was to a constellation of uncontrollable, fatally powerful women from the ancient past that Lewis and her circle returned again and again: Medusa, Pandora, Zenobia, Cleopatra. Hosmer's most famous sculpture, for example, the 1859 *Zenobia in Chains*, was not only well received but its subject was widely understood to be a close thematic and even biological relative of Cleopatra, and several of the other women in Hosmer's and Lewis's group experimented with representing Cleopatra; as has already been noted, at the same 1876 exhibition where Lewis displayed her Cleopatra her expatriate Roman neighbor Margaret Foley also displayed a Cleopatra, though only a bust and carefully executed as white, awake, and alive. [163]

And thus it is finally crucial to understand Lewis and her sculpture as occupying a central site in the complicated interplay of race, gender, and sexuality that characterized the birth of the queer. "This mutation took place at the turn of the nineteenth century," wrote Foucault in 1976; "it opened the way for many other transformations that derived from it." [164] In other words, it has of course become virtually axiomatic that it was during the second half of the nineteenth century—over the course of Lewis's life—that the homosexual was created. That is, it is now widely recognized that it was during this period that the conceptual developments occurred that eventually produced the conditions of possibility for the operations of what could be—and to some extent still are—understood as modern gay and lesbian identities. And even though Sedgwick points out that "an unfortunate side effect of this move has been implicitly to underwrite the notion that 'homosexuality' . . . itself comprises a coherent definitional field rather than a space of overlapping, contradictory, and conflictual definitional forces," this convenient periodization "has provided," as she also discerns, "a rhetorically necessary fulcrum point for the denaturalizing work on the past done by many historians," and this strategy has only been further entrenched since the publication of her 1990 *Epistemology of the Closet*.[165]

"The historicizing project of this generation," observes Scott Bravmann, writing more recently, "has revealed . . . the discontinuities between cultural conceptions of homosexuality across time and space," but he presents what for both Sedgwick and himself remains a central problem: "these texts have in turn tended to reify certain current conceptions of homosexuality which are unified and stabilized by contrasting them to an utterly different past."[166] In other words, "they have created categories of bodily, psychic, social, and political experience on either side of this divide between past and present that are not only fundamentally different from each other but are also fundamentally similar to themselves. . . . Although social constructionist theory is dynamic and promising in relationship to understanding both the past and the present, these studies of the emergence of lesbian and gay identity have been relatively unsuccessful at recognizing race, gender, and class (among other) antagonisms 'within' that identity."[167] For Bravmann, as for Sedgwick, the historicizing projects of late-twentieth-century queer scholarship preserve the radicalism of what Sedgwick, eyeing Foucault, calls "the historical search for a Great Paradigm Shift" only to undermine its further implications. "In foregrounding diachronic or historical ruptures between social constructions of 'homosexuality,'" Bravmann writes, "these related projects have underemphasized the synchronic or contemporary ruptures between social constructions of homosexuality and their own specific histories, rife with contradictions of their own."[168] In other words, queer historiography is both too scholarly and not scholarly enough; in writing itself into history, queerness in this mode runs the risk of writing itself out again.

All of this is relevant for my discussion for this reason: my study of Edmonia Lewis can be located precisely within the space created by such tensions in queer historiography. Any account of Lewis and her life must, it seems, depend in part on the historical contexts provided by the research performed within the very frameworks about which scholars such as Sedgwick and Bravmann express such careful misgivings: Lillian Faderman, for example, or her student Dede Mousseau. Before the publication of Lisa Merrill's 1999 study of Cushman's *When Romeo Was a Woman*, Faderman's influential 1981 *Surpassing the Love of Men* provided what was the most pointedly political account of the homosocial circle of expatriate American women sculptors within which Lewis found herself enmeshed in Rome, and Mousseau's 1992 thesis on the partnership of Anne Whitney and Adeline Manning was by far the most sexually attentive account of that section of the Cushman/Hosmer group.[169] Important as these earlier studies are, however, equally clear is the extent to which accounts such as Faderman's and Mousseau's partake of the historiographic solipsism identified by theorists such as Sedgwick and Bravmann. "Despite the way they complicate notions of 'gay identity,' and show how there is no such unitary phenomenon as 'the' homosexual," Bravmann writes during his discussion of a series of gay and lesbian historiographies, which includes Faderman's 1991 *Odd Girls and Twilight Lovers*, "all of these studies remain deeply concerned with questions of same-sex sexuality. . . . the 'modern' category of homosexuality nonetheless provides the thread that sutures together the diverse, unstable, contradictory, and shifting histories recounted within each book."[170]

Yet therein lie the problems and contradictions that produced my study: there exists shamefully little scholarship, historical or otherwise, by which to place Lewis in the fullness of a context she so obviously deserves, and what does exist is firmly situated in the interpretive traditions of what Sedgwick identifies as the seperatist-feminist ones rooted in the 1970s and in the wake of what Bravmann calls Sedgwick's "rather strong dismissal of feminist theory's usefulness to gay theory" to boot.[171] Even given the revolution in queer studies over the last quarter century, for a variety of reasons most of the extant scholarship on the nineteenth-century emergence of what would come to be understood as early modern lesbian identities has been conducted on white women, white communities, and white-authored texts. "No comparable body of evidence," writes Karen Hansen in one of the few available primary source studies, "exists for Black women in the nineteenth century."[172] For a figure such as Lewis—self-identified as both African American and Native American yet educated in and surrounded by mostly white communities her entire adult life, a female sculptor regularly addressing pointedly American themes yet choosing to live almost exclusively as an expatriate in Rome after reaching adulthood, a nonwhite woman romantically and erotically involved in interracial relationships at least from the time of the early scandal at Oberlin—there are even fewer frameworks within which to place a critical study. More to the point, as common in queer historiography as calls for historiographic responsibility are calls for racial diversity, yet studies of Lewis find her trapped, as perhaps this study is trapped, between lesbian histories that are white and black histories that are straight.[173]

Clearly, however, Lewis lived and created during a period of critical change in American sexual identities, one obviously related to that which Duggan, echoing the critical consensus, identifies as "the changing nexus of gender identity and sexuality" of the 1890s, yet one almost a full half century earlier. "The content of the identities 'man' and 'woman' shifted from their Victorian to their modern configurations," Duggan summarizes of the end of the nineteenth century, "and the heterosexual/homosexual polarity emerged as a newly central preoccupation of gendered stories of identity." [174] Yet what Lewis's *The Death of Cleopatra* shows is how explicitly engaged some women from midcentury on were with the discourses that immediately predated those that soon were to produce the modern lesbian—especially insofar as they produced her as inverted and pathological. "Contests over the meanings of stories of lesbian identity expressed profound social anxiety over the boundary masculine/feminine itself," writes Duggan, and, as exhibited by countless students of the life of Cleopatra, the same was regularly said about the Egyptian queen as well.[175] What makes the efforts of Lewis so remarkable, however, are the clear indications that she herself regularly addressed questions of what many of us might today recognize as "queer historiography." In particular, these issues seem to be what informed the creation of *The Death of Cleopatra*.

In the first place, Lewis's Cleopatra, like all neoclassical sculpture, was a mode of writing history, a self-consciously current engagement with contemporary history masquerading as an anachronistic intervention into ancient historiography. Indeed, such sculptures were deliberate announcements of an awareness on the part of the women who created them of the differences between history and historiography; like their peers in the fields of the written word, sculptural students of antiquity were debating during a period when the moralistic manipulation of the historical record was a matter of public record, even personal pride. Neither Jacob Abbott nor Mrs. Jameson seemed reluctant to join the long tradition of political propaganda regarding interpretations of the life of Cleopatra, and the visibility with which Cleopatra's image was shaped to fit the needs of a given position in what were such obviously polemical debates is proof enough that a pronounced slippage between veracity and a liberal interpretation was nothing new in the life of the Egyptian queen. In this milieu, a savvy self-fashioner such as Lewis, who was more than a little accustomed to fabricating elements of her own biography for political purposes, was more than a little aware of the flexibilities of historical scholarship, more than a little queer in her style.

In the second place, Lewis's imaging practices seem uncannily attuned to the historical liberties taken in the name of sexual taxonomy. Even as neoclassical precedents were being sought to give authority to the homosocial structures of nineteenth-century life — the homoerotic identifications of Hellenophile Johann Winckelmann being one, the eventual hegemony of the very term "Lesbian" being another — Lewis seems to signify on both these precedents and on the racial connotations they imply. "In . . . using ancient Greece as the raw material for fashioning new possibilities for homosexual existence," writes Bravmann, "these conceptual models of Greek antiquity have been neither historically inevitable nor politically innocent. . . . This investigation of lesbian and gay uses of the Greek past seems particularly authorized at a time when recent public debates on race, ethnicity, and multiculturalism have so thoroughly problematized notions of culture, identity, and history." [176] Obviously Lewis anticipated such concerns.

As, in fact, did many of the rest of her circle: from her own 1869 sculpture of the racially othered, sexually ostracized, and more abjectly Egyptian Hagar to Foley's bust of Cleopatra and perhaps the most famous of all the Cushman/Hosmer group's efforts, Hosmer's own *Zenobia in Chains* (based on the powerful Palmyran queen who had claimed to be a descendant of Cleopatra), the range of non-Greek and non-Roman references to suffrage and female sexual power exhibited by "the white, marmorean flock" in the 1850s and 1860s presents a startling array of possible alternative identifications for both black and white women engaged in erotic relationships with other women in the days before Sappho.[177] In the very period that predates the emergence of the appellation "Lesbian" and thus shares, however conditionally, in the Greco-Roman decisions already being made in male homoerotic communities at the same time, the nonwhite Lewis sculpts as her symbol of antique sexual transgression not a proper Greek nor a proper Roman but an improper Egyptian.

Thus, while it would be a historical misreading to characterize Lewis's sculpture as an intervention into "lesbian" culture per se, what I am proposing is this: Lewis's *The Death of Cleopatra* was an intervention into some of the most pronounced and powerful discourses regarding race and sexuality that predated, anticipated, and eventually produced the invention of the modern lesbian. Lewis is signifying on what at the time were some of the most effective discursive influences on the construction of the modern woman and "her" sexuality: heteronormativity, sexual appetite, sexual "inversion," the rise of medical pathology. That Lewis would be only too aware of not only these pressures but the extent to which they—especially in their scientistic modes—relied on similar aggressions toward the bodies and cultures of African Americans and Native Americans in general is altogether clear from both her biography and her choices of sculptures. Masculine women in chains stand next to martyred abolitionists, and African American slaves plead for the ability to make their own choices as Cleopatra sags under the weight of hers.

To claim Lewis as a lesbian is thus to engage in the same kind of historical rewriting in which she herself was fully invested and which she regularly employed, yet with which she obviously had some serious reservations and recurrent conflicts; one can imagine Edmonia Lewis dressed in the identity of a twenty-first-century lesbian even as she clothed her nineteenth-century woman in neoclassical drag. Lewis predates lesbianism precisely as Cleopatra predates feminism; she sculpts a deliberate anachronism, drawing attention to the problems raised by its historical difference even as she relies on such difference for its coherence. She takes the current fashion for historical anachronisms and uses it for her own purposes, even as she tacitly critiques the ethnocentrism implied by such references to the neoclassical past. And creating from within a circle of white Americans both male and female, both "queer" and "straight," all concerned to represent Cleopatra in one form or another, Lewis's *The Death of Cleopatra* is at once race play, gender play, and chronoplay. Like her choice of subject in the first place, then, that her Cleopatra seems exhausted to death in the face of such efforts should come as no surprise. Lewis's Cleopatra seems to have died not just from the war that had recently ended but also from the wars yet to come.

# CHAPTER FIVE

# Egypt Land

### SLAVERY, UPRISING,

### AND SIGNIFYING

### THE DOUBLE

Sometime in the summer of 1824, a free African American man living somewhere in the northeast visited Rembrandt Peale's Museum and Gallery of the Fine Arts in Baltimore, viewed the first dynastic Egyptian mummy ever to be imported across American borders, and in April 1827 published some reflections on his experience in an anonymous article in the abolitionist weekly *Freedom's Journal*. "During a recent visit to the Egyptian Mummy," the author relates, "my thoughts were insensibly carried back to former times, when Egypt was in her splendor, and the only seat of chivalry, science, arts, and civilization. As a descendant of Cush, I could not but mourn over her present degradation, while reflecting upon the mutability of human affairs, and upon the present condition of a people who, for more than one thousand years, were the most civilized and enlightened." [1] What is striking about this passage is how succinctly it presents the central tension in nineteenth-century American Egyptomania: ancient Egypt, the land of "splendor and civilization," is placed face to face with a signifier of race. Moreover, it presents the dualistic logic and twin shapes of the American Egypt: the Egypt of "enlightenment" is considered next to the Egypt of "degradation," and the gulf between the two is shaped to carry echoes of a theory of history, a story of human origin, and an intentionally provocative relationship between the Egypt of secular scholarship and the Egypt of the Bible. "History informs us that Cush and Menes (the Misriam of Scripture) were the sons of Ham," our writer explains. "Mankind generally allows that all nations are indebted to the Egyptians for the introduction of the arts and sciences; but they are not willing to acknowledge the present race of Africans."[2] The figure of this multilayered Egypt stands in for an overall indictment of American race relations: of slavery, slavery's justification, and the terms of its continuance. The free black spectator of Peale's encased Egyptian offers his existential reflection as both cause and effect of the complex politics of the racialized land he sees: Egypt's "obelisks and pyramids," he writes, "which attest her greatness still remain, amid the grandeur of the desert, full of magnificence and death, at once a trophy and a tomb."[3]

What is also striking is how historically early this piece presents its complexities: in 1827, American Egyptomania was only beginning to gain shape—Peale's mummies, for example, had only come to America a few years before—and the fever pitches that are usually associated with its more famous high points—the 1840s and 1850s, the 1890s, and even the 1920s—were still decades away. But all of the pieces are in place: Egyptian artifacts are presented in a setting that is not quite gaudy but not quite perfectly respectable, either—that is to say, they are antiquities that are being popularized—but for all their ambivalence as popular attractions they are presented in a way that is nevertheless very pointedly marked. In numerous ways, ranging from Peale's associations with upper-class American politicians to its uses of a very particular kind of American imagery, Peale's Museum was marked as more or less explicitly white. In the article in Freedom's Journal, our writer marks this tacit whiteness as such—indeed, as political—and makes it all too relevant for the politics of slavery. In "former times," he writes, the kings of Egypt erected their tombs "to preserve [their] bodies from sacrilegious hands."[4] Today, though, he asks, "where are they? Have they not been torn from their 'vaulted sepulchres,' and exhibited to a gazing world? Have not they too been bought and sold?"[5]

Our anonymous contributor refuses the context of Peale's presentation—indeed, seizes on it, turns it on its head, signifies on it—and places his mummies on the very image of the auction block. He does not imagine himself as a black Egyptian prince, as so many others in this tradition, in every decade of the nineteenth century, had already done and would continue to do, but instead places the ancient Africans with which he is claiming kinship in his own land, the land of American slavery. Moreover, the Egypt with which he is familiar is even more removed from that of Peale; his Egyptian mummies are not just from the land of pharaohs and gold, not just secular artifacts or curiosities in a museum of natural history, but from the land of Cush, products of a history that is specifically biblical. "It is, I conceive, generally known that the first great monarchy of Assyria was founded by the descendents of Ham," our writer asserts, "who are . . . descended from Cush, our great progenitor."[6] As the son of Ham, the grandson of Noah, the biblical account of Cush and his family marked a moment of historical origin—one including, of course, the account of the children of Ham populating what most people on both sides understood to be northern Africa, even as, in the "Curse of Ham," it provided a justification for slavery, and our writer makes it clear that his indictment is of both white historiography and its proslavery innovations. "Who can convince us that the intellectual powers of man are inferior, because nature's God has tinged his complexion with a darker hue?" he asks. "The doctrine is contrary to all the evidences we have of the creation."[7]

Our contributor's mummies are from this land, the land of what was even then both the explanation for the differences between the races and the justification for the institution of slavery. Cush is both black and a pharaoh, both a prince and a slave. Our writer understands precisely what is at stake in this, his appropriation of Peale's presentation of the mummies. The issues he raises, both implicitly and explicitly, turn on the relationship among competing versions of history, competing versions of progress, competing versions of Egypt, and the politics of racialized difference. They also present what will be the primary concern of the bulk of this chapter, a central paradigm in the theorization of African American discourses of ancient Egypt: the discursive formation of ancient Egypt into a sign of the radical double, a doubled double of race, history, and the political uses of unresolved contradictions.

## "The Egyptians Were Africans
## or Coloured People, Such as We Are"

In the beginning, there were two Egypts. That is to say, at least since the beginning of the nineteenth century there have always been at least two strains of representations of ancient Egypt in the cultural traditions of African Americans. They are both largely familiar, I would imagine: Egypt the *dark* land, the land of Hebrew bondage, the home of slavery and the throne of Ol' Pharaoh; and Egypt the *black* land, a great African civilization, the land of Nefertiti and powerful black rulers. "Twas not long since I left my native shore / The land of errors, and Egyptian gloom," Phillis Wheatley wrote in 1773, yet in 1925, Langston Hughes would proudly proclaim that "I looked upon the Nile and raised the pyramids above it." [8] Indeed, at times it seems possible to weave the story of black Americans using only these two threads of self-expression: Egypt as the land from which we must escape and Egypt as the land to which we must return.

For all our familiarity with these traditions, however, surprisingly little attention has been given to the interactions between the overlapping sides of this doubled figure of African American Egypt Land. Often, of course, the narrative provided to explain such apparent disparities is that suggested by my choice of examples: Wheatley, writing almost 150 years before Hughes, merely existed in an earlier time—perhaps, the implication goes, in a time somehow less secular than others—and, as the history of African American political resistance developed, so did black understandings of the importance of ancient Egypt. These waters, however, are ones I will attempt to trouble in this chapter. Richly textured and extremely varied, there is a range of nineteenth-century black representations of what was even then the doubled world of the Arab world and the Holy Land, which has gone scarcely noticed in scholarship on the period. From at least the earliest days of Christianization, enslaved Africans and their descendants in America have been aware of the complicated set of interrelated and often contradictory relationships Egyptians in ancient history have had with the United States, and it is with those interrelations and frequent contradictions that this chapter is concerned.

Attempts at systematizing the disparate and often strikingly complex African American representations of ancient Egypt have usually resulted in a system of various "modes": vindicationist, redemptionist, antimodernist. "Vindicationism has often been concerned with presenting African history in a heroic or monumental mode," writes Wilson Jeremiah Moses. "It emphasizes the spectacular past and monumental contributions of the ancient civilizations of the Nile, including Ethiopia, Egypt, and Meroe."[9] Yet often accounts of this tradition diverge sharply from accounts of what is at the very least an equally recognizable mode, that of an Exodus *from* Egypt. "Without doubt, the Exodus story was the most significant myth for American black identity, whether slave or free," writes Albert Raboteau. "White Americans had always thought of themselves as Israel, of course, but as Israelites in Canaan, the Promised Land. Black Americans were Israelites in Egypt."[10] It is my argument here that the relationship suggested by this tension—between Egypt the black land and Egypt the dark—forms one of the most critical figures in African American cultural history. Far from being able to be neatly contained, as some scholars have attempted to do, African American interests in ancient Egypt are as heterogeneous and complex as anything found in contemporaneous white writings, and their intricacies and contradictions describe a resistance to easy classification as committed as the people who hold them. Rather than occupying points on a linear timeline, smoothly transitioning from one stage to the next, and rather than politely coexisting in segregated neighborhoods—one more sacred, one more secular, than the other—it is the argument of this chapter that a primary site for nineteenth-century African American racial theorizing occurred through articulations of the relationships between the often divergent, often convergent, multilayered figure of ancient Egypt, and that a principal site for formations of resistance, revolution, and racial identity occurred in the doubled figure of African American Egypt Land.

This doubled Egypt Land would be one of the principal concerns of David Walker's 1829 *Appeal to the Coloured Citizens of the World, but in Particular, and Very Expressly, to Those of the United States of America*. Walker's *Appeal* is both an example of an early black nationalist political pamphlet and a moment in a long history of African American religious insurrection. It is also, however, a text that complicates both of these traditions. The web of references to the biblical story of Egyptian Hebrew slavery in the book of Exodus by African Americans in general, and by revolutionary leaders in particular, was always already about both Egypt and America, both history and the politics of race.[11] Walker, however, takes both the terms of a specific black nationalism and the terms of a specifically black Christianity and inverts them, even as he relies on them to structure the shape of his argument. The *Appeal* is an extremely rich example of the signifying practices of African American religious and political discourse. The central site of this signifying is Egypt Land.

Arranged in four articles, with a preamble, the *Appeal* opens with these words:

> *My dearly beloved Brethren and Fellow Citizens.*
>
> Having travelled over a considerable portion of these United States, and having, in the course of my travels, taken the most accurate observation of things as they exist—the result of my observations has warranted the full and unshaken conviction, that we, (coloured people of these United States), are the most degraded, wretched, and abject set of beings that ever lived since the world began; and I pray God that none like us ever may live again until time shall be no more. They tell us of the Israelites in Egypt, the Helots in Sparta, and of the Roman Slaves, which last were made up from almost every nation under heaven, whose sufferings under those ancient and heathen nations, were, in comparison with ours, under this enlightened and Christian nation, no more than a cypher—or, in other words, those heathen nations of antiquity, had but little more among them than the name and form of slavery; while wretchedness and endless miseries were reserved, apparently in a phial, to be poured out upon our fathers, ourselves and our children, by *Christian* Americans![12]

Among all of the other things that are going on in this paragraph, Walker is establishing for African Americans a condition of epistemological uniqueness: "We coloured people of these United States," he writes, "are the most degraded, wretched, and abject set of beings that ever lived since the world began." Walker invokes the ancient Israelites, as well as the slaves of Greece and Rome, and claims not a similarity between them and African Americans but a radical difference. American slaves are far *worse* in their condition than any of their historical predecessors, and for Walker the point is so clear that Egypt becomes almost a footnote. "I will not here speak of the destruction which the Lord brought upon Egypt," he writes in his very next mention of the land of Old Testament bondage, "in consequence of the oppression and consequent groans of the oppressed—of the hundreds and thousands of Egyptians whom God hurled into the Red Sea for afflicting his people in their land."[13] Rather than identifying with the Hebrews, constructing a sympathetic relationship between their situation and those of his "brethren and fellow citizens," Walker goes to great lengths to distance himself from them. In fact, Walker works to devalue the sufferings of the Israelites relative to those he sees in America. "I only made this extract to show how much lower we are held, and how much more cruel we are treated by the Americans, than were the children of Jacob, by the Egyptians," [14] he writes, and throughout he seems less interested in easily relying on the political capital of either the trope of Egypt the black or Egypt the dark than in complicating their rates of exchange.

This is especially clear when Walker directly engages the intersections between biblical history and secular ethnology; in the comparison constructed between Americans and Egyptians, Walker's relationship to the characters in the Old Testament becomes complicated indeed. "Some of my brethren do not know who Pharaoh and the Egyptians were," Walker explains. "I know it to be a fact, that some of them take the Egyptians to have been a gang of *devils*, not knowing any better, and that they (Egyptians) having got possession of the Lord's people, treated them *nearly as* cruel as *Christian Americans* do us, at the present day. For the information of such, I would only mention that the Egyptians, were Africans or coloured people, such as we are—some of them yellow and others dark—a mixture of Ethiopians and the natives of Egypt—about the same as you see the coloured people of the United States at the present day." [15] In 1829, Walker is almost nonchalantly presenting a claim that to this day remains very controversial—that the pharaohs were black—and is doing it in what is a widely recognized moment in the history of black nationalism, but he is doing it in the service of an uprising against the structural position held by the black pharaoh. Walker's position vis-à-vis Pharaoh is that he was both black *and* a villain, and yet still relatively insignificant in the politics of slave uprisings. "But what need have I to refer to antiquity," Walker asks his readers of the appropriateness of insurrection, "when Hayti, the glory of the blacks and terror of tyrants, is enough to convince [you]?" [16] Clearly, this is not a simple matter.

A somewhat more general reading of this problematic might suggest what scholars such as Raboteau and Moses have: that African Americans during this period as well as others seized on tropes of Christian typology and envisioned themselves as analogues to the ancient Hebrews. African Americans were in Egypt, waiting for Moses, searching for the Promised Land. [17] The typological vision of African American Christianity could thus imagine any number of possible deliverances, each of which was deferred, or, more precisely, reinscribed, as either the surrounding context did not change — slavery, after all, did not end in 1829 — or a new context developed in which the traditions of typological imagery could make sense again. But for Walker this is absolutely not the case. Walker is doing something that is not noticed nearly as often in studies of African American religious and political oratory: he is saying that his people are *not* slaves in Egypt. They are not even close. Walker is constructing the justifications for insurrection on the basis of a secular identity that takes precisely the religious identity most traditionally related to images of American bondage and refuses it, asserting over and over again that American slaves are *not* Hebrew children.

This is not to suggest, however, that the *Appeal* is not a religious document. Far from it: it is in fact an extended sermon — revolutionary, political, and historiographic — and by far the overriding motivation of the text is one of divine commandment. "God rules in the armies of heaven and among the inhabitants of the earth, having his ears continually open to the cries, tears and groans of his oppressed people," Walker writes with apocalyptic energy, "and being a just and holy Being will at one day appear fully in behalf of the oppressed, and arrest the progress of the avaricious oppressors. Will the Lord suffer this people to go on much longer, taking his holy name in vain? Will he not stop them, PREACHERS and all? O Americans! Americans!!! I call God — I call angels — I call men, to witness, that your DESTRUCTION *is at hand*, and will be speedily consummated, unless you REPENT." [18] So we have a revolutionary Christian writing like an Old Testament prophet, distancing himself and his audience from an easy identification with the most important victims in the Old Testament. We also have an incredibly skilled orator and writer carefully avoiding virtually any use of metaphor, especially that of what is sometimes considered the root metaphor of African American Christianity. What, then, is the logic of the *Appeal*?

The *Appeal* is an example of a carefully controlled chronological strategy composed of a two-part sense of time: one that is, on the one hand, radically linear; and one that is, on the other hand, radically circular. It is a religious pamphlet that is also a document of secular history, and it is a lesson in biblical history that makes its points through characters that appear nowhere in the Bible. It is a Jeremiad that resists the terms of the Jeremiad, and an advocate of a material history which is unrepentantly millennial. It is constructed around a central split — between a religious modality and secular historiography — and it enacts an overall semiotic instability, *per-*

*forms* it, and through an oscillation between these two modes produces a sign that today we call "race." Race itself is configured as a radically complicated thing, not biological, or even cultural, but constructed by a very fluid set of signifying practices, only one of which is understood as time.

Indeed, Walker declaims his investment in theorizing chronology at every turn. The *Appeal* is just as much a history textbook as it is a religious exhortation, and there are long passages on the history of Greece and Rome, Haiti, the early Spanish slave trade, and Henry Clay's African Colonization Society. One of its primary functions, in fact, can be seen to be historical education. Walker's claims for the historical singularity of American slaves rests, after all, on his reading of history, and the history he presents is factual, empiricist, academic. It is, however, a secular history that begins and ends with the Lord. Walker alternates, then, between secular historiography and biblical millenarianism — he writes of "the Americans looking for the Millennial day" — that is, between a history that is linear and a history that is typological and cyclical. Yet, as I suggest above, this is typological history of a very particular sort. Biblical figures so often known as types — Adam, Jesus, Moses, and, of course, the Hebrew slaves and Pharaoh — are, for Walker, even while writing in a typological tradition, not exactly traditional types at all. Rather, they are points of comparison for proving the differential status of African Americans — American slaves are *not* Hebrew children but worse; Moses was an inspiration, but, Walker writes, we are not like Moses. So Walker both invokes biblical typology and dismisses it with a single motion, both writes repetition into history and erases it. Likewise, he points at secular history but only to point to God; he draws a straight line, only to have it loop back around.

This double structure of history is precisely the structure of African American Egypt Land. This is neither the drama of mutual exclusivity between secular history and biblical truth which structures white secular Egyptology during this same period, nor the dream of eventual reconciliation between the discoveries along the Nile and the authority of the scriptures which structures white Christianity. Neither is it the chronological police state inhabited by either architectural revivalism or Edgar Allan Poe. Both secular and sacred, both linear and typological, both slave and pharaoh, Walker's text is structured by the simultaneous elaboration of ostensibly competing versions of history, and the oscillation between the two poles produces, in miniature, examples of the traditions we have come to know as "metaphor" or "rationalism." Identification with the slaves of the

Old Testament is not so much a process as an *effect*, produced by the discursive play between competing or alternating versions of the meanings of ancient Egypt. It is the use of one figure or the other that both draws the relationship and draws it into question. In other words, this is the sign of Cush, under which our contributor to *Freedom's Journal* placed his reading of Peale's mummies. It is the very model of an irreducible instability. It is the strategic space par excellence for the dislodging of both claims about the whiteness of ancient Egypt *and* claims about biblical justifications for slavery. The sign of Cush is the sign of Egypt: it is both secular *and* sacred, both the invocation of a tradition of white supremacy and an intervention into that tradition. It is also, and perhaps most importantly, the mark of *dialogue*, between black and white, between pharaoh and slave, and between Egypt and America.

## "The Pharaohs Are on Both Sides of the Blood-Red Waters!"

This structure was one that Henry Highland Garnet would later work into the very model of Egyptomanic signifying. Given in 1843 to the National Negro Convention in Buffalo, Garnet's "Address to the Slaves of the United States of America" was published five years later in the same pamphlet as Walker's 1829 *Appeal to the Coloured Citizens of the World*, and most scholars understand both the ideological and material relationships between these two texts to share much in the way of similarities.[19] Equal parts history text and theological exclamation, the "Address" is built around the same central tension as the *Appeal*, between secular historiography and religious oratory. Opening with a brief history of the Negro National Conventions, Garnet writes in his first paragraph that "We have been contented in sitting still and mourning over your sorrows, earnestly hoping that before this day your sacred liberties would have been restored. But, we have hoped in vain. Years have rolled on, and tens of thousands have been borne on streams of blood and tears to the shores of eternity."[20] Garnet, like Walker, understands his role to be just as much one of historian as of theologian. "Two hundred and twenty-seven years ago the first of our injured race were brought to the shores of America," he writes, "But they came with broken hearts . . . and were doomed to unrequited toil and deep degradation. Nor did the evil of their bondage end at their emancipation by death. Succeeding generations inherited their chains, *and millions have come from eternity into time."* [21]

Garnet includes a list of famous resisters to oppression, both black and white, complete with dates and details: Denmark Vesey, Nat Turner, Joseph Cinque, Madison Washington.[22] But just as importantly he also elaborates a theory of history: "Mankind are becoming wiser, and better, the oppressor's power is fading, and you, every day, are becoming better informed, and more numerous."[23] Throughout the "Address," Garnet reveals himself to be irreducibly teleological, a positivist with unshakable faith in the upward progress of an abstracted History. For a Christian abolitionist, however, this faith, it would seem, would be sorely tested:

> Humanity supplicated with tears for the deliverance of the children of Africa. Wisdom urged her solemn plea. The bleeding captive plead his innocence, and pointed to Christianity who stood weeping at the cross. Jehovah frowned upon the nefarious institution, and thunderbolts, red with vengeance, struggled to leap forth to blast the guilty wretches who maintained it. But all was vain. Slavery had stretched its dark wings of death over the land, the Church stood silently by—the priests had prophesied falsely, and the people loved to have it so. Its throne is established, and now it reigns triumphant.[24]

This passage is indicative of much of the register of the "Address": highly abstracted historical forces move across a stage of enlightenment positivism, with the heroes and opponents of progress divided in polar corners, and all are delivered in an idiom that is forcibly and pointedly that of the religious revival. This, then, is another way of framing the central tension in the text: the upward progress of a teleological history, wedded to a faith in emancipatory Christianity, must explain what is, after all, the central problematic of the piece, slavery.

Indeed, this tension between a secular teleology and a sacred typology produces some noticeable effects: for a religious tract, Garnet's "Address" contains surprisingly few actual quotations from the Bible. "God," like the terms "History" and "Wisdom" and "Humanity," is mostly abstracted, highly general, and for the most part nonspecific. There are in fact only three direct references to the Bible, and, interestingly enough, they are all made precisely to the figures a straight typological reading might expect—that is, to Egypt and Hebrew slavery. One is strictly historical, to

Moses; Garnet places him in his list of humanity's emancipators, along with William Tell, Toussaint L'Ouverture, and George Washington. The other two are to Pharaoh. In the penultimate paragraph, Garnet imagines an inversion of American race relations: "If the scale was turned," he writes, "and black men were the masters and white men the slaves, every destructive agent and element would be employed to lay the oppressor low. *Yes, the tyrants would meet with plagues more terrible than those of Pharaoh.*" [25] Like Walker, Garnet is using the image of Pharaoh only to show how the Egypt of *America* is, or at least would be, all the worse than the Egypt of the Old Testament. American slaves are, once again, *not* like their biblical progenitors at all. Moreover, there is also even more distancing going on here; in Garnet's apocalyptic vision, "the plagues more terrible than those of Pharaoh" would come only when "*black* men were the masters and *white* men the slaves"—that is, if and when the slaves to whom the "Address" is addressed were, in fact, Pharaohs.

By far, however, the highest point of Garnet's text comes exactly at the moment of the third invocation of Egypt. "Brethren," the long paragraph begins, "the time has come when you must act for yourselves. . . . You can plead your own cause, and do the work of emancipation better than any others." [26] Garnet builds his passage slowly, dramatically, invoking images of "loving wives," "poor children," and "the torture and disgrace of your noble mothers." [27] He first suggests that his audience "go to your lordly enslavers, and tell them plainly, that you *are determined to be free*," and then propose a new economic relationship with them, "promis[ing] them renewed diligence in the cultivation of the soil, if they will render to you an equivalent for your services." [28] If, however, this does not work—and Garnet's strategy implies that he knows full well how this offer would be received—the stakes must be increased:

> Tell them in language which they cannot misunderstand of the exceeding sinfulness of slavery, and of a future judgment, and of the righteous retributions of an indignant God. Inform them that all you desire is FREEDOM, and that nothing else will suffice. Do this, and forever after cease to toil for the heartless tyrants, who give you no other reward but stripes and abuse. If they then commence work of death, they, and not you, will be responsible for the consequences. You had far better all die— *die immediately*, than live slaves, and entail your wretchedness upon your posterity.[29]

But then, with his imagined audience primed, the passage becomes a shriek:

> If you must bleed, let it all come at once—rather *die freemen than live to be slaves*. It is impossible, like the children of Israel, to make a grand exodus from the land of bondage. The Pharaohs are on both sides of the blood-red waters![30]

The image of Egypt and of Exodus that Garnet deploys is one of radical disidentification; he applies precisely the typological image with which, as a preacher, he is so intimately familiar and which, indeed, his audience and his idiom almost *demand* he use, and he denies that it applies. "It is impossible" for African Americans to be "like the children of Israel"; there is no Red Sea crossable, there is no Promised Land reachable: "*the Pharaohs are on both sides of the blood-red waters!*" For Garnet, the image with the greatest impact is that which insists on contradicting its own connotations. Like that of Walker's *Appeal*, the Egypt of Garnet's "Address" is one that holds histories of both blackness *and* darkness and one that is, most importantly, not rent asunder by its seeming split.

Yet famous as Garnet's "Address" is, it was by no means his ultimate expression of the political exigencies of the doubled figure of African American Egypt Land. In fact, as in the "Address," sometimes the complexity of African American constructions of ancient Egypt is best seen in large-scale differences between radically opposed visions of ancient Egypt, and, seen from a certain distance, there are indeed important distinctions to be made between cotemporal shapes in the landscape of African America. Sometimes, however, the complexities of nineteenth-century black thought can be tracked in a single paragraph. "We learn from Herodotus, that the ancient Egyptians were black, and had woolly hair," wrote Garnet five years after his "Address," in what was by then a very familiar refrain in the call and response structure of nineteenth-century black historiography. "These people astonished the world with their arts and sciences, in which they revelled with unbounded prodigality."[31] But what begins as a standard catechism in the composition of Afrocentricity becomes, somewhat unexpectedly, a warning against the consequences of great power: "They became the masters of the East, and lords of the Hebrews. No arm less powerful than Jehovah's, could pluck the children of Abraham from their hands. The plagues were marshalled against them, and the pillars of cloud and fire, and at last the resistless sea."[32] Garnet is now representing *both* Egypt the black land *and* Egypt the dark, both secular scholarhip and the traditions of sacred scripture. Egypt is at once a site of an antiracist intervention, a site of the invocation of a pre-Christian authority, a territorial maneuver on the battlefield of civilizationism, *and* at the same time a site of a stern biblical admonition against the very terms of secular progress and civilization.

Like that of his "Address," Garnet's Egypt is here a double land. But Garnet does not complete his history lesson on even such a double note. "But the kingdom of the Pharaohs was still great," he equivocates, and "the most exalted moral eulogium that could be spoken of Moses, was, that he was learned in all the learning of the Egyptians. It was from them that he gathered the materials with which he reared that grand super-structure, partaking of law, poetry, and history, which has filled the world with wonder and praise." [33] For Garnet, Moses was great because he used the very power of the Egyptians against them. This is a kind of merging, where "greatness"—that is, a secular greatness measured by the values of a nineteenth-century civilizationism—is gauged by its effects on a bibli-cal figure—in fact, the figure who will famously reveal that greatness to be false—and power is measured by the extent to which it prepares, if un-wittingly, the instrument of its downfall to bring about its own destruc-tion. For the revolutionary Garnet, writing in the black abolitionist press in 1848, the connections between strength and self-destruction, between power and vulnerability, all metaphorized through the figures of ancient Egypt and the image of slavery, were entirely the point.

Yet Garnet still has more to say about the role of ancient Egypt in history, and, strikingly, he takes as his next point the very incident of self-destruction so obviously resonating with his abolitionist audience. "Mournful reverses of fortune have passed over that illustrious people," he writes. "The star that rose in such matchless splendor above the east-ern horizon has had its setting. But Egypt, Africa's dark-browed queen, still lives. Her pyramid tombs—her sculptured columns, dug from the sands to adorn modern architecture—the remnants of her once impreg-nable walls—the remains of her hundred-gated city, rising over the wide-spread ruins, as if to guard the fame of the race that gave them existence, all proclaim what she once was." [34] This rhetorical shape—of a ruined past haunting an eager and attentive present—emerges at the end of this single paragraph like an emblem in miniature of the heterogeneity of African American attitudes toward ancient Egypt.

As melancholy and Romantic as Shelley's buried Ozymandias, as secular and historiographic as a popularizing Egyptologist, as moralistic and scriptural as the preacher Garnet was, this passage switches through virtually all of the different modes available to nineteenth-century African Americans. Sentimentalist, vindicationist, monumentalist, redemptionist, and, especially, racialist, Garnet's Egypt seems expressly designed to operate in all of the supposedly competing modes of nineteenth-century black historical thought at once, and yet it somehow refuses them each in turn; his chronological contortionism seems calculated to declare his awareness of the complexities of dealing with the signs and wonders of ancient Egypt yet also to indicate some nagging inadequacies about the options they all present. His narrative is an unlikely manifesto of historiographic theory, almost dismissible because of its brevity and almost cavalier in its treatment of its subject, yet there is something obviously deadly serious about both its occasion and its content. "Briefly and imperfectly I have noticed the former condition of the colored race," he concludes. "Let us turn for a moment to survey our present state. . . . The woeful volume of our history, as it now lies open to the world, is written with tears and bound with blood. As I trace it, my eyes ache and my heart is filled with grief. No other people have suffered so much, and none have been more innocent. If I might apostrophize that bleeding country, I would say, O Africa, thou has bled, freely bled, at every pore! Thy sorrow has been mocked, and thy grief has not been heeded."[35] Garnet seems to turn away from history, at the close of his short article, yet even as he does so he returns to its lessons. "Hell itself cannot overmatch a deed like this," he writes of the horrors of American slavery, at the close of this article, which began by discussing the ancient world, "and dark damnation shudders as it sinks into its bosom and seeks to hide itself from the indignant eye of God."[36]

Part of what is being described here is a process of improvisation. Walker, Garnet, the contributor to *Freedom's Journal*, and the traditions of which they are a part represent a complicated strategy of improvisational hermeneutics, invoking related but diverging, and at times even contradictory, sets of images and connotations of ancient Egypt, at times weaving them together, at times wrenching them apart. Fluidity is paramount, as is the flexibility to deploy and redeploy types and icons that in some contexts signify oppression and in others liberation. And for a tradition that is heavily invested in both typology and linear history, the figure of ancient Egypt provides a vital vocabulary. Or, better, the idiom I want to use here is not so much linguistic — "vocabulary" — as musical; in my use of the term *improvisation*, the musical connotations are intentional. The improvisational skills rendered so richly by Walker and Garnet are of course closely related to their more strictly musical versions, one of which is referenced by the title of this chapter and this book.

Spirituals in general, and of course "Go Down, Moses" in particular, occupy precisely the space I am here attempting to describe: that of the relationship between discourses of race and characters in the Bible, and ways of thinking about time. Spirituals are, after all, ways of structuring time—not just in their lyrical aspects, and in the relationship to history that those lyrics represent, but in their status as *musical strategies*, as musical forms, as rhythmic and performative manipulations. They are sites for the practical and theoretical elaboration of notions about the ways time can work, the ways it can be shaped, addressed, constructed, and reconstructed. Improvisational and highly structured, highly fluid and highly fixed, spirituals render the space they inhabit linear *and* circular, mark their expression as both progressive and repetitious.[37] Spirituals, like the *Appeal* and the "Address," are mediums for theorizing time, even as they are vehicles for theorizing Egypt Land.

## "Way Down in Egypt's Land"

Near the midpoint of Pauline Hopkins's magazine novel *Of One Blood; or, The Hidden Self*, Dianthe Lusk, a former soloist with the Fisk Jubilee Singers, suddenly and unexpectedly crosses a crowded room at an upper crust party in high-society Boston, sits down at a piano, and, "unattended," begins to play and sing:

> Go down, Moses, way down in Egypt's land,
> Tell ol' Pharaoh, let my people go.[38]

No one seems more surprised at Dianthe's performance than the singer herself, and the effort of her performance takes a toll on her that far surpasses the physical: "The singer sang on, her voice dropping sweet and low . . . and at the closing word, she fell back in a dead faint."[39]

This moment of surprise and collapse is but one episode in a string of such instances that Hopkins uses to indicate the disruptive power of ancient Egypt and its representations in *Of One Blood*. Dianthe's husband has, only paragraphs before, left Boston on an archaeological expedition to study the history of ancient Egypt, causing "a perceptible break in [their] social circle," and the things he will discover will radically alter the lives of every character in the novel. What Dianthe's performance of the spiritual represents, however, is an irruption not only in the body of Dianthe or the plot of *Of One Blood* but in the very traditions of nineteenth-century American representations of Egypt as well. The Egypt to which Dianthe's husband journeys is represented as thoroughly scientific, structured by the discourses of archaeology, biology, and narrative history. The Egypt of which Dianthe sings is one of slavery, religion, and the Old Testament. The relationship between these two Egypts reveals *Of One Blood* to be one of the most important examples of African American constructions of the figure of the double.

Hopkins's novel was published in the *Colored American Magazine* between the Novembers of 1902 and 1903 and is often cited as an early-twentieth-century example of what has come to be known as Afrocentricity.[40] Her African American explorer hero will travel to Meroe, the capital city of ancient Ethiopia, will discover a hidden city of fantastic wealth and culture, and will establish for himself, and for Hopkins's readers, the "fact that Egypt drew from Ethiopia all the arts, sciences and knowledges of which she was mistress."[41] This is, moreover, a discovery with implications that are acutely racialized: "All records of history, sacred and profane," one of her scientists will pronounce, "unite in placing the Ethiopian as the primal race."[42] Ethiopia is a sign of explosive transgression for Hopkins, a site of absolute evidence for the history of the world and the politics of American race relations, but it is a sign that is buried, hidden, concealed. A critical term in the formulation of American racial identity, Ethiopia must be excavated to be understood. Both obvious and mysterious, manifest and submerged, declarative and secretive, in the unfolding of Hopkins's narrative its structure becomes the structure both of American racial identity and of the text itself.

At times a kind of showroom for scientific theories of human development, and for Hopkins's familiarity with them, *Of One Blood* is one of a large number of texts written by African Americans that by 1903 had placed Ethiopia as the point of origination for humankind. These texts were at once interventions into scholarly arguments about human origin and sites of resistance against the political implications those arguments were widely seen to have; ancient Egypt had long been claimed by white scholars as a "white" civilization, and ancient Ethiopia, simultaneously marked as "black," was denigrated, dismissed, or ignored. In this field of politicized history, Ethiopia was used by nineteenth-century African American intellectuals in two major ways. Sometimes it was used to perpetuate this binary racial distinction: Egypt was to Ethiopia as white was to black, and ancient Egypt was only a pale copy of Ethiopian greatness. In this model, Ethiopia was the undiscovered or repressed source of Egyptian—and, by white scholars' own extension, "white"—civilization, a point of hidden origin. It was a land whose study would reveal the structure of racist history even as it utilized the terms of that history. Sometimes it was used to deconstruct the binarism: ancient Egypt was seen to be an undiluted descendant of Ethiopia, and Egypt itself was thus presented as a product of what Americans would be either proud or horrified to understand as "blacks." "Great Scott!" one of Hopkins's white characters exclaims, "you don't mean to tell me that all this was done by *niggers?*"[43]

While these controversies have been explored at length elsewhere in this book, it is certainly worthwhile to note Hopkins's place in this long lineage of anxiously racialized debate. Sometimes thought to be a relatively recent controversy in the field of ancient history, Hopkins's text in fact stands at a point in this debate that is now equidistant from the time of its inception and our own. What particularly interests me here, however, is something that is unique to *Of One Blood*. It represents a crucial moment in the development of racialized American discourses of ancient Egypt, and particularly in those generated by African Americans. Egypt, Ethiopia, and the civilizations of ancient Africa were—and, indeed, still are—critical terms in the racialized politics of ancient historiography, but for these signs the mode of scientific representation marks only *one* strain of representation in Hopkins's text. The other is that which irrupts with such dramatic effect in the party in Boston. The Egypt/Ethiopia dyad is not only a mark of the politics of black and white, but for African Americans it is also a mark of the politics of the sacred and the secular. Hopkins's novel is written precisely at the point when Afrocentric Egyptology is making a transition from a grassroots, religiously informed, Bible-based social movement to an increasingly professionalized, highly centralized, scientifically invested, relatively secular program, and the entirety of her text can be seen to be concerned with this transition. In a period that can be seen as anxiously divided between binary terms like *black* and *white*, *biblical* and *nonbiblical*, and *Egypt* and *Ethiopia*, it is the space *between* these terms that is occupied by *Of One Blood*.

Both in the interactions between European Americans and African Americans and in the relationship between African American religious traditions and black secular historiography, the figure of Egypt becomes a figure for the cultural politics of race.

The figure of the scientist's Egypt is initially to be found in the archaeological voyage of Hopkins's main protagonist, in his expedition and its party; the figure of the Egypt of "Go Down, Moses"—the Egypt, quite explicitly, of the slave—is in the spiritual sung not once in the text but a total of three times. But the story of Dianthe and her world in Boston becomes itself an archaeological narrative, a series of revelations of buried secrets, and the voyage, placed so firmly under the sign of the knowable, becomes disrupted by its double, its hidden truth. Egypt is a land of hidden secrets and uncovered truths, but so, Hopkins makes clear, is America. Hopkins's text plays between these figures and the narratives that develop them, which number either two, four, or one; the ancient Egypt of Africa becomes a figure for race in America, and the American in ancient Africa becomes the main figure in Egypt's land. In his journey to a historicized Africa, Hopkins's protagonist becomes a character in biblical history, and in her invocation of a biblical figure his wife becomes an actor in the politics of "race" as a product of the secular.

What I wish to draw attention to is how, in *Of One Blood*, Egypt is represented as a figure of the double. It is at once both itself and America, both a land of historical pride and a land of religious shame, both a starting point for political controversy and an end, both a site of literal excavation and a metaphor for the problematic of African American racial identity. It is a land of freedom, in the form of a historical truth that will free America from the slavery of lies. It is also a land of oppression, in the form of a biblical truth about slavery, both of Hebrews and of Africans. In other words, as Hopkins's text oscillates between treatments of it as a site of enslavement and a site of liberation Egypt is a land of enormous ambivalence. Egypt is rendered here a *double* land: bifurcated, along the lines of, on the one hand, literal scientific artifact, eminently and patently knowable, and, on the other, as a sign of American slavery, radically and explosively metaphorical, irruptive, disruptive, and uncontainable. Egypt is both the signifier and the signified of what is here both slavery and freedom, both the content and the context of the transition from the sacred to the secular. Hopkins's novel is structured by the duality of what is, for her, both subject and object.

## "Many Things Herein Lie Buried"

1903 was no stranger to African American discourses of the double. It was the year that saw the publication of what has become the most famous formulation of African American duality, W. E. B. Du Bois's *The Souls of Black Folk*. "It is a peculiar sensation," the now familiar passage reads, "this double-consciousness, this sense of always looking at one's self through the eyes of others. . . . One ever feels his two-ness—an American, a Negro; two souls, two thoughts, two unreconciled strivings; two warring ideals in one dark body, whose dogged strength alone keeps it from being torn asunder."[44] As is well known, the section of *Souls* which presents Du Bois's formulation had actually appeared some six years prior, in the 1897 essay "Strivings of the Negro People," and this passage which is so often quoted was repeated verbatim from the earlier piece.[45] Hopkins thus announces throughout *Of One Blood* a strident intertextuality with the work of Du Bois and, moreover, with the intellectual traditions that shaped and influenced her more famous contemporary. *Of One Blood* is no less a sustained meditation on duality and African American identity than "Strivings" or *Souls*, and Hopkins's novelized structure of this meditation is, at the very least, a fictionalized counterpart to the essays that would become such a watershed in the history of race and race theory in America. Hopkins can even be seen to be making a wry inside joke about her relationship to Du Bois, early in the novel; "Lucky dog!" her hero "growl[s], enviously" at a friend marked by a position of relative wealth and privilege, "you have a greater gift of duality than I."[46] In fact, this main character in *Of One Blood* can be seen as a fictionalized figure of Du Bois: trained at Harvard and a disciple of William James.

An essay by James inaugurates the action of *Of One Blood*, although both its title and its authorship are disguised, and most recent scholars who have written on Hopkins's novel have commented on this threefold relationship among Hopkins, James, and Du Bois.[47] The overt placement of the James essay, even camouflaged as it is, the sustained treatment of the theme of African American duality in a work so contemporaneous with that of Du Bois, and the canonically recognized influence of James on Du Bois make these connections virtually foundational in current scholarly placements and understandings of *Of One Blood*. What is remarkable, however, in the history of the reception of the novel is how these relationships very often circumscribe the discursive presentation of the text as a whole, providing not only the beginnings but the end of critical investigation. This is testimony, no doubt, to the robustness of the theories of James and Du Bois but also to their accessibility and critical acceptance. Hopkins, I would claim, not only has a specificity of her own, apart from the influences of these more famous men, but is, moreover, attempting to write her way *through* these relationships in a way that is scarcely recognized.[48] *Of One Blood* is not only about psychology and biological constructions of race; it is also a text structured by a problematic that underwrites these themes, a problematic that is patently and manifestly *archaeological*. Hopkins's text is organized within an economy of the hidden, to be sure, but the discourses of psychology that have featured so prominently in recent criticism can themselves be seen to be only half of a dual construction; underneath is something perhaps more materialist, certainly more historicist, and concerned not, as it were, with the archaeologies of identities but with the identities of the archaeological. And, to gesture once more to Du Bois, this situation might very well be said to structure the reception of *Souls* itself; "many things which if read with patience may show the strange meaning of being black here in the dawning of the Twentieth Century," writes Du Bois in "The Forethought" to *his* work of 1903, "[h]erein lie buried."[49]

The action of *Of One Blood* is divided into roughly two parts, moving from Boston to Ethiopia. In Boston, the narrative develops the concentrated psychologism that frames the relationships among the major characters: Reuel Briggs, a brilliant but pointedly abject medical student, interested in mesmerism, spiritualism, and the "unclassified residuum" of the disguised James essay; Aubrey Livingston, a white Southern aristocrat whose slaveholding father practiced hypnotism on his slaves and who is a skilled mesmerist himself; and Dianthe, who after performing in Boston is injured, thought dead, but brought back to consciousness by Briggs by way of a spectacular display of mesmeric powers and, while yet amnesiac, is revealed to be suffering from what Briggs calls, via Alfred Binet, a "*dual* mesmeric trance."[50] Identity is immediately rendered flamboyantly dualized in these opening scenes, segmented along the lines of the new psychology of Binet and James. Its bifurcation is accessed in mesmeric trances, its binary construction a model of repression. Hopkins takes discourses that were not at all concerned with the problematic of "race" as such and enacts a politics of a racialized burial of identity.[51] These split figures—

Dianthe, Briggs, Livingston—will, as the narrative unfolds, come to be understood not as merely psychological case studies but as products of the politics of race. Their subjectivities will thus be the first installments in an extended development of the figure of Egypt: buried, hidden, excavated, and revealed.

Indeed, the mechanisms of repression shape for Hopkins the most concise example of the issues at stake in the psychologism of *Of One Blood*: race, memory, and the histories of slaves. At a party at the home of Charlie Vance, Aubrey Livingston tells a story of his slaveholding father and his father's favorite slave, of whom the elder Livingston was so fond of placing in a trance:

> "One day there was a great dinner party given at our place, and the élite of the country were bidden. It was about two years before the civil war, and our people were not expecting war. . . . When the feasting and mirth began to lag, someone called for Mira—the maid—and my father sent for her to come and amuse the guests.
>
> "My father made the necessary passes and from a serious, rather sad Negress, very mild with everyone, Mira changed to a gay, noisy, restless woman, full of irony and sharp jesting. In this case this peculiar metamorphosis always occurred. Nothing could be more curious to see her and hear her. 'Tell the company what you see, Mira,' commanded my father.
>
> " 'You will not like it, captain; but if I must, I must. All the women will be widows and the men shall sleep in early graves. They come from the north, from the east, from the west, they sweep to the gulf through a trail of blood. Your houses shall burn, your fields shall be laid waste, and a downtrodden race shall rule in your land. For you, captain, a prison cell and a pauper's grave.'
>
> "The dinner party broke up in a panic, and from that time my father could not abide the girl. He finally sold her just a few months before the secession of the Confederate States, and that was the last we ever knew of her." [52]

Mira is called to "amuse" but performs a role that is precisely the opposite. Mesmerism, a tool of the psychic archaeologist, here is a site of intended control but unexpected resistance, a return of the repressed with a supernatural vengeance. A figure of racialized coercion, Mira's split self becomes a site of excavation and one with devastating results. Mira is the destructive power of the truth unleashed. Asked to play the minstrel, Mira instead be-

comes a trickster, but she is a trickster with only two sides. On the stage of
the plantation, double consciousness is performed by New World Africans
as a symptom of their condition. In this, its most succinct manifestation,
it is explosive, prophetic, and all too acutely racialized.

"Race" thus becomes the signifier of the split subjectivity of the enslaved African. Especially in the face of the careful deconstructions of the
categories of *biological* definitions of race that Hopkins performs throughout *Of One Blood*, these split subjectivities become what in the text is presented under the sign of "race." The sign of race—which is the symptom
of the split self—renders African American subjectivity as such and vice
versa. To be doubled is to be black. And, to be sure, the analogy is made,
equally early in the novel, between the doubled consciousness of Dianthe,
the Livingstons' slaves, and the figure of Briggs, who, "[n]one of the students kn[owing] aught of [his] origin," is passing as white. As Cynthia
Schrager writes, "Reuel's fascination with 'the hidden self lying quiescent
in every human soul' can be seen, then, as a trope for the situation of the
African American who is 'passing.' "[53] It is not the color of Briggs's skin
that marks him as "black"; it is the dualized shape of his divided self. Hopkins takes a model of unstable subjectivity, presents it in a shape that is
profoundly archaeological, and displays it as a paradigm of race, of African American racial identity. This is Jamesian psychology turned, as for Du
Bois, into a model of racialized subjectivity.

For all its mysteriousness and scandalous unorthodoxy, however, this
psychological dualism is surprisingly easy to recognize. *Of One Blood* is a
text in which double consciousness loops through its characters, suturing
them all together in a network of bifurcated subjectivities. This intimacy
will come to have increasingly Gothic overtones as the novel continues,
but the dualisms are presented by Hopkins as altogether rather obvious in
their accessibility, curiously available as a split text to be read by almost
any given character—both of the Livingstons, Briggs, an unnamed woman
in a traveling sideshow. Hopkins even says as much, having Briggs suggest a radically democratic constituency for mesmerically knowable double
consciousness. "Perhaps the superstitious masses came nearer to solving
the mysteries of creation," he chides a skeptic, "than the favored elect will
ever come."[54] There is, however, another movement to the text, one that
sharply rarefies the currency of dualism and is in fact carefully and elaborately antidemocratic. Indeed, it is monarchical, and takes place during
the archaeological voyage to Africa. Just as African American subjectivity

is seen as divided, and just as the text itself is divided in its plot, the discourses of identity as such are divided, too: the second half of the novel is the site of revelation, of transformation, and, even dualized as it is, the psychologism of its first half is only the space of the manifest.

## "Go Down, Moses"

Dianthe is the hinge between Africa and America, not just in her doubled identity as both herself and Queen Candace—the identical, safely non-incestuous wife to be whom Briggs discovers along with his fantastic city and for whom Dianthe serves as prototype—but as the singer of the spiritual "Go Down, Moses." Virtually every character in *Of One Blood* is doubled in some way—racially, psychologically, familially—and virtually every one of them has some spectral or clairvoyant manifestation of this doubling; Briggs, for example, travels between Africa and America in astral form, as does the ghostly figure of his dead mother. But only Dianthe sings "Go Down, Moses," and "Go Down, Moses" is the only spiritual that is sung more than once and has its lyrics transcribed in the text. She is the character who first opens the space between the Africa of her husband's expedition and the Africa of something else, and that something else is precisely what is addressed in "Go Down, Moses."

The spiritual is performed first onstage, in the scene that introduces her both to the reader and to Briggs and Livingston (although she had been fantastically introduced to us and Briggs as a spirit figure only hours before), and then, weeks later, at the party. The second time, she is in fact onstage again, in a way that intentionally foreshadows the apocalyptic performance of the slave girl Mira, not performing under the auspices of the Jubilee Singers but under the social pressure of powerful whites looking for amusement. "There was a call for music," Hopkins writes. "Molly mentally calculated her available talent and was about to give up the idea and propose something else, when she was amazed to see Dianthe rise hurriedly from her seat on an ottoman, go to the piano unattended and sit down. Unable to move with astonishment she watched in fascination the slender white fingers flash over the keys."[55] As becomes clear, Dianthe is herself in the throes of a kind of psychological surfacing, a vehicle for the violent appearance of an identity repressed, in fact in a heightened degree of the trance state that has come to define her dualized consciousness. Indeed, this second performance presents one of the most attenuated passages of supernatural doubling in *Of One Blood*:

> There was a strange rigid appearance about the girl that was un-
> earthly. . . .
> Scarcely was the verse begun when every person in the room started
> suddenly and listened with eager interest. As the air proceeded, some
> grew visibly pale, and not daring to breathe a syllable, looked horri-
> fied into each other's faces. "Great heaven!" whispered Mr. Vance to his
> daughter, "do you not hear another voice beside Mrs. Briggs'?"
> It was true, indeed. A weird contralto, veiled as it were, rising and fall-
> ing upon every wave of the great soprano, and reaching the ear as from
> some strange distance. The singer sang on, her voice dropping sweet and
> low, the echo following it, and at the closing word, she fell back in a
> dead faint.[56]

The Egypt of which Dianthe sings is the Egypt of Moses and Pharaoh, and it marks the point of contact between Dianthe's doubled consciousnesses. This is also Egypt marking its ascent—into Dianthe, the text, and the land of the *American* Pharaohs—under the sign of liberation from slavery. Dianthe's performance is also, unlike the performance of Mira, not a sign of the mutual exclusion of divided African American selves—their binary oscillation describing an economy of repression—but a figure of their mutual sustainability. Through the figure of the spiritual, Dianthe per-forms her divided self, both parts at once. The effort takes its toll, of course, signifying her ultimate inability to withstand its pressures, but the "weird contralto," "the echo," and "another voice beside Mrs. Briggs' " are marks of the doubled Dianthe, and they are uniquely marks of the slaves' spiri-tual's Egypt.

Egypt is here rendered the central figure of the novel. Its secular impli-cations have already been hinted at, and soon will be revealed, and Hop-kins's model of African American subjectivity has already been elaborately structured by an archaeo-logic. Briggs has just departed for Ethiopia, and his voyage of discovery will dominate the second half of the text. Like-wise, the hidden secrets of all Hopkins's major characters will come to be uncovered only after this point. Dianthe's singing of "Go Down, Moses" christens this action, signals its commencement. It marks the space of the intersection of the secular agenda of Briggs's expedition and the reli-gious significance of Egypt in America—specifically its significance for traditions of African American Christianity—and, crucially, this intersection is represented as explosive, overwhelming, and dangerously unstable. Dianthe can, in fact, be seen to be singing to Briggs, imploring him to "go down, way down in Egypt's land"—where he is of course going, to the land that is forever marked by its relationship to Egypt—and asking him to become Moses, to become the deliverer from all the forms of oppression that so deeply mark Dianthe and the racialized situation she represents. The spiritual is an appeal for rupture, for an act of heroism of literally Biblical proportions. As the novel progresses, this role of messiah is precisely the one that Briggs will come to occupy. Briggs will go down—literally, raciologically, and archaeologically—into Egypt Land.

"Go Down, Moses" is an updated plea, configured in part by the Afrocentric designs of Briggs's Ethiopian expedition. It is an appeal to the archaeological orientation of Afrocentric Egyptology but is one made through the discourses of the Christian Bible. It takes a division that characterized it in the past, that between ancient Hebrew slavery and modern African slavery, and adds to it a coexisting division within African American cultural politics, that between Egypt as the sign of oppression and Egypt as the sign of liberation. Through this very relationship, it is a figure in miniature of the sign of the double. At once sacred and secular, ancient and modern, a reference both to the historical condition of enslaved Africans in America and to the specific cultural moment at which she writes, the "Go Down, Moses" of Of One Blood, the doubled sign of the "Egypt's land" of Hopkins's America, becomes the structuring principle of her formulation of racial identity and racial politics at the beginning of the twentieth century.

Singing the spiritual activates and deactivates Dianthe's amnesia; it structures her memory, forming a border on each side. "Can you tell me what has happened," she asks Livingston, "since I last sang the song I sang here tonight?"[57] It is only in the figure of "Go Down, Moses" that the boundaries of Hopkins's doubled identities can seem to be marked. The spiritual—the musical power of which is described as so generally powerful throughout the text—provides the therapy that none of the new psychology could supply. "Go Down, Moses" is the mark of the point of contact between Dianthe's "dual trance" and her awakening from it, and significantly enough she sings it and recovers only after Briggs has arrived in Africa. This representation of Egypt provides a stage for Hopkins's version of what Du Bois called the Veil, a musical representation of his "peculiar sensation"—"a weird contralto, veiled as it were, rising and falling upon every wave of the great soprano, and reaching the ear as from some strange distance"—and the veil, it seems, not only describes Dianthe's "two-ness" but divides her place of performance from her husband's place of adventure. It even, in fact, divides Egypt from itself.

A patient with amnesia, a subject of white philanthropy, an object of sexual oppression and a victim of rape and incest, prone to fits of melancholy and fainting, seemingly dead but brought back to life, Dianthe is the very model of instability. Performing the double, and paradigmatically unstable, she is Hopkins's great artist of Egypt Land. She is also, finally, a tragic mulatta with an Egyptomanic structure. She, like Briggs, is caught in a drama of passing—her amnesia having hidden her background from her friends and herself, at least until her performance at the party—and, save for one crucial exception, has gone unknown as black. "We are surprised as anyone," says Dianthe's Boston hostess, "we never knew that Mrs. Briggs was musical until this evening."[58] The singing of the spiritual thus controls the movement of the archaeology of identity, invokes the emergence of Dianthe's hidden self; its metaphoricity commands the appearance of the pretraumatic real. The irruption of her pretraumatic identity occurs as she is passing, so to speak, through the land of slavery. Musical, disruptive, and doubled: this is Hopkins's Egypt.


### "What Puzzles Me Is Not the Origin of the Blacks, but of the Whites"

As the text makes clear, however, Dianthe and her performance are only half of the twinned representations of ancient Africa, and in her African expedition party Hopkins includes a character who represents the rendering of Africa as scientific artifact. A mouthpiece for the nascent Afrocentricity that is so often mentioned in discussions of *Of One Blood*, slyly presented as a white British intellectual, Professor Stone is also a figure of a kind of radical positivism:

> "You and I, Briggs, know that the theories of prejudice are swept away by the great tide of facts. It is a *fact* that Egypt drew from Ethiopia all the arts, sciences and knowledge of which she was mistress. The very soil of Egypt was pilfered by the Nile from the foundations of Meroe. I have

even thought . . . that black was the original color of man in prehistoric times. You remember that Adam was made from the earth; what more natural than that he should have retained the color of the earth? What puzzles me is not the origin of the Blacks, but of the Whites. . . . But of this we are sure — all records of history, sacred and profane, unite in placing the Ethiopian as the primal race." [59]

Professor Stone represents not just the stability of the scientific but its structure as well. His discourses are not only positivistic but acutely linear: history, genealogy, naturalism. Dianthe, through her inscriptions of "Go Down, Moses," represents the radically metaphorical. In this metaphorical space, Hopkins locates the irruptive — the sudden, the unexpected, the nonlinear — and through this irruption, not through the scientific positivism of Professor Stone, she describes the archaeological.

Stone, as his comments make clear, is a figure of unity — not racial or psychological but discursive. His narrative takes schools of thought that are marked as explicitly antagonistic and weaves them together to the point of alliance with one another. "Sacred and profane," Aryanist and Afrocentrist, racist and antiracist: Professor Stone negotiates traditions that are widely divergent and has them support one another in a discursive high point of epistemic stability. Indeed, it is the discourses of the sacred and the secular that Professor Stone has to spend the most time uniting. "I know that in connecting Egypt with Ethiopia, one meets with most bitter denunciation from most modern scholars," he admits. "Science has done its best to separate the race from Northern Africa. . . . But the Biblical tradition is paramount to all." [60] Throughout his "story of ancient Ethiopia, told in broken sentences," Stone has to reach back and forth, across the discursive divide between the biblical and the nonbiblical, enlisting each to support the other: "We associate the name 'Chaldea' with the sciences of astronomy and philosophy and chronology. It was to the Wise Men of the East to whom the birth of Christ was revealed; they were Chaldeans — of the Ethiopians." [61] In particular, Stone appeals to the science of linguistics to validate his account: "These conclusions have lately received important and unexpected confirmation from the results of linguistic research. . . . Comparative philology appears to confirm old traditions." [62] As his comments make clear, however, the burden of proof is on the modern, the secular; "old traditions" — Biblical traditions — are there to be confirmed. The Bible as authority is never questioned. And, at its most crucial moment, the interpretive stitches between the Bible and Stone's science are made explicit, the transition from one to the other baldly marked.

> "But the Biblical tradition is paramount to all. In it lies the greatest authority that we have for the affiliation of nations, and it is delivered to us very simply and plainly: 'The sons of Ham were Cush and Mizraim and Phut and Canaan . . . and Cush begat Nimrod.' . . . It is the best interpretation of this passage to understand it as asserting that the four races — Egyptians, Ethiopians, Libyans and Canaanites — were ethnically connected, being all descended from Ham; and the primitive people of Babylon were a subdivision of one of these races; namely, of the Cushite or Ethiopian." [63]

As I showed in chapter one, Stone tells in many ways a very standard and traditional nineteenth-century ethnographic account of racialized types. From the perspective of a biblically informed Afrocentrist — not to mention from that of a black folk ethnography — the pro-Hamitic upshot of this narrative was even more traditional, familiar, and immediately recognizable. A scientist who relies heavily on the biblical account, Stone constructs something of a narrative chimera, all the more remarkable for its impetus toward seamlessness.

Stone's hybridized narrative repositions history as such, allowing sacred history to authorize the postbiblical and allowing postbiblical positivism to appear active in a time which predates its inception: "For three thousand years the world has been mainly indebted for its advancement to the Romans, Greeks, Hebrews, Germans, and Anglo-Saxons; but it was otherwise in the first years. Babylon and Egypt — Nimrod and Mizraim — both descendants of Ham — led the way, and acted as the pioneers of mankind in the untrodden fields of knowledge." [64] "The untrodden fields of knowledge" are what Nimrod and his Babylonian countrymen "pioneer," and this is a sign of the positivistic if ever there was one. As Hopkins's biblically literate readers were sure to realize, however, Stone's narrative is completely rewriting the traditional biblical account on which he so heavily draws: that period of human history that culminated in the building of the Tower of Babel. "The Babylonians early developed the energy of mind which made their country the first abode of civilization," Stone explains. "Canals covered the land, serving the purposes of traffic, defense and irrigation. Lakes were dug and stored with water, dykes built along the banks of rivers to fertilize the land, and it is not surprising to learn that from the earliest times Babylonia was crowded with populous cities. This grandeur was brought about by Nimrod the Ethiopian."[65] What Stone neglects to mention, of course, is that the "energy of mind" he so glowingly describes is in the Bible an unforgivable arrogance punished by God.[66] In fact, Hopkins's text contains no mention whatsoever of the Tower of Babel. Stone's account presents early human history as a classic positivist bedtime story: human intelligence and its quest for knowledge reaches ever upward, since the dawn of time, progress infinitely progressing, without, it seems, ever making a mistake. Hopkins thus uses Stone as one pole in a binary construction, one explicitly placed in the shadow of ancient Egypt, and, like the structure of the text, the structure of her characters' selves, and the structure of Stone's object of study, there will come a counterpart.

In many ways, *Of One Blood* represents a moment of close relation to the other major work of African American Egyptology discussed in this project, Martin Delany's *Principia of Ethnology*.[67] Published some twenty-three years before *Of One Blood*, the arguments in the *Principia* bear a remarkable resemblance to the narrative of Egypt and Ethiopia presented by Hopkins: the racially differentiated sons of Noah populate the postdiluvian earth, the sons of Ham were the builders of the pyramids, and the sons of their sons were the founders of civilization. The Bible is a source text, supremely valuable because it is both a historical document *and* unimpeachable in its authority. And, as I argue in chapter one, the publication of the *Principia* marks a watershed moment in the history of Afrocentrism precisely because of the relationship that is represented by Professor Stone in *Of One Blood*: it draws on both white notions of the biology of race and black traditions of the historical interpretation of scripture; its proHamitic narrative of human civilization allows both a European model of teleological progress and an African American inversion of the terms of that model (black as inferior, white as superior), and its impulse is both one of radical intellectualism and radical social activism. Aside from Du Bois, it is with Delany that Hopkins is most deeply in dialogue in *Of One Blood*.

There is, however, one crucial difference. Whereas in Delany's *Principia of Ethnology* the most important moment of all is the story of the Tower of Babel, Hopkins, as we have seen, avoids the story altogether. Indeed, this absence is shared in the novel by another, closely related: Hopkins makes no mention of the other great cataclysm associated with this section of the book of Genesis, the other great act of a vengeful God. This is the act, in fact, that is responsible for the ethnic differentiation the subsequent history of which is told by Professor Stone: the flood of Noah. Stone's story begins just after the Flood—with the story of Ham—and concludes just before the destruction of the Tower of Babel. So the two moments of biblical apocalypse that frame the narrative presented by Professor Stone—and treated with such importance by Delany—are in Hopkins's text nowhere to be found. It is as if all instances of divine retribution associated with early human history as recounted in the Old Testament are completely erased from *Of One Blood*—all, that is, except one. The only story that does remain is the one invoked in "Go Down, Moses."

This is ancient African history being shaped into its double self. Egypt is developing into a secular term of immense importance to turn-of-the-century African Americans, but, dependent as it is on the Bible for its authorization, it is in a position of extreme ambivalence. Hopkins could, of course, have continued, unproblematically, in the tradition represented by Delany and later by Marcus Garvey and a host of others—that is, selectively represent the history of Egypt as progressive and utopian, treat the Bible primarily as a secular document, and glorify the achievements of Egyptian civilization according to a model based either on secular positivism or African spirituality. And, if recent scholarly treatments of *Of One Blood* are any indication, this is what most modern critics seem to believe she does.[68]

But Hopkins's novel is structured around a *divided* representation of ancient Egypt, just as it addresses the African American divided self. As Dianthe's singing of "Go Down, Moses," makes only too clear, the Egypt of "Ol' Pharaoh," the Egypt of slave religion, returns if repressed. *Of One Blood* describes this shape, this relationship between the burgeoning secularism of Afrocentric Egyptology and the new psychology and the irruptive metaphoricity of African American Christianity's "Egypt Land." At the midpoint of the novel, for example, Charlie Vance looks out the door of his tent and gazes out at the landscape: "It was not a simple thing to come all these thousand of miles to look at a pile of old ruins that promised nothing of interest to him after all. This was what he had come for—the desolation of an African desert, and the companionship of human fossils and savage beasts of prey. The loneliness made him shiver. It was a desolation that doubled desolateness."[69] This is also the space that is addressed by the novel's title. "Of One Blood" refers, on the one hand, to the discourses of science, the problematic of racialized biology, on the other to the verse from the book of Acts. It is, after all, to the Bible that the ghostly figure of the slave-mother Mira returns again and again—a figure shaped both by the discourses of the science of mesmerism and by the gravity of the book of the religion of the enslaved. And the passage that Hopkins places under the final sign of Mira is metaphorical and biblical, but it is also *archaeological*: "For there is nothing covered that shall not be revealed, nothing hid that shall not be known."[70] Like African American subjectivity itself, the figure of Egypt describes a double space.

My argument here is borne out by Hopkins's inclusion of the character of Aunt Hannah. Hoodoo doctor, conjure woman, and grandmother to all the major characters, Aunt Hannah is Hopkins's holder of all buried secrets. She is also in every way an inverted double of Professor Stone: black to his white, female to his male, unschooled to his scholasticism, spiritual to his scientific, biblical to his secular. Stone has no evidence but an audience to listen; Hannah holds epiphanies she has not been allowed to speak. If there is a figure antithetical to Stone, it is Aunt Hannah. Stone is the figure of hidden truths suspected but unconfirmed; Hannah is the figure of truth revealed. In the very structure of knowledge itself, Hopkins scripts a duality. When Dianthe sings "Go Down, Moses" one last time, it is in a scene of melancholy, of mourning, of resignation, and this scene marks the end of the archaeological motions of the text. She sings only after her meeting with Aunt Hannah, only after her lineage has been revealed to her and the hidden secrets of the novel uncovered, only after, in effect, she has gone down to her own Egypt Land. This is the archaeology of identity, but for Dianthe it is lethal. It is thus Dianthe, not the explicitly marked "voodoo witch" Aunt Hannah, who is the conjure woman in *Of One Blood*. Dianthe's tripartite singing of "Go Down, Moses" structures the text as a whole—beginning, middle, end—and conjures all of the discoveries of the text into existence. The most obvious and pivotal instance of this conjuring—the episode which opened my reading of this novel—is only the most dramatic.

## "He Would Lose Himself in the Pyramid"

It remains for Briggs to represent the other figure of the archaeological, archaeology triumphant, archaeology as vengeance. Briggs is situated in the space not of identity as archaeological—the space that proves so deadly for Dianthe—but in the doubled space made whole, in the space of archaeology as identity. If Dianthe makes a journey to the Egypt of her divided self, so, no doubt, does Briggs. But, as with Hopkins's relationship to the traditions of Delany, once again there is a crucial difference. It is Briggs who does indeed "go down," like Moses, "way down in Egypt's land." But he, more like Moses than Dianthe, survives. In the second half of the text, Briggs becomes much more than a magazine novel's archaeologist hero. He becomes a deliverer from post-Reconstruction bondage. *Of One Blood* is a parable of the tragedies of the dualized subjectivities of African American double consciousness, but it is also a parable of a savior. The secular history of such importance to Afrocentrism will only be discovered by Hopkins's typological figure, by Briggs-as-Moses, by the deliverer from Old Testament slavery. Positivist archaeology becomes religious deliverance.

Initially, Briggs is brought along to Ethiopia only reluctantly. A last-minute decision on his part, resulting from his marriage to Dianthe and sinister manipulations by Aubrey Livingston, makes his interest in the voyage sheerly practical. The intent of the expedition is known to him, but not only is his role solely one of medical support but his hidden blackness has already established a conspicuous avoidance of all questions concerning race in America. "I have a horror of discussing the woes of unfortunates," he states early in the novel, "tramps, stray dogs and cats and Negroes— probably because I am an unfortunate myself." [71] Familiar in a general academic way with the discourses that frame the trip, nevertheless he is at best an accidental archaeologist. In his attempt to discover the archaeological secrets of Meroe, Stone is pointedly thwarted. Possessing a map and all the knowledge his scientific training will provide, Stone searches for weeks for his treasures—both material and intellectual—and finds only frustration. The secrets of Meroe, for the likes of Professor Stone, "were successfully hidden from searchers, and would remain a mystery." [72] It is Briggs, the doubled, who, looking one night only to end his own life, uncovers the space of Hopkins's hidden Africa.

Briggs's discoveries are produced, inadvertently, through the machinations of Livingston. The other of the two main holders of the secrets of others in the text, Livingston has conspired to use his knowledge to remove Briggs from Boston and possess Dianthe as his own. In so doing, however, Livingston must kill his own fiancée and fake the death of Dianthe. It is the arrival of the news of his wife's apparent accident that drives Briggs to suicide among the ruins of Meroe: "That night Reuel rose, took his revolver and ammunition, and leaving a note for Vance telling him he had gone to the third pyramid and not to worry, he rowed himself over to Meroe. He had no purpose, no sensation. Once he halted and tried to think. His love was dead:—that was the one fact that filled his thoughts at first. Then another took its place. Why should he live? Of course not; better rejoin her where parting was no more. He would lose himself in the pyramid. The manuscript had spoken of dangers—he would seek them."[73] While Briggs is in this state of utter despair, Hopkins makes an overt analogy between her hero and her land of hidden secrets. Among the ruins of Meroe, Hopkins marks an explicit sympathy with the remains of ancient Africa and the remains of Briggs's shattered, ruined life, a life lived in racialized secrecy: "Fragments of marble lay about him. It seemed to the lonely watcher that he could hear the sound of the centuries marching by in the moaning wind and purposeless dust. . . . The silence and sadness lay on him like a pall and seemed to answer to the desolation of his own life."[74] Briggs sinks to the level of Hopkins's supposedly exhausted archaeological site. The desolation of the ruins is "the desolation of his own life." He is ancient Africa. He is, as a song that Dianthe might sing might say, lost in the wilderness. He is at a point that fuses spiritual despair and secular gloom, a point Hopkins uses to combine her exterior narrative of historical decline and her interior one of psychic collapse. He is also, at this point, saved. His intent is only one of aimless wandering, and the bleakness that comes to characterize him does so only in the absence of a desire to discover. As Hopkins's Christian readers would quickly recognize, Briggs was in the dark night of his soul. He is looking for nothing. As Hopkins develops at length, his role as hero is primarily one that is unwilling. It is only after this point of total abjection that Briggs becomes Hopkins's figure of the archaeological. In other words, archaeological revelation here has the shape of religious conversion.

Briggs's passage into the hidden city is slow at first. "For a while he rambled aimlessly from wall to wall," detached, mechanical. It concludes, however, suddenly, with an aporia: "He was cold and damp, and turned suddenly to retrace his steps, when just in front of him to the left the candle's light fell full on the devilish countenance of the Ethiopian Sphinx. He moved quickly toward it. . . . 'As he stepped backward his foot crushed through a skull; he retreated with a shudder. . . . He turned to retrace his steps; something came out of the darkness like a hand, passed before his face emitting a subtle odor as it moved; he sank upon the ground and consciousness left him."[75] Briggs's discovery of the way to the hidden city renders archaeology as, at least, accident. Better, it is unwelcome, violent, an assault. The passage from the world of the manifest to the world of the hidden is, as for Dianthe, taken against his will, a site of the unknowable, taken in mystery. At its most obvious, this is a surface-depth model of discovery, a literal archaeologicism providing a referent for the novel's earlier psychologism. The sharpest similarity, however, between the psychological model and the archaeological one is in the transgressive power of the point of contact. Dianthe begins to know her psychological depths through trance-state singing; Briggs enters his archaeological ones in a state of unconsciousness.

This moment of excavation, discovery, revelation, and chronological collapse is what I describe in chapter two as the Egyptian moment. This is the moment that both explodes and contains the moment of contact between surface and depth, past and present, and it is here rendered precisely as a feature of the narrative, as an episodic break in the text. It is a moment of terror *and* enlightenment, attraction and repulsion, departure and arrival, closure and continuation, and mutual transgression. It calls Briggs's identity into focus only to destroy it: "The American man is familiar with many things because of his range of experience, and Reuel Briggs was devoid of fear, but in that moment he tasted the agony of pure, physical terror."[76] And, like those of the white imperialist adventure narratives on which Hopkins is obviously signifying, this Egyptian moment enacts a scene that manifests all the characteristics of colonialist anxiety—the self and the Other being only too proximate but only too different. In *Of One Blood*, however, this trope is curiously rescripted. The difference that Briggs discovers is no difference at all. Unlike the treatment of the Egyptian moment by European American authors, the terror of the unknown, of the ancient, of the racialized space of the point of colonial contact is quickly dissipated and replaced only by comfort. Briggs's transgression is in fact a homecoming.

## Egypt Land

In the hidden city of Telassar, after Briggs awakens, the second section of the novel begins in earnest. Briggs finds himself to have been abducted by a mysterious group of "unreal strangers" whose appearance is immediately described in the language of racialized ethnology: "Dark-visaged, he noticed that they ranged in complexion from a creamy tint to purest ebony;

the long hair which fell upon their shoulders, varied in texture from soft, waving curls to the crispness of the most pronounced African type." [77] His nonthreatening captors are revealed to be the representatives of the racialized civilization Professor Stone had so longed to discover. "You are in the hidden city Telassar," the group's leader tells him. "In my people you will behold the direct descendants of the inhabitants of Meroe." [78]

The situation in which Briggs finds himself is one of infinite comforts — "Was ever man more gorgeously housed than this?" [79] — and the "combination of Oriental and ancient luxury" is lavishly described as indication of the advanced learning of the ancient Ethiopians. But Briggs's first impression on awakening in Telassar, aside from his awareness of the racialized typologies of the group and a quick apprehension of "bewildering beauty that filled him with dazzling awe," is not of his physical surroundings but of a social system, represented by the group's leader, Ai: "In years the speaker was still young, not being over forty despite his patriarchal bearing. . . . But the most striking thing about the man was his kingly countenance, combining force, sweetness and dignity in every feature. The grace of a perfect life invested him like a royal robe." [80] The language of description of the figure of Ai is the language of royalty. Briggs has found himself in the land of monarchy.

Identifying himself as "of the priestly caste," Ai at the outset does two things that are of primary importance to the argument I am advancing here. He provides an account of the destruction of ancient Ethiopia and he invokes Psalm 68:31: "Destroyed and debased because of her idolatries, Ethiopia's arrogance and pride have been humbled in the dust. Utter destruction has come upon Meroe the glorious, as was predicted. But there was a hope held out to the faithful worshippers of the true God that Ethiopia should stretch forth her hand unto Eternal Goodness, and that then her glory should again dazzle the world." [81] Meroe, Ai explains, was "destroyed and debased because of her idolatries." In other words, Ai understands what Professor Stone did not, that the ways of radical positivism, the religion, so to speak, of progress, was for God "arrogance and pride." Ancient Ethiopia was "humbled in the dust." For Hopkins, the point of contact between the representations of ancient Africa as figure of secular splendor and the representations of it as an actor in the world of a vengeful Christian God is, once again, a disruptive one.

Of even more importance to the plot of the novel, however, is the invocation of the psalm. "That Ethiopia should stretch her hand unto Eternal Goodness" is Ai's loose quotation of what Albert Raboteau calls "the most quoted verse in black religious history," the foundational scripture of the African American social, political, and religious movement known as Ethiopianism: "Princes shall come out of Egypt; Ethiopia shall soon stretch out her hands to God."[82] As the African section of *Of One Blood* unfolds, it becomes clear that Ai and his fellow Telassarians are waiting "for the coming of our king who shall restore to the Ethiopian race its ancient glory."[83] That messiah is Briggs.

In his groundbreaking 1994 study *Conjuring Culture: Biblical Formations of Black America*, Theophus Smith charts the relationship between what he terms the Exodus figure, the Ethiopia figure, and the Egypt figure, and the Exodus configuration and the Ethiopia configuration, in African American religious, political, and social history.[84] In dialogue in part with the work of Werner Sollors,[85] Smith traces the history of Ethiopianism as it moves from an African American interpretive tradition regarding the biblical figure of Egypt—Egypt as the land of oppression—to the "post-Christian cultural nationalism" of Edward Wilmot Blyden—Egypt as the site of a sort of radical improvisation in the role of the prophesy of the psalm—to the full reversal of the earlier phase, to the figure of Egypt as the epitome of black nationalist expression—Egypt as the land of liberation: "the negative valuation of Egypt, which conventionally operates in Exodus configuration, is reversed in mature developments of Ethiopianism. For historically informed Ethiopianists ancient Egypt was understood to be a civilization of black rulers instead of a prison house of black slaves."[86]

In Smith's analysis, the figures of Egypt and Ethiopia are seen as readily identifiable features of a religious-discursive "configural repertory," tropes that are at once foundational elements in an ethnogenetic typology and fluid, appropriatable vehicles for cultural transformation.[87] Writing of the Ethiopian configuration, Smith highlights how two such ostensibly antithetical constructions of African American social and religious identity— Egypt as the land of bondage and Egypt as the land of greatness—could coexist and even draw strength from one another. In this repertory, which is characterized by such apparent opposition, "the Exodus and Ethiopia figures alternate as if to increase the amplitude—the imaginative or iconic power—of correspondences between black experience and biblical narrative. . . . The configural imagination can envision the return to Africa as a crossing of "the Red Sea"—*back to Egypt!* But . . . rather than a place of bondage Egypt is transvalued by black cultural nationalists as a positive representation of African greatness and potential destiny. By means of such improvisational transformation, a new Exodus is envisioned which leads out of captivity or exile in the New World."[88] Egypt and Ethiopia, "alternating," are at times mutually exclusive, at times mutually supportive. The improvisational hermeneutics of African American cultural traditions render them central terms, if contested ones. They are ambivalent twins. In other words, Egypt and Ethiopia, their figures and configurations, share a relationship that is doubled.

It is precisely this space, of improvisation, unpredictable alliance, and the cultural politics of hermeneutic transformation, that Hopkins addresses in *Of One Blood*. As Smith points out, "Psalm 68:31 features both Egypt and Ethiopia as figures for prophetic fulfillment,"[89] and, as we have seen, both Egypt and Ethiopia are characters in Hopkins's text. The psalm itself, then, is bifurcated, doubled, and Hopkins indeed treats it as much. In fact, the entirety of *Of One Blood* can be seen as a novelized rendering of the cultural politics of the two-part psalm. On the one hand, she treats the figure of Egypt—which, not incidentally, is itself one of irruption: "Princes *shall come out* of Egypt." This is at once biblical prophecy and secular politics, even, as "Go Down, Moses" makes only too plain, as America is Egypt *and* Egypt is Egypt. On the other hand, there is the figure of Ethiopia: scientifically secular and biblically endorsed. So, like the psalm, Hopkins's text has a *doubled* double structure. Each two parts of America has two parts, too (the land of the slaves' doubled song and the land of the African American doubled self), and both halves of Ethiopia are themselves divided in half (the Ethiopia of science is the Ethiopia of God, and the Ethiopia on the surface has its Ethiopia underneath). Smith writes of "the transition from a specifically religious figuration of Psalm 68:31 . . . to its political impact in black nationalism."[90] In its fusion of the secular glorification of Egypt as a black civilization and the biblical traditionalism of African American religious hermeneutics, in its elaborate construction of African American double consciousness and twinned inclusion of an unexpected Afrocentric adventure tale, and especially in its radical vision of the unstable power of the figure of ancient Egypt, *Of One Blood* is the most pronounced fictional text extant of that process of transition.

It is in this context that Briggs becomes Moses. He is at once the fulfillment of the prophesy of the psalm and also the figure of the deliverer from bondage. "In the Afro-American figural tradition," Smith writes, "it appears that all . . . liberation efforts can be configured . . . as dramatic reenactments of Exodus, and their leaders envisioned as approximate types of Moses."[91] At the same time, the "Egypt's land" to which Dianthe's spiritual urges Briggs is the land of the hidden Ethiopia. Briggs becomes a typological savior, a figure who is both the figure of the spiritual and the figure of the psalm. In classic Ethiopianist tradition, the exodus of which Dianthe's spiritual sings is an exodus, in the text, to Ethiopia.

To be sure, of course, Briggs's elevation enacts a colonialist fantasy: crowned as king, revered as a god, and Christianizing his subjects—all on the authority of birthright—Briggs is a veritable superhero for early-twentieth-century African American colonizationist movements.[92] But, curiously, this is a domination that presupposes a widespread submission by the "colonizers"—who, as far as the text is concerned, were only missing children returning home—to the wonders of the advanced Telassar. Hopkins's Africa, after all, is not peopled by savages but by their binary inversion. This is a colonialism that wants to declare its own inferiority. Moreover, this is a fantasy of a scope that is radically contained, utterly sealed, not forever punctured and wild in its desires. Although after returning to Ethiopia Briggs "spends his days in teaching his people all that he has learned in years of contact with modern culture," his conquest begins and ends with Telassar. He is a colonialist who wishes only to disappear. Hopkins even gives her text an ominous close, which turns on the encroaching spectre of colonial violence: Briggs "views . . . with serious apprehension, the advance of mighty nations penetrating the dark, mysterious forces of his native land."[93] A vague colonialism, perhaps, but one which, one assumes, must be seen as other than black. In this fable of reverse colonization, it is only Christianity that Briggs seems to have to offer to the land that gave it birth.

This, it seems, is a product of the ideology of Ethiopianism—Ethiopia stretching out her hands to God—but it is also a structural coda to the figure of the double, the conduit formed by the intersection of African American Christianity and Afrocentric Egyptology. African American Christianity still provides the point of contact between slave resistance and secular historiography. Briggs, the figure of the doubled black mesmerist, becomes, in the land of the double made whole, the figure of the bringer of Christian truth. The double, Hopkins suggests, reveals both ways. Hopkins's archaeological narrative produces a radical distinction between the hyperbolic materiality of the discourses of Egyptology and the elaborate ephemerality of African American song, yet this distinction is produced only to make it dissolve. Like the oscillations between her other figures, and like the meaning of her novel's title, Hopkins's archaeologic implies a certain unity. This is the movement from the authority of the Bible to the authority of science, from the narratives of the sacred to the narratives of the secular, from the figure of Egypt to the figure of Ethiopia, from the land of bondage to the land of freedom. It is also the movement back again. This is the space of Egypt Land.

# Notes

## Acknowledgments

1  Amelia Edwards, *A Thousand Miles up the Nile* (Philadelphia: Henry T. Coates, 1877), 2.

## Preface: "An Inspired Frenzy or Madness"

1  Emil Kraepelin, *Lectures on Clinical Psychiatry*, edited by Thomas Johnstone (London: Baillière, 1904), Lecture 3, "Dementia Praecox (Insanity of Adolescence)," 21–24.

2  See John T. Irwin, *American Hieroglyphics: The Symbol of the Egyptian Hieroglyphics in the American Renaissance* (Baltimore: Johns Hopkins University Press, [1980] 1983), 195–205.

3  For examples of these gaps, see, in addition to Irwin, the essays collected in Nancy Thomas et al., *The American Discovery of Ancient Egypt* (Los Angeles: Los Angeles County Museum of Art, 1995).

4  See Dana D. Nelson, *National Manhood: Capitalist Citizenship and the Imagined Fraternity of White Men* (Durham: Duke University Press, 1998); Malini Johar Schueller, *U.S. Orientalisms: Race, Nation, and Gender in Literature, 1790–1890* (Ann Arbor: University of Michigan Press, 1998); Theophus H. Smith, *Conjuring Culture: Biblical Formations of Black America* (New York: Oxford University Press, 1994); Teresa Goddu, *Gothic America: Narrative, History, and Nation* (New York: Columbia University Press, 1997); Wilson Jeremiah Moses, *Afrotopia: The Roots of African American Popular History* (Cambridge: Cambridge University Press, 1998); Shawn Michelle

Smith, *American Archives: Gender, Race, and Class in Visual Culture* (Princeton: Princeton University Press, 1999); Eddie S. Glaude Jr., *Exodus! Religion, Race, and Nation in Early Nineteenth-Century Black America* (Chicago: University of Chicago Press, 2000); Hilton Obenzinger, *American Palestine: Melville, Twain, and the Holy Land Mania* (Princeton: Princeton University Press, 1999); Maurice O. Wallace, *Constructing the Black Masculine: Identity and Ideality in African American Men's Literature and Culture, 1775–1995* (Durham: Duke University Press, 2002); Reina Lewis, *Gendering Orientalism: Race, Femininity, and Representation* (New York: Routledge, 1996); John Davis, *The Landscape of Belief: Encountering the Holy Land in Nineteenth-Century American Art and Culture* (Princeton: Princeton University Press, 1996); Inderpal Grewal, *Home and Harem: Nation, Gender, Empire, and the Cultures of Travel* (Durham: Duke University Press, 1996); Bruce A. Harvey, *American Geographics: U.S. National Narratives and the Representation of the Non-European World, 1830–1865* (Stanford: Stanford University Press, 2001); Jean-Marcel Humbert et al., *Egyptomania: Egypt in Western Art, 1730–1930* (Ottowa: National Gallery of Canada, 1994); Thomas, et al., *The American Discovery of Ancient Egypt*; Holly Edwards, ed., *Noble Dreams, Wicked Pleasures: Orientalism in America, 1870–1930* (Princeton: Princeton University Press, 2000); and Susan Walker and Peter Higgs, eds., *Cleopatra of Egypt: From History to Myth* (Princeton: Princeton University Press, 2001).

5 The most obvious and best-known recent example of this is the work of Martin Bernal; on Bernal and his multivolume study *Black Athena*, see the introduction.

6 See, for example, the work of Albert Raboteau: *A Fire in the Bones: Reflections on African-American Religious History* (Boston: Beacon Press, 1995); and "The Black Experience in American Evangelicism," in Timothy E. Fulop and Albert J. Raboteau, eds., *African-American Religion: Interpretive Essays in History and Culture* (New York: Routledge, 1997), 90–106.

## Introduction: "This Egypt of the West"

1 Paschal Beverly Randolph, *Pre-Adamite Man: Demonstrating the Existence of the Human Race upon This Earth 100,000 Years Ago!* (Toledo: Randolph, 1863), 141.

2 Ibid., 51–53.

3 Ibid., 23.

4 On the Washington Monument and its architect, Robert Mills, see especially John M. Bryan, ed., *Robert Mills, Architect* (Washington, D.C.: American Institute of Architects Press, 1989). On Edwin Blashfield and his 1895 Dome Collar mural entitled "The Evolution of Civilization," see Leonard N. Amico, *The Mural Decorations of Edwin Howland Blashfield (1848–1936)* (Williamstown: Sterling and Francis Clark Art Institute, 1978). The scene of the singing of "Go Down, Moses" appears in William Wells Brown, *The Negro in the American Rebellion* (Boston: A. G. Brown, 1880), 118–19, and is quoted in Eileen Southern, *The Music of Black Americans: A History* (New York: W. W. Norton, 1983), 214.

5 E. S. Addy, "National Sin," *The Colored American*, April 19, 1838.

6 *The Colored American*, June 13, 1840.

7 Quoted in Marcia Y. Riggs, ed., *Can I Get a Witness? Prophetic Voices of African American Women: An Anthology* (Maryknoll, NY: Orbis Books, 1997), 21.

8 See James D. McCabe, *The Illustrated History of the Centennial Exposition* (Philadelphia: National Publishing Company, 1876).

9 Martin Robison Delany, *The Origin and Objects of Ancient Freemasonry; Its Introduction into the United States, and Legitimacy among Colored Men* (Pittsburgh: W. S. Haven, 1853; rpt. Xenia, Ohio: A. D. Delany, 1904), 12, 37.

10 W. E. B. Du Bois, *The World and Africa: An Inquiry into the Part Which Africa Has Played in World History* (New York: International Publishers, [1946] 1965), 99.

11 As might be guessed, the reference here is to what has become known as "the *Black Athena* controversy," the social and intellectual one surrounding Cornell philologist Martin Bernal and his *Black Athena: The Afroasiatic Roots of Classical Civilization* (New Brunswick, N.J.: Rutgers University Press, 1987). The details and publication history of the controversy are far too dense and convoluted to be addressed in any comprehensive way here, but there are, however, several aspects of the argument of this book that overlap those of Bernal, and readers are likely to find much here that is in general sympathy with what can be understood to be the overall political positions supported by *Black Athena*. It must also be said, however, that while there are obvious agreements between *Black Athena* and *Egypt Land*, Bernal's project and mine diverge quite sharply in terms of subject matter, theoretical orientation, and both practical and critical methodologies; as is often forgotten, for example, *Black Athena* is almost completely silent on the two questions of most importance to me—that of the nineteenth century and that of the United States—and for scholars of either the rise of racialization or the history of "Western" interest in ancient Egypt this is of no small significance. (For an important earlier treatment on Bernal's lack of attention to nineteenth-century American Egyptomania, see Robert J. C. Young, *Colonial Desire: Hybridity in Theory, Culture, and Race* [New York: Routledge, 1995], 118–41. My thanks to Bernal himself for drawing my attention to Young's essay.) For the primary sources of the controversy see *Black Athena*—of which there are currently two volumes published—as well as the collection of follow-up responses to his detractors, *Black Athena Writes Back*, edited by Martin Bernal and David Chioni Moore (Durham: Duke University Press, 2001), and the major works that can be said to represent the opposing camp, commonly identified with Wellesley classicist Mary Lefkowitz: Mary Lefkowitz, *Not Out of Africa: How Afrocentrism Became an Excuse to Teach Myth as History* (New York: Basic Books, 1996); and Mary Lefkowitz and Guy MacLean Rogers, eds., *Black Athena Revisited* (Chapel Hill: University of North Carolina Press, 1996).

12 Josiah Clark Nott and George Robins Gliddon, *Types of Mankind: or, Ethnological Researches, Based upon the Ancient Monuments, Paintings, Sculptures, and Crania of Races, and upon their Natural, Geographical, Philological, and Biblical History* (Philadelphia: Lippincott, Grambo, 1854), 263.

13  Adah Isaacs Menken, "Hear, O Israel!" *Infelicia* (New York, 1868); rpt. in *Infelicia and Other Writings*, edited by Gregory Eiselein (Peterborough, Ontario: Broadview, 2002), 92, 94.

14  Edward Wilmot Blyden, *Philip and the Eunuch*, in *Christianity, Islam, and the Negro Race*, 2nd ed. (rpt. Baltimore: Black Classic Press, [1888] 1994), 176.

15  George Robins Gliddon, *Ancient Egypt: Her Monuments, Hieroglyphics, History, and Archaeology, and Other Subjects Connected with Hieroglyphical Literature*, 10th ed. (New York: William Taylor, 1847), 59.

16  David Dorr, *A Colored Man Round the World*, edited by Malini Johar Schueller (Ann Arbor: University of Michigan Press, [1858] 1999), 134.

17  Gliddon, *Ancient Egypt*, 40.

18  The lineage here referred to consists of Perry Miller, *Errand into the Wilderness* (Cambridge: Harvard University Press, 1956); Sacvan Bercovitch, *The American Jeremiad* (Madison: University of Wisconsin Press, 1978); and Werner Sollors, *Beyond Ethnicity: Consent and Descent in American Culture* (New York: Oxford University Press, 1986), but it has recently undergone further elaboration by Davis in *The Landscape of Belief*, Obenzinger in *American Palestine*, and Glaude in *Exodus!*

19  On the history of the white Masons, see Mark Carnes, *Secret Ritual and Manhood in Victorian America* (New Haven: Yale University Press, 1989); Lynn Dumenil, *Freemasonry and American Culture, 1880–1930* (Princeton: Princeton University Press, 1984); and Bobby J. Dermott, *Freemasonry in American Culture and Society* (Lanham, Md.: University Press of America, 1986).

20  John Ledyard to Thomas Jefferson, September 10, 1788, in *The Papers of Thomas Jefferson*, edited by Julian P. Boyd et al. (Princeton: Princeton University Press, 1988), 13:596.

21  Ibid., 595.

22  Ibid.

23  John Lloyd Stephens, *Incidents of Travel in Egypt, Arabia Petræa, and the Holy Land* (Norman: University of Oklahoma, [1837] 1970), 135.

24  Herman Melville, journal entry, January 3, 1857, in *The Writings of Herman Melville*, vol. 15: *Journals*, edited by Harrison Hayford et al. (Evanston: Northwestern University Press, 1989), 75–78.

25  For a proposed timeline of the life of this passage, see ibid. On Melville in this context, see especially Carol Colatrella, *Literature and Moral Reform: Melville and the Discipline of Reading* (Gainesville: University Press of Florida, 2002). For a more extended treatment of the question of the sublime in relation to nineteenth-century American images of ancient Egypt, see Patricia Dawes Pierce, "Deciphering Egypt: Four Studies in the American Sublime," PH.D. diss., Program in American Studies, Yale University, 1980.

26  Abraham Lincoln, Annual Message to Congress, December 1, 1862, in *Abraham Lincoln, Speeches and Writings, 1859–1865* (New York: Library of America, 1989), 405–6.

27  Ibid.

28  Ibid.

29  Ibid.

30  Ibid.

31  John Overton, advertisement for Memphis, Tennessee, *The Port Folio*, 1820, reproduced in John E. Harkins et al., *Metropolis of the American Nile: An Illustrated History of Memphis and Shelby County* (Woodland Hills: Windsor Publications, 1982), 34.

32  Edward Fontaine, *How the World Was Peopled: Ethnological Lectures* (New York: D. Appleton, 1877), 201, 47.

33  John Lloyd Stephens, *Incidents of Travel in Yucatán*, new ed., edited by Karl Ackerman (Washington, D.C.: Smithsonian Institution Press, 1996), 47, 74–75. On Stephens, see the introductions to the two sets of the reissued *Incidents* (the 1996 Smithsonian edition as well as the two-volume 1962 University of Oklahoma edition, edited and with an introduction by Victor Wolfgang von Hagen); as well as C. M. Hinsley, "Hemispheric Hegemony in Early American Anthropology, 1841–1851: Reflections on John Lloyd Stephens and Lewis Henry Morgan," in *Social Contexts of American Ethnology, 1840–1984*, edited by June Helm (Washington, D.C.: American Ethnological Society, 1985), 28–40; and Larzer Ziff, *Return Passages: Great American Travel Writing, 1780–1910* (New Haven: Yale University Press, 2000).

34  "Discoveries of Mummies at Durango, Mexico," *The Colored American*, January 19, 1839.

35  Herman Melville, *White-Jacket; or, The World in a Man-of-War* (Chicago: Northwestern University Press, 1970), 151.

36  Glaude, *Exodus!* 62.

37  Sollors, *Beyond Ethnicity*, 59.

38  Obenzinger, *American Palestine*, 5, x.

39  Davis, *The Landscape of Belief*, 22; Obenzinger, *American Palestine*, 24–38.

40  Martin Robison Delany, *Principia of Ethnology: The Origin of Races and Color, with an Archaeological Compendium of Ethiopian and Egyptian Civilization, from Years of Careful Examination and Inquiry* (Philadelphia: Harper and Brothers, 1879), 55. For more on Delany and his book, see chapter one.

41  Quoted in Richard S. Patterson and Richardson Dougall, *The Eagle and the Shield: A History of the Great Seal of the United States* (Washington, D.C.: Bureau of Public Affairs, 1976), 85.

42  Frederick Douglass, "Athens, Greece to Naples, Italy, Sunday, March 23, 1887," Frederick Douglass Papers, Manuscript Division, Library of Congress, Travels Folder 29.

43  Ibid.

44  Ibid. On Douglass's trip of 1887, see Robert S. Levine, "Road to Africa: Frederick Douglass's Rome," *African American Review* 34:2 (summer 2000): 217–31. Special thanks is here due to Bob Levine for bringing my attention to his excellent article, as well as for his singular generosity regarding this project.

45  Dorr, *A Colored Man Round the World*, 11–12.

46  Ibid., 175.

47  Ibid., 169–70.

48  Ibid., 170.

49  Edward Wilmot Blyden, "Mohammedanism and the Negro Race," *Fraser's Magazine*, new series, 12 (November 1875): 598–615; rpt. in Blyden, *Christianity, Islam, and the Negro Race*, 1.

50  Ibid.

51  Edward Wilmot Blyden, *From West Africa to Palestine* (Freetown: Manchester, 1873); rpt. in *Black Spokesman: Selected Published Writings of Edward Wilmot Blyden*, edited by Hollis R. Lynch (New York: Humanities Press, 1971).

52  On Blyden, see Hollis R. Lynch, *Edward Wilmot Blyden: Pan-Negro Patriot, 1832–1912* (London: Oxford University Press, 1967); V. Y. Mudimbe, *The Invention of Africa: Gnosis, Philosophy, and the Order of Knowledge* (Bloomington: Indiana University Press, 1988); Paul Gilroy, *The Black Atlantic: Modernity and Double Consciousness* (Cambridge: Harvard University Press, 1993); and Obenzinger, *American Palestine*.

53  Blyden, "Mohammedanism and the Negro Race," 13–14.

54  Richard Brent Turner, "Edward Wilmot Blyden and Pan-Africanism: The Ideological Roots of Islam and Black Nationalism in the United States," *The Muslim World* 87:2 (April 1997): 178.

55  Blyden, "Mohammedanism and the Negro Race," 9.

56  Turner, "Edward Wilmot Blyden and Pan-Africanism," 173.

57  Turner, "Edward Wilmot Blyden and Pan-Africanism," 173. See Ronald A. T. Judy, *(Dis)Forming the American Canon: African-Arabic Slave Narratives and the Vernacular* (Minneapolis: University of Minnesota Press, 1993); Allan D. Austin, ed., *African Muslims in Antebellum America: Transatlantic Stories and Spiritual Struggles* (New York: Routledge, 1997); Richard Brent Turner, *Islam in the African-American Experience* (Indianapolis: Indiana University Press, 1997); and Sylviane A. Diouf, *Servants of Allah: African Muslims Enslaved in the Americas* (New York: New York University Press, 1998).

58  Gayraud S. Wilmore, *Black Religion and Black Radicalism: An Interpretation of the Religious History of Afro-American People*, 2d ed. (Maryknoll, NY: Orbis Books, 1983), 116.

59  Schueller, *U.S. Orientalisms*, 106–7. Special thanks is here due to Malini Johar Schueller for her support of this project in both its first and its last stages.

60  Dorr, *A Colored Man Round the World*, 123.

61  Douglass, "Athens, Greece to Naples, Italy, Sunday, March 23, 1887."

62  Lisa Lowe, *Critical Terrains: French and British Orientalisms* (Ithaca: Cornell University Press, 1991), 5.

63  "The Old Girl of Cairo Town," in Richard M. Dorson, *Buying the Wind: Regional Folklore in the United States* (Chicago: University of Chicago Press, 1964), 413–14. Special thanks go to Margaret Yocom for this reference.

64 Schueller, *U.S. Orientalisms*; Russ Castronovo, *Necro Citizenship: Death, Eroticism, and the Public Sphere in the Nineteenth-Century United States* (Durham: Duke University Press, 2001), 160. Castronovo's work appeared after the primary research for this project had drawn to a close, but his text presents a wealth of observations that bear in fascinating ways on many of the arguments being made here. For his argument, see 108–14.

65 Castronovo, *Necro Citizenship*, 160–66.

66 John Patrick Deveney, *Paschal Beverly Randolph: A Nineteenth-Century Black American Spiritualist, Rosicrucian, and Sex Magician* (Albany: SUNY Press, 1997), 254.

67 The reference here is to Deveney; see *Paschal Beverly Randolph*. For an account of Randolph's suicide, see 237–40.

68 Emma Hardinge, *Modern American Spiritualism: A Twenty Years' Record of the Communion between Earth and the World of Spirits* (New Hyde Park, N.Y.: University Books, [1870] 1970).

69 H. P. Blavatsky, *Isis Unveiled: A Master-Key to the Mysteries of Ancient and Modern Science and Theology* (Pasadena: Theosophical University Press, 1972), 1:573, 515, 561.

70 Ibid., 2:436–37.

71 The reference here is of course to Bernal, *Black Athena*.

72 In this context, it is interesting to note that in 1891 John Wesley Gilbert, the first African American archaeologist, received his diploma from Brown University. Born the son of a slave in Hepzibah, Georgia, in 1864, Gilbert received some attention from a wealthy white minister, who in 1886 loaned him the money to enroll at Brown. After several years of study, Gilbert excelled as a classicist and on winning a scholarship became the first African American admitted to the American School in Athens. Gilbert spent several years in Greece, excavating in Eretria, writing a scholarly thesis, and working as a tour guide. He also conducted explorations in the Mediterranean, traveled to the Congo to establish a Methodist mission, and toured Europe. In 1891, he received his M.A. from Brown. After returning to the United States, Gilbert went to Augusta, Georgia, entered the ministry, and began teaching at Paine College, where he eventually became dean of theology and a full professor of Greek. See Vivian Ovelton Sammons, *Blacks in Science and Medicine* (New York: Hemisphere, 1990), 100; Martin Rywell et al., *Afro-American Encyclopedia* (North Miami: Educational Book Publishers, 1974), 4:1063; and Henry F. Kletzing and William H. Crogman, *Progress of a Race; or, the Remarkable Advancement of the Afro-American from the Bondage of Slavery, Ignorance and Poverty to the Freedom of Citizenship, Intelligence, Affluence, Honor and Trust* (Atlanta: J. L. Nichols, 1897; rpt. New York: Negro Universities Press, 1969).

73 On Dobson, see Jennifer Brody, "The Returns of Cleopatra Jones," *Signs* 25:1 (1999): 91–121.

74 Ignatius Donnelly, *Atlantis: The Antediluvian World*, rev. ed. (New York: Gramercy, [1882] 1949), 273. On Donnelly and Atlantis mania, see Stephen Williams,

*Fantastic Archaeology: The Wild Side of North American Prehistory* (Philadelphia: University of Pennsylvania Press, 1991); and Richard Ellis, *Imagining Atlantis* (New York: Knopf, 1998).

75  Donnelly, *Atlantis*, 183.

76  Ibid., 1.

77  Ibid., 246.

78  Ibid., 189.

79  Ibid., 58.

80  Ibid., 243.

81  On Cole and *The Course of Empire*, see especially Angela Miller, *The Empire of the Eye: Landscape Representation and American Cultural Politics, 1825–1875* (Ithaca: Cornell University Press, 1993).

82  Josiah C. Nott, *Two Lectures on the Connection between the Biblical and Physical History of Man* (New York: Negro Universities Press, [1849] 1969), 86.

83  Ariel [Buckner H. Payne], *The Negro: What Is His Ethnological Status? Is He the Progeny of Ham? Is He a Descendant of Adam and Eve? Has He a Soul? Or Is He a Beast in God's Nomenclature? What Is His Status as Fixed by God in Creation? What Is His Relation to the White Race?* (Cincinnati, 1867), 36; rpt. in *Anti-Black Thought, 1863–1925*, edited by John David Smith (New York: Garland, 1993), 5:36.

84  A. Hoyle Lester, *The Pre-Adamite; or, Who Tempted Eve? Scripture and Science in Unison as Respects the Antiquity of Man* (Philadelphia: J. B. Lippincott, 1875), 97; rpt. in Smith, *Anti-Black Thought*, 6:227. For a highly original reading of some of these issues, see Michael Lieb, *Children of Ezekiel: Aliens, UFOs, the Crisis of Race, and the Advent of End Time* (Durham: Duke University Press, 1998).

85  Ibid.

86  John H. Van Evrie, *White Supremacy and Negro Subordination; or, Negroes a Subordinate Race, and (So-Called) Slavery Its Normal Condition*, 2d ed. (New York: Van Evrie, Horton, 1868), 65.

87  Ibid.

88  Ibid., v–vii.

89  Fontaine, *How the World Was Peopled*, 184. Following this sentence, penciled in the margin of the copy of this text housed in the Perkins Library of Duke University, is the following phrase, of unknown author and date: "I would like to live to see that day!"

90  Transcribed in James Weldon Johnson, *The Books of American Negro Spirituals* (New York: Viking, 1925), 39. Dialect typography in the original.


Chapter 1: "A Veritable He-Nigger after All"

1  George Robins Gliddon, *Otia Ægyptiaca: Discourses on Egyptian Archaeology and Hieroglyphical Discoveries* (Philadelphia: John Penington, 1849), 76.

2  Bob Brier, *Egyptian Mummies: Unwrapping the Secrets of an Ancient Art* (New York: Quill, 1994), 173.

3  Luke Burke, "Introduction," in Gliddon, *Otia Ægyptiaca*, 49.

4  My version of this incident is based mainly on the account provided in William Stanton, *The Leopard's Spots: Scientific Attitudes toward Race in America, 1815–1859* (Chicago: University of Chicago Press, 1960), 145–50, as well as on several contemporaneous newspaper accounts that recounted the week's events: *Boston Courier*, May 15, 1850; *Boston Daily Advertiser*, May 20, June 4, and June 6, 1850; *Boston Cultivator*, June 8 and June 15, 1850; and *Daily Evening Traveller*, June 4, June 5, June 6, June 7, June 8, and June 14, 1850.

5  Gliddon, *Otia Ægyptiaca*, 77.

6  Ibid.

7  *The North Star*, June 27, 1850. Gliddon's Boston mummy was named Got Thothi Aunk, was "Chief of the Artificers of the Abode of Ammon," died during the Twenty-Third Dynasty in 989 B.C.E. of unknown causes, and was acquired by a colleague of Gliddon's named Anthony Harris from an unidentified site, named by Gliddon as Werda, in Thebes. The mummy was actually one of a pair obtained in the 1840s by Gliddon (the other was, ironically, that of a woman) and after the Tremont disaster Gliddon donated them both to the Anatomical Museum of the University of Louisiana (now Tulane University)—after publicly unrolling the second—at the suggestion of his friend and collaborator Josiah Clark Nott, whose brother Gustavus was dean of the Medical School there at the time of the donation. These mummies were then more or less lost to scholarship for 150 years before being rediscovered in 1997 in the basement of Tulane's Howard-Tilton Memorial Library by anthropology graduate student Guido Lombardi. They were then placed in the holdings of Tulane University's Special Collections, where as of this writing they remain. Lombardi's generosity and enthusiasm regarding his research into these mummies deserves special mention here; see his "Egyptian Mummies at Tulane University: An Anthropological Study," M.A. thesis, Tulane University, 1999; and Heather Pringle, *The Mummy Congress: Science, Obsession, and the Everlasting Dead* (New York: Theia Books, 2001), 162–87. For more on Nott and his relationship with Gliddon, see below.

8  Nott and Gliddon, *Types of Mankind*, 49.

9  Nott, *Two Lectures*, 18.

10  Ibid.

11  Ibid.

12  Ibid., 17.

13  Nott and Gliddon, *Types of Mankind*, 189.

14  Ibid., 241–44.

15  On the history of American Egyptology, see John A. Wilson, *Signs and Wonders upon Pharaoh: A History of American Egyptology* (Chicago: University of Chicago Press, 1964); and the essays in Thomas et al., *The American Discovery of Ancient Egypt*.

16  Young, *Colonial Desire*, 126.

17  Henry S. Patterson, "Memoir of the Life and Scientific Labors of Samuel George Morton," in Nott and Gliddon, *Types of Mankind*, xli.

18  The standard texts on the history of the American School are Stanton, *The Leopard's Spots*; Stephen Jay Gould, *The Mismeasure of Man* (New York: W. W. Norton, 1981); and Thomas F. Gossett, *Race: The History of an Idea in America* (Dallas: Southern Methodist University Press, 1963). Recently, however, there have been an increasing number of studies that take into account the connections between the rise of Egyptology and the rise of racialized science: in addition to the citations included in the introduction, see especially Susan Gillman, "Pauline Hopkins and the Occult: African-American Revisions of Nineteenth-Century Sciences," *American Literary History* 8:1 (spring 1996): 57–82. On Nott in particular, see Reginald Horsman, *Josiah Nott of Mobile: Southerner, Physician, and Racial Theorist* (Baton Rouge: Louisiana State University Press, 1987).

19  Young, *Colonial Desire*, 127.

20  Ibid., 59.

21  Josiah Nott, "Prefatory Letter. To J. D. B. De Bow, Esq.," in Nott, *Two Lectures*, 6.

22  Ibid., 50–51.

23  Nott, *Two Lectures*, 6.

24  Nott and Gliddon, *Types of Mankind*, 53.

25  Nott, *Two Lectures*, 68.

26  Nott and Gliddon, *Types of Mankind*, 50–51.

27  Ibid., 54.

28  Nott, *Two Lectures*, 85–86.

29  Nott and Gliddon, *Types of Mankind*, 95–96.

30  Gliddon, *Ancient Egypt*, 47.

31  Nott and Gliddon, *Types of Mankind*, 59–60.

32  "Caucasian" [Reverend William H. Campbell], *Anthropology for the People: A Refutation of the Theory of the Adamic Origin of All Races* (Richmond: Everett Waddey, 1891), 207–8.

33  Anonymous, *The Six Species of Men* (New York: Van Evrie, Horton, 1866); rpt. in Smith, *Anti-Black Thought*, 1:132, 140.

34  Nott and Gliddon, *Types of Mankind*, 210.

35  Ibid., 52.

36  Ibid., 212.

37  Samuel George Morton, *Crania Americana; or, a Comparative View of the Skulls of Various Aboriginal Nations of North and South America* (Philadelphia: John Pennington, 1839), 29.

38  Nott and Gliddon, *Types of Mankind*, xxxvii.

39  Gliddon, *Otia Ægyptiaca*, 77.

40  Ibid., 215–17.

41  Gliddon, *Ancient Egypt*, 42–46.

42  Ibid., 58.

43  Ibid.

44  "What an Old Lady Thought about Mummies," *Chicago Times*, September 3,

1863, quoted in Stanley B. Kimball, "New Light on Old Egyptiana: Mormon Mummies, 1848–71," *Dialogue: A Journal of Mormon Thought* 16:4 (1983): 78–79.

45 Gen. 9:18–27, King James Version.

46 Fontaine, *How the World Was Peopled*, 199–200.

47 Edward Wilmot Blyden, *Philip and the Eunuch*, 176.

48 In the nineteenth century, the African American Christian abolitionist James W. C. Pennington devoted the first chapter of his *A Text-Book of the Origin and History of the Colored People* (Hartford: L. Skinner, 1841) to a discussion of the (black) Sons of Ham and Cush (5–18) and the next two to a problack history of ancient Egypt and Ethiopia (19–31). In the twentieth, St. Clair Drake provided an extended discussion of the Ham(ite)-Cush(ite)-blackness interpretive network in the Hebrew/Judaic tradition in *Black Folk Here and There* (Los Angeles: Center for Afro-American Studies, 1990), 2:1–30; also see Charles B. Copher, "Three Thousand Years of Biblical Interpretation with Reference to Black Peoples," in *African American Religious Studies: An Interdisciplinary Anthology*, edited by Gayraud Wilmore (Durham: Duke University Press, 1989), 106–28; and David N. Livingstone, "The Preadamite Theory and the Marriage of Science and Religion," *Transactions of the American Philosophical Society* 82:3 (1992). And finally, as this manuscript was going to press, Stephen R. Haynes published a much-needed book-length study of the racialized politics of the curse, with which, unfortunately, I was unable to engage in these pages; see *Noah's Curse: The Biblical Justification of American Slavery* (New York: Oxford University Press, 2002).

49 Gliddon, *Ancient Egypt*, 40.

50 Harvey Johnson, *The Hamite* (Baltimore: J. F. Weishampel, 1889), 52.

51 Gliddon, *Ancient Egypt*, 41.

52 Fontaine, *How the World Was Peopled*.

53 See Thomas Virgil Peterson, "The Myth of Ham among White, Antebellum Southerners," PH.D. diss., Stanford University, 1975. The phrase "microdynamics of differentiation" is closely related to a coinage of Barbara Herrnstein Smith, "microdynamics of incommensurability"; see *Belief and Resistance: Dynamics of Contemporary Intellectual Controversy* (Cambridge: Harvard University Press, 1997), 125–52.

54 Frederick Douglass, "The Claims of the Negro Ethnologically Considered," in *The Life and Writings of Frederick Douglass*, Volume 2: *Pre-Civil War Decade, 1850–1860*, edited by Philip S. Foner (New York: International Publishers, 1950), 299.

55 See especially the studies cited in the introduction, chapter five, and below.

56 J. Theodore Holly, "Thoughts on Hayti," *The Anglo-African Magazine* 1:6 (June 1859); rpt. New York: Arno Press, 1968, 186.

57 Ibid.

58 Henry Highland Garnet, "On the Past and Present Condition, and Destiny of the Colored Race," *The North Star*, June 16, 1848.

59 Wilson Armistead, *A Tribute for the Negro: Being a Vindication of the Moral, Intel-*

lectual, and Religious Capabilities of the Colored Portion of Mankind; with Particular Reference to the African Race (Manchester: William Irwin, 1848), 121.

60 Garnet, "On the Past and Present Condition, and Destiny of the Colored Race."

61 Ibid.

62 William Wells Brown, The Black Man, His Antecedents, His Genius, and His Achievements (New York: Thomas Hamilton, 1863), 32–33.

63 H. S. Fulkerson, The Negro as He Was; as He Is; as He Will Be (Vicksburg, Miss.: Commercial Herald, 1887), 81; rpt. Smith, Anti-Black Thought, vol. 10.

64 For examples of such African American community-based race theory, see Johnson, The Hamite; Harvey Johnson, The Question of Race: A Reply to W. Cabell Bruce, Esq. (Baltimore: J. F. Weishampel, 1891); and Caesar A. A. Taylor, The Negro Race, Retrospective and Prospective; or, the Negro's Past and Present, and His Future Prospects (Johnstown, Pa.: Harry M. Benshoff, 1890).

65 Thomas Hamilton, "Apology," Anglo-African Magazine 1:1 (January 1859): 4.

66 Frederick Douglass, My Bondage and My Freedom (New York: Miller, Orton, and Mulligan, 1855), 38–39; rpt. Urbana: University of Illinois Press, 1987.

67 See George W. Stocking, Jr.'s introduction to the 1973 edition of Prichard's The Natural History of Man, Comprising Inquiries into the Modifying Influence of Physical and Moral Agencies on the Different Tribes of the Human Family, "From Chronology to Ethnology: James Cowles Prichard and British Anthropology, 1800–1850," 2 vols. (Chicago: University of Chicago Press, 1973), ix-cx.

68 Michael A. Chaney, "Picturing the Mother, Claiming Egypt: My Bondage and My Freedom as Auto(bio)ethnography," African American Review 35:3 (fall 2001): 391.

69 James McCune Smith, "Introduction," in Douglass, My Bondage and My Freedom, 22.

70 Ibid., 22–23.

71 Ibid., 22.

72 Van Evrie, White Supremacy and Negro Subordination, 201.

73 Smith, "Introduction," 22.

74 Ibid., 23.

75 Brown, The Black Man, 205.

76 On Smith, see Sammons, Blacks in Science and Medicine, 215–16; Dumas Malone, ed., Dictionary of American Biography (New York: Charles Scribner's Sons, 1935), 17:288–89; Martin Kaufman et al., eds., Dictionary of American Medical Biography (Westport, Conn.: Greenwood Press, 1984), 2:693; A. A. Schomburg, "Dr. James McCune Smith," Negro History Bulletin 9:2 (November 1945): 41–42; and Kelly Miller, "The Historic Background of the Negro Physician," Journal of Negro History, 1:2 (April 1916): 99–109.

77 Wallace, Constructing the Black Masculine, 56. On African American Free-masonry, also see, especially, Joanna Brooks, "Colonization, Black Freemasonry, and the Rehabilitation of Africa," in Messy Beginnings: Postcolonialism and Early Ameri-

can Studies, edited by Malini Johar Schueller and Edward Watts (New Brunswick: Rutgers University Press, 2003); and Joanna Brooks, "Prince Hall, Freemasonry, and Genealogy," *African American Review* 34:2 (summer 2000), 197–216; William A. Muraskin, *Middle-Class Blacks in a White Society: Prince Hall Freemasonry in America* (Berkeley: University of California Press, 1975); George W. Crawford, *Prince Hall and His Followers: Being a Monograph on the Legitimacy of Negro Masonry* (New York: Crisis, 1914); and William Henry Grimshaw, *Official History of Freemasonry among the Colored People in North America* (New York: Negro Universities Press, [1903] 1989).

78 Delany, *The Origin and Objects of Ancient Freemasonry*, 40.

79 Ibid., 24.

80 Ibid., 35.

81 Ibid.

82 Ibid., 15–18.

83 Ibid., 40.

84 Ibid.

85 See Moses, *Afrotopia*.

86 Wallace, *Constructing the Black Masculine*, 53, 65.

87 Ibid., 68.

88 Ibid.

89 Delany, *The Origin and Objects of Ancient Freemasonry*, 33.

90 The best discussions of Delany are now found in Wallace, *Constructing the Black Masculine*; and Robert S. Levine, *Martin Delany, Frederick Douglass, and the Politics of Representative Identity* (Chapel Hill: University of North Carolina Press, 1997). But also see Victor Ullman, *Martin R. Delany: The Beginnings of Black Nationalism* (Boston: Beacon Press, 1971); Cyril Griffith, *The African Dream: Martin R. Delany and the Emergence of Pan-African Thought* (University Park: Pennsylvania State University Press, 1975); and Gilroy, *The Black Atlantic*.

91 Delany, *Principia of Ethnology*, 9. This edition was reprinted in 1991 as *The Origin of Races and Color* (Baltimore: Black Classic Press), and has also recently been included in Robert Levine's landmark edited collection *Martin R. Delany: A Documentary Reader* (Chapel Hill: University of North Carolina Press, 2003); my notes, however, refer to the original edition, and I refer to this work throughout under its main title, *Principia of Ethnology*.

92 Delany, *Principia of Ethnology*, 21.

93 Ibid., 20–21.

94 Ibid., 14–17.

95 Ibid., 17–22.

96 Ibid., 44.

97 Ibid., 49–50.

98 The Ethiopianist-Egyptological arguments Delany puts forward in the last chapters of the monograph also appear, in a differently arranged and much less

elaborate form, in his *The International Policy of the World towards the African Race* of more than ten years before (in Frank [Frances] Rollin, *Life and Public Services of Martin R. Delany* [Boston: Lee and Shepard, 1883]; rpt. in the Schomburg Library of Nineteenth-Century Black Women Writers' volume, *Two Biographies by African-American Women*, edited by Henry Louis Gates Jr. [New York: Oxford University Press, 1991], 316–26). For more on Ethiopianism and Delany, see chapter five.

99  Delany, *Principia of Ethnology*, 50.

100  Ibid., 52–53.

101  Nott and Gliddon, *Types of Mankind*, 95.

102  Delany, *Principia of Ethnology*, 33.

103  Ibid., 25.

104  Ibid., 26.

105  Ibid., 26–27.

106  Ibid., 26.

107  Ibid., 27.

108  See, for example, Ullman, *Martin R. Delany*; Griffith, *The African Dream*; and Gilroy, *The Black Atlantic*.

109  Delany, *Principia of Ethnology*, 26.

110  See Bernal, *Black Athena*, especially volume 1, *The Fabrication of Ancient Greece, 1785–1985*, chapters 5–9, 224–399.

111  Bruno Latour, *The Pasteurization of France*, translated by Alan Sheridan and John Law (Cambridge: Harvard University Press, 1988), 166. For assistance in thinking through this period in the history of American science, I am especially indebted to the works of Latour, particularly *The Pasteurization of France* and *Science in Action: How to Follow Scientists and Engineers through Society* (Cambridge: Harvard University Press, 1987). Also central are the works of Barbara Herrnstein Smith (on which see below). Work in sympathy or dialogue with Latour's should also be mentioned here, with the assurance that this is a partial (in both senses of the term) and somewhat arbitrary list: Andrew Pickering, *The Mangle of Practice: Time, Agency, and Science* (Chicago: University of Chicago Press, 1995); Malcolm Ashmore, *The Reflexive Thesis: Wrighting Sociology of Scientific Knowledge* (Chicago: University of Chicago Press, 1989); Donna Haraway, *Simians, Cyborgs, and Women: The Reinvention of Nature* (New York: Routledge, 1991); the essays in B. H. Smith and Arkady Plotnitsky, eds., *Mathematics, Science, and Postclassical Theory* (South Atlantic Quarterly, special issue 94:2 [Spring 1995]); the essays in Andrew Pickering, ed., *Science as Culture and Practice* (Chicago: University of Chicago Press, 1992); and the essays in John Law, ed., *A Sociology of Monsters: Essays on Power, Technology and Domination*, Sociological Review Monographs 38 (London: Routledge, 1991).

112  Nott and Gliddon, *Types of Mankind*, 59.

113  Nott, *Two Lectures*, 21.

114  *The African Observer: A Monthly Journal, Containing Essays and Documents Illustra-*

tive of the General Character, and Moral and Political Effects, of Negro Slavery (Sixth Month, 1827); rpt. Westport: Negro Universities Press, 1970), nos. 1–12 (1827–28), 65–96.

115 Thomas Jefferson, Notes on the State of Virginia, edited by William Peden (Chapel Hill: University of North Carolina Press, 1982), 138–39.

116 And thus in yet other words this period in racially constituted ethno-Egyptology provides a textbook example of what Barbara Herrnstein Smith has analyzed as "epistemic self-privileging." See Smith, Belief and Resistance, esp. xi–xx, 37–51; and Barbara Herrnstein Smith, Contingencies of Value: Alternate Perspectives for Critical Theory (Cambridge: Harvard University Press, 1988), esp. 36–42.

117 The reference here is multifold: to Bernal, to the highly influential work of Gould in Mismeasure of Man; and to the essays in Sandra Harding, ed., The "Racial" Economy of Science: Toward a Democratic Future (Bloomington: Indiana University Press, 1993), all of which are understood here to be fully invested in the legacy of positivism.

118 Anonymous [Carlyle McKinley], An Appeal to Pharaoh: The Negro Problem, and Its Radical Solution (New York: Fords, Howard, and Hulbert, 1889), 32; rpt. in Smith, Anti-Black Thought, Volume 11:32.

## Chapter 2: The Egyptian Moment

1 Howard Carter and A. C. Mace, The Tomb of Tut.ankh.Amen, Discovered by the Late Earl of Carnarvon and Howard Carter (London: Cassell, 1923), 1:97–98.

2 Mary Louise Pratt, Imperial Eyes: Travel Writing and Transculturation (New York: Routledge, 1992), 205.

3 The published account is found in Carter and Mace, The Tomb of Tuk.ankh. Amen, 95–96. The passage from Carter's diary is taken from the Carter Diary, Griffith Institute, Ashmolean Museum, Oxford University, and is quoted in H. V. F. Winstone, Howard Carter and the Discovery of the Tomb of Tutankhamen (London: Constable, 1991), 142.

4 Pratt, Imperial Eyes, 204.

5 In addition to the adventurer's texts themselves, see Frederick Bradnum, The Long Walks: Journeys to the Sources of the White Nile (London: Victor Gollancz, 1969).

6 Schueller, U.S. Orientalisms, 29, 33.

7 Pratt, Imperial Eyes, 201.

8 The obvious reference here is to J. Gerald Kennedy and Liliane Weissberg, eds., Romancing the Shadow: Poe and Race (New York: Oxford University Press, 2001), but much of the current work in Poe scholarship that attends to issues of race began with Dana Nelson's chapter on Poe in The Word in Black and White: Reading "Race" in American Literature, 1638–1867 (New York: Oxford University Press, 1992); and Joan Dayan's famous essay "Amorous Bondage: Poe, Ladies, and Slaves," American Literature 66 (June 1994): 239–73.

9  William F. Lyon, *The Hollow Globe; or, The World's Agitator and Reconciler: A Treatise on the Physical Conformation of the Earth* (Chicago: Sherman and Lyon, 1875), 9.

10  Ibid., 10, 343–44.

11  See Paul K. Alkon, *Origins of Futuristic Fiction* (Athens: University of Georgia Press, 1987); Paul K. Alkon, *Science Fiction before 1900: Imagination Discovers Technology* (New York: Twayne, 1994); David Seed, ed., *Anticipations: Essays in Early Science Fiction and Its Precursors* (Liverpool: Liverpool University Press, 1995); and Allienne R. Becker, *The Lost Worlds Romance: From Dawn to Dusk* (Westport: Greenwood Press, 1992). For collections of nineteenth-century speculative fiction, see H. Bruce Franklin, ed., *Future Perfect: American Science Fiction of the Nineteenth Century—An Anthology*, rev. ed. (New Brunswick, N.J.: Rutgers University Press 1995); and Carol Farley Kessler, ed., *Daring to Dream: Utopian Stories by United States Women, 1836–1919* (Boston: Pandora Press, 1984).

12  Edgar Allan Poe, "The Murders in the Rue Morgue," in *Edgar Allen Poe: Poetry, Tales, and Selected Essays* (New York: Library of America, 1996), 397.

13  Irwin, *American Hieroglyphics*, 44.

14  The obvious temptation to go into greater detail here regarding the implications of the narrative of analysis presented in "The Murders in the Rue Morgue" is of course a strong one, and certainly the relationship among Dupin, his hieroglyphical rationalism, and the wildly racialized figure of the orangutan at the heart of the story is a provocative one, and one with no small connection to the argument of this chapter. Unfortunately, however, size and scope limitations have forced me to forgo such an analysis in favor of a more streamlined one focusing on those narrative shapes involving the expeditionary tale and what I am here thematizing as the racial rupture. Recently, though, several important studies have appeared that address many of the racialized issues that organize "Rue Morgue": see, for example, Loisa Nygaard, "Winning the Game: Inductive Reasoning in Poe's 'Murders in the Rue Morgue,' " *Studies in Romanticism* 33 (summer 1994): 223–54; Lindon Barrett, "Presence of Mind: Detection and Racialization in 'The Murders in the Rue Morgue' "; and Elise Lemire, " 'The Murders in the Rue Morgue': Amalgamation Discourses and the Race Riots of 1838 in Poe's Philadelphia" (the latter two are in Kennedy and Weissberg, *Romancing the Shadow*, 157–76 and 177–204, respectively).

15  See Mary Louise Pratt, "Fieldwork in Common Places," in *Writing Culture*, edited by James Clifford and George Marcus (Berkeley: University of California Press, 1987).

16  Edgar Allan Poe, "The Gold-Bug," in Poe, *Poetry, Tales, and Selected Essays*, 578.

17  Ibid., 578.

18  See, for example, Irwin, *American Hieroglyphics*.

19  Toni Morrison, *Playing in the Dark: Whiteness and the Literary Imagination* (New York: Vintage, 1992), 33.

20 Ibid., 32. For Morrison's comments on this text, and of the figure of Jupiter in particular, see 57–58.

21 On Sullivan's Island—the setting of "The Gold-Bug"—see Liliane Weissberg, "Black, White, and Gold," in Kennedy and Weissberg, *Romancing the Shadow*, 127–56.

22 Edgar Allan Poe, "MS. Found in a Bottle," in Poe, *Poetry, Tales, and Selected Essays*, 199.

23 "MS. Found in a Bottle" appeared in the October 19, 1833, issue of the Baltimore *Saturday Visitor*. There were several other previously published but unsigned pieces, now attributed to Poe, but this was his first signed publication, and so for a variety of reasons I am choosing to understand the trajectory of his professional career beginning with it.

24 John Cleves Symmes, "Circular Number 1," reproduced in Herman J. Viola and Carolyn Margolis, eds., *Magnificent Voyagers: The U.S. Exploring Expedition, 1838–1842* (Washington, D.C.: Smithsonian Institution Press, 1985), 10.

25 Captain Adam Seaborn [John Cleves Symmes], *Symzonia: A Voyage of Discovery* (New York: Seymour, 1820), 13–18.

26 See Victoria Nelson, "Symmes Hole, or the South Polar Romance," *Raritan* 17:2 (fall 1997): 136–66.

27 John Cleves Symmes and James McBride, *Symmes Theory of Concentric Spheres and Polar Voids: Demonstrating That the Earth is Hollow, Habitable Within, and Widely Open at the Poles* (Cincinnati: Morgan, Lodge and Fischer, 1826).

28 Symmes, "Circular Number 1."

29 On Symmes and the expedition, see Viola and Margolis, *Magnificent Voyages*; William Stanton, *The Great United States Exploring Expedition of 1838–1842* (Berkeley: University of California Press, 1975); and Charles Wilkes, *Voyage Round the World, Embracing the Principal Events of the Narrative of the United States Exploring Expedition. In One Volume* (Philadelphia: George W. Gorton, 1849). On *Symzonia*, see Goddu, *Gothic America*; and three works by J. O. Bailey: *Pilgrims through Space and Time: Trends and Patterns in Scientific and Utopian Fiction* (New York: Argus Books, 1947); "An Early American Utopian Fiction," *American Literature* 14 (1942): 285–93; and "Introduction," in the 1965 edition of Symmes's *Symzonia* (Gainesville: Scholars' Facsimiles and Reprints, 1965).

30 Symmes, *Symzonia*, 97.

31 Ibid., 108.

32 Ibid., 110.

33 A number of critics have noted the relationship between Poe and Symmes. In addition to the works of Goddu and Bailey, see William E. Lenz, "Poe's *Arthur Gordon Pym* and the Narrative Techniques of Antarctic Gothic," *CEA Critic* 53:3 (spring–summer 1991): 30–38; David Kadlec, "The Flowering of Miss Jack Tar: *Symzonia, Pym,* and Paul Metcalf's *Both*," *Sagetrieb* 12:1 (spring 1993): 83–94; and both Richard Wilbur, "Introduction," in the 1973 David R. Godine edition, and

Harold Beaver, "Introduction," in the 1975 Penguin edition of *Pym*. As these works note, Symmes's theory actually got most of its exposure not from Symmes himself but from his friend and fellow Ohioan Jeremiah Reynolds; the Wilkes Expedition owes virtually its entire transition from a theory first set forth in Symmes's circular of 1818 to its embarkation in 1838 to Reynolds. On Reynolds, see Stanton, *Exploring Expedition*. On his relationship with Poe, see Robert F. Almy, "J. N. Reynolds: A Brief Biography with Particular Reference to Poe and Symmes," *The Colophon*, new series, 2 (1937): 227–45; and Aubrey Starke, "Poe's Friend Reynolds," *American Literature* 11 (1939): 152–66. For more on *Pym*, see below.

34 "Bedloe's contact with the Orient begins with his enacting the trope of discovery," writes Malini Johar Schueller of "A Tale of the Ragged Mountains," "both of the New World and of the Orient, the ostensible goal of Columbus's quest" (*U.S. Orientalisms*, 112). On this, also see John Carlos Rowe, "Edgar Allan Poe's Imperial Fantasy and the American Frontier," in Kennedy and Weissberg, *Romancing the Shadow*, 75–105.

35 Pratt, *Imperial Eyes*, 216.

36 Edgar Allan Poe, "A Descent into the Maelström," in Poe, *Poetry, Tales, and Selected Essays*, 433.

37 Ibid., 443.

38 See, for example, the works of Nelson, Dayan, Morrison, and Goddu, as well as the essay by Gerald Kennedy in Kennedy and Weissberg, *Romancing the Shadow*, " 'Trust No Man': Poe, Douglass, and the Culture of Slavery," 225–57. For a more diverse overview of the history of *Pym*, see Richard Kopley, ed., *Poe's Pym: Critical Explorations* (Durham: Duke University Press, 1992).

39 Stephen Dougherty, "Prophecy, Racial Paranoia, and the Figure of Egypt in Antebellum America," *Arizona Quarterly* 56:3 (autumn 2000): 17.

40 Edgar Allan Poe, *The Narrative of Arthur Gordon Pym*, in Poe, *Poetry, Tales, and Selected Essays*, 1129.

41 Goddu, *Gothic America*, 81.

42 Nelson, *The Word in Black and White*, 96. Extra special thanks are here due to Dana Nelson for her conversations with me over the years regarding Poe and American race science, as well as for her early, ongoing, and unflagging support of this project.

43 In her discussion of *Pym*, Goddu warns against just this kind of interpretation; she argues that "it was not until the 1850s that an inherent inequality between the races was accepted as scientific fact," that "this acceptance was not regionally based," and that "to read [*Pym*] as an allegory of racial difference is to project upon it an 1850s discourse of polygenism" (*Gothic America*, 84). While her points—especially concerning regionalism and allegoricizing—are well taken, her support for them does bear some clarification. Even though she writes that "from the early eighteenth century through the 1830s, monogenism, the belief in the original sameness of men, was the dominant racial ideology" and that the "gradual shift from monogenism to polygenism . . . was occurring on the national

level as Poe wrote *Pym*" (83–84), this is not, strictly speaking, the case. As Goddu herself admits, the intellectual developments that led to the canonization of the polygenic proslavery American School of Ethnology were already being formed by 1838, and even at this relatively early date they were far more widespread and influential than she suggests. Moreover, not only was the controversy over multiple origins well in play as early as the 1820s, and not only was polygeny also frequently used by proslavery antiscience Christians, but there was never such a thing as a "gradual shift" from monogeny to polygeny. Rather, there was a continual and continually uneven conflict between monogenism and polygenism—neither one of which was ever fully identified as more thoroughly "social" or "biological" than the other—throughout the whole of the nineteenth century. (And this conflict is not by any means resolved yet.) In short, at no point was racial inequality ever simply "accepted as scientific fact," as Goddu suggests, nor was racism or even polygenism ever the sole province of science. What makes *Pym* so remarkable, in fact, is its sophisticated understanding of the constituent terms of nineteenth-century ethnology—and their implications—at such an early point in their dissemination. Poe is engaging and intervening in the very discourses that already constituted American racialization and would continue to operate indefinitely into the future. Radical racialization, like Poe's Pym, was by 1838 well under way. For more on these issues, see chapter one.

44  See William E. Lenz, *The Poetics of the Antarctic: A Study in Nineteenth-Century American Cultural Perceptions* (New York: Garland, 1995); and Paul Simpson-Housley, *Antarctica: Exploration, Perception, and Metaphor* (New York: Routledge, 1992).

45  Poe, *Pym*, 1026.

46  My discussion here obviously owes a great deal to that of Nelson: "Racialist polarities structure the island of Tsalal," she writes. "Tsalal in effect underwrites the color line of the antebellum South" (*The Word in Black and White*, 96).

47  Poe, *Pym*, 1181. It has become a subfield of Poe and *Pym* studies to debate over the references included in the inscriptions: see, for example, Joseph J. Moldenhauer, "*Pym*, the Dighton Rock, and the Matter of Vinland," in Kopley, ed., *Poe's Pym*, 75–94.

48  Poe, *Pym*, 1179.

49  The Egyptomanic structure of *The Narrative of Arthur Gordon Pym* was literalized some years later by none other than Jules Verne, who in 1897 wrote a "conclusion" to *Pym* called *Les Sphinx des Glaces: The Sphinx of the Ice*. In this little read story, Verne scripts a sequel in which the *Jane Guy* is revealed to have been drawn into the white barrier by the magnetic force of a great hunk of Antarctic ice, inexplicably found to be in the shape of a Sphinx. "We beheld a huge mound," Verne's narrator recounts, "reared above the plain to a height of three hundred feet, with a circumference of from two to three hundred feet. In its strange form this great mound resembled an enormous sphinx; the body upright, the paws stretched out, crouching in the attitude of the winged monster which Grecian Mythology has placed upon the way to Thebes" (Jules Verne, *An Antarctic Mystery*, translated

by Cashel Hoey [Philadelphia: J. B. Lippincott, 1899; rpt. Boston: Gregg Press, 1975], 317). For a reading of Verne's text, see an earlier version of this discussion, in chapter three of Scott Trafton, "Egypt Land: Race and the Cultural Politics of American Egyptomania, 1800–1900," ph.d. diss., Department of English, Duke University, 1998.

50 See David R. Oldroyd, *Thinking about the Earth: A History of Ideas in Geology* (Cambridge: Harvard University Press, 1996); and Alice Turner, *The History of Hell* (New York: Harcourt Brace, 1993).

51 Richard Hamblyn, "Private Cabinets and Popular Geology: The British Audiences for Volcanoes in the Eighteenth Century," in *Transports: Travel, Pleasure, and Imaginative Geography, 1600–1830*, edited by Chloe Chard and Helen Langdon (New Haven: Yale University Press, 1996), 188.

52 For a critique of geographical determinism, see Martin W. Lewis and Kären E. Wigen, *The Myth of Continents: A Critique of Metageography* (Berkeley: University of California Press, 1997).

53 W. J. Shaw, *Cresten, Queen of the Toltus; or, Under the Auroras: A Marvellous Tale of the Interior World* (New York: Excelsior, 1888), 28.

54 Ibid., 3.

55 Ibid., 116–17.

56 Ibid., 116.

57 Ibid., 145–46.

58 Ibid.

59 Ibid., 175.

60 Ibid., 183.

61 Ibid.

62 Ibid., 170, 177.

63 Val Gough, "Lesbians and Virgins: The New Motherhood in *Herland*," in Seed, *Anticipations*, 196, 206.

64 J. Wood, *Pantaletta: A Romance of Sheheland* (New York: American News Company, 1882); John DeMorgan, *Bess: A Companion to Jess* (New York: Munro, 1887); Frank Cowan, *Revi-Lona: A Romance of Love in a Marvelous Land* (Pittsburgh: privately printed, ca. 1880). DeMorgan, in particular, was known for his parodies and satires of Haggard published in 1887 in the triweekly Munro's Library: *He, a Companion to She; It, a Wild, Weird History of Marvelous, Phantasmagorical Adventures in Search of He, She, & Jess, & Leading to the Finding of "It"; King Solomon's Wives; King Solomon's Treasures;* and more. For collections of parodies of Haggard — including DeMorgan's *Bess* — see two edited by Robert Reginald and Douglas Menville: *King Solomon's Children: Some Parodies of H. Rider Haggard,* and *They: Three Parodies of H. Rider Haggard's She* (both New York: Arno Press, 1978).

65 Cowan, *Revi-Lona*, i.

66 Jean Pfaelzer, "Utopians Prefer Blondes: Mary Lane's *Mizora* and the Nineteenth-Century Utopian Imagination," in Mary E. Bradley Lane, *Mizora: A Prophecy*

(New York: G.W. Dillingham, 1890; rpt. Syracuse: Syracuse University Press, 2000), xvi.

67 For more on Hale and Kaplan, see chapter four.

68 Lillian Frances Mentor, *The Day of Resis* (New York: G. W. Dillingham, 1897), 10.

69 Ibid.

70 Ibid., 9.

71 Mudimbe, *The Invention of Africa*, 17.

72 Mentor, *The Day of Resis*, 21–22.

73 Mudimbe, *The Invention of Africa*, 16.

74 Mentor, *The Day of Resis*, 57–58.

75 Ibid., 58–59.

76 Ibid., 67.

77 Ibid., 72.

78 Ibid., 270.

79 Ibid., 312–13.

80 Ibid., 314.

81 Ibid.

82 Ibid., 293–94.

83 Ibid., 322.

84 Ibid., 320.

85 Ibid., 331.

86 Ibid., 322.

## Chapter 3: The Curse of the Mummy

1 Traditional; quoted in Eugene Genovese, *Roll, Jordan, Roll: The World the Slaves Made* (New York: Vintage, 1976), 199. Dialect typography in the original.

2 Charles White, arr., *The Virginny Mummy: A Negro Farce* (New York, Happy Hours, n.d.), scene II, 5. White was one of the more famous blackface minstrelsy performers of the nineteenth century, leader of White's Minstrels and frequently associated with T. D. Rice. *The Virginny* (sometimes *Virginia* or *Virginian*) *Mummy* was, in fact, often listed as one of Rice's favorites, and its origin is usually credited to him, with Rice in the role of Ginger Blue; the play was one of the few he staged during his tour of England in 1836–37, alongside *The Peacock and the Crow* (in which Rice "jumped Jim Crow"). The version cited here, however, was arranged by White and lists as the cast the members of his standard company, with White in the role of Ginger. On this, see Gerald Bordman's brief mention of the play in his *American Musical Theatre: A Chronicle*, 3d ed. (New York: Oxford University Press, 2001), 11; as well as the documentation of Rice's performances at the Adelphi Theatre in London during the 1836–37 season, online as of this writing at http://www.emich.edu/public/english/adelphi_calendar/m36d.htm. The stan-

dard study of blackface minstrelsy is of course Eric Lott, *Love and Theft: Black-face Minstrelsy and the American Working Class* (New York: Oxford University Press, 1993), but by far the most thorough treatment of Charles T. White is found in Annemarie Bean et al., eds., *Inside the Minstrel Mask: Readings in Nineteenth-Century Blackface Minstrelsy* (Hanover, N.H.: Wesleyan University Press, 1996); in that collection William J. Mahar's article "Ethiopian Skits and Sketches: Contents and Contexts of Blackface Minstrelsy, 1840–1890" contains an extended discussion of White and several of his works, and the volume also reproduces the text of White's midcentury *The Hop of Fashion*, with a cast list almost identical to that of *The Virginny Mummy*.

3  White, *Virginny Mummy*, scene III, 7.

4  Ibid., scene IV, 8–16.

5  Lott, *Love and Theft*, 52.

6  White, *Virginny Mummy*, scene IV, 14–15.

7  Ibid., scene IV, 12.

8  On this, see Mahar, "Ethiopian Skits and Sketches," 204–5.

9  See, for example, William T. Alderson, ed., *Mermaids, Mummies, and Mastodons: The Emergence of the American Museum* (Washington, D.C.: American Association of Museums, 1992).

10  Horace Smith, "On a Stupendous Leg of Granite, Discovered Standing by Itself in the Deserts of Egypt, with the Inscription Inserted Below," in Horace Smith, *Amarynthus, the Nympholet: A Pastoral Drama, in Three Acts, with Other Poems* (London: Hurst, Rees, Orne, and Brown, 1821; rpt. New York: Garland, 1977). On Smith and Shelley, see Eugene M. Waith, "Ozymandias: Shelley, Horace Smith, and Denon," *Keats-Shelley Journal* 44 (1995): 22–28; and M. K. Bequette, "Shelley and Smith: Two Sonnets on Ozymandias," *Keats-Shelley Journal* 26 (1977): 29–31.

11  The 1819 first canto of Byron's *Don Juan* (canto I, stanza CCXIX) features the image in question:

> What are the hopes of man? Old Egypt's King
> Cheops erected the first Pyramid
> And largest, thinking it was just the thing
> To keep his memory whole, and mummy hid;
> But somebody or other rummaging
> Burglariously broke his coffin's lid:
> Let not a monument give you or me hopes,
> Since not a pinch of dust remains of Cheops.

12  For a general overview of the connections between mummies and early medicine, see the work of Bob Brier, especially *Egyptian Mummies* and *The Encyclopedia of Mummies* (Checkmark Books, 1998). For more on the "Ether Dome Mummy," which entered the United States in May 1823 but whose name went untranslated until 1960, see Joyce Haynes and R. Jackson Wilson, *Padihershef the Egyptian*

Mummy (Springfield, Mass.: Springfield Library and Museums Association, 1984); George E. Gifford, "The Case of the Ether Dome Mummy," *Harvard Medical Alumni Bulletin* (March-April 1977); Alderson, *Mummies, Mermaids, and Mummies*; and S. J. Wolfe and Robert Singerman, " 'As Cheap as Candidates for the Presidency': The Beginnings of Mummy Mania in America," manuscript, 2002. An excellent example of the slippages among popular Egyptology, race science, and medical artifacts that structured the display of ancient Egyptian mummies can be seen in the history of Got Thothi Aunk, the mummy unrolled by George Gliddon in Boston in June 1850, which, for almost fifty years, was on display at Tulane University's Anatomical Museum; on this, see Lombardi, "Egyptian Mummies at Tulane University," and my discussion of Gliddon in chapter one.

13   John Collins Warren, "Description of an Egyptian Mummy, Presented to the Massachusetts General Hospital with an Account of the Operation of Embalming, in Ancient and Modern Times," *Boston Journal of Philosophy and the Arts* 1 (1823): 284–85. Quoted in Wolfe and Singerman, " 'As Cheap as Candidates for the Presidency,' " 2–3. My thanks to S. J. Wolfe for permission to quote from her piece.

14   Louisa May Alcott, "Lost in a Pyramid, or The Mummy's Curse," *The New World* 1:1 (January 16, 1869); rpt. in John Richard Stephens, ed., *Into the Mummy's Tomb* (New York: Berkley Books, 2001), 41–42.

15   Mary Shelley, *Frankenstein or the Modern Prometheus* (Oxford: Oxford University Press, 1981).

16   Judith Halberstam, *Skin Shows: Gothic Horror and the Technology of Monsters* (Durham: Duke University Press, 1995), 85.

17   John Fanning Watson, *Extra-Illustrated Autograph Manuscript of "Annals of Philadelphia"* (Philadelphia: Library Company of Philadelphia, ca. 1830). Quoted in Wolfe and Singerman, " 'As Cheap as Candidates for the Presidency,' " 12–13.

18   For the century's earliest large-scale treatment of the figure of the reanimated mummy, see British writer Jane Webb Loudon's *The Mummy! A Tale of the Twenty-Second Century* (London: Henry Colburn, 1827; rpt. Ann Arbor: University of Michigan Press, 1994).

19   Alcott, "The Mummy's Curse." Though clearly related to them and written during the same period, this story was not included in the recent series of reissues of the works Elaine Showalter calls "alternative Alcott." Originally appearing in the January 16, 1869, issue of the periodical *The New World*, "The Mummy's Curse"—by which title I refer to the piece since the curse is arguably more the subject of the story than the brief episode in the pyramid—remained lost until 1998, when British scholar Dominic Montserrat rediscovered it in the Library of Congress and published it in the summer 1998 issue of the Egyptological journal KMT (9:2). It has since been reissued again, in Stephens, *Into the Mummy's Tomb*, 33–42, and my notes refer to this edition. For the Alcott reissues to which I refer, see the sequence of collections edited by Madeline Stern et al., beginning in 1975, but especially her latest and most complete, *Louisa May Alcott Unmasked:*

Collected Thrillers (Boston: Northeastern University Press, 1995); as well as Elaine Showalter, ed., *Alternative Alcott: Louisa May Alcott* (New Brunswick: Rutgers University Press, 1988).

20 Alcott, "The Mummy's Curse," quoted in Stephens, *Into the Mummy's Tomb,* 34.

21 Ibid., 36.

22 Ibid., 37.

23 Ibid., 38.

24 Ibid., 42.

25 Ibid.

26 Ibid., 36.

27 Ibid., 37.

28 Ibid., 42, 37.

29 Ibid., 40.

30 Ibid., 33, 42.

31 "The Effects of a Hearty Dinner after Visiting the Antediluvian Department at the Crystal Palace," *Punch,* February 3, 1855, 50. This image also appears in Martin J. S. Rudwick, *Scenes from Deep Time: Early Pictorial Representations of the Prehistoric World* (Chicago: University of Chicago Press, 1992), fig. 65, 151.

32 See Nelson, *National Manhood,* esp. 206–16; and Schueller, *U.S. Orientalisms,* 113; as well as Burton R. Pollin, "Poe's 'Some Words with a Mummy' Reconsidered," ESQ 60, Poe Supplement (fall 1970): 60–67; Michael Williams, *A World of Words: Language and Displacement in the Fiction of Edgar Allan Poe* (Durham: Duke University Press, 1988); David A. Long, "Poe's Political Identity: A Mummy Unswathed," *Poe Studies* 23:1 (June 1990): 1–22; and Irwin, *American Hieroglyphics,* 55–61.

33 Edgar Allan Poe, "Some Words with a Mummy," in Poe, *Edgar Allan Poe,* 807.

34 Ibid., 810.

35 Ibid., 808.

36 Ibid.

37 Ibid., 810.

38 Ibid.

39 Ibid.

40 Ibid.

41 Ibid., 813.

42 Ibid., 811.

43 Ibid., 812.

44 Ibid.

45 Ibid., 814.

46 Ibid., 817.

47 Ibid.

48 Nelson, *National Manhood,* 213.

49  Ibid., 211.

50  Ibid.

51  Poe, "Some Words with a Mummy," 807.

52  Ibid., 821.

53  Ibid., 820.

54  Schueller, *U.S. Orientalisms*, 113.

55  On mummy mania, see Wolfe and Singerman, "As Cheap as Candidates for the Presidency."

56  Giovanni Belzoni, *Narrative of the Operations and Recent Discoveries within the Pyramids, Temples, Tombs and Excavations in Egypt and Nubia* (London: John Murray, 1820).

57  Arthur Weigall, *The Glory of the Pharaohs* (London, 1923), 127–30.

58  Antonia Lant, "Haptical Cinema," *October* 74 (fall 1995): 52–53.

59  Philip Hone, *The Diary of Philip Hone, 1828–1851*, edited by Allan Nevins (New York: Dodd, Mead, 1927), February 14, 1838, quoted in Talbot Hamlin, *Greek Revival Architecture in America* (New York: Oxford University Press, 1944), 78.

60  Vincent Scully, *American Architecture and Urbanism*, new rev. ed. (New York: Henry Holt, 1988), 48, 74.

61  Edward W. Said, *Orientalism* (New York: Vintage, 1979), 84.

62  Quoted in Linda Nochlin, "The Imaginary Orient," *Art in America* 71:5 (May 1983): 123.

63  Said, *Orientalism*, 85.

64  It was a major architect of the Egyptian Revival, in fact, who published one of the earliest architect's guides in America, a genre that provided reproductions of classical structures and their details for the purpose of reference and modeling, as well as professional advice and instructions on technique. See John Haviland, *The Practical Builder's Assistant: Containing the Five Orders of Architecture, Selected from the Best Specimens of the Greek and Roman* (Philadelphia: John Bioren, 1818). On architectural guidebooks in general, see Jacob Landy, *The Architecture of Minard Lafever* (New York: Columbia University Press, 1970); and Pamela Scott, *Temple of Liberty: Building the Capitol for a New Nation* (New York: Oxford University Press, 1995). For more on Haviland, see below.

65  On these see John Sweetman, *The Oriental Obsession: Islamic Inspiration in British and American Art and Architecture, 1500–1920* (Cambridge: Cambridge University Press, 1988); Clay Lancaster, *Architectural Follies in America* (Rutland, Vt.: Charles E. Tuttle, 1960); and Patrick Conner, *Oriental Architecture in the West* (London: Thames and Hudson, 1979). Iranistan's architect was Leopold Eidlitz, the first professional Jewish architect to work in the United States; for more on Eidlitz, see Montgomery Schuyler, "A Great American Architect: Leopold Eidlitz," *Architectural Record* 24:3 (September 1903): 169.

66  Pamela Scott, "Robert Mills and American Monuments," in *Robert Mills, Architect*, edited by John M. Bryan (Washington, D.C.: American Institute of Archi-

tects Press, 1989), 158. Scott notes that the proposal for this structure comes from an undated manuscript, entitled "National Monument to Washington," housed in the Maryland Historical Society (176 n.46).

67 George Templeton Strong, in Allan Nevins and M. H. Thomas, eds., *The Diary of George Templeton Strong* (New York: Octagon, 1952), 1:297, quoted in Landy, *The Architecture of Minard Lafever*, 141.

68 "Halls of the Ancients: Purpose of the Queer Building on New York Avenue," unattributed newspaper clipping, n.d., "Halls of the Ancients" folder, Washingtoniana Division, Martin Luther King Jr. Memorial Library, Washington, D.C. The structure that occasioned this response was the Halls of the Ancients, an Egyptian Revival museum built in 1898 by wealthy Boston merchant Franklin Webster Smith, once located at 1312 New York Avenue N.W. but razed in 1926. Information on Smith and his building is scant; the best source material is collected at the Washingtoniana Division.

69 Norton P. Chipman, "Speech of Hon. Norton P. Chipman," in *Washington National Monument: Shall the Unfinished Obelisk Stand a Monument of National Disgrace and National Dishonor?* (Washington, D.C.: Government Printing Office, 1874), 11 (collected speeches made in the House of Representatives, June 4, 1874).

70 The thickly racialized politics of the history of the Washington Monument were further elaborated by the circumstances of the delay in its completion— which, as their title makes clear, was the occasion of Chipman's remarks. The long delay was due in part to the interruption caused by the Civil War, but construction began in 1854 and was soon forcibly halted by members of the antislavery anti-immigrant Republican splinter group, the Know Nothings. The Know Nothings objected to Catholic participation in the building of the monument, both in terms of the immigrant Irish labor that was being used to construct it and in terms of the enthusiasm for it voiced by Catholic leaders across the world. The group thus seized a symbolic "pope stone" sent from the Vatican as a symbol of international support for Mills's obelisk and threw it in the Potomac River. This, combined with the Know Nothings' subsequent ousting of the board in charge of the project, effectively scuttled construction until funding was diverted for the war; the monument was thus long associated both with the racialized politics of nativism and with abolitionism. On the "pope stone," see Scott, "Robert Mills"; on the Know Nothings, see Tyler Anbinder, *Nativism and Slavery: The Northern Know Nothings and the Politics of the 1850s* (New York: Oxford University Press, 1992); Noel Ignatiev, *How the Irish Became White* (New York: Routledge, 1995); and Eric Foner, *Free Soil, Free Labor, Free Men: The Ideology of the Republican Party before the Civil War* (New York: Oxford University Press, 1970).

71 James Stevens Curl, *Egyptomania: The Egyptian Revival, a Recurring Theme in the History of Taste* (Manchester: Manchester University Press, 1994), 180.

72 On Haviland and the Tombs, see Richard G. Carrott, *The Egyptian Revival: Its Sources, Monuments, and Meaning, 1808–1858* (Berkeley: University of California

Press, 1978); and Norman Johnston, "John Haviland," in *Pioneers in Criminology*, edited by Hermann Mannheim, 2d ed. (Montclair, N.J.: Patterson Smith, 1972), 116–17.

73 Thomas Ustick Walter, letter to the New York Architectural Committee, June 30, 1835. Quoted in Carrott, *The Egyptian Revival*, 156–57.

74 In their original form, the New York City Halls of Justice and House of Detention were located in what is now lower Manhattan, occupying the entire city block bounded by Leonard, Elm, Franklin, and Centre streets. The original complex was demolished in 1897 and replaced with another prison-courthouse complex ("Tombs II") in the same location in 1902, albeit in what Carrott calls "a not particularly original Renaissance style." That structure was torn down in 1948 and replaced with a third complex ("Tombs III") in what Carrott, writing in 1978, called "the rather boxy vernacular of the 1950s" and an example of the "undistinguished public architecture of our century par excellence" (*The Egyptian Revival*, 190). Further renovations then included the complete remodeling of the original site, called by the 1980s the Manhattan House of Detention (which in that form did not include the courthouse) and then later the South Tower, as a neighboring North Tower (which did contain the courthouse) opened in 1990. "Tombs III" was officially renamed the Manhattan Detention Complex in the 1970s and then renamed yet again The Bernard B. Kerik Complex (after a former commissioner of the New York Department of Corrections) in December 2001. It is crucial to recognize that, even given the succession of different buildings and names over the years, the complex continued (and continues) to be almost universally known as "the Tombs," regardless of its official name or architectural style. On the Tombs, see Carrott, *The Egyptian Revival*, especially appendix 3.

75 Alfred Trumble, *Secrets of the Tombs: Its Crimes, Romances, and Mysteries* (New York: Richard K. Fox, 1881), 5–6.

76 Carrott, *The Egyptian Revival*, 165.

77 Amazingly, in 2002 the official Web site of the New York Correction History Society not only presented this faulty account of the Tombs as authoritative but also seems to have lifted its text almost verbatim from Alfred Trumble's 1881 pulpy and sensationalistic (not to mention hard to find) real-life crime "history" *Secrets of the Tombs*, quoted above, with only another misspelling of Stephens's name to distinguish it. "Its design had been inspired by an ancient mausoleum," the Web site reads, "that a traveler to Egypt, John I. Stevens of Hoboken, N.J., illustrated and wrote about in his book 'Stevens' Travels.'" At the time of this writing, this narrative could be found at http://www.correctionhistory.org/html/chronicl/nycdoc/html/histry3a.html. For biographies of Stephens, see Victor Wolfgang von Hagen, "Editor's Introduction," in *Incidents of Travel in Yucatán* (Norman: University of Oklahoma Press, 1962), 1:vii–xxiii; and Ziff, *Return Passages*.

78 Carrott, *The Egyptian Revival*, 112.

79 Carrott himself is among those who make this mistake; while not nearly

as widely as in England, the revival was in fact utilized for domestic architecture in the United States. See, for example, Virginia McAlester and Lee McAlester, *A Field Guide to American Houses* (New York: Knopf, 1995), 231.

80  Haviland, *The Practical Builder's Assistant*, 89, quoted in Peggy McDowell and Richard E. Meyer, *The Revival Styles in American Memorial Art* (Bowling Green: Bowling Green State University Popular Press, 1994), 133.

81  Michel Foucault, *Discipline and Punish: The Birth of the Prison*, translated by Alan Sheridan (New York: Vintage, 1979), 26.

82  Ibid., 125.

83  Ibid., 123–24.

84  Haviland is perhaps most famous for his 1820s design and construction of the Eastern State Penitentiary outside Philadelphia, known as the Prison at Cherry Hill, which, though designed in the Gothic style, would become one of the most influential structures in the history of prison reform; see Norman Johnston, Kenneth Finkel, and Jeffrey A. Cohen, *Eastern State Penitentiary: Crucible of Good Intentions* (Philadelphia: Philadelphia Museum of Art, 1994). Haviland, however, understood the Tombs to be an improvement over Cherry Hill; on this, see Carrott, *The Egyptian Revival*.

85  On the Pennsylvania System and development of American penal reforms, see David J. Rothman, *The Discovery of the Asylum: Social Order and Disorder in the New Republic* (Boston: Little, Brown, 1971); Louis P. Masur, *Rites of Execution: Capital Punishment and the Transformation of American Culture, 1776–1865* (New York: Oxford University Press, 1989); Norval Morris and David J. Rothman, eds., *The Oxford History of the Prison: The Practice of Punishment in Western Society* (New York: Oxford University Press, 1995); and Mark Colvin, *Penitentiaries, Reformatories, and Chain Gangs: Social Theory and the History of Punishment in Nineteenth-Century America* (New York: St. Martin's, 1997).

86  James Mease, *Observations on the Penitentiary System, and Penal Code of Pennsylvania: With Suggestions for Their Improvement* (Philadelphia: Clark and Raser, 1828), 17.

87  Foucault, *Discipline and Punish*, 239.

88  Ibid.

89  Gershom Powers, Warden, New York State Prison at Auburn, *A Letter . . . in Answer to a Letter of the Hon. Edward Livingston* (Albany, 1829), 14, quoted in W. David Lewis, *From Newgate to Dannemora: The Rise of the Penitentiary in New York, 1796–1848* (Ithaca: Cornell University Press, 1965), 115.

90  Lewis, *From Newgate to Dannemora*, 115.

91  Ibid.

92  Mease, *Observations on the Penitentiary System*, 73–74.

93  Alfred H. Love, *Journal of the Pennsylvania Prison Society*, 1896/97, 14, quoted in Negley K. Teeters, *They Were in Prison: A History of the Pennsylvania Prison Society, 1787–1937* (Chicago: John C. Winston, 1937), 204.

94 Robert Turnbull, *Maryland Gazette*, October 31, 1788, quoted in Masur, *Rites of Execution*, 83.

95 See Carrott, *The Egyptian Revival*, 90–93.

96 On the evident tensions between Austin and the supervising committee, see ibid., 90–91.

97 1 Cor. 15:51–52, King James Version.

98 1 Cor. 15:16–17, King James Version.

99 On this see Carrott, *The Egyptian Revival*, 80–101. These gates were part of the large-scale change in American burial practices associated with what is now called the "rural cemetery movement"; on this, see David Charles Sloane, *The Last Great Necessity: Cemeteries in American History* (Baltimore: The Johns Hopkins University Press, 1991).

100 *Forest Hills Cemetery* (Roxbury, 1855), 123, quoted in Carrott, *The Egyptian Revival*, 93.

101 C. W. Walter, *Mount Auburn* (New York, 1850), 17, quoted in Carrott, *The Egyptian Revival*, 84–85.

102 "Rural Cemeteries," *North American Review* 53:113 (1842): 391–92, quoted in Carrott, *The Egyptian Revival*, 86.

103 James Gallier, "American Architecture," *North American Review* 43 (October 1836): 379.

104 Ibid.

105 Carrott, *The Egyptian Revival*, 83.

106 Gallier, "American Architecture," 379.

107 Ibid.

108 Carrott, *The Egyptian Revival*, 91.

109 Ibid., 92.

110 Scott, "Robert Mills," 149.

111 *Forest Hills Cemetery*, quoted in Carrott, *The Egyptian Revival*, 93.

112 Walter, *Mount Auburn*, 17, quoted in Carrott, *The Egyptian Revival*, 84.

113 Ibid.

114 Ibid., 85.

115 The literature on the influences of the monotheism of ancient Egypt on Judeo-Christian traditions is extremely interesting, although almost none of it directly addresses religious (or aesthetic) controversies in the United States; see, in particular, Jan Assmann, *Moses the Egyptian: The Memory of Egypt in Western Monotheism* (Cambridge: Harvard University Press, 1997). Much of the attention given to this issue has, not unexpectedly, centered on Sigmund Freud's *Der Mann Moses und die monotheistische Religion* (1939), published in English as *Moses and Monotheism* (in *Standard Edition of the Complete Psychological Works of Sigmund Freud*, translated by James Strachey, vol. 23 [London: Hogarth, 1959]). In addition to Assmann, see, for example, Michel de Certeau, *The Writing of History*, translated by Tom Conley (New York: Columbia University Press, 1988).

116  Walter, *Mount Auburn*, 17, quoted in Carrott, *The Egyptian Revival*, 85.

117  Ibid.

118  Nehemiah Cleveland, *Green-Wood* (New York, 1847), 71, quoted in Carrott, *The Egyptian Revival*, 84.

119  *Forest Hills Cemetery*, 123, quoted in Carrott, *The Egyptian Revival*, 84.

120  Gerald Massey, *The Natural Genesis; or Second Part of a Book of the Beginnings, Containing an Attempt to Recover and Reconstitute the Lost Origins of the Myths and Mysteries, Types and Symbols, Religion and Language, with Egypt for the Mouthpiece and Africa as the Birthplace* (London: R. Clay, Sons, and Taylor, 1883; rpt. Kila, Mont.: Kessinger, 1992), 2:437–38.

121  Ibid.

122  Josiah C. Nott, *Essay on the Natural History of Mankind, Viewed in Connection with Negro Slavery: Delivered before the Southern Rights Association, 14th December, 1850* (Mobile: Dade, Thompson, 1851), 26.

## Chapter 4: Undressing Cleopatra

1  Jacob Abbott, *The History of Cleopatra, Queen of Egypt* (New York: Harper and Brothers, 1851), 317.

2  Anna Brownell Jameson, *Memoirs of Celebrated Female Sovereigns* (New York: Harper and Brothers, 1842), 1:31–32.

3  Ibid., 32. On Jameson, see Kimberly Vanesveld Adams, *Our Lady of Victorian Feminism: The Madonna in the Work of Anna Jameson, Margaret Fuller, and George Eliot* (Athens: Ohio University Press, 2001); Judith Johnston, *Anna Jameson: Victorian, Feminist, Woman of Letters* (Aldershot: Ashgate Press, 1997); and Clara Thomas, *Love and Work Enough: The Life of Anna Jameson* (Toronto: University of Toronto Press, 1978).

4  Abbott, *The History of Cleopatra*; Sarah Josepha Hale, "Cleopatra," in *Woman's Record; or, Sketches of All Distinguished Women, from "The Beginning" till A.D. 1850* (New York: Harper and Brothers, 1853), 31–32; Mary Cowden Clarke, "Cleopatra," in *World-Noted Women; or, Types of Womanly Attributes of All Lands and Ages* (New York: Appleton, 1857), 61–85; and Lydia Hoyt Farmer, "Cleopatra," in *The Girl's Book of Famous Queens* (New York: Thomas Y. Crowell, 1887), 33–94.

5  See Mary Hamer, *Signs of Cleopatra: History, Politics, Representation* (New York: Routledge, 1993).

6  Ibid., 34.

7  Hamer argues that prior to the nineteenth century, especially in Europe, the two most foundational representations of Cleopatra were her suicide and her banquet with Antony—recounted in Boccaccio, who adapted it from book 9 of Pliny's *Historia Naturalis*—in which, on a wager, she supposedly dissolved one of her priceless pearl earrings in a glass of wine and drank it. See ibid., chapter 3.

8  Julia Wiggin King, "Cleopatra: The Queen, the Mistress, the Suicide," *Cosmopolitan Art Journal* 3:1 (1858): 42.

9 Nathaniel Hawthorne, *The Marble Faun; or, The Romance of Monte Beni* (New York: Penguin, 1990), 125–26.

10 Lucy Hughes-Hallett, *Cleopatra: Histories, Dreams, and Distortions* (New York: HarperPerennial, 1991), 151.

11 In addition to the work of Hughes-Hallett and Hamer, see the National Gallery of Canada's massive exhibition catalog: Jean-Marcel Humbert et al., eds., *Egyptomania: Egypt in Western Art, 1730–1930* (Ottawa: National Gallery of Canada, 1994); and Susan Walker and Peter Higgs, eds., *Cleopatra of Egypt: From History to Myth* (Princeton: Princeton University Press, 2001).

12 Hughes-Hallet, *Cleopatra,* 151.

13 Hamer, *Signs of Cleopatra,* 72.

14 Grewal, *Home and Harem,* 25–27.

15 Anne McClintock, *Imperial Leather: Race, Gender, and Sexuality in the Colonial Contest* (New York: Routledge, 1995), 26; Michel Foucault, *The Birth of the Clinic: An Archaeology of Medical Perception,* translated by A. M. Sheridan Smith (New York: Vintage, 1994), 107.

16 Farmer, "Cleopatra," *The Girl's Book of Famous Queens,* 94.

17 William James, *The Principles of Psychology* (New York: Holt, 1890), vol. 2, chapter 17, 1.

18 Foucault, *The Birth of the Clinic,* 135–36. On nineteenth-century American visual representations of bodily interiority, see especially Alexander Nemerov, *The Body of Raphaelle Peale: Still Life and Selfhood, 1812–1824* (Berkeley: University of California Press, 2001).

19 Schueller, *U.S. Orientalisms,* 5.

20 Joseph A. Boone, "Vacation Cruises; or, The Homoerotics of Orientalism," PMLA 110:1 (January 1995): 92.

21 "M. S.," in *The Adamic Race: Reply to "Ariel," Drs. Young and Blackie, on the Negro* (New York: Russell Bros., 1868), 30; rpt. in Smith, *Anti-Black Thought,* 5:150.

22 "C.," "Cleopatra's Complexion," *The Nation,* December 4, 1890, 441.

23 Farmer, "Cleopatra," in *The Book of Famous Queens* (New York: Thomas Y. Crowell, 1887), 11. This version of Farmer's biography of Cleopatra is not to be confused with her other "Cleopatra," which is also cited throughout this chapter. Though published in the same year by the same publisher, *The Book of Famous Queens* and *The Girl's Book of Famous Queens* are closely related but contain many significant differences at the levels of both their texts and their illustrations; this passage, for example, appears only in *The Book of Famous Queens.* For more on *The Girl's Book of Famous Queens,* see below.

24 Abbott, *The History of Cleopatra,* 13–14.

25 George Robins Gliddon, "The Monogenists and the Polygenists," in *Indigenous Races of the Earth; or, New Chapters of Ethnological Inquiry* (Philadelphia: J. B. Lippincott, 1857), 491.

26 "C.," "Cleopatra's Complexion." Those familiar with the *Black Athena* controversy of the 1990s will recognize some obvious similarities between these pas-

sages and those in chapter two of Mary Lefkowitz's *Not Out of Africa*, in which she devotes much of the chapter to addressing the question "Was Cleopatra Black?" (34 ff.).

27  Edward Everett Hale, *Ninety Days' Worth of Europe* (Boston: Walker and Wise, 1861), 145.

28  Farmer, "Cleopatra," *The Girl's Book of Famous Queens*, 12.

29  Garnet, "On the Past and Present Condition, and Destiny of the Colored Race."

30  Ibid.

31  Charlotte Forten Grimké, journal entry, Friday, July 6, 1888, in *The Journals of Charlotte Forten Grimké*, edited by Brenda Stevenson (New York: Oxford University Press, 1988), Journal Five, 534.

32  Anna Julia Cooper, *A Voice from the South* (New York: Oxford University Press, 1988), 276.

33  Robert Reid-Pharr, *Conjugal Union: The Body, the House, and the Black American* (New York: Oxford University Press, 1999), 60.

34  Hale, *Ninety Days' Worth of Europe*, 145.

35  Hawthorne, *The Marble Faun*, 126–27.

36  Henry James, *William Wetmore Story and His Friends: From Letters, Diaries, and Recollections* (London: William Blackwood and Sons, 1903), 2:75, 80. See also Lorado Taft, *The History of American Sculpture* (New York: Macmillan, 1903), 153.

37  Joy Kasson, *Marble Queens and Captives: Women in Nineteenth-Century American Sculpture* (New Haven: Yale University Press, 1990), 217.

38  See Jan M. Seidler, "A Critical Reappraisal of the Career of William Wetmore Story (1819–1895): American Sculptor and Man of Letters," ph.d. diss., Boston University, 1985.

39  Charles Swann, *Nathaniel Hawthorne: Tradition and Revolution* (Cambridge: Cambridge University Press, 1991), 186.

40  See Grewal, *Home and Harem*, esp. 24–56.

41  Nancy Bentley, "Slaves and Fauns: Hawthorne and the Uses of Primitivism," ELH 57 (1990): 910.

42  Hawthorne, *The Marble Faun*, 22–23.

43  Bentley, "Slaves and Fauns," 917.

44  Obviously my use of this phrase recalls the title of Werner Sollors's *Neither Black nor White yet Both: Thematic Explorations of Interracial Literature* (Cambridge: Harvard University Press, 1997); it is in fact Sollors who helpfully points out that such a Cleopatran intertext plays a role at the end of the century in Charles Chesnutt's 1898 short story "The Wife of His Youth." Sollors realized that, when the light-skinned main character of Chesnutt's story is confronted by the dark-skinned titular character, he is reading a book of Tennyson poems opened to a page featuring an illustration of Cleopatra, of which Tennyson himself had complained that the artist "has made a mulatto of her. . . . I know perfectly well that she was a Greek" (416 n.49). The illustration at which Sollors suggests Chesnutt's

Mr. Ryder is looking was created by pre-Raphaelite artist John Everett Millais and was included in the most popular illustrated edition of Tennyson's poems. " 'Swarthy' merely means sunburnt," Tennyson goes on to say, in reference to Millais's interpretation of the language of his poem. "I should not have spoken of her breast as 'polished silver' if I had not known her as a white woman. Read 'sunburnt' if you like it better" (416 n.49).

45  Reid-Pharr, Conjugal Union, 41–42.

46  Hawthorne, The Marble Faun, 126.

47  On race and The Marble Faun, see Blythe Ann Tellefson, " 'The Case with My Dear Native Land': Nathaniel Hawthorne's Vision of America in The Marble Faun," Nineteenth-Century Literature 54:4 (March 2000): 455–79; Anna C. Brickhouse, " 'I Do Abhor an Indian Story': Hawthorne and the Allegorization of Racial 'Commixture,' " ESQ 42:4 (1996): 233–53; Peter M. McCluskey, " 'The Recovery of the Sacred Candlestick': Jewish Imagery and the Problem of Allegory in The Marble Faun," Publications of the Arkansas Philological Association 18:2 (1992): 14–27; and T. Walter Herbert Jr., "The Erotics of Purity: The Marble Faun and the Victorian Construction of Sexuality," Representations 36 (fall 1991): 114–32. Some attention has also been paid to trying to "actually" identify the source for the character of Miriam; see, for example, Patrick Brancaccio, "Emma Abigail Solomons: Hawthorne's Miriam Identified," Nathaniel Hawthorne Journal 8 (1978): 95–103.

48  John Lord, "Cleopatra: The Woman of Paganism, 69–30 B.C.E.," in Great Women (New York: Fords, Howard, and Hulbert, 1886), 25.

49  William Wetmore Story, letter from Villa Palmeri, Leghorn, October 12, 1863, 10–11, Story Papers, Harry Ransom Humanities Research Center, University of Texas at Austin. These remarks were directed not at Lord but at the writer of a review of the second edition of his Roba di Roma, which had appeared in the London Quarterly Review; see William Wetmore Story, Roba di Roma (London: Chapman and Hall, 1863).

50  William Wetmore Story, letter from Villa Palmeri, 10–11.

51  Hale, Ninety Days' Worth of Europe, 145.

52  It is also worth noting that Story's first Cleopatra was conceived and created as half of an ideological pair of "racial" sculptures, together with his 1862 The Libyan Sibyl, which was inspired by a tale told to Story by Harriet Beecher Stowe and was meant to be a representation of Sojourner Truth. "Already his mind had begun to turn to Egypt in search of a type of art which should represent a larger and more vigorous development of nature than the cold elegance of Greek lines," wrote Stowe. "The history of Sojourner Truth worked in his mind and led him into the deeper recesses of the African nature—those unexplored depths of being and feeling, mighty and dark as the gigantic depths of tropical forests, mysterious as the hidden rivers and mines of that burning continent whose life-history is yet to be" (Harriet Beecher Stowe, "Sojourner Truth, the Libyan Sibyl," Atlantic Monthly vol. 2, no. 11 [April 1863], 473). On this, see Nell Irvin Painter, Sojourner Truth: A Life, a Symbol (New York: W. W. Norton, 1996).

53 Mary Hamer, "Black and White? Viewing Cleopatra in 1862," in *The Victorians and Race*, edited by Shearer West (Scolar Press, 1997), 61. Hamer explores her reactions to the racialized politics of the American Cleopatra at further length, and with particular attention to the *Black Athena* controversy, in "Queen of Denial: On the Uses of Cleopatra," *Transition* 6:4 (winter 1996): 80–92.

54 Reid-Pharr, *Conjugal Union*, 44.

55 Ibid.

56 Hamer, *Signs of Cleopatra*, 26.

57 Abbott, *The History of Cleopatra*, 228–29.

58 Plutarch, "Caesar," in *Fall of the Roman Republic: Six Lives by Plutarch*, translated by Rex Warner (New York: Penguin, 1972), 290. Plutarch's "Caesar" was originally presented as part of his *Parallel Lives*; in the nineteenth century, the most commonly used translation was probably that of John Dryden. For Dryden's "Caesar," see Plutarch, *Plutarch's Lives: The Dryden Translation*, edited by Arthur Hugh Clough (New York: The Modern Library, 2001), 2:199–244.

59 Plutarch, "Caesar," 49, 1. In Plutarch, *Plutarch's Lives*, ed. Bernadotte Perrin (New York: G. P. Putnam's Sons, [1919] 1927), 7:558–59. The complete phrase is Κἀκείνη παραλαβοῦσα τῶν φίλων Ἀπολλόδωρον τὸν Σικελιώτην μόνον, which translates literally (if inelegantly) as "And so taking from among her friends Apollodorus the Sicilian only" (my translation). The specificity regarding the connotation of the phrase τῶν φίλων (if indeed clarification would have been needed for such a recognizable cognate as philo-) is made all the sharper by Plutarch's use of the word οἰκέτης later in the same section (in reference to Caesar's barber), which usually translates as "house slave" (558–59).

60 Clarke, "Cleopatra," 62. North's translation was actually published in 1579, but, like Dryden's (who chooses the word "confidant"), it was widely used throughout the nineteenth century; see, for example, Walter W. Skeat, *Shakespeare's Plutarch: Being a Selection from the Lives in North's Plutarch Which Illustrate Shakespeare's Plays* (London: Macmillan, 1875).

61 Jameson, *Memoirs of Celebrated Female Sovereigns*, 1:36.

62 Abbott, *The History of Cleopatra*, 134.

63 Hale, "Cleopatra," 31.

64 Leonard Cassuto, *The Inhuman Race: The Racial Grotesque in American Literature and Culture* (New York: Columbia University Press, 1997), 6–8.

65 Abbott, *The History of Cleopatra*, 134.

66 Ibid., 135.

67 Hughes-Hallett, *Cleopatra*, 219.

68 Ibid., 210.

69 Farmer, *The Book of Famous Queens*, 11. The illustration appears in Farmer, *The Girl's Book of Famous Queens*, 34.

70 See Hamer, *Signs of Cleopatra*, chapter 2, "Cleopatra: Housewife," 24–44.

71 William Gilmore Simms, "The Death of Cleopatra," in *Poems: Descriptive, Dramatic, Legendary, and Contemplative* (Redfield, 1853), 2:332.

72 William Wetmore Story, "Cleopatra," in *Graffiti d'Italia* (London: William Blackwood and Sons, 1868). Story's verse "Cleopatra" was composed during roughly the same period in which he was revising his marble one (which process would eventually result in his second sculpted queen of 1869)—that is, circa 1864–65—but the details of its publication are convoluted and the year of its origin is often misdated; on this, see Seidler, "A Critical Reappraisal of the Career of William Wetmore Story," 496–98.

73 Story, "Cleopatra."

74 *Watson's Weekly Art Journal* 4 (February 10, 1866), 258, quoted in Seidler, "A Critical Reappraisal of the Career of William Wetmore Story," 498.

75 Story, "Cleopatra."

76 See Hughes-Hallett, *Cleopatra*, 201–24.

77 Story, "Cleopatra."

78 Boone, "Vacation Cruises," 89.

79 Edward Strahan [Earl Shinn], *Gérome: A Collection of the Works of J. L. Gérome in One Hundred Photogravures* (New York: Samuel L. Hall, 1881), vol. 6, pl. 4.

80 Ibid.

81 William L. Vance, *America's Rome* (New Haven: Yale University Press, 1989), 1:211.

82 On Powers, see Richard P. Wunder, *Hiram Powers: Vermont Sculptor, 1805–1873*, vol. 1 (Newark: University of Delaware Press, 1991); Vance, *America's Rome*; and Goddu, *Gothic America*, 97–105.

83 Mary E. Phillips, *Reminiscences of William Wetmore Story* (Chicago: Rand McNally, 1897), 229.

84 On this, see Nochlin, "The Imaginary Orient," 118–91; Lynne Thornton, *Women as Portrayed in Orientalist Painting* (Paris: ACR Édition Internationale, 1995); Lewis, *Gendering Orientalism*; and Holly Edwards, "A Million and One Nights: Orientalism in America, 1870–1930," in Edwards, *Noble Dreams, Wicked Pleasures*, 11–57.

85 Frederick Arthur Bridgman, *Winters in Algeria* (New York: Harper and Brothers, 1890), 45.

86 In Bridgman's 1880s *Afternoon, Algeria*, for example, two dark-skinned and heavily covered black women sing and play the oud for a family of four much lighter skinned girls and women, each shown in various degrees of complexion, relaxation, and undress; in his 1878 *The First Steps*, a virtually white infant is helped toward his just barely less white mother across a lavishly imagined Algerian room by a smiling and servile dark-skinned black woman—his Oriental mammy. See Frederick Arthur Bridgman, *Afternoon, Algeria*, and *The First Steps*, in Gerald Ackerman, *American Orientalists* (Paris: ACR, 1994), 29 and 34.

87 It is worth noting that, in the words of Michael Neill, "it is a telling paradox of the play's stage history that, despite Shakespeare's clearly envisaging Cleopatra as a North African Queen whose skin is either 'tawny' or 'black,' there is no history of black Cleopatras as there has been . . . a series of striking black Othellos" ("Introduction," in *Antony and Cleopatra* [London: Oxford Univer-

sity Press, 1994], 65, quoted in Francesca T. Royster, "Cleopatra as Diva: African-American Women and Shakespearean Tactics," in *Transforming Shakespeare: Contemporary Women's Re-Visions in Literature and Performance*, edited by Marianne Novy [New York: St. Martin's, 1999], 108). On the history of Shakespeare in the United States, see Lawrence Levine, *Highbrow/Lowbrow: The Emergence of Cultural Hierarchy in America* (Cambridge: Harvard University Press, 1988). On the issues of "race" as they relate to Shakespeare's Cleopatra, see Joyce Green MacDonald, "Sex, Race, and Empire in Shakespeare's *Antony and Cleopatra*," *Literature and History* 5:5 (spring 1996): 60–77; Kim F. Hall, *Things of Darkness: The Economies of Race and Gender in Early Modern England* (Ithaca: Cornell University Press, 1995); and the essays in John Drakakis, ed., *New Casebooks*: Antony and Cleopatra (New York: St. Martin's, 1994).

88  Robert Browning, "Fifine at the Fair," in *Robert Browning: The Poems*, edited by John Pettigrew (New Haven: Yale University Press, 1981), vol. 2, stanza XX, 14.

89  Mary Hamer, "The Myth of Cleopatra since the Renaissance," in Walker and Higgs, *Cleopatra of Egypt*. On the importance of the nude to nineteenth-century American sculpture, see Chloe Chard, "Nakedness and Tourism: Classical Sculpture and the Imaginative Geography of the Grand Tour," *Oxford Art Journal* 18:1 (1995): 14–28. For some contexts on the representations of breasts in art history, see Margaret R. Miles, "The Virgin's One Bare Breast: Nudity, Gender, and Religious Meaning in Tuscan Early Renaissance Culture," in *The Female Body in Western Culture: Contemporary Perspectives*, edited by Susan Suleiman (Cambridge: Harvard University Press, 1986), 193–208; and Marilyn Yalom, *A History of the Breast* (New York: Ballantine, 1997).

90  Simms, "The Death of Cleopatra," 332.

91  James, *William Wetmore Story and His Friends*, 80–82. Vance argues that James, writing a biography authorized by Story's family, was confronted with "the delicate task" of discussing what he considered Story's "fondness for the draped body and his too liberal use of drapery," seen especially in the first *Cleopatra*, and resolved it by turning his entire analysis of Story's neoclassicism into an extended discussion of the two competing traditions of nudity and drapery. See Vance, *America's Rome*, 248–51.

92  Kasson, *Marble Queens and Captives*, 243.

93  Strahan, *Gérome*, vol. 10, pl. 6.

94  Abbott, *The History of Cleopatra*, 134–37.

95  Hughes-Hallett, *Cleopatra*, 214.

96  Translated and quoted in Christiane Ziegler, "Cleopatra and Caesar," in Humbert et al., *Egyptomania*, 574.

97  Strahan, *Gérome*, vol. 10, pl. 6. Gerald Ackerman points out that the final 1866 version of *Cleopatra and Caesar* was actually predated by at least two preliminary sketches of the previous year in which the figure of Cleopatra was not shown standing, nor with her slave at her feet, but rather was shown reclining on the floor, reaching up to a standing Caesar, with her slave squatting above and be-

hind her; see Ackerman, *La vie et l'oeuvre de Jean-Léon Gérôme* (Paris, 1986), 218; and Ziegler's entry on the finished Gérôme painting in her "Cleopatra and Caesar."

98 "Cicerone" [Earl Shinn], "American Art Galleries VI: Collection of D. O. Mills, Esq.," *The Art Amateur* 3:4 (1880), 72. Gérôme's *Cleopatra and Caesar* has, in fact, an important American connection: originally painted by Gérôme on silk, "ordered and executed for one of the sumptuous modern hôtels of Paris, that of Mme. de Païva, being intended as a transparency to be lowered or raised midway of a long saloon," as Shinn explains, the painting, after being sold by de Païva, made its way to the United States, entering the collection of Darius Ogden Mills — banker, industrialist, and namesake of Millbrae, California, where the painting was long displayed — and it has remained in American collections ever since. It is by Shinn, both in his *Gérome* and in this pseudonymous article, that the painting's early history is most authoritatively documented; in Ziegler's footnotes to her 1994 essay "Cleopatra and Caesar," she establishes that it is "now in a private collection in the United States" (575 n.3).

99 Edward Strahan [Earl Shinn], *The Masterpieces of the Centennial International Exposition, Illustrated*, vol. 1: *Fine Art* (Philadelphia: Gebbie and Barrie, 1876), 144.

100 Hughes-Hallett, *Cleopatra*, 214. Gérôme in fact transformed the queen quite literally into a slave, naked before the gaze of her master. Not only is Cleopatra's pose virtually identical to that of the slave girl in Gérôme's even more famous *The Slave Market* (1867) — exposed, naked, ready for inspection before men — but the actual faces and bodies of the two figures are exactly the same as well: the model Gérôme used for the slave girl in his market was the same model he used to pose for Cleopatra. "The painter previously, in his 'Cleopatra before Caesar,' had used the same model employed for the female slave," wrote Shinn of the later painting, "and the likeness of the two faces, queen and bondwoman, is identical" (Strahan, *Gérome*, vol. 6, pl. 7).

101 King, "Cleopatra," 43.

102 "Cicerone," "American Art Galleries VI."

103 Ibid.

104 King, "Cleopatra," 42–43.

105 Hale, "Cleopatra," 32.

106 Farmer, "Cleopatra," *The Girl's Book of Famous Queens*, 92–93.

107 Ibid., 93.

108 *Cosmopolitan Art Journal* 3:1 (1858).

109 King, "Cleopatra," 42. King, writing under the matrimonial Mrs. Starr King, was née Julia Wiggin, the wife of prominent Boston Unitarian and Universalist minister Thomas Starr King; this article was written at approximately the same time she and her husband relocated to California in the late 1850s.

110 Ibid.

111 When Rembrandt Peale, visiting Rome and copying the works of the Italian masters in 1829, reworked the *Cleopatra* of Guido Reni from almost two hun-

dred years before, he prefigured the concerns of later white feminists and took great pains to cover her iconic breasts. Peale even went so far as to remove the additional icon of Reni's Cleopatra, the asp; all that one sees when looking at his American Cleopatra is a full-faced white woman gazing upward, her deep-necked wrap spilling off her left shoulder to expose as much of her chest as possible without actually revealing her nipples. "Rembrandt took some liberties," writes Lillian Miller, of Peale's copy of Reni. "He covered up Cleopatra's partial nakedness and eliminated the deadly asp that gives meaning to the story. . . . Especially since we do not see the means of her death . . . we can only understand the event through our associations with the title" (Lillian B. Miller, in Miller et al., *In Pursuit of Fame: Rembrandt Peale, 1778–1860* [Washington: National Portrait Gallery, 1992], 200). Cleopatra, as it happens, was painted several times by Reni circa 1630–40, in varying positions, and, as Miller notes, it is unclear exactly which version Peale saw (300 n.58). Yet characteristic of all Reni's Cleopatras were the traditional bared breast(s); compare, for example, the version in Hughes-Hallett (*Cleopatra*, pl. 11) with that in Miller (200, fig. 89). For more on Reni and Peale, see D. Stephen Pepper, *Guido Reni: A Complete Catalogue of His Works with an Introductory Text* (New York, 1984); Rembrandt Peale, *Notes on Italy* (Philadelphia: Carey and Lea, 1831); and Carol E. Hevner, "Rembrandt Peale's Dream and Experience of Italy," in *The Italian Presence in American Art, 1760–1860*, edited by Irma B. Jaffe (New York: Fordham University Press, 1989), 9–25.

112  Carol Farley Kessler, "Introduction," in Elizabeth Stuart Phelps, *The Story of Avis*, edited by Carol Farley Kessler (New Brunswick, N.J.: Rutgers University Press, 1985), xxiii.

113  On Vedder's 1863 *The Questioner of the Sphinx*, see Hugh Honour, *The Image of the Black in Western Art*, Vol. 4: *From the American Revolution to World War I*, part 1: *Slaves and Liberators* (Cambridge: Harvard University Press, 1989), 229–34.

114  Deborah Barker, *Aesthetics and Gender in American Literature* (Lewisburg: Bucknell University Press, 1998), chapter 3, "The Riddle of the Sphinx: Elizabeth Stuart Phelps's *The Story of Avis*," 86. On Phelps, see Lori Duin Kelly, *The Life and Works of Elizabeth Stuart Phelps, Victorian Feminist Writer* (Troy: Whitston, 1983); Carol Farley Kessler, *Elizabeth Stuart Phelps* (Boston: Twayne, 1982), as well as her introduction; and Jack H. Wilson, "Competing Narratives in Elizabeth Stuart Phelps' *The Story of Avis*," *American Literary Realism, 1870–1910* 26:1 (1993): 60–75.

115  Phelps, *The Story of Avis*, 82–83.

116  See Amy Kaplan, "Manifest Domesticity," *American Literature* 70:3 (1998): 581–606. For more on these issues, see also Louise Michele Newman, *White Women's Rights: The Racial Origins of Feminism in the United States* (New York: Oxford University Press, 1999).

117  Phelps, *The Story of Avis*, 83.

118  Abbott, *The History of Cleopatra*, 13.

119  Ibid.

120  Hamer, *Signs of Cleopatra*, 30.

121 Marylynne Diggs, "Romantic Friends or a 'Different Race of Creatures'? The Representation of Lesbian Pathology in Nineteenth-Century America," *Feminist Studies* 21:2 (summer 1995), 323.

122 Abbott, *The History of Cleopatra*, 179.

123 Ibid., 55.

124 King, "Cleopatra," 43.

125 Horatio Robinson Storer, *The Causation, Course, and Treatment of Reflex Insanity in Women* (Boston: Lee and Shepard, 1871), 86.

126 G. W. Simpson, *The Female Instructor and Guide to Health* (Baltimore, 1875), 158.

127 Ibid., 78–79.

128 Mary E. Wilkins Freeman, untitled short story ca. 1890, in Diggs, "Romantic Friends or a 'Different Race of Creatures'?" 336. Originally quoted in Edward Foster, *Mary E. Wilkins Freeman* (New York: Hendricks House, 1956), 143.

129 In addition to Diggs, on this also see Nelson, *National Manhood*, chapter 4, "Gynecological Manhood: The Worries of Whiteness and the Disorders of Women," 135–75; Deborah Kuhn McGregor, *From Midwives to Medicine: The Birth of American Gynecology* (New Brunswick, N.J.: Rutgers University Press, 1998); Terri Kapsalis, *Public Privates: Performing Gynecology at Both Ends of the Speculum* (Durham: Duke University Press, 1997); John S. Haller Jr. and Robin M. Haller, *The Physician and Sexuality in Victorian America*, new ed. (Carbondale: Southern Illinois University Press, 1995); G. J. Barker-Benfield, *The Horrors of the Half-Known Life: Male Attitudes toward Women and Sexuality in Nineteenth-Century America* (New York: Harper Colophon, 1976); and Laura Briggs, "The Race of Hysteria: 'Overcivilization' and the 'Savage' Woman in Late Nineteenth-Century Obstetrics and Gynecology," *American Quarterly* 52:2 (June 2000), 246–73.

130 Diggs, "Romantic Friends or a 'Different Race of Creatures'?" 320.

131 Lisa Duggan, "The Trials of Alice Mitchell: Sensationalism, Sexology, and the Lesbian Subject in Turn-of-the-Century America," *Signs* 18:4 (summer 1993): 795. For another overview of this, also see Patricia E. Stevens and Joanne M. Hall, "A Critical Historical Analysis of the Medical Construction of Lesbianism," *International Journal of Health Services* 21:2 (1991): 291–307.

132 Diggs, "Romantic Friends or a 'Different Race of Creatures'?"

133 Josiah Nott, Letter to Ephraim Squier, August 19, 1848, Squier Papers, Library of Congress, quoted in Nelson, *National Manhood*, 135.

134 Nelson, *National Manhood*, 136.

135 Diggs, "Romantic Friends or a 'Different Race of Creatures'?" 334.

136 On these and related clusters of issues, also see Lisa Cartwright, *Screening the Body: Tracing Medicine's Visual Culture* (Minneapolis: University of Minnesota Press, 1995); Ludmila Jordanova, *Sexual Visions: Images of Gender in Science and Medicine between the Eighteenth and Twentieth Centuries* (Ann Arbor: University of Michigan Press, 1993); Giuliana Bruno, "Spectatorial Embodiments: Anatomies of the Visible and the Female Bodyscape," *Camera Obscura* 28 (1992), 239–62; and the

essays in Mary Jacobus, Evelyn Fox Keller, and Sally Shuttleworth, eds., *Body/ Politics: Women and the Discourses of Science* (New York: Routledge, 1990), as well as those in Catherine Gallagher and Thomas Laqueur, eds., *The Making of the Modern Body: Sexuality and Society in the Nineteenth Century* (Berkeley: University of California Press, 1987).

137 Eve Kosofsky Sedgwick, *Epistemology of the Closet* (Berkeley: University of California Press, 1990), 11.

138 The most authoritative account of Lewis's biography is still found in the chapter on her in Romare Bearden and Harry Henderson, *A History of African American Artists from 1792 to the Present* (New York: Pantheon, 1993), 54–77, but important documentary evidence has also been uncovered by Kirsten Pai Buick, in her dissertation (the first full-length study ever written on Lewis), "The Sentimental Education of Mary Edmonia Lewis: Identity, Culture, and Ideal Works," Department of the History of Art, University of Michigan, 1999, as well as by Marilyn Richardson in "Edmonia Lewis's *The Death of Cleopatra*," *International Review of African American Art* 12:2 (1995): 36–52. Buick, however, has emerged as the most active scholar of Lewis; see also her "Edmonia Lewis in Art History: The Paradox of the Exotic Subject," in *Three Generations of African American Women Sculptors: A Study in Paradox*, edited by Leslie King-Hammond and Tritobia Hayes Benjamin (Philadelphia: Afro-American Historical and Cultural Museum, 1996). There is, not surprisingly, some confusion as to the exact date of Lewis's birth. Though Bearden and Henderson use the date July 14, 1845, Buick cites Lewis's passport application from 1865, which lists it as July 4, 1844 (helpfully reproduced in Rinna Evelyn Wolfe's biography of Lewis written for a young adult audience, *Edmonia Lewis: Wildfire in Marble* [Parsippany: Dillon Press, 1998], 13, and showing Lewis's occupation listed as "spinster"). To make matters more complicated, when Lewis traveled from Rome to New York in 1876 to attend the unveiling of *The Death of Cleopatra* at the Centennial Exhibition, she listed her year of birth on the passenger manifest as 1842 (microfiche in the National Archives, Washington, D.C.; cited in Buick, "Sentimental Education," 93 n.2), and even Bearden and Henderson admit that in 1895, as a visitor to the Rome Consulate, Lewis gave her birth year as 1854 (485 n.3). So, at the very least, the details regarding Lewis's early life are vague at best—a situation on which Lewis herself repeatedly relied. For more on this, see below.

139 For an account of the incident and the subsequent proceedings, see especially Bearden and Henderson, *A History of African American Artists from 1972 to the Present*; and Buick, "Sentimental Education."

140 Quoted in Henry Wreford, "A Negro Sculptress," *The Athanaeum*, March 3, 1866.

141 Ibid.

142 On Garrison and Brackett, see Bearden and Henderson, *A History of African American Artists from 1792 to the Present*; and Buick, "Sentimental Education." On Cushman and Hosmer, see below.

143 Lydia Maria Child to Annie Adams Fields, November 25, 1865. Quoted in Buick, "Sentimental Education," 63.

144 Lydia Maria Child to Harriet Winslow Sewall, July 10, 1868, in Patricia G. Holland and Milton Merzer, eds., *Collected Correspondence of Lydia Maria Child, 1817–1880* (Millwood: Kraus Microform), quoted in Dolly Sherwood, *Harriet Hosmer: American Sculptor, 1830–1908* (Columbia: University of Missouri Press, 1991), 259.

145 On Child, see Carolyn L. Karcher, *The First Woman in the Republic: A Cultural Biography of Lydia Maria Child* (Durham: Duke University Press, 1994); and Deborah Pickman Clifford, *Crusader for Freedom: A Life of Lydia Maria Child* (Boston: Beacon Press, 1992).

146 Laura Curtis Bullard, "Edmonia Lewis," *The Revolution*, April 20, 1871.

147 William Wetmore Story to James Russell Lowell, February 11, 1853. 28 Corso was the address of Harriet and her father Hiram Hosmer's first apartment in Rome, which became a gathering place for the expatriate women artists with which "Hatty" was so famously associated. The "Wood" to whom Story refers is British sculptor and writer Shakspere Wood, with whom Harriet Hosmer in particular shared a close friendship. (This letter is partially reproduced in James, *William Wetmore Story and His Friends*, 1:253–57, but James discreetly abbreviates Wood's name to W.) On Wood, and for the uncensored section of Story's letter, see Sherwood, *Harriet Hosmer*, 53 and passim.

148 Lisa Merrill, *When Romeo Was a Woman: Charlotte Cushman and Her Circle of Female Spectators* (Ann Arbor: University of Michigan Press, 1999), 171–76. This circle, in addition to Cushman, Hosmer, and Lewis, also included the sculptor couple Anne Whitney and Adeline Manning, Louise Lander, Margaret Foley, Florence Freeman, and Cushman's last longtime partner and eventual biographer Emma Stebbins. On the lives and art of this group of women, see, in addition to Merrill and James, Eric W. Baumgartner, *A Marvellous Repose: American Neoclassical Sculpture, 1825–1876* (New York: Hirschl and Adler Galleries, 1997); Dede Mousseau, "Anne Whitney: Her Life, Her Art, and Her Relationship with Adeline Manning," M.A. thesis, California State University, Fresno, 1992; Sherwood, *Harriet Hosmer*; William H. Gerdts Jr., *The White, Marmorean Flock: Nineteenth-Century American Women Neoclassical Sculptors* (Poughkeepsie: Vassar College Art Gallery, 1972); Joseph Leach, *Bright Particular Star: The Life and Times of Charlotte Cushman* (New Haven: Yale University Press, 1970); Lillian Faderman, *Surpassing the Love of Men: Romantic Friendship and Love between Women from the Renaissance to the Present* (New York: Quill, 1981); Emma Stebbins, *Charlotte Cushman: Her Letters and Memories of Her Life* (New York: Blom, [1878] 1972); Sara Foose Parrott, "Networking in Italy: Charlotte Cushman and 'The White Marmorean Flock,'" *Women's Studies* 14:4 (1988): 305–38; and the entries on the individual artists in Charlotte Streifer Rubinstein, *American Women Artists: From Early Indian Times to the Present* (Boston: G. K. Hall, 1982).

149 James, *William Wetmore Story and His Friends*, 258.

150 On Howard, see Buick, "Sentimental Education," 59–61; the reference

to Gales appears in the *Diary of Frederick Douglass, 1886–94* (Library of Congress, Manuscript Division, Frederick Douglass Papers, Microfilm Reel No. 1), and is quoted in Bearden and Henderson, *A History of African American Artists from 1792 to the Present*, 76.

151  Buick, "Sentimental Education," 214.

152  Ibid.

153  Edmonia Lewis, *The Death of Cleopatra*, Smithsonian American Art Museum, Smithsonian Institution, Washington, D.C.; gift of the Historical Society of Forest Park, Illinois. The history of Lewis's sculpture after the Centennial Exhibition is just as complicated and conflicted as its creator. After 1876, Cleopatra went on tour and was exhibited at various locations in the United States, ultimately ending up on display in Chicago in 1878. Lewis, like most artists working with large marble forms at the time, had financial problems relating to her choice of medium: she had a difficult time selling her sculpture and was unable to fund the shipment of its two tons back to Rome and so was forced to put it in storage in Chicago while she continued her travels. Cleopatra was thus effectively abandoned, and her history becomes quickly hazy for over one hundred years. In 1892, *The Death of Cleopatra* was reported as being on display in a bar near what is now Chicago's Magnificent Mile, and sometime later it was purchased by a local gangster, who placed it atop the grave of one of his racehorses, which happened to be buried in front of the grandstand of his racetrack in what is now Forest Park and which happened to be named Cleopatra. Before the gangster's death, he specified that the sculpture remain on the property in perpetuity, and so it did, for some sixty years, until the site, after various incarnations (including a golf course and a World War II torpedo factory), became home to a U.S. postal facility, at which point *The Death of Cleopatra* was removed to a contractor's storage yard in a neighboring suburb, where it was eventually noticed by a local fire inspector, who as a project had his son's Boy Scout troop clean and paint it. At this point, things moved more quickly, if no less strangely: in 1985, the sculpture was acquired by the Forest Park Historical Society and identified as the work of Lewis; shortly thereafter—and completely coincidentally—art historian Marilyn Richardson began making inquiries into the career of Lewis; a curator at the New York Metropolitan Museum of Art who had been contacted by the historical society put Richardson in touch with them; soon Richardson traveled to Forest Park, and discovered Cleopatra in a storeroom in a local shopping mall. The sculpture then made its way into the holdings of the National Museum of American Art (now the Smithsonian American Art Museum) and, under the guidance of curator George Gurney, was finally restored in 1995. The rediscovery of *The Death of Cleopatra* became, thankfully, something of a cause célèbre in some late-twentieth-century American and African American art circles and resulted in what was for a time something of a sensation. For accounts of Cleopatra's rescue and subsequent renovation—which also serve as documents of the excitement its rediscovery caused—see Stephen May, "The Object at Hand," *Smith-*

*sonian* 27 (September 1996): 16–20; Lois E. Nesbitt, "Cleopatra at the Mall," *Art-News* 87:8 (October 1988): 18–20; and Richardson, "Edmonia Lewis's *The Death of Cleopatra*." At the time of this writing, online access to images of Lewis's Cleopatra were available on the SAAM Web site "Edmonia Lewis: Lost and Found," at http://americanart.si.edu/collections/exhibits/lewis.

154 William J. Clark, *Great American Sculptures* (Philadelphia: Gebbie and Barrie, 1878), 141.

155 The nose of Lewis's Cleopatra, in particular, excites both Richardson's and Buick's interest as a sign of her ethnological accuracy, especially insofar as that nose appears on several Roman coins. On this, see Richardson, "Edmonia Lewis's *The Death of Cleopatra*"; and Buick, "Sentimental Education." These items are reprinted in Hamer, *Signs of Cleopatra*; Hughes-Hallett, *Cleopatra*; and Walker and Higgs, *Cleopatra of Egypt*. It must also be noted, however, that even at the time viewers were not entirely united over identifying the race of Lewis's Cleopatra; "the features were not even Egyptian in their outline," wrote one reviewer, "but of a decidedly Jewish cast" (J. S. Ingram, *The Centennial Exposition* [Philadelphia: Hubbard Bros., 1876], 372, quoted in Bearden and Henderson, *A History of African American Artists from 1792 to the Present*, 74).

156 Clark, *Great American Sculptures*, 141.

157 Bullard, "Edmonia Lewis."

158 Buick, "Sentimental Education," 2.

159 "Cleopatra Had a Jazz Band" (New York: Leo Feist, 1917), lyrics by James Lewellyn Morgan and Jack Coogan and music by Jack Coogan, Columbia Records A2472, recorded December 7, 1917. Special thanks to James Wolf of the Recorded Sound Division of the Library of Congress for his help in obtaining this recording, as well as for other forms of friendship too numerous to catalog.

160 Merrill, *When Romeo Was a Woman*, 199.

161 Bearden and Henderson, *A History of African American Artists from 1792 to the Present*, 65.

162 Anne Whitney, letter to Adeline Manning, August 9, 1864, Anne Whitney Papers, Wellesley College Archives, Margaret Clapp Library, quoted in Buick, "Sentimental Education," 45. To be fair, Merrill does hint at the frictions that must have existed between Lewis and the controlling and often condescending Cushman along the lines of privilege and patronage. "[A]lthough in later years Charlotte was credited with unqualified support for Lewis," Merrill writes, "to modern readers there is a decidedly patronizing tone in the famous white actress's promotion of her countrywoman" (*When Romeo Was a Woman*, 200).

163 Hosmer's *Zenobia in Chains* represents something of a high-water mark in the ongoing dialogue between the feminists associated with the women artists living in Rome and the American writers who were their contemporaries and peers; from Poe to Hawthorne to James to Margaret Fuller, the association of the Palmyran queen with the lesbians and feminists of the mid–nineteenth century was a virtual trope of American Renaissance literature; for a recent treatment of

this, see Castronovo, *Necro Citizenship*, 142–49. On Hawthorne and Fuller, see especially Thomas R. Mitchell, *Hawthorne's Fuller Mystery* (Amherst: University of Massachusetts Press, 1998). For more on Hosmer's *Zenobia in Chains*, see Sherwood, *Harriet Hosmer*; and Kasson, *Marble Queens and Captives*.

164  Michel Foucault, *The History of Sexuality, Volume I: An Introduction* (New York: Vintage, 1990), 117.

165  Sedgwick, *Epistemology of the Closet*, 45.

166  Scott Bravmann, *Queer Fictions of the Past: History, Culture, and Difference* (Cambridge: Cambridge University Press, 1997), 5.

167  Ibid.

168  Ibid.

169  See Merrill, *When Romeo Was a Woman*; Faderman, *Surpassing the Love of Men*; and Mousseau, "Anne Whitney." Merrill's book is, however, an extremely important exception to the general problematic I identify here, and Merrill herself draws attention to these same issues (*When Romeo Was a Woman*, 1–14).

170  Bravmann, *Queen Fictions of the Past*, 41.

171  Ibid., 17.

172  Karen V. Hansen, " 'No Kisses Is Like Youres': An Erotic Friendship between Two African-American Women during the Mid–Nineteenth Century," *Gender and History* 7:2 (August 1995), 159. The letters originally collected by Hansen have recently been released in their entirety in a volume edited by Farah Jasmine Griffin, though Griffin's editorial comments are more historical and biographical than theoretical; see her *Beloved Sisters and Loving Friends: Letters from Rebecca Primus of Royal Oak, Maryland, and Addie Brown of Hartford, Connecticut, 1854–1868* (New York: Ballantine, 1999).

173  The most egregious example of the closeting of Lewis is, ironically, the one that also stands as such a landmark in studies of her life. Buick's "Sentimental Education" makes virtually no mention of Lewis's romantic or sexual history and in fact seems to go to great lengths to avoid discussing these issues at all; see especially the passages on Adeline Howard. It must be said, however, that Buick is by no means unusual in this regard; while she has slowly been given a more visible role in accounts of nineteenth-century African American (and) women artists, virtually no studies of Lewis attempt to understand her as an important figure in lesbian history or queer art history; see, for example, Bearden and Henderson, *A History of African American Artists from 1792 to the Present*; and Richardson, "Edmonia Lewis's *The Death of Cleopatra*."

174  Duggan, "The Trials of Alice Mitchell," 794.

175  Ibid. Especially helpful in this context is another piece by Marylynne Diggs; see her "Surveying the Intersection: Pathology, Secrecy, and the Discourses of Racial and Sexual Identity," in *Critical Essays: Gay and Lesbian Writers of Color*, edited by Emmanuel S. Nelson (New York: Haworth, 1993).

176  Bravmann, *Queer Fictions of the Past*, 49.

177  For more on the issue of race, Hellenophilia, and queer sexuality, also

see Alex Potts, *Flesh and the Ideal: Winckelmann and the Origins of Art History* (New Haven: Yale University Press, 1996); and Mandy Merck's chapter, "The Amazons of Ancient Athens," in *Perversions: Deviant Readings* (New York: Routledge, 1993), 121–61.

## Chapter 5: Egypt Land

1 "Mutability of Human Affairs," *Freedom's Journal*, April 6, 1827. This article was published in three parts, on April 6, 13, and 20, 1827, under the same title each week. Portions of it appear in Wilson Jeremiah Moses, ed., *Classical Black Nationalism: From the American Revolution to Marcus Garvey* (New York: New York University Press, 1996), though this edition is incomplete; Moses's reprint includes only two of the three parts, the first and the third, and omits the middle section of April 13. Accordingly, my quotations are taken from the original versions in *Freedom's Journal*.

2 Ibid.

3 Ibid.

4 Ibid.

5 Ibid. The mummy was that of Padihershef, the famous traveling artifact otherwise known as "the Ether Dome mummy," which was eventually housed in the Massachusetts General Hospital (in the Ether Dome, or operating theater), and was exclusively displayed in Baltimore by Peale from June 14 to July 24, 1824. On this, see my discussion of Padihershef and the trope of the mummy in chapter three, as well as Alderson, *Mermaids, Mummies, and Mastodons*. For studies of Peale, his family, and their museums, see Edgar P. Richardson et al., eds., *Charles Willson Peale and His World* (New York: Harry N. Abrams, 1982); Lillian B. Miller and David C. Ward, eds., *New Perspectives on Charles Willson Peale: A 250th Anniversary Celebration* (Pittsburgh: University of Pittsburgh Press, 1991); and Lillian B. Miller, ed., *The Peale Family: Creation of a Legacy, 1770–1790* (Washington, D.C.: National Portrait Gallery, 1996).

6 "Mutability of Human Affairs," April 13, 1827.

7 This pattern of racialized Egyptological dialogics would be repeated years later during what is arguably the most famous mummy exhibit in American history, that of "The Treasures of Tutankhamun" of the late 1970s. On this, see Melani McAlister, " 'The Common Heritage of Mankind': Race, Nation, and Masculinity in the King Tut Exhibit," *Representations* 54 (1996): 80–103. For more on the Ham/Canaan/Cush/Curse quadrangle, see chapter one.

8 Phillis Wheatley, "To the University of Cambridge, in New-England," in *Poems on Various Subjects, Religious and Moral* (London: Bell, 1773); rpt. in *The Collected Works of Phillis Wheatley*, edited by John Shields (New York: Oxford University Press, 1988), 15; Langston Hughes, "The Negro Speaks of Rivers," in *The New Negro*, edited by Alain Locke (New York: Albert and Charles Boni, 1925), 141.

9 Moses, *Afrotopia*, 24. This tradition of systematization I refer to here does of

course emerge from the disciplines within which its most influential proponents were trained; also see Drake, *Black Folk Here and There.*

10 Raboteau, "The Black Experience in American Evangelicism," 101. The scholarship on the Exodus figure in African American religious and cultural history is of course incredibly expansive; on the period under discussion here, see especially Eddie S. Glaude Jr., *Exodus!*; Smith, *Conjuring Culture*; Wilson Jeremiah Moses, "The Poetics of Ethiopianism: W. E. B. Du Bois and Literary Black Nationalism," *American Literature* 47:3 (November 1975), 411–26; George Fredrickson, *Black Liberation: A Comparative History of Black Ideologies in the United States and South Africa* (New York: Oxford University Press, 1995); Wilmore, *Black Religion and Black Radicalism*; and Cornel West, *Prophesy Deliverance! An Afro-American Revolutionary Christianity* (Philadelphia: Westminster, 1982).

11 On Walker, see Peter Hinks's edition of David Walker, *Appeal to the Coloured Citizens of the World* (University Park: Pennsylvania State University Press, 2000); as well as his *To Awaken My Afflicted Brethren: David Walker and the Problem of Antebellum Slave Resistance* (University Park: Pennsylvania State University Press, 1997); Sterling Stuckey, *Slave Culture: Nationalist Theory and the Foundations of Black America* (New York: Oxford University Press, 1987); Ian Finseth, "David Walker, Nature's Nation, and Early African-American Separatism," *Mississippi Quarterly* 54:3 (summer 2001): 337–62; Dolan Hubbard, "David Walker's *Appeal* and the American Puritan Jeremiadic Tradition," *Centennial Review* 30:3 (summer 1986): 331–46; and Sean Wilentz, "The Mysteries of David Walker," which appears as the introduction to his edition of Walker's *Appeal to the Coloured Citizens of the World* (New York: Hill and Wang, 1995), vii–xxiii.

12 David Walker, *David Walker's Appeal, in Four Articles; Together with a Preamble, to the Coloured Citizens of the World, but in Particular, and Very Expressly, to Those of the United States of America*, edited by Sean Wilentz (New York: Hill and Wang, 1995), 1.

13 Ibid., 3–4.

14 Ibid., 9.

15 Ibid., 8.

16 Ibid., 21.

17 See for example Raboteau, *A Fire in the Bones*; Wilson Jeremiah Moses, *Black Messiahs and Uncle Toms: Social and Literary Manipulations of a Religious Myth*, rev. ed. (University Park: Pennsylvania State University Press, 1993); and Wilmore, *Black Religion and Black Radicalism*. Likewise, although his study is considerably more nuanced than most, Eddie Glaude partakes in large part of this general tendency toward periodization; see *Exodus!*, 3–104, and, for his disagreements with Moses, 12–15 ff.

18 Walker, *David Walker's Appeal*, 5, 44.

19 On Garnet, see Joel Schor, *Henry Highland Garnet: A Voice of Black Radicalism in the Nineteenth Century* (Westport: Greenwood Press, 1977); Glaude, *Exodus!*; and Stuckey, *Slave Culture.*

20 Henry Highland Garnet, "An Address to the Slaves of the United States

of America," in *The Norton Anthology of African American Literature*, edited by Henry Louis Gates Jr. and Nellie Y. McKay (New York: W. W. Norton, 1997), 280.

21 Ibid., 281.

22 Ibid., 284–85.

23 Ibid., 280.

24 Ibid., 281.

25 Ibid., 285.

26 Ibid., 283.

27 Ibid.

28 Ibid.

29 Ibid.

30 Ibid.

31 Garnet, "On the Past and Present Condition, and Destiny of the Colored Race."

32 Ibid.

33 Ibid.

34 Ibid.

35 Ibid.

36 Ibid.

37 In addition to Stuckey and Smith, see Samuel A. Floyd Jr., *The Power of Black Music: Interpreting Its History from Africa to the United States* (New York: Oxford University Press, 1995); Paul F. Berliner, *Thinking in Jazz: The Infinite Art of Improvisation* (Chicago: University of Chicago Press, 1994); Jon Michael Spencer, *Protest and Praise: Sacred Music of Black Religion* (Minneapolis: Fortress Press, 1990); William C. Turner Jr., "The Musicality of Black Preaching: A Phenomenology," *Journal of Black Sacred Music* 2:1 (spring 1988): 21–33; and Southern, *The Music of Black Americans*.

38 Pauline Elizabeth Hopkins, *Of One Blood; or, The Hidden Self*, in *Colored American Magazine* 6:1–11 (November 1902–November 1903); rpt. *The Magazine Novels of Pauline Hopkins*, edited by Hazel B. Carby (New York: Oxford University Press, 1988), 502.

39 Ibid.

40 The term *Afrocentricity* has a close and at times complicated relationship with another term often named in studies of *Of One Blood* and its cultural traditions, *Pan-Africanism* — the term that was actually in use in 1903. Both are usually used to signal moments in the history of another closely related set of discourses, *black nationalism*. These terms are sometimes used interchangeably and sometimes to mark professional, political, philosophical, or idiomatic differences, but taken as a group they are highly intertextual and their connotations densely interlaced. With this in mind, the central texts for their study span several fields. The self-identified figurehead of contemporary American Afrocentricity is of course Molefi Kete Asante, and his 1980 *Afrocentricity* has since gone through several revised and expanded editions; the most recent is the third (Trenton: Africa World Press, 1988); also see his *The Afrocentric Idea* (Philadelphia: Temple University Press, 1987).

As is well known, however, Asante's cultural legacy involves several other key figures, among them George G. M. James and his 1954 *Stolen Legacy: Greek Philosophy Is Stolen Egyptian Philosophy* (Trenton: Africa World Press, 1992); Chiekh Anta Diop and his large body of work, including the 1955 *The African Origin of Civilization* (New York: Lawrence Hill, [1955] 1974); and Yosef A. A. ben-Jochannan, whose 1970 *Black Man of the Nile and His Family* (rpt. Baltimore: Black Classics Press, [1970] 1989) remains his most widely read. As with most of the issues under discussion in this book, however, Afrocentrism, Pan-Africanism, and black nationalism have popular and scholarly histories that extend far beyond the scope of the nineteenth century; accordingly, I have attempted to keep my citations in this chapter limited to sources that treat this historical period in some detail. See Stephen Howe, *Afrocentrism: Mythical Pasts and Imagined Homes* (London: Verso, 1998); Wilson Jeremiah Moses, *The Golden Age of Black Nationalism, 1850–1925* (New York: Oxford University Press, 1978); P. Olisanwuche Esedebe, *Pan-Africanism: The Idea and Movement, 1776–1963* (Washington, D.C.: Howard University Press, 1982); and Eric J. Sundquist, *To Wake the Nations: Race in the Making of American Literature* (Cambridge, Mass.: Belknap, 1993). Regarding the distinctions between Afrocentricity and Pan-Africanism in the case of *Of One Blood*, the historiographically accurate rubric of Pan-Africanism notwithstanding, it is entirely unclear where to locate the *Pan-* in Hopkins's *Africanism*, and it is the particularly spiritualized figure of her Africa with which I am concerned here. This spiritualism, I would argue, is a critical distinction between the histories of Pan-Africanism and Afrocentricity, and, given the ways the cultural politics of these terms played out in the last half of the twentieth century, it is under the heading of the latter that I place my reading of *Of One Blood*.

41  Hopkins, *Of One Blood*, 520.

42  Ibid., 521.

43  Ibid., 532.

44  W. E. B. Du Bois, *The Souls of Black Folk: Essays and Sketches* (New York: Library of America, 1990), 8–9.

45  W. E. B. Du Bois, "Strivings of the Negro People," *Atlantic Monthly* 80 (August 1897): 194–98. The quoted passage appears on page 194. For more on the figure of the double, see especially Nahum Dimitri Chandler, *The Economy of Desedimentation: W. E. B. Du Bois and the Discourses of the Negro* (Stanford: Stanford University Press, forthcoming).

46  Hopkins, *Of One Blood*, 447.

47  See Cynthia D. Schrager, "Pauline Hopkins and William James: The New Psychology and the Politics of Race," in *The Unruly Voice: Rediscovering Pauline Elizabeth Hopkins*, edited by John Cullen Gruesser (Urbana: University of Illinois Press, 1996), 182–209; Sundquist, *To Wake the Nations*; Thomas J. Otten, "Pauline Hopkins and the Hidden Self of Race," ELH 59 (1992): 227–56; and Claudia Tate, *Domestic Allegories of Political Desire: The Black Heroine's Text at the Turn of the Century* (New York: Oxford University Press, 1992). As these studies note, Hopkins took the subtitle

of *Of One Blood* from the essay of James that opens the novel *The Hidden Self*, which first appeared in *Scribner's* in 1890 and is collected in *The Works of William James: Essays in Psychology*, edited by Frederick H. Burkhardt et al. (Cambridge: Harvard University Press, 1983), 247–68.

48 An exception to the tendencies of the studies mentioned above is an article by Susan Gillman, which both engages the psychologism of *Of One Blood* and attempts to think the text along these lines without reducing it to a fictionalized version of a lecture by William James; see "Pauline Hopkins and the Occult."

49 Du Bois, *The Souls of Black Folk*, 3. The work on Du Bois and double consciousness is enormous, but most salient in this context are Arnold Rampersad, *The Art and Imagination of W. E. B. Du Bois* (New York: Schocken, 1990); Tom Lutz, *American Nervousness, 1903: An Anecdotal History* (Ithaca: Cornell University Press, 1991); and Dickson D. Bruce Jr., "W. E. B. Du Bois and the Idea of Double Consciousness," *American Literature* 64:2 (June 1992): 299–309. Indispensable, however, is an earlier piece by Nahum Chandler, which appears in revised form in a forthcoming book of this same name but is significant in its own right: "The Economy of Desedimentation: W. E. B. Du Bois and the Discourses of the Negro," *Callaloo* 19:1 (winter 1996): 78–93.

50 Hopkins, *Of One Blood*, 471. It was Binet who in 1889 published *On Double Consciousness: Experimental Psychological Studies* (Chicago: Open Court, 1896). This connection is also noted by Otten, "Pauline Hopkins and the Hidden Self of Race," 254; Sundquist, *To Wake the Nations*, 570–71; and Gillman, "Pauline Hopkins and the Occult," 71.

51 In her discussion of the new psychology, Gillman points out that the relationship between James and Binet was not sympathetic but antagonistic and that the space of contention was located around the question of repression. James understood subconscious states to be " 'immensely complex and fluctuating' " and potentially if not generally positive and therapeutic. He "thus opposed . . . Binet . . . for whom the phenomena of the unconscious . . . were . . . rare and pathological, an essentially 'degenerative' part of the human personality" ("Pauline Hopkins and the Occult," 73). As Gillman recognizes, *Of One Blood* is most closely related to James, but Hopkins's own understanding of the politics of repression seems to be at least as complicated as the feud between the Anglo-Americans and the French; it is in fact with the politics of the *construction* of the repressed, racialized, subject — not only its post facto existence and treatment — that the novel is most concerned. For more on the question of psychology and racialized science, see 74–75.

52 Hopkins, *Of One Blood*, 486–87. Cynthia Schrager notes that Hopkins took this example of polar opposite dual personality from a case study of Pierre Janet's, a discussion of which figures prominently in James's "The Hidden Self"; see her "Pauline Hopkins and William James," 205 n.18. Needless to say, however, the political context of both Mira's prophetic ability and its specificity are of Hopkins's own invention.

53 Schrager, "Pauline Hopkins and William James," 188.

54 Hopkins, *Of One Blood*, 469.

55 Ibid., 501.

56 Ibid., 501–2.

57 Ibid., 503.

58 Ibid., 502.

59 Ibid., 520–21.

60 Ibid., 532–53.

61 Ibid., 532.

62 Ibid., 533–34.

63 Ibid., 533.

64 Ibid., 531.

65 Ibid., 532.

66 The passage recounting the construction and abandonment of the Tower of Babel occurs in Gen. 11:1–9 (King James Version):

> And the whole earth was of one language, and of one speech. . . . And they said, Go to, let us build us a city, and a tower, whose top may reach unto heaven; and let us make us a name, lest we be scattered abroad upon the face of the whole earth. And the Lord came down to see the city and the tower, which the children of men builded. And the Lord said, Behold, the people is one, and they have all one language; and this they begin to do: and now nothing will be restrained from them, which they have imagined to do. Go to, let us go down, and there confound their language, that they may not understand one another's speech. So the Lord scattered them abroad from thence upon the face of all the earth: and they left off to build the city. Therefore is the name of it called Babel; because the Lord did there confound the language of all the earth: and from thence did the Lord scatter them abroad upon the face of all the earth.

67 Delany, *Principia of Ethnology*. For more on this, see the discussion of Delany and his book in chapter one.

68 See, for example, Otten, "Pauline Hopkins and the Hidden Self of Race," 240–41; and Sundquist, *To Wake the Nations*, 569.

69 Hopkins, *Of One Blood*, 526.

70 Ibid., 598. The passage is from Luke 12:2.

71 Ibid., 449.

72 Ibid., 542.

73 Ibid.

74 Ibid., 543.

75 Ibid., 544.

76 Ibid.

77 Ibid., 545.

78 Ibid., 546–47.

79  Ibid., 548.

80  Ibid., 546.

81  Ibid., 547–48.

82  Psalms 68:31, King James Version. The literature on Ethiopianism is widespread, but any survey of it should begin with the work of Raboteau, including *Slave Religion: The "Invisible Institution" in the Antebellum South* (New York: Oxford University Press, 1978); and *A Fire in the Bones*. This latter volume includes " 'Ethiopia Shall Soon Stretch Forth Her Hands': Black Destiny in Nineteenth-Century America" (37–56), from which my quotation is taken (42).

83  Hopkins, *Of One Blood*, 547.

84  Smith, *Conjuring Culture*, 63–70.

85  See Sollors, *Beyond Ethnicity*.

86  Smith, *Conjuring Culture*, 65–66.

87  On Smith's definition of "repertory," see ibid., 66–67.

88  Ibid., 70.

89  Ibid., 65.

90  Ibid., 69.

91  Ibid., 67.

92  On African American emigration and colonization movements, see Wilmore, *Black Religion and Black Radicalism*; and Moses, *The Golden Age of Black Nationalism*.

93  Hopkins, *Of One Blood*, 621.

# Works Cited

Abbott, Jacob. *The History of Cleopatra, Queen of Egypt*. New York: Harper and Brothers, 1851.

Ackerman, Gerald. *American Orientalists*. Paris: ACR, 1994.

———. *La Vie et l'oeuvre de Jean-Léon Gérôme*. Paris: ACR, 1986.

Adams, Kimberly Vanesveld. *Our Lady of Victorian Feminism: The Madonna in the Work of Anna Jameson, Margaret Fuller, and George Eliot*. Athens: Ohio University Press, 1978.

Addy, E. S. "National Sin." *The Colored American*, April 19, 1838.

Alcott, Louisa May. "Lost in a Pyramid, or The Mummy's Curse." *The New World* 1:1 (January 16, 1869). Rpt. in *Into the Mummy's Tomb*, edited by John Richard Stephens. New York: Berkley Books, 2001.

Alderson, William T., ed. *Mermaids, Mummies, and Mastodons: The Emergence of the American Museum*. Washington, D.C.: American Association of Museums, 1992.

Alkon, Paul K. *Origins of Futuristic Fiction*. Athens: University of Georgia Press, 1987.

———. *Science Fiction before 1900: Imagination Discovers Technology*. New York: Twayne, 1994.

Almy, Robert F. "J. N. Reynolds: A Brief Biography with Particular Reference to Poe and Symmes." *The Colophone*, new series, 2 (1937): 227–45.

Amico, Leonard. *The Mural Decorations of Edwin Howland Blashfield (1848–1936)*. Williamstown: Sterling and Francis Clark Art Institute, 1978.

Anbinder, Tyler. *Nativism and Slavery: The Northern Know Nothings and the Politics of the 1850s*. New York: Oxford University Press, 1992.

Anonymous [Carlyle McKinley]. *An Appeal to Pharaoh: The Negro Problem, and Its Radi-*

cal Solution. New York: Fords, Howard, and Hulbert, 1889. Rpt. in Smith, Anti-Black Thought, Vol. 11.

Ariel [Buckner H. Payne]. *The Negro: What Is His Ethnological Status? Is He the Progeny of Ham? Is He a Descendant of Adam and Eve? Has He a Soul? Or Is He a Beast in God's Nomenclature? What Is His Status as Fixed by God in Creation? What Is His Relation to the White Race?* Cincinnati, 1867. Rpt. in Smith, *Anti-Black Thought*, vol. 5.

Armistead, Wilson. *A Tribute for the Negro: Being a Vindication of the Moral, Intellectual, and Religious Capabilities of the Colored Portion of Mankind; with Particular Reference to the African Race.* Manchester: William Irwin, 1848.

Asante, Molefi Kete. *Afrocentricity.* 3d ed. Trenton: Africa World Press, 1988.

———. *The Afrocentric Idea.* Philadelphia: Temple University Press, 1988.

Ashmore, Malcolm. *The Reflexive Thesis: Wrighting Sociology of Scientific Knowledge.* Chicago: University of Chicago Press, 1989.

Assmann, Jan. *Moses the Egyptian: The Memory of Egypt in Western Monotheism.* Cambridge: Harvard University Press, 1997.

Austin, Allan D., ed. *African Muslims in Antebellum America: Transatlantic Stories and Spiritual Struggles.* New York: Routledge, 1997.

Bailey, J. O. "An Early American Utopian Fiction." *American Literature* 14 (1942): 285–93.

———. "Introduction." In John Cleves Symmes, *Symzonia: A Voyage of Discovery.* Gainesville: Scholars' Facsimiles and Reprints, 1965.

———. *Pilgrims through Space and Time: Trends and Patterns in Scientific and Utopian Fiction.* New York: Argus Books, 1947.

Barker, Deborah. *Aesthetics and Gender in American Literature.* Lewisburg: Bucknell University Press, 1998.

Barker-Benfield, G. J. *The Horrors of the Half-Known Life: Male Attitudes toward Women and Sexuality in Nineteenth-Century America.* New York: HarperColophon, 1976.

Barrett, Lindon. "Presence of Mind: Detection and Racialization in 'The Murders in the Rue Morgue.' " In Kennedy and Weissberg, *Romancing the Shadow,* 157–76.

Baumgartner, Eric W. *A Marvellous Repose: American Neo-Classical Sculpture, 1825–1876.* New York: Hirschl and Adler Galleries, 1997.

Bean, Annemarie, et al., eds. *Inside the Minstrel Mask: Readings in Nineteenth-Century Blackface Minstrelsy.* Hanover, N.H.: Wesleyan University Press, 1996.

Bearden, Romare, and Harry Henderson. *A History of African American Artists from 1792 to the Present.* New York: Pantheon, 1993.

Beaver, Harold. "Introduction." In Edgar Allan Poe, *The Narrative of Arthur Gordon Pym of Nantucket.* Baltimore: Penguin Books, 1975.

Becker, Allienne R. *The Lost Worlds Romance: From Dawn to Dusk.* Westport: Greenwood Press, 1992.

Belzoni, Giovanni. *Narrative of the Operations and Recent Discoveries within the Pyramids, Temples, Tombs and Excavations in Egypt and Nubia.* London: John Murray, 1820.

ben-Jochannan, Josef A. A. *Black Man of the Nile and His Family.* Baltimore: Black Classics Press, [1970] 1989.

Bentley, Nancy. "Slaves and Fauns: Hawthorne and the Uses of Primitivism." ELH 57 (1990): 901–37.

Bequette, M. K. "Shelley and Smith: Two Sonnets on Oxymandias." *Keats-Shelley Journal* 26 (1977): 29–31.

Berkovitch, Sacvan. *The American Jeremiad.* Madison: University of Wisconsin Press, 1978.

Berliner, Paul F. *Thinking in Jazz: The Infinite Art of Improvisation.* Chicago: University of Chicago Press, 1994.

Bernal, Martin. *Black Athena: The Afroasiatic Roots of Classical Civilization,* Vol. 1: *The Fabrication of Ancient Greece, 1785–1985.* New Brunswick, N.J.: Rutgers University Press, 1987.

Bernal, Martin, and David Chioni Moore, eds. *Black Athena Writes Back.* Durham: Duke University Press, 2001.

Binet, Alfred. *On Double Consciousness: Experimental Psychological Studies.* Chicago: Open Court, 1896.

Blavatsky, H. P. *Isis Unveiled: A Master-Key to the Mysteries of Ancient and Modern Science and Theology.* 2 vols. Pasadena: Theosophical University Press, 1972.

Blyden, Edward Wilmot. *Black Spokesman: Selected Published Writings of Edward Wilmot Blyden.* Edited by Hollis R. Lynch. New York: Humanities Press, 1971.

———. *Christianity, Islam, and the Negro Race.* Baltimore: Black Classic Press, [1888] 1994.

———. *From West Africa to Palestine.* Rpt. in Blyden, *Black Spokesman.*

———. *Philip and the Eunuch.* In *Christianity, Islam, and the Negro Race.* Baltimore: Black Classic Press, 1994.

Boone, Joseph A. "Vacation Cruises; or, The Homoerotics of Orientalism." PMLA 110:1 (January 1995): 89–107.

Bordman, Gerald. *American Musical Theatre: A Chronicle.* 3d ed. New York: Oxford University Press, 2001.

Boyd, Julian P., et al., eds. *The Papers of Thomas Jefferson.* Princeton: Princeton University Press, 1988.

Bradnum, Frederick. *The Long Walks: Journeys to the Sources of the White Nile.* London: Victor Gollancz, 1969.

Brancaccio, Patrick. "Emma Abigail Solomons: Hawthorne's Miriam Identified." *Nathaniel Hawthorne Journal* 8 (1978): 95–103.

Bravmann, Scott. *Queer Fictions of the Past: History, Culture, and Difference.* Cambridge: Cambridge University Press, 1997.

Brickhouse, Anna C. " 'I Do Abhor an Indian Story': Hawthorne and the Allegorization of Racial 'Commixture.' " ESQ 42:4 (1996): 233–53.

Bridgman, Frederick Arthur. *Winters in Algeria.* New York: Harper and Brothers, 1890.

Brier, Bob. *Egyptian Mummies: Unwrapping the Secrets of an Ancient Art.* New York: Quill, 1994.

———. *The Encyclopedia of Mummies.* New York: Checkmark Books, 1998.

Briggs, Laura. "The Race of Hysteria: 'Overcivilization' and the 'Savage' Woman in Late Nineteenth-Century Obstretrics and Gynecology." *American Quarterly* 52:2 (June 2000): 246–73.

Brody, Jennifer. "The Returns of Cleopatra Jones." *Signs* 25:1 (1999): 91–121.

Brooks, Joanna. "Colonization, Black Freemasonry, and the Rehabilitation of Africa." In *Messy Beginnings: Postcolonialism and Early American Studies*, edited by Malini Johar Schueller and Edward Watts. New Brunswick, N.J.: Rutgers University Press, 2003.

———. "Prince Hall, Freemasonry, and Genealogy." *African American Review* 34:2 (summer 2000): 197–216.

Brown, William Wells. *The Black Man, His Antecedents, His Genius, and His Achievements.* New York: Thomas Hamilton, 1863.

———. *The Negro in the American Rebellion.* Boston: A. G. Brown, 1880.

Browning, Robert. "Fifine at the Fair." In *Robert Browning: The Poems.* Vol. 2. Edited by John Pettigrew. 2 vols. New Haven: Yale University Press, 1981.

Bruce, Dickson D., Jr. "W. E. B. Du Bois and the Idea of Double Consciousness." *American Literature* 64:2 (June 1992): 299–309.

Bruno, Giuliana. "Spectatorial Embodiments: Anatomies of the Visible and the Female Bodyscape." *Camera Obscura* 28 (1992): 239–62.

Bryan, John M., ed. *Robert Mills, Architect.* Washington, D.C.: American Institute of Architects Press, 1989.

Buick, Kirsten Pai. "Edmonia Lewis in Art History: The Paradox of the Exotic Subject." In *Three Generations of African American Women Sculptors: A Study in Paradox*, edited by Leslie King-Hammond and Tritobia Hayes Benjamin. Philadelphia: Afro-American Historical and Cultural Museum, 1996.

———. "The Sentimental Education of Mary Edmonia Lewis: Identity, Culture, and Ideal Works." ph.d. diss., Department of the History of Art, University of Michigan, 1999.

Bullard, Laura Curtis. "Edmonia Lewis." *The Revolution,* April 20, 1871.

"C." "Cleopatra's Complexion." *The Nation,* December 4, 1890.

Campbell, William H. *Anthropology for the People: A Refutation of the Theory of the Adamic Origin of All Races.* Richmond: Everett Waddey, 1891.

Carnes, Mark. *Secret Ritual and Manhood in Victorian America.* New Haven: Yale University Press, 1989.

Carrott, Richard G. *The Egyptian Revival: Its Sources, Monuments, and Meaning, 1808–1858.* Berkeley: University of California Press, 1978.

Carter, Howard, and A. C. Mace. *The Tomb of Tut.ankh.Amen, Discovered by the Late Earl of Carnarvon and Howard Carter.* London: Cassell, 1923.

Cartwright, Lisa. *Screening the Body: Tracing Medicine's Visual Culture.* Minneapolis: University of Minnesota Press, 1995.

Cassuto, Leonard. *The Inhuman Race: The Racial Grotesque in American Literature and Culture.* New York: Columbia University Press, 1997.

Castronovo, Russ. *Necro Citizenship: Death, Eroticism, and the Public Sphere in the Nineteenth-Century United States*. Durham: Duke University Press, 2001.

de Certeau, Michel. *The Writing of History*. Translated by Tom Conley. New York: Columbia University Press, 1988.

Chandler, Nahum Dimitri. *The Economy of Desedimentation: W. E. B. Du Bois and the Discourses of the Negro*. Stanford: Stanford University Press, forthcoming.

————. "The Economy of Desedimentation: W. E. B. Du Bois and the Discourses of the Negro." *Callaloo* 19:1 (winter 1996): 78–93.

Chaney, Michael A. "Picturing the Mother, Claiming Egypt: *My Bondage and My Freedom* as Auto(bio)ethnography." *African American Review* 35:3 (fall 2001): 391–408.

Chard, Chloe. "Nakedness and Tourism: Classical Sculpture and the Imaginative Geography of the Grand Tour." *Oxford Art Journal* 18:1 (1995): 14–28.

Chipman, Norton P. "Speech of Hon. Norton P. Chipman." In *Washington National Monument: Shall the Unfinished Obelisk Stand a Monument of National Disgrace and National Dishonor?* Washington, D.C.: Government Printing Office, 1874.

"Cicerone" [Earl Shinn]. "American Art Galleries VI: Collection of D. O. Mills, Esq." *The Art Amateur* 3:4 (1880): 72–73.

Clark, William J. *Great American Sculptures*. Philadelphia: Gebbie and Barrie, 1878.

Clarke, Mary Cowden. "Cleopatra." In *World-Noted Women; or, Types of Womanly Attributes of All Lands and Ages*. New York: Appleton, 1857.

Cleveland, Nehemiah. *Green-Wood*. New York, 1847.

Clifford, Deborah Pickman. *Crusader for Freedom: A Life of Lydia Maria Child*. Boston: Beacon Press, 1992.

Colatrella, Carol. *Literature and Moral Reform: Melville and the Discipline of Reading*. Gainesville: University Press of Florida, 2002.

Colwin, Mark. *Penitentiaries, Reformatories, and Chain Gangs: Social Theory and the History of Punishment in Nineteenth-Century America*. New York: St. Martin's, 1997.

Connor, Patrick. *Oriental Architecture in the West*. London: Thames and Hudson, 1979.

Cooper, Anna Julia. *A Voice from the South*. New York: Oxford University Press, 1988.

Copher, Charles B. "Three Thousand Years of Biblical Interpretation with Reference to Black Peoples." In *African American Religious Studies: An Interdisciplinary Anthology*, edited by Gayraud Wilmore. Durham: Duke University Press, 1989.

Cowan, Frank. *Revi-Lona: A Romance of Love in a Marvelous Land*. Pittsburgh: privately printed, ca. 1880.

Crawford, George W. *Prince Hall and His Followers: Being a Monograph on the Legitimacy of Negro Masonry*. New York: Crisis, 1914.

Curl, James Stevens. *Egyptomania: The Egyptian Revival, a Recurring Theme in the History of Taste*. Manchester: Manchester University Press, 1994.

Davis, John. *The Landscape of Belief: Encountering the Holy Land in Nineteenth-Century American Art and Culture*. Princeton: Princeton University Press, 1996.

Dayan, Joan. "Amorous Bondage: Poe, Ladies, and Slaves." *American Literature* 66 (June 1994): 239–73.

Delany, Martin Robison. *The Origin and Objects of Ancient Freemasonry; Its Introduction into the United States, and Legitimacy among Colored Men.* Pittsburgh: W. S. Haven, 1853. Rpt. Xenia, Ohio: A. D. Delany, 1904.

———. *Principia of Ethnology: The Origin of Races and Color, with an Archaeological Compendium of Ethiopian and Egyptian Civilization, from Years of Careful Examination and Inquiry.* Philadelphia: Harper and Brothers, 1879.

DeMorgan, John. *Bess: A Companion to Jess.* New York: Munro, 1887.

Dermott, Bobby J. *Freemasonry in American Culture and Society.* Lanham, Md.: University Press of America, 1986.

Deveney, John Patrick. *Paschal Beverly Randolph: A Nineteenth-Century Black American Spiritualist, Rosicrucian, and Sex Magician.* Albany: State University of New York Press, 1997.

Diggs, Marylynne. "Romantic Friends or a 'Different Race of Creatures'? The Representation of Lesbian Pathology in Nineteenth-Century America." *Feminist Studies* 21:2 (summer 1995): 317–40.

———. "Surveying the Intersection: Pathology, Secrecy, and the Discourses of Racial and Sexual Identity." In *Critical Essays: Gay and Lesbian Writers of Color,* edited by Emmanuel S. Nelson. New York: Haworth, 1993.

Diop, Chiekh Anta. *The African Origin of Civilization.* New York: Lawrence Hill, [1955] 1974.

Diouf, Sylviane A. *Servants of Allah: African Muslims Enslaved in the Americas.* New York: New York University Press, 1998.

"Discoveries of Mummies at Durango, Mexico." *The Colored American,* January 19, 1839.

Donnelly, Ignatius. *Atlantis: The Antediluvian World.* New York: Harper and Brothers, 1882. Rpt. New York: Gramercy, 1949.

Dorr, David. *A Colored Man Round the World.* Ed. Malini Johar Schueller. Ann Arbor: University of Michigan Press, [1858] 1999.

Dorson, Richard M. *Buying the Wind: Regional Folklore in the United States.* Chicago: University of Chicago Press, 1964.

Dougherty, Stephen. "Prophecy, Racial Paranoia, and the Figure of Egypt in Antebellum America." *Arizona Quarterly* 56:3 (autumn 2000): 1–28.

Douglass, Frederick. "Athens, Greece to Naples, Italy, Sunday, March 23, 1887." Manuscript Division, Library of Congress. Frederick Douglass Papers, *Travels* Folder 29.

———. "The Claims of the Negro Ethnologically Considered." In Foner, *The Life and Writings of Frederick Douglass.*

———. *My Bondage and My Freedom.* New York: Miller, Orton, and Mulligan, 1855. Rpt. Urbana: University of Illinois Press, 1987.

Drakakis, John, ed. *New Casebooks: Antony and Cleopatra.* New York: St. Martin's. 1994.

Drake, St. Clair. *Black Folk Here and There*. 2 vols. Los Angeles: Center for Afro-American Studies, 1990.

Du Bois, W. E. B. *The Souls of Black Folk: Essays and Sketches*. New York: Library of America, 1990.

———. "Strivings of the Negro People." *Atlantic Monthly* 80 (August 1897).

———. *The World and Africa: An Inquiry into the Part Which Africa Has Played in World History*. New York: International Publishers, 1965.

Duggan, Lisa. "The Trials of Alice Mitchell: Sensationalism, Sexology, and the Lesbian Subject in Turn-of-the-Century America." *Signs: Journal of Women in Culture and Society* 18:4 (summer 1993): 791–814.

Dumenil, Lynn. *Freemasonry and American Culture, 1880–1930*. Princeton: Princeton University Press, 1984.

Edwards, Amelia. *A Thousand Miles up the Nile*. Philadelphia: Henry T. Coates, 1877.

Edwards, Holly. "A Million and One Nights: Orientalism in America, 1870–1930." In Edwards, *Noble Dreams, Wicked Pleasures*, 11–57.

Edwards, Holly, ed. *Noble Dreams, Wicked Pleasures: Orientalism in America, 1870–1930*. Princeton: Princeton University Press, 2000.

"The Effects of a Hearty Dinner after Visiting the Antediluvian Department at the Crystal Palace." *Punch*, February 3, 1855, 50.

Ellis, Richard. *Imagining Atlantis*. New York: Knopf, 1998.

Esedebe, P. Olisanwuche. *Pan-Africanism: The Idea and Movement, 1776–1963*. Washington, D.C.: Howard University Press, 1982.

Faderman, Lillian. *Surpassing the Love of Men: Romantic Friendship and Love between Women from the Renaissance to the Present*. New York: Quill, 1981.

Farmer, Lydia Hoyt. "Cleopatra." In *The Book of Famous Queens*. New York: Thomas Y. Crowell, 1887.

———. "Cleopatra." In *The Girl's Book of Famous Queens*. New York: Thomas Y. Crowell, 1887.

Finseth, Ian. "David Walker, Nature's Nation, and Early African-American Separatism." *Mississippi Quarterly* 54:3 (summer 2001): 337–62.

Floyd, Samuel A., Jr. *The Power of Black Music: Interpreting Its History from Africa to the United States*. New York: Oxford University Press, 1995.

Foner, Eric. *Free Soil, Free Labor, Free Men: The Ideology of the Republican Party before the Civil War*. New York: Oxford University Press, 1970.

Foner, Philip S., ed. *The Life and Writings of Frederick Douglass*. Vol. 2: *Pre–Civil War Decade, 1850–1860*. New York: International Publishers, 1950.

Fontaine, Edward. *How the World Was Peopled: Ethnological Lectures*. New York: Appleton, 1877.

*Forest Hills Cemetery*. Roxbury, 1855.

Foster, Edward. *Mary E. Wilkins Freeman*. New York: Hendricks House, 1956.

Foucault, Michel. *The Birth of the Clinic: An Archaeology of Medical Perception*. Translated by A. M. Sheridan Smith. New York: Vintage, 1994.

————. *Discipline and Punish: The Birth of the Prison.* Translated by Alan Sheridan. New York: Vintage, 1979.

————. *The History of Sexuality, Volume I: An Introduction.* Translated by Robert Hurley. New York: Vintage, 1990.

Franklin, H. Bruce, ed. *Future Perfect: American Science Fiction of the Nineteenth Century —An Anthology.* Rev. ed. New Brunswick, N.J.: Rutgers University Press, 1995.

Fredrickson, George. *Black Liberation: A Comparative History of Black Ideologies in the United States and South Africa.* New York: Oxford University Press, 1995.

Freud, Sigmund. *Moses and Monotheism.* In *Standard Edition of the Complete Psychological Works of Sigmund Freud,* vol. 23. Translated by James Strachey. London: Hogarth, 1959.

Fulkerson, H. S. *The Negro as He Was; as He Is; as He Will Be.* Vicksburg, Miss.: Commercial Herald, 1887. Rpt. in Smith, *Anti-Black Thought,* vol. 10.

Fulop, Timothy E., and Albert J. Raboteau, eds. *African-American Religion: Interpretive Essays in History and Culture.* New York: Routledge, 1997.

Gallagher, Catherine, and Thomas Laqueur, eds. *The Making of the Modern Body: Sexuality and Society in the Nineteenth Century.* Berkeley: University of California Press, 1987.

Gallier, James. "American Architecture." *North American Review* 43 (October 1836).

Garnet, Henry Highland. "An Address to the Slaves of the United States of America." In *The Norton Anthology of African American Literature,* edited by Henry Louis Gates Jr. and Nellie Y. McKay. New York: W. W. Norton, 1997.

————. "On the Past and Present Condition, and Destiny of the Colored Race." *The North Star,* June 16, 1848.

Genovese, Eugene. *Roll, Jordan, Roll: The World the Slaves Made.* New York: Vintage, 1976.

Gerdts, William H., Jr. *The White, Marmorean Flock: Nineteenth-Century American Women Neoclassical Sculptors.* Poughkeepsie: Vassar College Art Gallery, 1972.

Gifford, George E. "The Case of the Ether Dome Mummy." *Harvard Medical Alumni Bulletin,* March–April 1977.

Gillman, Susan. "Pauline Hopkins and the Occult: African-American Revisions of Nineteenth-Century Sciences." *American Literary History* 8:1 (spring 1996): 57–82.

Gilroy, Paul. *The Black Atlantic: Modernity and Double Consciousness.* Cambridge: Harvard University Press, 1993.

Glaude, Eddie S., Jr. *Exodus! Religion, Race, and Nation in Early Nineteenth-Century Black America.* Chicago: University of Chicago Press, 2000.

Gliddon, George Robins. *Ancient Egypt: Her Monuments, Hieroglyphics, History, and Archaeology, and Other Subjects Connected with Hieroglyphical Literature.* 10th ed. New York: William Taylor, 1847.

————. "The Monogenists and the Polygenists." In *Indigenous Races of the Earth; or, New Chapters of Ethnological Inquiry.* Philadelphia: J. B. Lippincott, 1857.

————. *Otia Ægyptiaca: Discourses on Egyptian Archaeology and Hieroglyphical Discoveries.* Philadelphia: John Penington, 1849.

Goddu, Teresa. *Gothic America: Narrative, History, and Nation.* New York: Columbia University Press, 1997.

Gossett, Thomas F. *Race: The History of an Idea in America.* Dallas: Southern Methodist University Press, 1963.

Gough, Val. "Lesbians and Virgins: The New Motherhood in *Herland.*" In Seed, *Anticipations.*

Gould, Stephen Jay. *The Mismeasure of Man.* New York: W. W. Norton, 1981.

Grewal, Inderpal. *Home and Harem: Nation, Gender, Empire, and the Cultures of Travel.* Durham: Duke University Press, 1996.

Griffin, Farah Jasmine. *Beloved Sisters and Loving Friends: Letters from Rebecca Primus of Royal Oak, Maryland, and Addie Brown of Hartford, Connecticut, 1854–1868.* New York: Ballantine, 1999.

Griffith, Cyril. *The African Dream: Martin R. Delany and the Emergence of Pan-African Thought.* University Park: Pennsylvania State University Press, 1975.

Grimké, Charlotte Forten. *The Journals of Charlotte Forten Grimké.* Edited by Brenda Stevenson. New York: Oxford University Press, 1988.

Grimshaw, William Henry. *Official History of Freemasonry among the Colored People in North America.* New York: Negro Universities Press, [1903] 1989.

Halberstam, Judith. *Skin Shows: Gothic Horror and the Technology of Monsters.* Durham: Duke University Press, 1995.

Hale, Edward Everett. *Ninety Days' Worth of Europe.* Boston: Walker and Wise, 1861.

Hale, Sarah Josepha. "Cleopatra." In *Woman's Record; or, Sketches of All Distinguished Women, from "The Beginning" Till A.D. 1850.* New York: Harper and Brothers, 1853.

Hall, Kim F. *Things of Darkness: The Economies of Race and Gender in Early Modern England.* Ithaca: Cornell University Press, 1995.

Haller, John S., Jr., and Robin M. Haller. *The Physician and Sexuality in Victorian America.* New ed. Carbondale: Southern Illinois University Press, 1995.

Hamblyn, Richard. "Private Cabinets and Popular Geology: The British Audiences for Volcanoes in the Eighteenth Century." In *Transports: Travel, Pleasure, and Imaginative Geography, 1600–1830,* edited by Chloe Chard and Helen Langdon. New Haven: Yale University Press, 1996.

Hamer, Mary. "Black and White? Viewing Cleopatra in 1862." In *The Victorians and Race,* edited by Shearer West. Aldershot, Hampshire: Scolar Press, 1997.

————. "The Myth of Cleopatra since the Renaissance." In Walker and Higgs, *Cleopatra of Egypt.*

————. "Queen of Denial: On the Uses of Cleopatra." *Transition* 6:4 (winter 1996): 80–92.

————. *Signs of Cleopatra: History, Politics, Representation.* New York: Routledge, 1993.

Hamilton, Thomas. "Apology." *The Anglo-African Magazine* 1:1 (January 1859): 1–5.

Hamlin, Talbot. *Greek Revival Architecture in America.* New York: Oxford University Press, 1944.

Hansen, Karen V. " 'No Kisses Is Like Youres': An Erotic Friendship between Two African-American Women during the Mid–Nineteenth Century." *Gender and History* 7:2 (August 1995): 153–81.

Harding, Sandra, ed. *The "Racial" Economy of Science: Toward a Democratic Future.* Bloomington: Indiana University Press, 1993.

Hardinge, Emma. *Modern American Spiritualism: A Twenty Years' Record of the Communion between Earth and the World of Spirits.* New Hyde Park, N.Y.: University Books, [1870] 1970.

Harkins, John E., et al. *Metropolis of the American Nile: An Illustrated History of Memphis and Shelby County.* Woodland Hills: Windsor Publications, 1982.

Harvey, Bruce A. *American Geographics: U.S. National Narratives and the Representation of the Non-European World, 1830–1865.* Stanford: Stanford University Press, 2001.

Haviland, John. *The Practical Builder's Assistant: Containing the Five Orders of Architecture, Selected from the Best Specimens of the Greek and Roman.* Philadelphia: John Bioren, 1818.

Hawaway, Donna. *Simians, Cyborgs, and Women: The Reinvention of Nature.* New York: Routledge, 1991.

Hawthorne, Nathaniel. *The Marble Faun; or, The Romance of Monte Beni.* New York: Penguin, 1990.

Hayford, Harrison, et al., eds. *The Writings of Herman Melville.* Vol. 15. Evanston: Northwestern University Press, 1989.

Haynes, Joyce, and R. Jackson Wilson. *Padihershef the Egyptian Mummy.* Springfield, Mass.: Springfield Library and Museums Association, 1984.

Haynes, Stephen R. *Noah's Curse: The Biblical Justification of American Slavery.* New York: Oxford University Press, 2002.

Herbert, T. Walter, Jr. "The Erotics of Purity: The Marble Faun and the Victorian Construction of Sexuality." *Representations* 36 (fall 1991): 114–32.

Hevner, Carol E. "Rembrandt Peale's Dream and Experience of Italy." In *The Italian Presence in American Art, 1760–1860,* edited by Irma B. Jaffe. New York: Fordham University Press, 1989.

Hinks, Peter. *To Awaken My Afflicted Brethren: David Walker and the Problem of Antebellum Slave Resistance.* University Park: Pennsylvania State University Press, 1997.

Hinsley, C. M. "Hemispheric Hegemony in Early American Anthropology, 1841–1851: Reflections on John Lloyd Stephens and Lewis Henry Morgan." In *Social Contexts of American Ethnology, 1840–1984,* edited by June Helm. Washington, D.C.: American Ethnological Society, 1985.

Holland, Patricia G., and Milton Merzer, eds. *Collected Correspondence of Lydia Maria Child, 1817–1880.* Millwood: Kraus Microform.

Holly, J. Theodore. "Thoughts on Hayti." *The Anglo-African Magazine* 1:6 (June 1859). Rpt. New York: Arno Press, 1968.

Hone, Philip. *The Diary of Philip Hone, 1828–1851.* Edited by Allan Nevins. New York: Dodd, Mead, 1927.

Honour, Hugh. *The Image of the Black in Western Art.* Vol. 4: From the American Revolution to World War I, Part 1: Slaves and Liberators. Cambridge: Harvard University Press, 1989.

Hopkins, Pauline Elizabeth. Of One Blood; or, The Hidden Self. In The Magazine Novels of Pauline Hopkins, edited by Hazel V. Carby. New York: Oxford University Press, 1988.

Horsman, Reginald. Josiah Nott of Mobile: Southerner, Physician, and Racial Theorist. Baton Rouge: Louisiana State University Press, 1987.

Howe, Stephen. Afrocentrism: Mythical Pasts and Imagined Homes. London: Verso, 1998.

Hubbard, Dolan. "David Walker's Appeal and the American Puritan Jeremiadic Tradition." Centennial Review 30:3 (summer 1986): 331–46.

Hughes, Langston. "The Negro Speaks of Rivers." In The New Negro, ed. Alain Locke. New York: Albert and Charles Boni, 1925.

Hughes-Hallett, Lucy. Cleopatra: Histories, Dreams, and Distortions. New York: Harper-Perennial, 1991.

Humbert, Jean-Marcel, et al., eds. Egyptomania: Egypt in Western Art, 1730–1930. Ottawa: National Gallery of Canada, 1994.

Ignatiev, Noel. How the Irish Became White. New York: Routledge, 1995.

Irwin, John T. American Hieroglyphics: The Symbol of the Egyptian Hieroglyphics in the American Renaissance. Baltimore: The Johns Hopkins University Press, [1980] 1983.

Jacobus, Mary, Evelyn Fox Keller, and Sally Shuttleworth, eds., Body-Politics: Women and the Discourses of Science. New York: Routledge, 1990.

James, George G. M. Stolen Legacy: Greek Philosophy Is Stolen Egyptian Philosophy. Trenton: Africa World Press, [1954] 1992.

James, Henry. William Wetmore Story and His Friends: From Letters, Diaries, and Recollections. 2 vols. London: William Blackwood and Sons, 1903.

James, William. "The Hidden Self." In The Works of William James: Essays in Psychology. Edited by Frederick H. Burkhardt et al. Cambridge: Harvard University Press, 1983.

———. The Principles of Psychology. 2 Volumes. New York: Holt, 1890.

Jameson, Anna Brownell. Memoirs of Celebrated Female Sovereigns. Vol. 1. New York: Harper and Brothers, 1842.

Jefferson, Thomas. Notes on the State of Virginia. Edited by William Peden. Chapel Hill: University of North Carolina Press, 1982.

Johnson, Harvey. The Hamite. Baltimore: J. F. Weishampel, 1889.

———. The Question of Race: A Reply to W. Cabell Bruce, Esq. Baltimore: J. F. Weishampel, 1891.

Johnson, James Weldon. The Books of American Negro Spirituals. New York: Viking, 1925.

Johnston, Judith. Anna Jameson: Victorian, Feminist, Woman of Letters. Aldershot: Ashgate Press, 1997.

Johnston, Norman. "John Haviland." In *Pioneers in Criminology*, edited by Hermann Mannheim, 2d ed. Montclair, NJ: Patterson Smith, 1972.

Johnston, Norman, Kenneth Finkel, and Jeffrey A. Cohen. *Eastern State Penitentiary: Crucible of Good Intentions*. Philadelphia: Philadelphia Museum of Art, 1994.

Jordanova, Ludmila. *Sexual Visions: Images of Gender in Science and Medicine between the Eighteenth and Twentieth Centuries*. Ann Arbor: University of Michigan Press, 1993.

Judy, Ronald A. T. *(Dis)Forming the American Canon: African-Arabic Slave Narratives and the Vernacular*. Minneapolis: University of Minnesota Press, 1993.

Kadlec, David. "The Flowering of Miss Jack Tar: *Symzonia, Pym*, and Paul Metcalf's *Both*." *Sagetrieg* 12:1 (spring 1993): 83–94.

Kaplan, Amy. "Manifest Domesticity." *American Literature* 70:3 (1998): 581–606.

Kapsalis, Terri. *Public Privates: Performing Gynecology at Both Ends of the Speculum*. Durham: Duke University Press, 1997.

Karcher, Carolyn L. *The First Woman in the Republic: A Cultural Biography of Lydia Maria Child*. Durham: Duke University Press, 1994.

Kasson, Joy. *Marble Queens and Captives: Women in Nineteenth-Century American Sculpture*. New Haven: Yale University Press, 1990.

Kaufman, Martin, et al., eds. *Dictionary of American Medical Biography*. 2 vols. Westport, Conn.: Greenwood Press, 1984.

Kelly, Lori Duin. *The Life and Works of Elizabeth Stuart Phelps, Victorian Feminist Writer*. Troy: Whitston, 1983.

Kennedy, J. Gerald. " 'Trust No Man': Poe, Douglass, and the Culture of Slavery." In Kennedy and Weissberg, *Romancing the Shadow*, 225–57.

Kennedy, J. Gerald, and Liliane Weissberg, eds. *Romancing the Shadow: Poe and Race*. New York: Oxford University Press, 2001.

Kessler, Carol Farley. *Elizabeth Stuart Phelps*. Boston: Twayne, 1982.

———. "Introduction." In Elizabeth Stuart Phelps, *The Story of Avis*. Edited by Carol Farley Kessler. New Brunswick, N.J.: Rutgers University Press, 1985.

———, ed. *Daring to Dream: Utopian Stories by United States Women, 1836–1919*. Boston: Pandora Press, 1984.

Kimball, Stanley B. "New Light on Old Egyptiana: Mormon Mummies, 1848–71." *Dialogue: A Journal of Mormon Thought* 16:4 (1983): 72–90.

King, Mrs. Starr [Julia Wiggin King]. "Cleopatra: The Queen, the Mistress, the Suicide." *Cosmopolitan Art Journal* 3:1 (1858): 42–3.

Kletzing, Henry F., and William H. Crogman, *Progress of a Race; or, the Remarkable Advancement of the Afro-American from the Bondage of Slavery, Ignorance and Poverty to the Freedom of Citizenship, Intelligence, Affluence, Honor and Trust*. Atlanta: J. L. Nichols, 1897; rpt. New York: Negro Universities Press, 1969.

Kopley, Richard, ed. *Poe's Pym: Critical Explorations*. Durham: Duke University Press, 1992.

Kraepelin, Emil. *Lectures on Clinical Psychiatry*. Edited by Thomas Johnstone. London: Baillière, 1904.

Lancaster, Clay. *Architectural Follies in America*. Rutland, Vt.: Charles E. Tuttle, 1960.

Landy, Jacob. *The Architecture of Minard Lafever*. New York: Columbia University Press, 1970.

Lant, Antonia. "Haptical Cinema." *October* 74 (1995): 45–73.

Latour, Bruno. *The Pasteurization of France*. Translated by Alan Sheridan and John Law. Cambridge: Harvard University Press, 1988.

———. *Science in Action: How to Follow Scientists and Engineers through Society*. Cambridge: Harvard University Press, 1987.

Law, John, ed. *A Sociology of Monsters: Essays on Power, Technology and Domination*, Sociological Review Monographs 38. London: Routledge: 1991.

Leach, Joseph. *Bright Particular Star: The Life and Times of Charlotte Cushman*. New Haven: Yale University Press, 1970.

Lefkowitz, Mary. *Not Out of Africa: How Afrocentrism Became an Excuse to Teach Myth as History*. New York: Basic Books, 1996.

Lefkowitz, Mary, and Guy MacLean Rogers, eds., *Black Athena Revisited*. Chapel Hill: University of North Carolina Press, 1966.

Lemire, Elise. " 'The Murders in the Rue Morgue': Amalgamation Discourses and the Race Riots of 1838 in Poe's Philadelphia." In Kennedy and Weissberg, *Romancing the Shadow*, 177–204.

Lenz, William E. "Poe's *Arthur Gordon Pym* and the Narrative Techniques of Antarctic Gothic." *CEA Critic* 53:3 (spring–summer 1991): 30–38.

———. *The Poetics of the Antarctic: A Study in Nineteenth-Century American Cultural Perceptions*. New York: Garland, 1995.

Lester, A. Hoyle. *The Pre-Adamite; or, Who Tempted Eve? Scripture and Science in Unison as Respects the Antiquity of Man*. Philadelphia: J. B. Lippincott, 1875. Rpt. in Smith, *Anti-Black Thought*, vol. 6.

Levine, Lawrence. *Highbrow/Lowbrow: The Emergence of Cultural Hierarchy in America*. Cambridge: Harvard University Press, 1988.

Levine, Robert S. *Martin Delany, Frederick Douglass, and the Politics of Representative Identity*. Chapel Hill: University of North Carolina Press, 1997.

———. *Martin R. Delany: A Documentary Reader*. Chapel Hill: University of North Carolina Press, 2003.

———. "Road to Africa: Frederick Douglass's Rome." *African American Review* 34:2 (summer 2000): 217–231.

Lewis, Martin W., and Kären Wigen. *The Myth of Continents: A Critique of Metageography*. Berkeley: University of California Press, 1997.

Lewis, Reina. *Gendering Orientalism: Race, Femininity, and Representation*. New York: Routledge, 1996.

Lewis, W. David. *From Newgate to Dannemora: The Rise of the Penitentiary in New York, 1796–1848*. Ithaca: Cornell University Press, 1965.

Lieb, Michael. *Children of Ezekiel: Aliens, UFOs, the Crisis of Race, and the Advent of End Time*. Durham: Duke University Press, 1998.

Lincoln, Abraham. *Speeches and Writings, 1859–1865*. New York: Library of America, 1989.

Livingstone, David N. "The Preadamite Theory and the Marriage of Science and Religion." *Transactions of the American Philosophical Society* 82:3 (1992).

Locke, Alain, ed. *The New Negro*. New York: Albert and Charles Boni, 1925.

Lombardi, Guido. "Egyptian Mummies at Tulane University: An Anthropological Study." M.A. thesis, Tulane University, 1999.

Long, David A. "Poe's Political Identity: A Mummy Unswathed." *Poe Studies* 23:1 (June 1990): 1–22.

Lord, John. "Cleopatra: The Woman of Paganism, 69–30 B.C.E." In *Great Women*. New York: Fords, Howard, and Hulbert, 1886.

Lott, Eric. *Love and Theft: Blackface Minstrelsy and the American Working Class*. New York: Oxford University Press, 1993.

Loudon, Jane Webb. *The Mummy! A Tale of the Twenty-Second Century*. London: Henry Colburn, 1827. Rpt. Ann Arbor: University of Michigan Press, 1994.

Lowe, Lisa. *Critical Terrains: French and British Orientalisms*. Ithaca: Cornell University Press, 1991.

Lutz, Tom. *American Nervousness, 1903: An Anecdotal History*. Ithaca: Cornell University Press, 1991.

Lynch, Hollis R. *Edward Wilmot Blyden: Pan-Negro Patriot, 1832–1912*. London: Oxford University Press, 1967.

Lynch, Hollis R., ed. *Black Spokesman: Selected Published Writings of Edward Wilmot Blyden*. New York: Humanities Press, 1971.

Lyon, William F. *The Hollow Globe; or, The World's Agitator and Reconciler: A Treatise on the Physical Conformation of the Earth*. Chicago: Sherman and Lyon, 1875.

Mahar, William J. "Ethiopian Skits and Sketches: Contents and Contexts of Blackface Minstrelsy, 1840–1890." In Bean, *Inside the Minstrel Mask*.

Malone, Dumas, ed. *Dictionary of American Biography*. New York: Charles Scribner's Sons, 1935.

Massey, Gerald. *The Natural Genesis; or Second Part of a Book of the Beginnings, Containing an Attempt to Recover and Reconstitute the Lost Origins of the Myths and Mysteries, Types and Symbols, Religion and Language, with Egypt for the Mouthpiece and Africa as the Birthplace*. Vol. 2. London: R. Clay, Sons, and Taylor, 1883. Rpt. Kila, Mont.: Kessinger, 1992.

Masur, Louis P. *Rites of Execution: Capital Punishment and the Transformation of American Culture, 1776–1865*. New York: Oxford University Press, 1989.

May, Stephen. "The Object at Hand." *Smithsonian* 27 (September 1996): 16–20.

McAlester, Virginia, and Lee McAlester. *A Field Guide to American Houses*. New York: Knopf, 1995.

McAlister, Melani. " 'The Common Heritage of Mankind': Race, Nation, and Masculinity in the King Tut Exhibit." *Representations* 54 (1996): 80–103.

McCabe, James D. *The Illustrated History of the Centennial Exposition*. Philadelphia: National Publishing Company, 1976.

McClintock, Anne. *Imperial Leather: Race, Gender, and Sexuality in the Colonial Contest.* New York: Routledge, 1995.

McCluskey, Peter M. " 'The Recovery of the Sacred Candlestick': Jewish Imagery and the Problem of Allegory in *The Marble Faun.*" *Publications of the Arkansas Philological Association* 18:2 (1992): 14–27.

McDonald, Joyce Green. "Sex, Race, and Empire in Shakespeare's *Antony and Cleopatra.*" *Literature and History* 5:5 (spring 1996): 60–77.

McDowell, Peggy, and Richard E. Meyer. *The Revival Styles in American Memorial Art.* Bowling Green: Bowling Green State University Popular Press, 1994.

McGregor, Deborah Kuhn. *From Midwives to Medicine: The Birth of American Gynecology.* New Brunswick, N.J.: Rutgers University Press, 1998.

Mease, James. *Observations on the Penitentiary System, and Penal Code of Pennsylvania: With Suggestions for Their Improvement.* Philadelphia: Clark and Raser, 1828.

Melville, Herman. *White-Jacket; or, The World in a Man-of-War.* Chicago: Northwestern University Press, 1970.

Menken, Adah Isaacs. *Infelicia.* New York, 1868. Rpt. in *Infelicia and Other Writings,* edited by Gregory Eiselein. Peterborough: Broadview, 2002.

Mentor, Lillian Frances. *The Day of Resis.* New York: G. W. Dillingham, 1897.

Merck, Mandy. "The Amazons of Ancient Athens." In *Perversions: Deviant Readings.* New York: Routledge, 1993.

Merrill, Lisa. *When Romeo Was a Woman: Charlotte Cushman and Her Circle of Female Spectators.* Ann Arbor: University of Michigan Press, 1999.

Miles, Margaret R. "The Virgin's One Bare Breast: Nudity, Gender, and Religious Meaning in Tuscan Early Renaissance Culture." In *The Female Body in Western Culture: Contemporary Perspectives,* edited by Susan Suleiman. Cambridge: Harvard University Press, 1986.

Miller, Angela. *The Empire of the Eye: Landscape Representation and American Cultural Politics, 1825–1875.* Ithaca: Cornell University Press, 1993.

Miller, Kelly. "The Historic Background of the Negro Physician." *Journal of Negro History* 1:2 (April 1916): 99–109.

Miller, Lillian B. *In Pursuit of Fame: Rembrandt Peale, 1778–1860.* Washington: National Portrait Gallery, 1992.

————, ed. *The Peale Family: Creation of a Legacy, 1770–1790.* Washington, D.C.: National Portrait Gallery, 1996.

Miller, Lillian B., and David C. Ward, eds. *New Perspectives on Charles Willson Peale: A 250th Anniversary Celebration.* Pittsburgh: University of Pittsburgh Press, 1991.

Miller, Perry. *Errand into the Wilderness.* Cambridge: Harvard University Press, 1956.

Mitchell, Thomas R. *Hawthrone's Fuller Mystery.* Amherst: University of Massachusetts Press, 1998.

Morgan, James Lewellyn, and Jack Coogan. "Cleopatra Had a Jazz Band." Columbia Records A2472 (rec. December 7, 1917).

Morris, Norval, and David J. Rothman, eds. *The Oxford History of the Prison: The Practice of Punishment in Western Society.* New York: Oxford University Press, 1995.

Morrison, Toni. *Playing in the Dark: Whiteness and the Literary Imagination*. New York: Vintage, 1992.

Morton, Samuel George. *Crania Ægyptiaca*. Philadelphia: J. Penington, 1844.

———. *Crania Americana: or, a Comparative View of the Skulls of Various Aboriginal Nations of North and South America*. Philadelphia: John Pennington, 1839.

Moses, Wilson Jeremiah. *Afrotopia: The Roots of African American Popular History*. Cambridge: Cambridge University Press, 1998.

———. *Black Messiahs and Uncle Toms: Social and Literary Manipulations of a Religious Myth*. Rev. ed. University Park: Pennsylvania State University Press, 1993.

———. *The Golden Age of Black Nationalism, 1850–1925*. New York: Oxford University Press, 1978.

———. "The Poetics of Ethiopianism: W.E.B. Du Bois and Literary Black Nationalism." *American Literature* 47:3 (November 1975): 411–26.

———, ed. *Classical Black Nationalism: From the American Revolution to Marcus Garvey*. New York: New York University Press, 1996.

"M.S." In *The Adamic Race: Reply to "Ariel," Drs. Young and Blackie, on the Negro*. New York: Russell Bros., 1868. Rpt. in Smith, *Anti-Black Thought*, vol. 5.

Mousseau, Dede. "Anne Whitney: Her Life, Her Art, and Her Relationship with Adeline Manning." M. A. thesis, California State University, Fresno, 1992.

Mudimbe, V. Y. *The Invention of Africa: Gnosis, Philosophy, and the Order of Knowledge*. Bloomington: Indiana University Press, 1988.

Muraskin, William A. *Middle-Class Blacks in a White Society: Prince Hall Freemasonry in America*. Berkeley: University of California Press, 1975.

"Mutability of Human Affairs." *Freedom's Journal*, April 6–20, 1827.

Neill, Michael. "Introduction." In William Shakespeare, *Antony and Cleopatra*. London: Oxford University Press, 1994.

Nelson, Dana D. *National Manhood: Capitalist Citizenship and the Imagined Fraternity of White Men*. Durham: Duke University Press, 1998.

———. *The Word in Black and White: Reading "Race" in American Literature, 1638–1867*. New York: Oxford University Press, 1992.

Nelson, Victoria. "Symmes Hole, or the South Polar Romance." *Raritan* 17:2 (fall 1997): 136–66.

Nemerov, Alexander. *The Body of Raphaelle Peale: Still Life and Selfhood, 1812–1824*. Berkeley: University of California Press, 2001.

Nesbitt, Lois E. "Cleopatra at the Mall." *ArtNews* 87:8 (October 1988): 18–20.

Nevins, Allan, and M. H. Thomas, eds. *The Diary of George Templeton Strong*. 4 vols. New York: Macmillan Company, 1952.

Nochlin, Linda. "The Imaginary Orient." *Art in America* 71:5 (May 1983): 46–59.

Nott, Josiah Clark. *Essay on the Natural History of Mankind, Viewed in Connection with Negro Slavery: Delivered before the Southern Rights Association, 14th December, 1850*. Mobile: Dade, Thompson, 1851.

———. *Two Lectures on the Connection between the Biblical and Physical History of Man*. New York: Negro Universities Press, [1849] 1969.

Nott, Josiah Clark, and George Robins Gliddon. *Types of Mankind; or, Ethnological Researches, Based upon the Ancient Monuments, Paintings, Sculptures, and Crania of Races, and upon their Natural, Geographical, Philological, and Biblical History*. Philadelphia: Lippincott, Grambo, 1854.

Nygaard, Loisa. "Winning the Game: Inductive Reasoning in Poe's 'Murders in the Rue Morgue.' " *Studies in Romanticism* 33 (summer 1994): 223–54.

Obenzinger, Hilton. *American Palestine: Melville, Twain, and the Holy Land Mania*. Princeton: Princeton University Press, 1999.

"The Old Girl of Cairo Town." In Richard M. Dorson, *Buying the Wind: Regional Folklore in the United States*, Chicago: University of Chicago Press, 1964.

Oldroyd, David R. *Thinking about the Earth: A History of Ideas in Geology*. Cambridge: Harvard University Press, 1996.

Otten, Thomas J. "Pauline Hopkins and the Hidden Self of Race." ELH 59 (1992): 227–56.

Painter, Nell Irvin. *Sojourner Truth: A Life, a Symbol*. New York: W. W. Norton, 1997.

Parrott, Sara Foose. "Networking in Italy: Charlotte Cushman and 'The White Mamorean Flock.' " *Women's Studies* 14:4 (1988): 305–38.

Patterson, Richard S., and Richardson Dougall. *The Eagle and the Shield: A History of the Great Seal of the United States*. Washington, D.C.: Bureau of Public Affairs, 1976.

Peale, Rembrandt. *Notes on Italy*. Philadelphia: Carey and Lea, 1831.

Pennington, James W. C. *A Text-Book of the Origin and History, &c. &c. of the Colored People*. Hartford: L. Skinner, 1841.

Pepper, D. Stephen. *Guido Reni: A Complete Catalogue of His Works with an Introductory Text*. New York: New York University Press, 1985.

Peterson, Thomas Virgil. "The Myth of Ham among White, Antebellum Southerners." PH.D. diss., Stanford University, 1975.

Pfaelzer, Jean. "Utopians Prefer Blondes: Mary Lane's *Mizora* and the Nineteenth-Century Utopian Imagination." In Mary E. Bradley Lane, *Mizora: A Prophecy*. Syracuse: Syracuse University Press, 2000.

Phillips, Mary E. *Reminiscences of William Wetmore Story*. Chicago: Rand McNally, 1897.

Pickering, Andrew. *The Mangle of Practice: Time, Agency, and Science*. Chicago: University of Chicago Press, 1995.

Pickering, Andrew, ed. *Science as Culture and Practice*. Chicago: University of Chicago Press, 1992.

Pierce, Patricia Dawes. "Deciphering Egypt: Four Studies in the American Sublime." PH.D. diss., Program in American Studies, Yale University, 1980.

Plutarch. "Caesar." In *Fall of the Roman Republic: Six Lives by Plutarch*. Translated by Rex Warner. New York: Penguin, 1972.

———. *Plutarch's Lives*. Edited and translated by Bernadotte Perrin. Vol. 7. New York: G. P. Putnam's Sons, [1919] 1927.

Poe, Edgar Allan. *Edgar Allan Poe: Poetry, Tales, and Selected Essays*. New York: Library of America, 1996.

————. "The Gold-Bug." In Poe, Edgar Allan Poe.

————. *The Narrative of Arthur Gordon Pym of Nantucket*. In Poe, Edgar Allan Poe.

————. "Some Words With a Mummy." In Poe, Edgar Allan Poe.

Pollin, Burton R. "Poe's 'Some Words with a Mummy' Reconsidered." ESQ 60, Poe supplement (fall 1970): 60–67.

Potts, Alex. *Flesh and the Ideal: Winckelmann and the Origins of Art History*. New Haven: Yale University Press, 1996.

Pratt, Mary Louise. "Fieldwork in Common Places." In *Writing Culture*, edited by James Clifford and George Marcus. Berkeley: University of California Press, 1987.

————. *Imperial Eyes: Travel Writing and Transculturation*. New York: Routledge, 1992.

Prichard, James Cowles. *The Natural History of Man: Comprising Inquiries into the Modifying Influence of Physical and Moral Agencies on the Different Tribes of the Human Family*. Edited by George W. Stocking Jr. Chicago: University of Chicago Press, 1973.

Pringle, Heather. *The Mummy Congress: Science, Obsession, and the Everlasting Dead*. New York: Theia Books, 2001.

Raboteau, Albert. "The Black Experience in American Evangelicism." In *The African-American Religion: Interpretive Essays in History and Culture*, edited by Timothy E. Fulop and Albert J. Raboteau. New York: Routledge, 1997.

————. *A Fire in the Bones: Reflections on African-American Religious History*. Boston: Beacon Press, 1995.

————. *Slave Religion: The "Invisible Institution" in the Antebellum South*. New York: Oxford University Press, 1978.

Rampersad, Arnold. *The Art and Imagination of W. E. B Du Bois*. New York: Schocken, 1990.

Randolph, Paschal Beverly. *Pre-Adamite Man: Demonstrating the Existence of the Human Race upon this Earth 100,000 Years Ago!* Toledo: Randolph, 1863.

Reginald, Robert, and Douglas Menville. *King Solomon's Children: Some Parodies of H. Rider Haggard*. New York: Arno Press, 1978.

————. *They: Three Parodies of H. Rider Haggard's She*. New York: Arno Press, 1978.

Reid-Pharr, Robert. *Conjugal Union: The Body, the House, and the Black American*. New York: Oxford University Press, 1999.

Richardson, Edgar P., et al., eds. *Charles Willson Peale and His World*. New York: Harry N. Abrams, 1982.

Richardson, Marilyn. "Edmonia Lewis's *The Death of Cleopatra*." *International Review of African American Art* 12:2 (1995): 36–52.

Riggs, Marcia Y., ed. *Can I Get a Witness? Prophetic Voices of African American Women: An Anthology*. Maryknoll, N.Y.: Orbis Books, 1997.

Rothman, David J. *The Discovery of the Asylum: Social Order and Disorder in the New Republic*. Boston: Little, Brown, 1971.

Rowe, John Carlos. "Edgar Allan Poe's Imperial Fantasy and the American Frontier." In Kennedy and Weissberg, *Romancing the Shadow*, 75–105.

Royster, Francesca T. "Cleopatra as Diva: African-American Women and Shakespearean Tactics." In *Literature and Performance*, edited by Marianne Novy. New York: St. Martin's, 1999.

Rudwick, Martin J. S. *Scenes from Deep Time: Early Pictorial Representations of the Prehistoric World*. Chicago: University of Chicago Press, 1992.

Rywell, Martin, et al. *Afro-American Encyclopedia*. North Miami: Educational Book Publishers, 1974.

Said, Edward W. *Orientalism*. New York: Vintage, 1979.

Sammons, Vivian Ovelton. *Blacks in Science and Medicine*. New York: Hemisphere, 1990.

Schomburg, A. A. "Dr. James McCune Smith." *Negro History Bulletin* 9:2 (November 1945): 41–42.

Schor, Joel. *Henry Highland Garnet: A Voice of Black Radicalism in the Nineteenth Century*. Westport: Greenwood, 1977.

Schrager, Cynthia D. "Pauline Hopkins and William James: The New Psychology and the Politics of Race." In *The Unruly Voice: Rediscovering Pauline Elizabeth Hopkins*, edited by John Cullen Gruesser. Urbana: University of Illinois Press, 1996.

Schueller, Malini Johar. *U.S. Orientalisms: Race, Nation, and Gender in Literature, 1790–1890*. Ann Arbor: University of Michigan Press, 1998.

Schuyler, Montgomery. "A Great American Architect: Leopold Eidlitz." *Architectural Record* 24:3 (September 1903): 164–79.

Scott, Pamela. "Robert Mills and American Monuments." In *Robert Mills, Architect*, edited by John M. Bryan. Washington, D.C.: American Institute of Architects Press, 1989.

———. *Temple of Liberty: Building the Capitol for a New Nation*. New York: Oxford University Press, 1995.

Scully, Vincent. *American Architecture and Urbanism*. New rev. ed. New York: Henry Holt, 1988.

Sedgwick, Eve Kosofsky. *Epistemology of the Closet*. Berkeley: University of California Press, 1990.

Seed, David, ed. *Anticipations: Essays in Early Science Fiction and Its Precursors*. Liverpool: Liverpool University Press, 1995.

Seidler, Jan M. "A Critical Reappraisal of the Career of William Wetmore Story, 1819–1895: American Sculptor and Man of Letters." Ph.D. diss., Boston University, 1985.

Shaw, W. J. *Cresten, Queen of the Toltus; or, Under the Auroras: A Marvellous Tale of the Interior World*. New York: Excelsior, 1888.

Shelley, Mary. *Frankenstein, or the Modern Prometheus*. Oxford: Oxford University Press, 1981.

Sherwood, Dolly. *Harriet Hosmer: American Sculptor, 1830–1908*. Columbia: University of Missouri Press, 1991.

Showalter, Elaine, ed. *Alternative Alcott: Louisa May Alcott*. New Brunswick, N.J.: Rutgers University Press, 1988.

Simms, William Gilmore. "The Death of Cleopatra." In *Poems: Descriptive, Dramatic, Legendary, and Contemplative*. Vol. 2. Redfield, 1853.

Simpson, G. W. *The Female Instructor and Guide to Health*. Baltimore, 1875.

Simpson-Housley, Paul. *Antarctica: Exploration, Perception, and Metaphor*. New York: Routledge, 1992.

*The Six Species of Men*. New York: Van Evrie, Horton, 1866. Rpt. in Smith, Anti-Black Thought, vol. 1.

Skeat, Walter W. *Shakespeare's Plutarch: Being a Selection from the Lives in North's Plutarch Which Illustrate Shakespeare's Plays*. London: Macmillan, 1875.

Sloan, David Charles. *The Last Great Necessity: Cemeteries in American History*. Baltimore: Johns Hopkins University Press, 1991.

Smith, Barbara Hernstein. *Belief and Resistance: Dynamics of Intellectual Controversy*. Cambridge: Harvard University Press, 1997.

———. *Contingencies of Value: Alternative Perspectives for Critical Theory*. Cambridge: Harvard University Press, 1988.

Smith, B. H., and Arkady Plotnitsky, eds. "Mathematics, Science, and Postclassical Theory." Special issue, *South Atlantic Quarterly* 94:2 (spring 1995).

Smith, Horace. *Amarynthus, the Nympholet: A Pastoral Drama, in Three Acts, with Other Poems*. London: Hurst, Rees, Orne, and Brown, 1821. Rpt. New York: Garland, 1977.

Smith, James McCune. "Introduction." In Douglass, *My Bondage and My Freedom*.

Smith, John David, ed. *Anti-Black Thought, 1863–1925*. 11 vols. New York: Garland, 1993.

Smith, Shawn Michelle. *American Archives: Gender, Race, and Class in Visual Culture*. Princeton: Princeton University Press, 1999.

Smith, Theophus H. *Conjuring Culture: Biblical Formations of Black America*. New York: Oxford University Press, 1994.

Sollors, Werner. *Beyond Ethnicity: Consent and Descent in American Culture*. New York: Oxford University Press, 1986.

———. *Neither Black nor White yet Both: Thematic Explorations of Interracial Literature*. Cambridge: Harvard University Press, 1997.

Southern, Eileen. *The Music of Black Americans: A History*. New York: W. W. Norton, 1983.

Spencer, Jon Michael. *Protest and Praise: Sacred Music of Black Religion*. Minneapolis: Fortress Press, 1990.

Stanton, William. *The Great United States Exploring Expedition of 1838–1842*. Berkeley: University of California Press, 1975.

———. *The Leopard's Spots: Scientific Attitudes toward Race in America, 1815–1859*. Chicago: University of Chicago Press, 1960.

Stark, Aubrey. "Poe's Friend Reynolds." *American Literature* 11 (1939): 152–66.

Stebbins, Emma. *Charlotte Cushman: Her Letters and Memories of Her Life*. New York: Blom, [1878] 1972.

Stephens, John Lloyd. *Incidents of Travel in Egypt, Arabia Petræa, and the Holy Land*. Norman: University of Oklahoma, [1837] 1970.

———. *Incidents of Travel in Yucatán*. Edited by Karl Ackerman. Washington, D.C.: Smithsonian Institution Press, 1996.

Stephens, John Richard, ed. *Into the Mummy's Tomb*. New York: Berkeley Books, 2001.

Stern, Madeline, et al. *Louisa May Alcott Unmasked: Collected Thrillers*. Boston: Northeastern University Press, 1995.

Stevens, Patricia E., and Joanne M. Hall. "A Critical Historical Analysis of the Medical Construction of Lesbianism." *International Journal of Health Services* 21:2 (1991): 291–307.

Stocking, George W., Jr. "From Chronology to Ethnology: James Cowles Prichard and British Anthropology, 1800–1850." In Prichard, *The Natural History of Man*.

Storer, Horatio Robinson. *The Causation, Course, and Treatment of Reflex Insanity in Women*. Boston: Lee and Shepard, 1871.

Story, William Wetmore. "Cleopatra." In *Graffiti d'Italia*. London: William Blackwood and Sons, 1868.

———. Letter from Villa Palmeri, Leghorn, October 12, 1863. Story Papers, Harry Ransom Humanities Research Center, University of Texas, Austin.

———. *Roba di Roma*. London: Chapman and Hall, 1863.

Stowe, Harriet Beecher. "Sojourner Truth, the Libyan Sibyl." *Atlantic Monthly* 11 (April 1863): 473–81.

Strahan, Edward [Shinn, Earl]. *Gérome: A Collection of the Works of J. L. Gérome in One Hundred Photogravures*. Multiple vols. New York: Samuel L. Hall, 1881.

———. *The Masterpieces of the Centennial International Exposition, Illustrated*. Vol. 1: *Fine Art*. Philadelphia: Gebbie and Barrie, 1876.

Stuckey, Sterling. *Slave Culture: Nationalist Theory and the Foundations of Black America*. New York: Oxford University Press, 1987.

Sundquist, Eric J. *To Wake the Nations: Race in the Making of American Literature*. Cambridge, Mass.: Belknap, 1993.

Swann, Charles. *Nathaniel Hawthorne: Tradition and Revolution*. Cambridge: Cambridge University Press, 1991.

Sweetman, John. *The Oriental Obsession: Islamic Inspiration in British and American Art and Architecture, 1500–1920*. Cambridge: Cambridge University Press, 1988.

Symmes, John Cleves. "Circular Number 1." Reproduced in Viola and Margolis, *Magnificent Voyagers*.

——— [Adam Seaborn]. *Symzonia: A Voyage of Discovery*. New York: Seymour, 1820. Rpt. Gainesville: Scholars' Facsimiles and Reprints, 1965.

Symmes, John Cleves and James McBride. *Symmes Theory of Concentric Spheres and Polar Voids: Demonstrating That the Earth Is Hollow, Habitable within, and Widely Open at the Poles*. Cincinnati: Morgan, Lodge and Fischer, 1826.

Taft, Lorado. *The History of American Sculpture*. New York: Macmillan, 1903.

Tate, Claudia. *Domestic Allegories of Political Desire: The Black Heroine's Text at the Turn of the Century*. New York: Oxford University Press, 1992.

Taylor, Caesar A. A. *The Negro Race, Retrospective and Prospective; or, the Negro's Past and Present, and His Future Prospects*. Johnstown, Pa.: Harry M. Benshoff, 1890.

Teeters, Negley K. *They Were in Prison: A History of the Pennsylvania Prison Society, 1787–1937*. Chicago: John C. Winston, 1937.

Tellefson, Blythe Ann. " 'The Case with My Dear Native Land': Nathaniel Hawthorne's Vision of America in *The Marble Faun*." *Nineteenth-Century Literature* 54:4 (March 2000): 455–79.

Thomas, Clara. *Love and Work Enough: The Life of Anna Jameson*. Toronto: University of Toronto Press, 1978.

Thomas, Nancy, et al., eds. *The American Discovery of Ancient Egypt*. Los Angeles: Los Angeles County Museum of Art, 1995.

Thornton, Lynne. *Women as Portrayed in Orientalist Paintings*. Paris: ACR Édition Internationale, 1995.

Trafton, Scott. "Egypt Land: Race and the Cultural Politics of American Egyptomania, 1800–1900." PH.D. diss., Department of English, Duke University, 1998.

Trumble, Alfred. *Secrets of the Tombs: Its Crimes, Romances, and Mysteries*. New York: Richard K. Fox, 1881.

Turner, Alice. *The History of Hell*. New York: Harcourt Brace, 1993.

Turner, Richard Brent. "Edward Wilmot Blyden and Pan-Africanism: The Ideological Roots of Islam and Black Nationalism in the United States." *The Muslim World* 87:2 (April 1997): 169–82.

———. *Islam in the African-American Experience*. Indianapolis: Indiana University Press, 1997.

Turner, William C., Jr. "The Musicality of Black Preaching: A Phenomenology." *Journal of Black Sacred Music* 2:1 (spring 1988): 21–33.

Ullman, Victor. *Martin R. Delany: The Beginnings of Black Nationalism*. Boston: Beacon Press, 1971.

Van Evrie, John H. *White Supremacy and Negro Subordination; or, Negroes a Subordinate Race, and (So-Called) Slavery Its Normal Condition*. 2d ed. New York: Van Evrie, Horton, 1868.

Vance, William L. *America's Rome*. 2 vols. New Haven: Yale University Press, 1989.

Verne, Jules. *An Antarctic Mystery*. Translated by Cashel Hoey. Philadelphia: J. B. Lippincott, 1899. Rpt. Boston: Gregg Press, 1975.

Viola, Herman J., and Carolyn Margolis, eds. *Magnificent Voyagers: The U.S. Exploring Expedition, 1838–1842*. Washington, D.C.: Smithsonian Institution Press, 1985.

von Hagen, Victor Wolfgang. "Editor's Introduction." In John Lloyd Stephens, *Incidents of Travel in Yucatán*, Volume One. Edited by Victor Wolfgang von Hagen. Norman: University of Oklahoma Press, 1962.

Waith, Eugene M. "Ozymandias: Shelley, Horace Smith, and Denon." *Keats-Shelley Journal* 44 (1995): 22–28.

Walker, David. *Appeal to the Colored Citizens of the World.* Edited by Peter Hinks. University Park: Pennsylvania State University Press, 2000.

———. *Appeal to the Coloured Citizens of the World.* Edited by Sean Wilentz. New York: Hill and Wang, [1829] 1995.

Walker, Susan, and Peter Higgs, eds. *Cleopatra of Egypt: From History to Myth.* Princeton: Princeton University Press, 2001.

Wallace, Maurice O. *Constructing the Black Masculine: Identity and Ideality in African American Men's Literature and Culture, 1775–1995.* Durham: Duke University Press, 2002.

Walter, C. W. *Mount Auburn.* New York, 1850.

Warren, John Collins. "Description of an Egyptian Mummy, Presented to the Massachusetts General Hospital with an Account of the Operation of Embalming, in Ancient and Modern Times." *Boston Journal of Philosophy and the Arts* 1 (1823).

Watson, John Fanning. *Extra-Illustrated Autograph Manuscript of "Annals of Philadelphia."* Philadelphia: Library Company of Philadelphia, ca. 1830.

Weigall, Arthur. *The Glory of the Pharaohs.* London, 1923.

Weissberg, Liliane. "Black, White, and Gold." In Kennedy and Weissberg, *Romancing the Shadow,* 127–56.

West, Cornel. *Prophesy Deliverance! An Afro-American Revolutionary Christianity.* Philadelphia: Westminster, 1982.

West, Shearer, ed. *The Victorians and Race.* Aldershot, Hampshire: Scolar Press, 1997.

Wheatley, Phillis. *Poems on Various Subjects, Religious and Moral.* Rpt. in *The Collected Works of Phillis Wheatley,* edited by John Shields. New York: Oxford University Press, 1988.

White, Charles, arr. *The Virginny Mummy: A Negro Farce.* New York: Happy Hours, n.d.

Wilbur, Richard. "Introduction." In Edgar Allan Poe, *The Narrative of Arthur Gordon Pym.* Boston: David R. Godine, 1973.

Wilkes, Charles. *Voyage Round the World, Embracing the Principal Events of the Narrative of the United States Exploring Expedition. In One Volume.* Philadelphia: George W. Gorton, 1849.

Williams, Michael. *A World of Words: Language and Displacement in the Fiction of Edgar Allan Poe.* Durham: Duke University Press, 1988.

Williams, Stephen. *Fantastic Archaeology: The Wild Side of North American Prehistory.* Philadelphia: University of Pennsylvania Press, 1991.

Wilmore, Gayraud S. *Black Religion and Black Radicalism: An Interpretation of the Religious History of Afro-American People.* 2d ed. Maryknoll, N.Y.: Orbis Books, 1983.

Wilson, Jack H. "Competing Narratives in Elizabeth Stuart Phelps' *The Story of Avis,*" *American Literary Realism, 1870–1910* 26:1 (1993): 60–67.

Wilson, John A. *Signs and Wonders upon Pharaoh: A History of American Egyptology.* Chicago: University of Chicago Press, 1964.

Winstone, H. V. F. *Howard Carter and the Discovery of the Tomb of Tutankhamen.* London: Constable, 1991.

Wolfe, Rinna Evelyn. *Edmonia Lewis: Wildfire in Marble.* Parsippany: Dillon Press, 1998.

Wolfe, S. J., and Robert Singerman. " 'As Cheap as Candidates for the Presidency': The Beginnings of Mummy Mania in America." Manuscript, 2002.

Wood, J. *Pantaletta: A Romance of Sheheland.* New York: American News Company, 1882.

Wreford, Henry. "A Negro Sculptress." *The Athanaeum,* March 3, 1866.

Wunder, Richard P. *Hiram Powers: Vermont Sculptor, 1805–1873.* 2 vols. Newark: University of Delaware Press, 1991.

Yalom, Marilyn. *A History of the Breast.* New York: Ballantine, 1997.

Young, Robert J. C. *Colonial Desire: Hybridity in Theory, Culture, and Race.* New York: Routledge, 1995.

Ziegler, Christiane. "Cleopatra and Caesar." In Humbert et al., *Egyptomania.*

Ziff, Larzer. *Return Passages: Great American Travel Writing, 1780–1910.* New Haven: Yale University Press, 2000.

# Index

Egypt (*continued*)

222–61; as sign of apocalypse, 33–39; as sign of civilization, 2–5, 48–59, 69–77, 129–30, 142–48, 222–61; as sign of historiographic anxiety, 16–20, 35–39, 54–62, 129–31, 137–48, 155–56, 162–64, 177–86; as sign of indecipherability, 106–8, 213–15; as sign of magic, 10, 27–31; as sign of paganism, 10, 24, 117, 129–30, 156–64; as sign of ruined civilization, 14, 33–39, 123–26, 143, 222–61; as slave society, 2–5, 7–9, 16–20, 22–23, 37, 49, 59–62, 147–48, 222–61; as split sign, 1–6, 10–12, 18–20, 34–35, 81–84, 93–108, 142–48, 184–85, 192–95, 222–61; as white, 8–10, 59–62, 177–78, 186–91

Egyptian moment: and adventure tales, 10–12, 99–120, 244–45; and archaeology, 85–89, 93–96, 244–45; as Egyptomanic puncture, 10–12, 85–96, 244–45; and Edgar Allan Poe, 96–113; as rupture in earth, 99–120; as rupture in identity, 89–93, 107–8, 244–45; and speculative fiction, 99–120, 244–45

Egyptian Revival, 131–32, 140–64, 169, 230, 235; and cemeteries, 148, 156–64, 291 n.99; and Christian resurrection, 153–64; as neoclassical style, 142–43; as "Oriental" style, 144–46; and prisons, 148–56; as sign of racializied anxiety, 146–48

Egyptology, xvii, 6, 31–33, 39, 48–84, 92–93, 110–13, 118–19, 129–30, 230, 271 n.15; and human origin, 48–54, 222–26, 237–40; and Orientalism, 20–27, 41–45

Egyptomania: and Afrocentrism, xvii–xviii, 20–27, 54–59, 62–84, 118–19, 222–61; and American identity, 1–27, 48–68, 93–96, 107–8, 132–40, 145–48, 162–64, 177–86, 201–4, 222–61; architectural, 140–64, 169, 287 n.65; black, xvii, 20–27, 165–68, 222–61;

British, 124; carceral logic of, 10–12, 125–26, 148–64, 222–37, 252–53, 256–61; in eighteenth century, 12–14, 123–26; European, xvii, 145, 169–71, 192, 292 n.7, 299 n.111; and the fantastic, 27–35, 108–120, 237–61; as figure of racial instability, 4–5, 8–12, 93–108, 129–31, 139–48, 175–80, 184–85, 192–95, 222–61; and mysticism, 27–35, 245–48; and Orientalism, xvii, 20–27, 142–48, 175, 191–201, 257; pre-racial, 172, 186–87, 190–91, 201–2, 292 n.7; and racial identity, 1–39, 62–77, 110–11, 118–20, 145–48, 177–80, 222–61; as site of racialized conflict, 2–12, 48–69, 76–77, 81–84, 177–91, 248–53; visual, 165–221; white, xvii, 85–120, 121–64, 169–204

Eidlitz, Leopold, 287 n.65

Emancipation Proclamation, 2, 15

Esedebe, P. Olisanwuche, 309 n.40

"Ether Dome Mummy." *See* Padihershef

Ethiopia, 76–77, 226, 238–39, 248–61. *See also* Afrocentrism; Black nationalism; Ethiopianism; Pan-Africanism

Ethiopianism, 12, 222–61, 275 n.98, 313 n.82. *See also* Afrocentrism; Black nationalism; Ethiopia; Pan-Africanism

Ethnology, 16–17, 45–84, 101–2, 105–8, 128, 177, 185, 206–7, 213–14, 228, 280 n.43

Exodus: and Afrocentrism, xvi–xviii, 222–37; and American identity, 18–20; and black antislavery activism, 222–37, 308 n.10; and Ethiopianism, 237–61

Faderman, Lillian, 218, 303 n.148, 306 n.169

Farmer, Lydia Hoyt, 170, 174, 177–78, 188–90, 201–2, 293 n.23

Feminism: and Cleopatra, 165–74, 201–21, 299 n.111; and lost race/hollow earth novels, 113–15; racial politics of, 113–15, 165–68, 201–4, 215–21

Floyd, Samuel A., Jr., 309 n.40

Howe, Stephen, 309 n.40
Hughes, Langston, 225
Hughes-Hallett, Lucy, 172–73, 188, 192, 198–99

Imperialism, 2–6, 10–12, 20–31, 85–96, 102–4, 120, 204. See also Colonialism
Improvisation, 10, 236–37, 258–59, 309 n.37
Interiority, 11–12; architectural, 140–64; bodily, 124–25, 165–76, 186–201, 205–9, 293 n.18; earthly, 89–104, 108–113; psychological, 241–56
Irwin, John, xvi, 94, 268 n.57, 278 n.18, 286 n.32
Islam, 23–25, 268 n.57
Israel, 18–20, 225–61
Israelites, 18–20, 225–61

James, George G. M., 309 n.40
James, Henry, 181, 196, 211–12
James, William, 175, 241–42, 244, 310 n.47, 311 n.51
Jameson, Anna Brownell, 169–70, 187, 204, 219, 292 n.3
Janet, Pierre, 311 n.52
Japheth, 32, 59–62, 72–77
Jefferson, Thomas, 13, 82
Jeremiad, 18–20, 229, 308 n.11
Johnson, Harvey, 61, 64
Johnson, James Weldon, 39, 270 n.90

Kaplan, Amy, 115, 204
Kaplan, Sidney, 104
Kasson, Joy, 181, 196
Kennedy, J. Gerald, 277 n.8, 280 n.38
Kessler, Carol Farley, 203
King, Julia Wiggin, 199–203, 206, 299 n.109
King, Mrs. Starr. See King, Julia Wiggin
King, Thomas Starr, 299 n.109
Know Nothings, 288 n.70
Kraepelin, Emil, xv, xix

Lander, Louise, 303 n.148
Lane, Mary E. Bradley, 115
Langston, John Mercer, 209
Lant, Antonia, 141

Latour, Bruno, 81, 276 n.111
Law of the father, 205
Ledyard, John, 13–14
Lefkowitz, Mary, 265 n.11, 293 n.26
Lesbianism. See Cleopatra; Lewis, Edmonia; Historiography, queer
Lester, A. Hoyle, 36–37
Levine, Lawrence, 297 n.87
Levine, Robert S., 267 n.44, 275 nn.90, 91
Lewis, Edmonia, 165–68, 175, 179–80, 196, 199, 208–21; and The Death of Cleopatra, 165–68, 179, 196, 209, 213–15, 219–21, 304 n.153; early life, 209–11, 302 n.138; and lesbianism, 211–21, 303 n.148, 306 n.173; in Rome, 211–16; and white peers, 210–12, 215–16. See also Cleopatra
Lewis, Reina, xvi
Lieb, Michael, 270 n.84
Lincoln, Abraham, 15–16, 142
Little Egypt (Illinois), 27
Lombardi, Guido, 271 n.7, 284 n.12
Lord, John, 179–80, 184
"Lost in the Pyramid, or The Mummy's Curse" (Alcott), 125–29
Lost race narratives, 89–120; parodies of, 114
Lott, Eric, 123, 283 n.2
Loudon, Jane Webb, 114, 133, 285 n.18
Lynching, 119
Lyon, William, 92, 109

Mahar, William, 283 n.2, 284 n.8
Manning, Adeline, 216, 218, 303 n.148
Marble Faun, The (Hawthorne), 166, 171–72, 180–86, 295 n.47
Masculinity: black, 26–27; white, 126–28, 138
Masons. See Freemasonry
Massey, Gerald, 162
McAlister, Melani, 307 n.7
McClintock, Anne, 173
Melville, Herman, 14; "Bartleby, the Scrivener," 149, 169
Memphis (Tennessee), 15
Menken, Adah Isaacs, 8, 215

Scott Trafton is an assistant professor of
English and African American Studies at George Mason University.

*Library of Congress Cataloging-in-Publication Data*

Trafton, Scott, 1968–
Egypt land : race and nineteenth-century American
Egyptomania / Scott Trafton.
p. cm.
Includes bibliographical references and index.
ISBN 0-8223-3375-9 (cloth : alk. paper)
ISBN 0-8223-3362-7 (pbk. : alk. paper)
1. Egypt—Study and teaching—United States—History—19th
century.   2. Egypt—Foreign public opinion, American—History—
19th century.   3. United States—Race relations—History—
19th century.   4. Racism—United States—History—19th century.
5. Slavery—Egypt.   6. Slavery—United States.   I. Title.
DT76.95.U6T73 2004
303.48′273032′09034—dc22
2004007962